THE CONTRADICTIONS OF CAPITAL
IN THE TWENTY-FIRST CENTURY

THE CONTRADICTIONS OF CAPITAL IN THE TWENTY-FIRST CENTURY

THE PIKETTY OPPORTUNITY

Edited by Pat Hudson and Keith Tribe

agenda

First published in 2016 by Agenda

Agenda Publishing Limited
The Core
Science Central
Bath Lane
Newcastle upon Tyne
NE4 5TF
www.agendapub.com

ISBN 978-1-911116-10-3 (hardcover)
ISBN 978-1-911116-11-0 (paperback)

British Library Cataloguing-in-Publication Data
A catalogue record for this book is available from the British Library

Typeset by T&T Productions Ltd, London
Printed and bound in the UK by CPI Group (UK) Ltd, Croydon, CR0 4YY

CONTENTS

Acknowledgements   *vii*

Contributors   *ix*

1. Introduction   1
   PAT HUDSON AND KEITH TRIBE

I. Concepts and Models   11

2. Capital and Wealth   13
   G. C. HARCOURT AND KEITH TRIBE

3. Inequality   29
   KEITH TRIBE

4. Models, Money and Housing   53
   AVNER OFFER

II. Piketty in Western National Contexts   65

5. French Idiosyncracies   67
   GAUTHIER LANOT

6. Fact or Fiction? Complexities of Economic Inequality
   in Twentieth-Century Germany   87
   JAN-OTMAR HESSE

7. Collective Wealth Formation: Conflict and Compromise
   in Sweden, 1950–2000   109
   YLVA HASSELBERG AND HENRY OHLSSON

8. A Confusion of Capital in the United States   131
   MARY A. O'SULLIVAN

9. Distributional Politics: The Search for Equality in Britain
   Since the First World War   167
   JIM TOMLINSON

III. Piketty: Global Commentaries 193

10. Looking at Piketty from the Periphery 195
LUIS BÉRTOLA

11. The Differences of Inequality in Africa 207
PATRICK MANNING AND MATT DRWENSKI

12. Income Distribution in Pre-war Japan 223
TETSUJI OKAZAKI

13. Piketty and India 237
PRASANNAN PARTHASARATHI

IV. Prospect 247

14. Goals and Measures of Development: The Piketty Opportunity 249
PAT HUDSON

15. Wealth and Income Distribution: New Theories Needed for a New Era 283
RAVI KANBUR AND JOSEPH E. STIGLITZ

Index 289

ACKNOWLEDGEMENTS

First and foremost we wish to thank Thomas Piketty and his international team of colleagues who have gathered so much new and very valuable data, particularly that relating to the World Top Incomes Database (WTID), a project that involved more than thirty scholars. Piketty's *Capital in the Twenty-First Century* (Cambridge, MA: Harvard University Press, 2014) is central to a spate of important books published in recent years that have placed inequality back at the heart of economic history and hopefully also at the heart of economics. Our motivation and approach, in different ways, owes a great debt to all of these, and to writers from a much earlier tradition, whose preoccupation with equality speaks to us from the past.

This volume was suggested to us by Steven Gerrard of Agenda Publishing and we are grateful to him and his colleagues for encouragement and support throughout the production process. The editors, and some of the contributors, benefitted from a panel session, centred on Piketty's work and thesis, at the 2015 Economic History Society conference at the University of Wolverhampton. We are grateful to Martin Daunton, who took part in the panel, alongside Keith Tribe, Jim Tomlinson and Avner Offer; to Rick Trainor, who, as the President of the Society, supported and chaired the session; and to the audience for an excellent discussion. We warmly thank the authors and Richard Baldwin, editor in chief of VoxEU.org, the policy portal of the Centre for Economic Policy Research, for permission to reproduce "Wealth and Income Distribution: New Theories Needed for a New Era" by Ravi Kanbur and Joseph E. Stiglitz, first published online on 18 August 2015. We also thank various journals and organizations for permission to reproduce figures and graphs (the copyright sources are given in the text).

The influence and generous encouragement of many other colleagues is also acknowledged, not least the dedication and enthusiasm of our international team of contributors.

Pat Hudson and Keith Tribe

CONTRIBUTORS

Luis Bértola is Professor in Economic History and Development Economics at Universidad de la República, Uruguay. He has been a visiting professor at several American and European universities. His *Economic Development of Latin America since Independence* (with José Antonio Ocampo) (2012) has been translated into Spanish (2013), Portuguese (2014) and Chinese (2016). His most recent book, co-edited with Jeffrey Williamson, is *Has Latin American Inequality Changed Direction? Looking Over the Long Run* (2016).

Matt Drwenski is a PhD student in world history at the University of Pittsburgh. His interests include social and economic inequality, the digital humanities and world history pedagogy.

G. C. Harcourt is Emeritus Reader in the History of Economic Theory at the University of Cambridge, Emeritus Fellow of Jesus College, Cambridge (since 1998), Professor Emeritus at the University of Adelaide (since 1988), and currently Visiting Professorial Fellow, School of Economics, University of New South Wales. His books include *Some Cambridge Controversies in the Theory of Capital* (1972), *The Structure of Post-Keynesian Economics* (2006), *Joan Robinson* (with Prue Kerr) (2009), *The Oxford Handbook of Post-Keynesian Economics* (two volumes) (co-editor with Peter Kriesler) (2013), and ten volumes of selected essays.

Ylva Hasselberg is Professor of Economic History at Uppsala University, Sweden, and director of the Uppsala University Science and Technology Studies Centre. She has published a monograph on the historiography of economic history in Sweden (*Industrisamhällets förkunnare. Eli Heckscher, Arthur Montgomery, Bertil Boëthius och svensk ekonomisk historia 1920–1950* (2007)) and another concerning the fate of professional identity in a commod-ified university setting (*Vetenskap som arbete. Normer och arbetsorganisation i den kommodifierade vetenskapen* (2012)). She is presently working on a biog-raphy of Eli Heckscher.

Jan-Otmar Hesse is Professor of Economic and Social History at the University of Bayreuth, Germany. He has held positions at the universities of Frankfurt, Goettingen and Bielefeld, and has also been the Alfred D. Chandler Visiting Professor in International Business History at Harvard Business School. His research focuses on modern German economic and business history as well as on the history of German economics. He has recently published on the Great Depression (together with Werner Plumpe and Roman Köster) and is the author of *Wirtschaftsgeschichte. Entstehung und Wandel der modernen Wirtschaft* (2013).

Pat Hudson is Emeritus Professor of Economic History at Cardiff University. She has published research on various aspects of industrialization in Britain, on historiography and historical methodology. Recent works include *The Routledge Handbook of Global Economic History* (co-edited with Francesco Boldizzoni) (2016) and *History by Numbers: An Introduction to Quantitative Approaches*, second edition (jointly with Mina Ishizu) (2016). Her 2014 Tawney Memorial Lecture entitled "Industrialisation, Global History and the Ghost of Rostow" is available as a podcast at www.ehs.org.uk/multimedia/tawney-lecture-2014-indu strialisation-global-history-and-the-ghost-of-rostow.

Ravi Kanbur is T. H. Lee Professor of World Affairs, International Professor of Applied Economics and Management, and Professor of Economics at Cornell University. His recent books include *International Development: Ideas, Experience, and Prospects* (co-editor with B. Currie-Alder, D. Malone and R. Medhora) (2014), *Inequality in Asia and the Pacific: Trends, Drivers, and Policy Implications* (co-editor with C. Rhee and J. Zhuang) (2014), *The Oxford Companion to the Economics of South Africa* (co-editor with H. Bhorat, A. Hirsch and M. Ncube) (2014) and *The Oxford Companion to the Economics of China* (co-editor with S. Fan, S. Wei and X. Zhang) (2014).

Gauthier Lanot is Professor of Economics in the Economics Department of Umeå School of Business and Economics, Sweden. He obtained his doctorate from the University Louis Pasteur, Strasbourg, France (now Université de Strasbourg) and taught at the universities of Keele, Laval Quebec and Queen's, Belfast, before moving to Umeå University in 2013. His research is in the fields of labour economics, taxation and public finance and it has appeared in several international economic journals. His current research is concerned with the measurement of the elasticity of taxable income, and with the interactions between the labour and housing markets.

Patrick Manning is Andrew W. Mellon Professor of World History (Emeritus) at the University of Pittsburgh. He is the author of many studies in African economic history, African population and migration since 1650, and the African diaspora. His *Big Data in History: A World-Historical Archive* was published in 2013. In 2016 he served as president of the American Historical Association.

Avner Offer is Chichele Professor Emeritus of Economic History at the University of Oxford. His chapter draws on work in the economic history of housing going back to his *Property and Politics 1870–1914* (1981); on his work in the history of economics, published (with Gabriel Söderberg) in *The Nobel Factor* (2016); and on his Tawney Memorial Lecture of 2016 to the Economic History Society about "The Market Turn", which is being readied for publication (see www.ehs.org.uk/multimedia/tawney-lecture-2016-the-market-turn-from-social-democracy-to-market-liberalism).

Henry Ohlsson is Deputy Governor at Sveriges Riksbank, the central bank of Sweden, and Professor of Economics at Uppsala University. He has a PhD from Umeå University. His recent research, which has appeared in several international academic journals, is within the fields of public economics, taxation, wealth inequality and intergenerational transfers.

Tetsuji Okazaki is Professor of Economics at the University of Tokyo. He has been the President of the International Economic History Association since 2015. His articles have appeared in major journals in economic history and economics, including *American Economic Review, Journal of Economic History, Economic History Review* and *Explorations in Economic History*.

Mary A. O'Sullivan is Professor of Economic History and the chair of the Department of History, Economics and Society at the University of Geneva. Her latest book, *Dividends of Development: Fits and Starts in the History of US Securities Markets, 1865–1919* (2016), analyses the development of US capital markets from the Civil War through the First World War. She is also author of *Contests for Corporate Control: Corporate Governance and Economic Performance in the United States and Germany* (2000).

Prasannan Parthasarathi is Professor of History at Boston College, Massachusetts. He has published on South Asian and global histories. His most recent book, *Why Europe Grew Rich and Asia Did Not: Global Economic Divergence, 1600–1850* (2011), was awarded the Jerry Bentley Book Prize of the World History Association.

Joseph E. Stiglitz is University Professor at Columbia University. In 2001 he was awarded the Nobel Memorial Prize in Economic Sciences for his analyses of markets with asymmetric information. His book *Globalization and Its Discontents* (2002) has been translated into thirty-five languages. His most recent books include *The Price of Inequality: How Today's Divided Society Endangers Our Future* (2012), *The Great Divide: Unequal Societies and What We Can Do*

About Them (2015) and *Rewriting the Rules of the American Economy: An Agenda for Growth and Shared Prosperity* (2015).

Jim Tomlinson is Professor of Economic and Social History at the University of Glasgow. He has published widely on the historical political economy of modern Britain. His latest book, *Dundee and the Empire: Juteopolis, 1850–1939* was published in 2014.

Keith Tribe retired as Reader in Economics from Keele University in 2002 and has since then worked as a professional translator and independent scholar, specializing in the history of economics. He recently published *The Economy of the Word* (2015) and a new translation of Friedrich Schiller's *On the Aesthetic Education of Man* (2016).

1

INTRODUCTION

Pat Hudson and Keith Tribe

Thomas Piketty's *Le Capital au XXIe siècle* was first published in Paris during the summer of 2013. On the appearance of an English edition in March 2014 it became an international blockbuster, being quickly translated into German, Spanish and Chinese. Sales of all copies by January 2015 were 1.5 million and rising, fuelled by popular concern about growing income inequality and the links between inequality and global economic instability. Thanks to Piketty, and to his large transnational team of colleagues, together with a spate of recent books on global wealth and income disparities, distribution is back at the centre of our concerns.[1]

PIKETTY'S PROMISE

In light of the mass of new comparative data contained in *Capital in the Twenty-First Century*, and in associated publications and appendices, it is clear that some common long-run trends in inequality across the developed world had not been sufficiently recognized. In particular, Piketty emphasizes the notable increase in income-generating wealth of top income earners in recent decades, together with rising pay. His study of top incomes, and their genesis, has unsettled the widely held assumption that capital's share in national income (via interest, dividends and capital gains) would always necessarily revert to a long-run constant. The social concentration of wealth through inheritance and its role in cumulatively ratcheting up incomes, and thus further increasing wealth in the top 10 per cent or so of the population, is now in the spotlight. It is this that underpins Piketty's dire prediction that, in the absence of fiscal and other measures to arrest the trend, things can only get worse. The new patrimonial class will increasingly engineer the political and legal process to further their economic interests, the rewards to merit and education in society will break down, and crises will ensue across the social democracies within a few decades.

Following the work of Simon Kuznets in the early 1950s, economists had generally assumed that modern economic growth would in the long run reduce the gap between rich and poor. In the early post-war years it was relatively easy to accept the inverted U-shaped curve of income distribution that Kuznets had identified for developed economies. Though based on flimsier evidence than we have today, tax and income data for the first half of the twentieth century, and mainly from the US, supported his argument that early industrial capitalism may, at first, have created greater economic and social inequality but that this was negated as capitalism matured, creating a more progressive balance of the rewards to labour compared with the shares of national income accruing to profits and rents.[2]

During the twentieth century there was a long and sophisticated tradition of writing about the ills of inequality and how to deal with it[3] but economists of the era following Kuznets showed little interest in the matter. Kuznets's thesis was presented during the period when neoclassical economic thinking was in the ascendant, and it was widely supposed that inequality was a necessary spur to aspiration and endeavour. Most economists of the period also assumed that, as economies tended towards stabilization at (or near) full employment, working people would earn what their skills and education entitled them to. As long as the engine of growth, sparked by continuous technical change, was given the freedom to keep going, the trickle-down effects of the rewards to capital would permeate throughout society. Hence the goal was growth, growth and more growth. And the main concern of economists was to identify the sources of economic growth, and how to increase and sustain it. Distribution was often seen as a pernicious distraction. Hence the statement of the Nobel Laureate Robert Lucas, writing as recently as 2004, that: "Of the tendencies that are harmful to sound economics the most seductive and ... the most poisonous is to focus on questions of distribution."[4]

The rationale for the market liberalization measures introduced during the 1980s and 1990s was faster growth, a view especially influential in the UK and the US. Instead, growth slowed, economic instability increased and the top layer of Western societies benefitted disproportionately from deregulation and privatization. Economists struggled to explain these contrary results. Then the global financial crisis of 2007–9 – accompanied by widespread protests about the iniquities, as well as the inequities, of liberalized globalization – unsettled popular faith in the core tenets of conventional economic theory. This was at last a real "legitimation crisis of capitalism", to borrow a phrase from German Marxists of the 1970s. The financial crisis undermined any idea that bankers, financial experts and corporate executives were doing sufficiently responsible and socially useful work to justify their explosively high remuneration. Furthermore, the dominant voices among academic economists had been unable to predict or even identify the causal forces at work during the crisis.[5] This was the "Piketty moment". By moving away from a preoccupation with economic growth and its determinants, by highlighting the large and growing gap between the wealth that societies have at their disposal and the human utility it generates, and by undermining the dominant view that free market capitalism spreads increases in wealth throughout society, Piketty promised a new perspective on the ills of modern economies.

In the reviews and discussions that followed the publication of *Capital in the Twenty-First Century,* major inconsistencies in Piketty's comparative data (arising inevitably from varied, complex and incomplete taxation and other records available in different national contexts) have been highlighted, alongside problems in his definitions of capital and his model of the dynamics of accumulation. He has been particularly held to account for neglecting the overriding importance of an array of political economy and technological factors at play in determining the vagaries of income and wealth distribution across countries and over time, especially since the 1980s, although he has clarified and contested this in subsequent publications.[6] His major thesis – that inequality in the long term is driven not by politics, technology, financialization, globalization or the specialization of economies but by rates of return on capital that exceed the level of economic growth – leads him to concentrate, in policy terms, largely upon a narrow range of radical fiscal solutions that critics have termed impractical (as indeed has Piketty himself) or naive. The aim of this collection of essays is to move on from this phase of endorsement or criticism of particular aspects of Piketty's argument and refocus attention on the larger questions he has raised.

CONSTRUCTIVE DIALOGUE

While criticism of Piketty's theory, method and data analysis can be found in this volume, in every case the purpose is constructively to highlight the complexities of aggregate cross-national comparative work of this kind using long-run time series data based on sources that are both country specific and temporally specific and are therefore hard to compare. We consider Piketty's arguments about wealth, capital and inequality with reference to the variability of political, historical and global contexts. Finally, we consider the opportunity that his work creates for rethinking some of the basic assumptions and methods of economics and of economic history.

First of all, attention is given to some foundational analytical concepts and models that are central to Piketty's work, in particular those concerning capital, wealth, inequality, money and real estate. The national-level sources and context of Piketty's data are then considered. Beginning with aspects of the fiscal and demographic history of France, we move on to consider how the specific developmental features of his other major sources (for Germany, Sweden, the US and Britain), together with the fiscal and welfare policies of these countries, might modify Piketty's general arguments regarding long-term movements in capital, wealth and income. In these chapters we go back to Piketty's definitions and data sources, examining the possibilities and limitations thrown up by historical national statistics and their intersection with the social and political history of the countries concerned.

Four shorter surveys then sketch out how Piketty's findings and thesis might bear on economic development outside the main twentieth-century Western industrial economies. These "global commentaries" consider the history of inequality in Latin America, Africa, Japan and India in the light of Piketty's work and ideas, suggesting that more attention be paid to cultural specificities and to the long-term impact of colonialism, resource depletion, unequal trade, patterns of primary, secondary and tertiary specialization, international financial flows and the power play of world politics. The book concludes with discussion of the dominant goals, measures and theories of growth and development that have been unsettled by Piketty's work, and considers their future prospects. Throughout, the assumption is that Piketty has provided an opportunity to re-examine the purposes and the jaded tool kit of current mainstream analysis in economics and economic history. It is in this spirit of dialogue that all contributions have been written.

A WORLD OF DIVERSE TRAJECTORIES

In the early nineteenth century European economies broke free of a number of political, economic and social constraints. Absolute monarchy gave way to republican and parliamentary regimes that, in the course of the century, reconstructed conceptions of equality and human rights. Economies that had for millennia been shackled to the agrarian cycles of dearth and plenty began a re-orientation to the rhythms of manufacture and commerce. Populations that had long been held in check by disease, warfare and food shortage began a secular increase, shifting away from rural occupations to urban employments. The rate at which this happened varied greatly from one country to another; England was already considered the model by the 1830s, and it was a Frenchman, Adolphe Blanqui, who in 1837 coined the idea that an "Industrial Revolution" was under way in Britain.[7]

But while England did exemplify the possibilities of economic and social change, it represented a developmental path that no other economy followed closely. Although Britain rapidly became a highly urbanized economy whose population was largely fed by imports paid for by its manufactured exports, one hundred years after Blanqui had written Europe still for the most part lived off its own agricultural produce. Germany, the most industrialized of Continential European economies, had in the 1930s around half of its population in rural areas.

If we, along with Piketty, add the US into this picture, matters become even more complicated. For almost a century after its foundation the first large-scale modern republic harboured the most profound inequality possible – that between free human beings and slaves – and even after the Civil War systematic racial discrimination was underwritten by statutes that prevailed for another hundred years. The northern states moved to a different rhythm, attracting successive waves of migrants from Europe and, in the wake of the Civil War, experiencing rapid westward territorial expansion combined with the rampant industrialization of the Gilded Age. Remote from international politics throughout the nineteenth century, the stance of the US changed with its involvement in the First World War: a war that scarred the major Western European economies but provided the platform upon which international American supremacy in the twentieth century was built. This was dramatically reinforced by its role in the Second World War, a conflict that was also a water-shed across the developed world in transforming ideas about the role of the state, national accounting, macroeconomic management and welfare provision. The rate at which this happened was not, however, uniform: Japan and West Germany, both occupied by American forces, proved most resistant to many of these ideas, despite contemporary critiques of American cultural imperialism.

Even sketched out roughly in this way, it becomes obvious that the core econ-omies upon which Piketty's analysis of wealth and inequality is based – France, Germany, Sweden, Britain and the US – have, since the early 1800s, diverged from each other as much as they have converged along a common develop-mental path. And once attention moves beyond these countries to the rest of the world, it becomes plain that any talk of common "global trends in inequality", to say nothing of their causation, forcibly aggregates a diversity of conditions and histories that escapes easy generalization.

This is not of course to say that trends in inequality do not exist, nor that the many dimensions upon which inequalities can be registered are simply a reflection of the human condition. Economists, in seeking to make sense of the world, naturally turn to simple models – in most cases growth models built around inputs of "capital" and "labour" – through which aggregated data can then be run to identify relationships and networks of causation. The simplicity of the models dictates the use of simplified aggregates: in its most reductive form, historical data often becomes merely the meat for an economic mincing machine. In this way aggregate trends are produced that reflect the pace and structure of development in none of the countries from which the data sets have been drawn: this is the danger to set against the great promise and insight of Piketty's work.

Most economists today are resolutely present-centred, viewing the recent past through current preoccupations, and imposing these preoccupations upon stylized versions of the longer run. That such self-confidence is ill-founded is now widely recognized. The appropriate response is not to replace "theory" with "history" but to look for better ways to link theory and history together. This is undoubtedly Piketty's aim, and the wealth of new and much-needed data that he provides, covering several regions of the world over two centuries, is a path-breaking achievement of historical reconstruction.[8] For a work of economic history, *Capital in the Twenty-First Century* has a refreshing absence of complex causal models and statistical regressions. Piketty carefully teases out common trends and national differences. In its methodological sympathies, at least, his work might be seen as a return to the aims and methods of historical economics: not narrow empiricism, but empiricism with a purpose – an "analytical histor-ical narrative", as Piketty himself terms it.[9] His "fundamental laws" of capitalist development might, in this light, be seen as an empirical generalization derived inductively from the mass of data assembled.[10]

That said, Piketty is an economist trained in the 1990s, sharing many of the reflexes of his peers. The concepts and terminology that he routinely employs have long and much-debated histories that he barely explores, and his causal thesis remains consciously embedded in an outdated neoclassical orthodoxy. His comparative national approach, rooted in close study of five major Western economies, inevitably sidelines the insights that might derive from a more connective or global historical analysis. And his emphasis upon common paths and experiences of development driven, in the last instance, by a common mechanism diverts attention from potentially more important, more varied and perhaps more tractable determinants of inequality. Thus, although Piketty's book is a landmark and a watershed for both economics and economic history, fully deserving of its huge readership and acclaim, it is justified to state that "Despite its great ambitions, his book is not the accomplished work of high theory that its title, length and reception (so far) suggest."[11]

Nevertheless, thanks to Piketty, to his immediate colleagues and also to the work of Bourguignon, Galbraith and Milanovic in particular, the transforma-tion and distribution of global wealth in the last 100 years, and the links between inequality and global economic and political stability, now sit at the top of the social science agenda. If we are to understand the implications of this observa-tion, we must use Piketty as a springboard to debate, but also to move beyond aggregated data sets to the institutions that produced the data, and the tasks that these institutions were set – new systems of taxation, state and private pensions, welfare benefits, unemployment, housing finance – in the emergent nation states of the nineteenth century, and in the more "mature" national and international economies of the twentieth and twenty-first centuries.

In a world of global liberalization and global financial flows, we also need a better understanding of the role of global connections in creating and endorsing inequalities.[12] Just as variations in wealth and income disparities over time within Piketty's core nations have been, and are being, strongly influenced by a variety of monopolistic and collusive practices, so also is the experience of income and wealth distribution transnationally. Colonial legacies, unbalanced growth, patterns of economic specialization, the location and use of R&D, technology gaps, economic and political volatility, and the exercise of transnational power: all of these must continue to be the focus of global inequality research beyond Piketty. As the chapters in this book make clear, to come to terms with the modern world, and its contradictions, we need history and politics as well as economics.

Notes for Chapter 1

1. Apart from Thomas Piketty's *Capital in the Twenty-First Century* (Cambridge, MA: Harvard University Press, 2014), a vast number of other publications (books, journal articles and online appendices) have been produced by Piketty and his colleagues working on the World Top Incomes Database (WTID); see www.wid.world/. For supplementary material to *Capital in the Twenty-First Century* see http://piketty. pse.ens.fr/en/capital21c2. Other major contributions on global inequality and on the causes and impact of inequality in recent years include: Anthony B. Atkinson, *Inequality: What Can be Done* (Cambridge, MA: Harvard University Press, 2015); François Bourguignon, *The Globalization of Inequality* (Princeton, NJ: Princeton University Press, 2015); Angus Deaton, *The Great Escape: Health, Wealth and the Origins of Inequality* (Princeton, NJ: Princeton University Press, 2013); James K. Galbraith, *Inequality and Instability: A Study of the World Economy Just Before the Great Crisis* (New York: Oxford University Press, 2012); Peter H. Lindert and Jeffrey G. Williamson, *Unequal Gains: American Growth and Inequality Since 1700* (Princeton, NJ: Princeton University Press, 2016); Branko Milanovic, *Global Inequality: A New Approach for the Age of Globalization* (Cambridge, MA: Harvard University Press, 2016); Robert Reich, *Saving Capitalism: For the Many, Not the Few* (New York: Knopf, 2015); Joseph E. Stiglitz, *The Price of Inequality: How Today's Divided Society Endangers Our Future* (London: Penguin, 2012); Joseph E. Stiglitz, *The Great Divide: Unequal Societies and What We Can Do About Them* (New York: W. W. Norton, 2015); Richard Wilkinson and Kate Pickett, *The Spirit Level: Why More Equal Societies Almost Always Do Better* (London: Allen Lane, 2009).

2. Simon Kuznets presented this argument in his 1954 Presidential Address to the American Economic Association, published as "Economic Growth and Income Inequality", *American Economic Review* 45 (1955), pp. 1–28. Kuznets is quite explicit that his observation concerning increasing income inequality in early industrialization is only a working assumption, since he had no data for this period (*ibid.*, p. 18).

The data that he discussed in his Presidential Address covers the period 1913–48, which, placed together with the presumed trend of the nineteenth century, creates the inverted U-curve that later became associated with his argument. Piketty more or less dismisses the Kuznets curve as a piece of Cold War propaganda (Piketty, *Capital*, pp. 13–14).

3. See Tribe in this volume, Chapter 3.

4. See p. 7 of Robert E. Lucas Jr, "The Industrial Revolution: Past and Future", *Economic Education Bulletin* XLIV(8) (August 2004), pp. 1–8.

5. For an account of the failure of mainstream economists to predict the economic crisis and what happened thereafter see Philip Mirowski, *Never Let a Serious Crisis go to Waste: How Neoliberalism Survived the Financial Meltdown* (London: Verso, 2013); for a study of the world economy leading up to the crisis, see Galbraith, *Inequality and Instability*.

6. Some of the data issues are discussed in Parts II and III of this volume. Reviews of Piketty are legion and multilingual. Many are referenced in footnotes throughout this volume. On Piketty's data, definitions and his growth model the main English language critiques include: Anthony B. Atkinson, "After Piketty?", *British Journal of Sociology* 65(4) (2014), pp. 619–38; J. Bradford DeLong, "Unjust Deserts", www.project-syndicate.org, 31 May 2014; J. Bradford DeLong, "Mr Piketty and the 'Neoclassics': A Suggested Interpretation", *National Tax Journal* 68(2) (June 2015), pp. 393–408; Jeffrey Frankel, "Piketty's Missing Rentiers", www.project-syndicate.org, 18 September 2014; James K. Galbraith, "Kapital for the Twenty-First Century?", *Dissent*, Spring 2015, www.dissentmagazine.org; David Harvey, "Afterthoughts on Piketty's *Capital in the Twenty-First Century*", *Challenge* 57(5) (2014), pp. 81–6; Stefan Homberg, "Critical Remarks on Piketty's *Capital in the Twenty-First Century*", *Applied Economics* 47(14), pp. 1401–6; Jane Humphries, "*Capital in the Twenty-First Century*", *Feminist Economics* 21(1) (2015), pp. 164–73; Paul Krugman, review in *New York Times*, 23 March 2014; Peter H. Lindert, "Making the Most of Capital in the 21st Century", NBER Working Paper 20232, June 2014; Michel Margairaz and Kenneth Mouré, "Les inégalités contemporaines: l'oeuvre de Thomas Piketty et les historien(ne)s", *Revue d'histoire moderne et contemporaine* 62(4) (2015), pp. 113–31; Robert Rowthorn, "A Note on Piketty's *Capital in the Twenty-First Century*", *Cambridge Journal of Economics* 38 (2014), pp. 1275–84; Robert Solow, "Thomas Piketty is Right: Everything You Need to Know about 'Capital in the Twenty-First Century'", *New Republic*, 22 April 2014; David Soskice, "*Capital in the Twenty-First Century*: A Critique", *British Journal of Sociology* 65(4) (2014), pp. 650–66; Joseph E. Stiglitz, "Democracy in the Twenty-First Century", www.project-syndicate.org, 1 September 2014; Joseph E. Stiglitz, "The Origins of Inequality and Policies to Contain It", *National Tax Journal* 68(2) (2015), pp. 425–48; Simon Szreter, "Wealth, Population, and Inequality: A Review Essay", *Population and Development Review* 42(2) (2015), pp. 343–68; Lance Taylor, "The Triumph of the Rentier? Thomas Piketty vs Luigi Pasinetti and John Maynard Keynes", *International Journal of Political Economy* 43 (2014), pp. 4–17; Lance Taylor, "Modeling Distribution and Growth: Replies to Garbellini and Wirkierman, Harcourt, and Nell", *International Journal of Political Economy* 43(3) (2014), pp. 44–54; Jim Tomlinson, "A New Political Arithmetic?", *Social History* 40 (2015), pp. 5–14; Keith Tribe, "Wealth and Inequality: Thomas Piketty's *Capital in the Twenty-First Century*", *Past & Present* 227 (2015), pp. 249–63; Yanis Varoufakis, "Egalitarianism's Latest Foe", *Real-World*

Economics Review 69 (October 2014), pp. 18–35. See also special issues of many journals on Piketty including: "Lire *Le capital* de Thomas Piketty", *Annales Histoire, Sciences Sociales* 70(1) (2015); *British Journal of Sociology* 65(4) (2014); and *Journal of Economic Perspectives* 29(1) (2015). For Piketty's responses and restatements see in particular: Thomas Piketty, "Putting Distribution Back at the Center of Economics: Reflections on *Capital in the Twenty-First Century*", *Journal of Economic Perspectives* 29(1) (2015), pp. 67–88; "*Capital in the Twenty-First Century*: A Multidimensional Approach to the History of Capital and Social Classes", *British Journal of Sociology* 65(4) (2014), pp. 736–47.

7. Adolphe Blanqui, *Histoire de l'économie politique en Europe depuis les anciens jusqu'à nos jours*, tome 2 (Paris: Guillaumin, 1837), pp. 166ff.

8. Piketty's varied data sources and the manipulations that he must make to get some degree of comparability from different national taxation records and national accounts are discussed to some degree in the book, but also in a plethora of online appendices. It is unlikely that researchers in Piketty's wake will read their way through all this material and there is therefore a strong likelihood that the figures will be quoted and re-used with fewer insights and qualifications than Piketty himself provides: a common phenomenon. It is also the case that Piketty's data visualizations can be criticized for enhancing the trends that fit with his thesis. This is particularly true with his choice of uneven horizontal scales in many of his time series graphs. See Noah Wright, "Data Visualization in *Capital in the 21st Century*", University of Texas Inequality Project ,Working Paper 70, May 2015.

9. Piketty, "Putting Distribution Back at the Center of Economics", p. 69.

10. See p. 593 of Michael Savage, "Piketty's Challenge for Sociology", *British Journal of Sociology* 65 (2014), pp. 591–606.

11. Galbraith, "Kapital for the Twenty-First Century?".

12. In different ways these are the preoccupations of several of the global studies of inequality listed in note 1.

PART I

CONCEPTS AND MODELS

2

CAPITAL AND WEALTH

G. C. Harcourt and Keith Tribe

The focus of Thomas Piketty's analysis of modern capitalism is the tremendous growth during the last forty years or so of inequality in income and wealth in the advanced industrial economies.[1] However, he places this forty-year period in the context of a much longer time frame; he argues that this divergence in the distribution of income and wealth is far from being a deviation from trend: it in fact represents a return to a normal path of development following a prolonged deviation during the twentieth century, especially during the long post-war boom ending in the mid 1970s. In approaching growth and inequality in this way Piketty has returned to the principal preoccupations of the political economy of the early nineteenth century: an attention to the long-term aspects of accumulation, distribution and growth associated with the writings of Robert Malthus, David Ricardo, John Stuart Mill and, of course, Karl Marx. Modern economists are on the whole forward looking, seeking to identify the trend of the next few years on the basis of data that has for the most part only been available since the middle of the twentieth century. While economic historians have sought to project a modern statistical framework backwards into the remote past, economists seek to extrapolate patterns from current data. In part, the attention that Piketty's book has received is owed to the way in which he takes the standard analytical framework used by modern economists but looks back, rather than forward. However, he shares with modern economists a paramount interest in the policy framework of the present and immediate future. Using masses of long-period data – and betraying the French origins of his work by his reliance on long runs of tax and estate duty data dating back to the early nineteenth century – he presents a new profile for the accumulation of capital during the process of industrialization and urbanization that created the wealth of today's advanced industrial nations. While he rejects the inferences about long-term growth drawn by nineteenth-century political economists, he nevertheless follows their lead in seeking to establish long-term laws of development (if not of motion) in modern economies.

Piketty devotes only fleeting attention to the long-term laws of development developed by nineteenth-century political economists, but it might here be useful to begin by sketching how these "laws" worked, for the idea that there is any kind of logic to capitalist development is not today argued over in the way that it used to be. Of course, the work of Karl Marx has been most influential in this area, and the title of Piketty's book alludes directly to Marx's own project to identify the long-term laws of motion of the capitalist mode of production. For much of the twentieth century, analysis of long-run trends in advanced economies was pursued either in the spirit of Marx or in opposition to his ideas, but the debates concerning accumulation, immiseration and crises that developed around his ideas have now faded; more recent invocations of Marx's *Capital* have been little more than gesture, paying scant attention to his analysis and arguments. Since Piketty does in fact espouse the idea that there is some kind of regularity in the past that can be projected into the future, but discusses this presumption only in a very specific manner, we can start by considering what nineteenth-century political economy made of the long-term prospects of capitalist development.

The "law of motion" embraced by Robert Malthus in his *Essay on Population* (1798) turned on biology, or, more exactly, on the behavioural outcomes of the biological constraints imposed by the confrontation between the geometric potential for human reproduction and the merely arithmetical potential for growth in the means of subsistence. The point of this argument was not to predict population change but to explain why the share of revenue taken by wages was limited by the availability of means of subsistence. Malthus sought to demonstrate that increasing wages as a response to rising prices would simply drive prices higher, and not resolve any food shortages suffered by the poor. In effect, he argued that the sum of real wages was fixed in the long run, and that only a reduction in the size of the working population could increase the wages received by individual workers. There are of course objections and qualifications that can be made in regard to this line of argument – involving, for example, the life cycle of the domestic household, technological change, or the changing impact of infant mortality – but the key point here was the contention that in the distribution of revenue between workers (wages), capitalists (profit) and landowners (rents), the total paid in real (rather than nominal) wages was fixed in the long run. Biology supplied the "law of motion" in demonstrating that no redistribution from richer to poorer could ameliorate the condition of the latter.

David Ricardo took up this idea and, in his *Principles of Political Economy, and Taxation* (1817), built it into a different kind of argument that turned on the problems of the long-run rate of profits; it therefore also became a question of the distribution of revenue. Responding to discussion in 1815 about the impact of legislation intended to protect grain producers, both Malthus and Ricardo had developed an analysis of the way in which increased investment in agriculture led to downward pressure on the general rate of profits. While Malthus was not prepared to face the consequences of his own logic, Ricardo was unequivocal that, in a closed agrarian economy, the pressure to increase domestic production of grain consequent on a growing population would place a downward pressure on the general rate of profits, divert increasing amounts of rental payments into the pockets of landowners, and at the same time pushing up the price of grain. This then was a different distributional problem: revenue was diverted from capitalists to landowners (not the same people, for "capitalists" were, here, "farmer-capitalists" renting their land from landlords), and the price of grain was maintained at a level such that there was a short-term rise in the subsistence wage, increasing costs for both manufacturers and farmers. The interests of the landlords were in this way set against both capitalists and workers: a conclusion that Malthus was reluctant to concede. From this basic dynamic in which rising agricultural investment drives down the general rate of profits, Ricardo derived the idea of a tendency for the rate of profits to fall to the point where the economy entered a stationary state: a purely theoretical conclusion that he used, in typically Ricardian fashion, to make arguments for the abolition of all protective tariffs on grain.

Ricardo's reasoning led from an analysis of distribution to a long-run decline in the rate of profits, and it would therefore be easy to assume that Marx drew on this element of Ricardo's thinking for his own proposition that the dynamic development of the capitalist mode of production resulted in a long-run decline in the rate of profits. In fact, Marx does not seem to have noticed this aspect of Ricardo's argument; nor did Marx himself identify any clear mechanism that would reliably generate such an outcome. Indeed, while Marx set out to identify the laws of motion of the capitalist mode of production, the chronology of capitalist development that he outlined in the first volume of *Capital* (1867) was purely historical, rather than theoretical, as with Ricardo. Nonetheless, Marxists subsequently sought to remedy this deficiency, drawing especially on the circuits of capital elaborated in the second (posthumous) volume of *Capital*, which Friedrich Engels assembled from manuscript drafts. In time, arguments about the accumulation of capital, crises of overproduction and underconsumption, immiseration, the reserve army of labour and the long-run decline in the rate of profits became the stock in trade of a Marxist economics developed in the course of the twentieth century and an "alternative" to mainstream economic analysis.[2]

The emergence of formal growth models centred upon the interaction of capital, labour and time in mainstream economics[3] ran in parallel with the elaboration of accounts of capitalist development that emphasized its crisis-ridden long-run tendencies. As already noted, economists were primarily concerned with the immediate future growth path, whereas Marxist critics of capitalism treated the future as the outcome of long-run underlying contradictions in the relation of capital and labour that were ultimately about distribution: the extraction of surplus value from the labour of working people and its re-embodiment in capital. Although this can only be a very sketchy account of the way in which, by the middle of the twentieth century, there were two principal and parallel accounts of the path of economic development in advanced economies, there is a difference between them that requires emphasis. Mainstream economic models were primarily short run as well as forward looking; while "Marxist" models, developed on the basis of nineteenth-century political economy, were long run, seeking "laws of capitalist development" that could underlie a projection of past outcomes in the accumulation of capital into a distant future. Piketty's work merges these two distinct approaches, although it is possible this has been done quite unconsciously since he is too young to have had personal experience of debates over inequality and capitalism, from the 1960s and the 1970s, that are now very remote. In 1980 he was nine years old, and there is more than a sense that he regards the time before 1980 as a kind of Stone Age, separating ancient from modern history.[4] Additionally, his economic education took place in the course of the 1990s rather than in the very different circumstances of the 1950s, 1960s and 1970s. Piketty is therefore personally detached from the period in which vigorous argument over capital and growth took place, and he blends the two analytical traditions outlined above: he works with conventional neoclassical growth models but places them within the scenario of capitalist development more familiar during the first three-quarters of the twentieth century as the stock in trade of Marxist economists.

Piketty is well advised in taking Simon Kuznets's account of income distribution as his foil. Kuznets's approach was multidimensional: an amalgam of applicable theory, careful measurement of the empirical counterparts to theoretical concepts, and an encyclopaedic knowledge applied to historical, sociological and political evidence. Like Nicholas Kaldor, he looked for "stylised facts" that needed explanation. He supported inferences from his hypotheses with exhaustive, careful analysis of the empirical evidence, much of which arose from his own painstaking search for and assembly of the appropriate data. Kuznets was very sceptical of the merits of pure theory and of the lasting universality of empirical laws. His extraordinary contributions over his long working life, "sixty years of professional work", more than justify Vibha Kapuria-Foreman and Mark Perlman's claim that he was "the *exemplar economic empiricist* of the century and possibly of all previous centuries".[5]

The main theoretical sections of Piketty's book seek to explain the Kaldor-type stylized facts his data have revealed using an aggregate production function model – the derivation of aggregate output from inputs of factors of production, chiefly capital and labour – that he attributes to Bob Solow (but not Trevor

Swan).[6] Piketty makes use of this model so that he might be understood by the mainstream, whose approach of choice it still is. He neglects, however, the careful provisos made by Solow and Swan concerning the limitations of the method: what it can and cannot achieve and, especially, the Harrod-type problems it was designed to tackle (dealt with below).

The aggregate production function has long been used to explain the relative contributions of the services of labour and capital to the creation of the national product, and of the distribution of that product as wages to wage-earners and profits to profit-receivers. In 1956 Solow and Swan independently argued that if the time series figures on national income, wages and profits could be viewed as if they were created by such a production process, and if this world could be viewed as if it were operating in a freely competitive environment, the relative shares of wages and profits could be viewed as the outcome of the contributions of the services of labour and capital, at the margin, in the creation of the total product, multiplied by the sizes of the employed labour supply and capital stock, respectively.

Modern interest in the process of growth over time was set in train by the seminal (and now classic) writings of Roy Harrod, the Oxford economist who was a close friend and follower of Maynard Keynes, and his first biographer. In 1939 he published a landmark article in the *Economic Journal*, "An Essay in Dynamic Theory", and in 1948 came a book, *Towards a Dynamic Economics*, which arose from lectures he had given at the London School of Economics. Harrod's analysis raised some major puzzles and problems. First, what conditions have to obtain if business people are to be satisfied, after the event, that they had, before the event, made the correct decisions concerning investment expenditure (accumulation)? He began from what he called the "warranted rate of growth", (G_w), "that rate of growth which, if it occurs, will leave all parties satisfied that they have produced neither more nor less than the right amount". Business people will then form expectations that will lead them to behave in such a way as to ensure this rate of growth continues.[7] Hence if the actual rate of growth (G_a) at one moment in time equalled G_w, the economy would continue to grow along this path. However, if this equality were not achieved, would the economy generate signals that would be recognized by business people and help form their expectations, thus leading them to take actions that brought G_a into line with G_w? Harrod showed that such stabilizing signals were not likely to occur; that, instead, signals would lead to an overall outcome that took G_a even further away from G_w: "A departure from equilibrium, instead of being self-righting, will be self-aggravating."[8] Hence, G_w was an unstable concept.[9]

Nor was this all. Harrod also identified what he named the natural rate of growth (G_n): the highest sustainable rate of growth emanating from the growth of the workforce, the improvement over time in the productivity of the workforce that resulted from accumulation, and the technical progress embodied in accumulation. The next main question was: even if the economy achieved G_w, would there be any forces (signals) that would bring the warranted rate of growth (G_w) and the actual rate of growth (G_a) to equality with the natural rate of growth (G_n), that is to say, to sustained full employment of the work force and the capital stock over time? While Keynes had analysed the short-period employment-creating effects of investment, Harrod was investigating key aspects of the capacity-creating effects of investment over the longer term.

Harrod's expression for G_w was $G_w = s/v$, where s is the overall average and marginal propensity to save and v is the desired capital–output ratio: linking savings to capital and output. There were two main early reactions to Harrod's problems: one concerned with the determinants of s and the other concerned with the determinants of v. Solow and Swan concentrated on v, asking whether there were forces (signals) to be found that would lead to decisions to change v when investment occurred, so as to bring G_a to equal G_w and, in turn, to equal G_n?

Both Solow and Swan explicitly assumed that an all-wise government always kept the economy at short-period full-employment equilibrium. This implied that G_n (abstracting from technical progress) matched the rate of growth of a fully employed work force. They asked: if G_a and G_w were not initially equal to G_n, would the relative prices of the services of labour and capital change in such a way as to induce business people to accumulate at the desired capital–output ratio that brought G_w ($= s/v$) to equality with G_n? They both showed that their simple, all-purpose, one-commodity Cobb–Douglas models[10] within this abstract setting did produce this result. Neither claimed that their analysis was descriptive of real economies, only that they had isolated tendencies at work that were stabilizing and that brought about abstract solutions to Harrod's problems. Alas, ever since, their models have been treated as if they are descriptive analysis – hence Piketty's decision to use this approach.

What is clear from the foregoing is that, in the middle of the twentieth century, economists developed some simple models of growth and distribution that worked in terms of given technologies and the contribution to aggregate output of varying amounts of capital and labour. The basic workhorse of the Cobb–Douglas model then provided a way of comparing and contrasting the effects on growth of changes in the productivity of labour or of capital. To keep things simple, in all of these models labour is estimated in person-hours per year (and not in wages), but capital is the total (depreciated) *value* of plant, equipment, buildings used in the production process, and is therefore, in fact, an accounting construct that may or may not reflect the real condition of invested capital. As we shall see, it was exactly the potential instability in the measurement of capital that led to significant arguments about the viability of the neoclassical growth model.

More recently, one of the prime rationales for privatization and public–private partnerships has been the real difficulty of estimating the output of hospitals, schools, railway systems and diverse utilities. Government spending in these areas does represent infrastructural investment, but government "investment" differs from private investment in that there is often no clearly identifiable market rate of return that makes it possible to assess the viability of any one project, or assign a realistic rate of depreciation and hence measure its future value.[11] There are of course various ways of circumventing this problem, but Piketty's approach is extremely radical: he discounts infrastructural assets by offsetting them against sovereign debt, arriving at the highly questionable conclusion that "public wealth in most developed countries is currently insignificant."[12]

Piketty adopted the standard economic models, but in order to do so he had to conflate his concept and measurement of wealth with those of capital in his theoretical arguments, although he cannot hide the fact that he is rather uncomfortable with the inappropriateness of this procedure.[13] Wealth in his reading includes land, housing and financial asset holdings as well as capital goods in the more usual sense of their presence in an aggregate production function. While there are clear problems with the measurement of capital, the problems arising from the measurement of wealth, especially over the long term, are very significant indeed. For example, the size of a pension fund, whether personal or corporate, is sensitive to the rates of return realized on the assets that make it up. What today looks like a solid asset can tomorrow be subject to a major writedown; conversely, imposing market valuations on diverse historical assets raises issues of fungibility and liquidity. The longer the time series, the greater these issues are; the relative significance of types of asset alters over time, and Piketty's argument depends on the identification of very long-run trends.

Piketty's principal explanation of his findings is presented as three "laws": (1) the rate of profits is greater than the rate of growth; (2) the capital to income ratio tends to rise; and (3) the share of profits in income tends to rise. Taken together, he argues that they imply greater and greater concentration of inherited wealth among relatively fewer people: a cumulative causation process that is leading to the re-establishment of what Jayati Ghosh astutely names "the resurgence of patrimonial capitalism"[14] (the resurgence of a feature of the eighteenth century). Lance Taylor has dubbed this "the triumph of the rentier",[15] as opposed to Keynes's desire for, and prediction of, the euthanasia of that class.[16] Keynes argued in *The General Theory* and elsewhere that as capital accumulated and so became abundant, its expected and actual return at the margin would approach zero. Accompanying this process would (or should) be measures to reduce the rate of interest to zero, eventually resulting in "the euthanasia of the rentier".

Keynes wrote: "I see, therefore, the rentier aspect of capitalism as a transitional phase which will disappear when it has done its work."[17] As we discuss below, Piketty's own approach has the euthanasia of the rentier as one of three possible outcomes, but that it is not the outcome that Piketty himself predicts.[18]

Here, as several reviewers have pointed out, Piketty runs into serious difficulties. In essence, his theories, when properly worked out, do not imply inferences that necessarily match his main findings. Among other requirements for his results to be rigorously established within his framework is that the value of the elasticity of substitution between capital and labour be greater than unity: that there be increasing returns to scale. He claims this to be not unreasonable, but most empirical studies suggest otherwise: that it is usually less than unity. Even if it were unity – that is to say, Cobb–Douglas – that would not predict his findings.[19]

So what of the use of the aggregate production function and, by implication, of the marginal productivity theory of distribution, to explain the systemic distribution of income that, in turn, leads to the unequal accumulation of capital and, more widely, wealth? Piketty is aware of the polemical debates between the two Cambridges about capital theory,[20] initially placed in an aggregate production function setting by Joan Robinson's "The Production Function and the Theory of Capital", which pointed out the problems inherent in measuring capital, and the instability that these problems introduce into any production function involving capital and labour.[21] Robinson raised three core questions in her paper.

First, what is the unit in which capital is measured in the aggregate production function? If the mainstream intuition that price is an index of scarcity is to be illuminating, we have to know, before any analysis starts, quite what "a lot" or "a little" capital might mean. If the amount of capital is then to be an explanator of the size of the rate of profits, it must be measured in a unit that is independent of distribution and prices. Otherwise, valuing overall capital in price terms means arguing in a circle: using a measure that includes itself to explain itself. So far, such a unit has never been found outside an all-purpose one-commodity model.

Second, Robinson criticized the methodology of using comparisons of equilibrium positions – differences – to explain *processes* (for example, accumulation) that take place over time.

And third, while analysing the problem of measurement, she regarded it as a corollary of the more fundamental question: what are the characteristics, "the rules of the game", of the society being analysed?

Piketty's reading of the issues and the outcome of "the capital controversy" is mistaken on at least two counts.[22] First, Piketty does not correctly identify the theoretical and empirical issues at stake. Second, his claim that MIT eventually won the argument is wrong: at a theoretical level MIT lost, as Paul Samuelson handsomely and graciously admitted in the 1966 Symposium on Capital-Reversing and Reswitching.[23] Alas, like the priest and the Levite, the profession has subsequently chosen to pass by on the other side.

The most serious theorists have moved on to a different terrain: can the initial results vitiate the most rigorous form of mainstream theory – that is, the intertemporal general equilibrium heterogeneous goods models associated with MIT? The final answer is not yet in, but our reading of what has happened so far (although we must admit that the formal aspects of the exchanges often pass way over our heads) is that the response should be a resounding "yes".[24] However, from our point of view, the moves that "save" the mainstream make its models incapable of explaining real-world findings on the distribution of income. Moreover, they remove from their model of society any concept of profit as it has traditionally been understood in analyses of capitalism.

It is a limitation of Piketty's understanding, given his excursions into the history of our trade and his use of a title for his book that suggests that a latter-day Marx is now among us, that he has failed to see that the principal issue at stake here is not the *measurement* of capital (that is a corollary of the main issue) but the *meaning* of capital: what "vision" of the economy does the analyst have in mind? There are two main claimants to this vision. The first is the mainstream Arrow–Debreu, Irving Fisher version, in which the consumer queen is the driving force of development over time, with all other agents and institutions serving to help her achieve her aim of maximizing her lifetime expected utility through her periodic allocation of income between consumption and saving over her lifetime.[25] The other "vision" arises from the political economists and Marx: here, the ruthless and swashbuckling capitalist class (including industrial, commercial and financial capitalists) rules the roost, production and distribution being determined by conflict between all classes in the economy, its institutions dancing to the tune of Capital as it endeavours to achieve the behavioural requirements of moneymaking and accumulation as ends in themselves, as a way of life whose only point is the continued accumulation of capital.

In the non-formal parts of Piketty's discussion there is an awareness of this background but, despite his disclaimers and the honest setting out of limitations, his chosen formal structure negates any impact that this might have. The economists initially involved in the debates were clearly aware of this distinction, and indeed Bob Solow, in his 1963 de Vries Lectures, *Capital Theory and the Rate of Return*, tried to overcome the puzzles thrown up by the measurement of capital by developing, both theoretically and empirically, Irving Fisher's concept of the social rate of return on investment. That he was not successful has been argued by both Joan Robinson[26] and Luigi Pasinetti[27]. Among the economists aligned with Cambridge England who early on perceived what was at stake were Amit Bhaduri[28] and Anwar Shaikh. The latter wrote his PhD dissertation at Columbia on these issues and published a classic paper on the humbug production function,[29] drawing on his theoretical discussion to criticize the arguments and practices of Solow's 1957 article in the *Review of Economics and Statistics*,[30] an article that spawned a huge literature on the relative contributions of capital deepening and technical progress to the growth of overall productivity.

As to the measurement and aggregation aspects of the debates, in addition to the external critique from a Marxist standpoint by Bhaduri and Shaikh, there have been internal critiques from within the mainstream approach. Franklin Fisher in particular has drawn attention to how stringent the conditions are for aggregation, and how inappropriate such an endeavour is in any case, because the empirical specifications in this literature are really no more than the manipulation of identities. John McCombie and Jesus Felipe (who has also collaborated with Fisher) have advanced this argument for many years, culminating in their comprehensive and definitive book.[31] Their book contains the history of the arguments from go to whoa and presents conclusions that, because they are irrefutably correct, are mostly ignored by the profession. If something is uncomfortable or does not square with received opinion, the natural reflex of the economist is to ignore it entirely and assume that it does not exist.

By using the marginal productivity theory of distribution in its aggregate form, Piketty subscribes to a Say's law[32] world over the long term: that is to say, to a world in which full employment of labour and of capital are ensured. In this way he automatically excludes the insights of Marx, Keynes and Kalecki regarding past and present historical events and findings. A number of economists have raised this point in their criticisms of Piketty's approach, introducing, for example, Keynes's analysis in *The General Theory*, as well as Pasinetti's contributions, which incorporate classical, Marxian, Keynesian, Kaleckian, Sraffian and Kaldorian insights into his own highly original system building. This is especially true of Lance Taylor's critique,[33] which is the core paper of a symposium on these issues in the Canadian *International Journal of Political Economy*. Taylor shows that, properly worked out, Piketty's own model and approach may result in either the euthanasia of the rentier (more involuntarily than voluntarily), or a steady state, or the triumph of the rentier, which is Piketty's principal claim. Introducing the insights of Keynes and Pasinetti results in a substantially more complex and relevant analysis that makes better sense of Piketty's findings, especially for the last forty years or so. Taylor combines the prospect of periods of time characterized by involuntary unemployment with Pasinetti's emphasis on the class nature of capitalist society and the implications of different spending and saving behaviour of the two principal classes: wage-earners and profit-receivers.

Our own take on this overlaps with, and is complementary to, Taylor's arguments. Keynes has shown us that there is no automatic tendency for capitalism, left to itself, to attain and sustain full employment: involuntary unemployment is always a distinct possibility. Marx's analysis reinforces this when he argues that the capitalist class will always take steps to make sure there exists a reserve army of labour, so as to be able to "discipline" the wage-earners by making dismissal an effective weapon. This argument was brought into the modern era in 1943 by Michal Kalecki in his classic article "Political Aspects of Full Employment".[34] He pointed out that there is a world of difference between the political economy of getting back to full employment from a deep slump, when all classes and the government benefit, and the political economy of sustained full employment. In the latter situation, political, economic and social power cumulatively passes from capital to labour, so that the power to hire and fire is no longer effective, and inflationary forces cumulatively increase. This prompts a reaction from the ruling class (and their hired prize-fighter economists) so that unemployment can be reinstated while claiming to be fighting inflation. Thomas Balogh and Nicholas Kaldor both pointed out in the 1970s that monetarism was "the incomes policy of Karl Marx",[35] that the shift in economic, political and social power from capital to labour over the long boom was no longer tolerated by the capitalist class the world over. Add to this the increasing dominance of world markets (and governments) by large multinational oligopolies and we might understand the events of the 1970s and 1980s as a concentrated attempt to create quiescent workforces on a worldwide scale (in the guise of controlling inflation). In the sphere of production this would increase the potential surplus available for accumulation in the sphere of distribution and exchange. Of course, one unintended consequence of these actions was often sluggish overall demand (as Taylor noted). "Animal spirits" were dimmed, and so the potential surplus was not realized owing to sluggish rates of accumulation; or it was only realized if governments stepped in to increase their own expenditure. Combining Taylor's analysis of these factors with Edward Nell's incisive comment on Taylor's article[36] yields a much more plausible narrative with which to interpret Piketty's findings than does his own analysis, trapped as it is within the neoclassical fairy tale.

Our reading of Piketty is that he is a progressive social democrat who, like Keynes, wants to save capitalism from itself. He says that he is not a member of any political party, that he is first and foremost a scholar deriving evidence-based accounts of the motions of society and proposing positive policies, which others might take up, with which to tackle the malfunctions he reveals. He advocates a worldwide wealth tax and/or progressive income taxes for individual countries: measures that any non-militant progressive would heartily agree with. But such a person would also agree with Piketty that, in the current global political climate, these are rather utopian proposals. Piketty makes up for this lack of realism by pointing out that major historical reforms have not, for the most part, come about as a result of the activities of well-trained technocrats in civil services; that wars and revolutions were often a necessary impulse; and that people like Piketty have at least to begin somewhere, to set debate in motion.

His admirable highlighting of the extent and causes of growing inequalities the world over has been well timed, striking a responsive chord. He has as a result quickly gained megastar status, with reviews of his book by many leading economists and, more recently, a symposium in the *Journal of Economic Perspectives* (2015), in which Piketty defends himself strongly as well as introducing some second thoughts.[37] We close with some comments and criticisms, including the limitations associated with his data sources.

First, as previously noted, his concept of wealth includes not only houses and land but also financial assets. As Galbraith has noted, the explicit concept of capital used by Piketty is neither that of Marx nor the physical capital as a factor of production found in the neoclassical model of economic growth. The book instead turns on the valuation placed on tangible and intangible assets, their distribution through time, and inheritance from one generation to the next.[38] Because of double-entry bookkeeping, financial assets reflect real capital goods that are also included in the totals, and of necessity valued at market prices. Does this mean that double-counting may be part of the overall totals?[39]

Second (and here we repeat our earlier argument for the sake of emphasis), if the distribution of income is to be explained by the use of "capital" and "its" marginal product – the principle embedded in the neoclassical models that Piketty employs – this requires that "capital" be measured in a unit that is independent of distribution and prices. But outside of an all-purpose one-commodity world – the "corn model" proposed by Piero Sraffa to interpret Ricardo's model of production and distribution[40] – valuation is required, and the prices used of necessity include profits and rate of profits components, so the argument is essentially circular. This point was put most succinctly by Piero Sraffa in response to Roy Harrod's review of his book:[41] "What good is a quantity of capital … which, since it depends on the rate of interest, cannot be used for its traditional purpose … to determine the rate of interest[?]."[42] This does not represent the failure, as is sometimes claimed, on the part of Sraffa (or of Joan Robinson) to understand the nature of mutual and/or simultaneous determination, but instead reflects the core distinction that has to be made between determining factors and determined outcomes. The rate of interest (or profits) cannot be at one and the same time a cause and an effect.

Third, there are limitations associated with the use of reported taxation and the impact upon such records of historical cost accounting conventions and procedures. This was an issue that was vigorously discussed in the 1960s, 1970s and 1980s. We could perhaps take the liberty of pointing out that in 1965 one of us published an article in *Oxford Economic Papers* in which it was shown that if an accountant were to be let loose in a Golden

Age where expected and actual rates of profit coincide because expectations are always realized, the accountant could, nevertheless, using his/her tools, give very misleading answers to the question of what rates of profit prevailed. Depending on the shape of the quasi-rents associated with each investment, the method of depreciation used, whether growth was occurring or not and, if so, how fast, and on the ratios of financial to real assets in the balance sheets of individual companies, then the discrepancies between the accountant's measure and the true figure could be very large indeed.[43] In the early 1980s Fisher and McGowan used the same argument, but expressed much more elegantly, to determine whether IBM was or was not making monopoly profits.[44] As there are no rough rules of thumb to correct for these effects in the figures, we have to take Piketty's findings on trust.

Finally, although Piketty realizes that much of the extreme inequality in leading economies is associated with the obscenely large salaries and bonuses of CEOs and managers, rather than the profits of traditional capitalists, he does not refer to the two classic volumes that started this literature: Robin Marris's *The Economic Theory of "Managerial" Capitalism* (1964) and Edith Penrose's *The Theory of Growth of the Firm* (1959).

As we have shown in the above, Piketty's analytical apparatus is rooted in neoclassical models that go back to the 1950s. By directing attention back to these, and the argument that has grown up for decades around them, we hope to have shown that the economic analysis of growth and distribution remains indebted to this earlier literature and earlier debates. In seeking a critical assessment of contemporary argument, we need to remind ourselves of awkward problems that remain unresolved, and largely ignored.

Notes for Chapter 2

1. Thomas Piketty, *Capital in the Twenty-First Century* (Cambridge, MA: Harvard University Press, 2014).

2. The most accessible example of this in English is Paul Sweezy's *Theory of Capitalist Development* (New York: Monthly Review Press, 1942).

3. See, for example, Part IV, "The Working of the Dynamic System", in J. R. Hicks, *Value and Capital: An Inquiry into Some Fundamental Principles of Economic Theory* (Oxford: Clarendon Press, 1939).

4. See his remarks on the degree of technological change since 1980 in *Capital*, pp. 95–6.

5. Vibha Kapuri-Foreman and Mark Perlman, "An Economic Historian's Economist: Remembering Simon Kuznets", *Economic Journal* 105 (1995), p. 1524 (emphasis in the original).

6. R. M. Solow, "A Contribution to the Theory of Economic Growth", *Quarterly Journal of Economics* 70 (1956), pp. 65–94; T. W. Swan, "Economic Growth and Capital Accumulation", *Economic Record* 32 (1956), pp. 343–61.

7. R. F. Harrod, "An Essay in Dynamic Theory", *Economic Journal* 49 (1939), p. 16.

8. *Ibid.*, p. 22.

9. As further explained in G. C. Harcourt, *The Structure of Post-Keynesian Economics: The Core Contributions of the Pioneers* (Cambridge: Cambridge University Press, 2006), pp. 104–9.

10. The Cobb–Douglas production function treats output as a function of inputs of capital and labour, each of which has a particular marginal product: the amount of additional output resulting from a given addition of capital or labour. When combined with the average amounts, their elasticities are formed. Assuming constant returns to scale, so that the elasticities of K and L sum to 1, the elasticities represent the respective shares in output.

11. The argument could be extended to include the contents of national museums and art galleries, investment by the government in ships, submarines, aircraft, assorted military hardware, and the increasing amount of funding devoted to intelligence and cyber-security.

12. Piketty, *Capital*, p. 48.

13. Soskice has argued that in his modelling Piketty effectively employs the standard economists' concept of capital as an input in the production of goods and services. See Soskice, "*Capital in the Twenty-First Century*: A Critique", p. 651.

14. Jayati Ghosh, "Piketty and the Resurgence of Patrimonial Capitalism", *Real-World Economics Review* 69(7) (2014), pp. 138–44.

15. Lance Taylor, "The Triumph of the Rentier? Thomas Piketty vs Luigi Pasinetti and John Maynard Keynes", *International Journal of Political Economy* 43 (2014), pp. 4–17.

16. Stephanie Blankenburg (to GCH 16/05/15) has noted that it was Michal Kalecki who brought back the role of the rentier into modern macroeconomic theory and that our mutual friend, Gabriel Palma, wrote of the return of the rentier in his "The Revenge of the Market on the Rentiers: Why Neo-liberal Reports of the End of History Turned out to be Premature", *Cambridge Journal of Economics* 33 (2009), pp. 829–69 (the special issue of the *Cambridge Journal of Economics* devoted to the global financial crisis).

17. J. M. Keynes, *The General Theory of Employment, Interest and Money, Collected Writings of John Maynard Keynes*, Volume VII (London: Macmillan, 1973), p. 376.

18. Taylor, "The Triumph of the Rentier?", p. 5.

19. With Cobb–Douglas, relative shares are always constant; a rise or fall in marginal contributions is exactly offset by the fall or rise in the employment of the services of labour or capital. The most relevant source on this is Bob Rowthorn's "A Note on Piketty's *Capital in the Twenty-First Century*", *Cambridge Journal of Economics* 38 (2014), pp. 275–84, for both the empirical findings and the theoretical argument.

20. Summarized in G. C. Harcourt, *Some Cambridge Controversies in the Theory of Capital* (Cambridge: Cambridge University Press, 1972).

21. Joan Robinson, "The Production Function and the Theory of Capital", *Review of Economic Studies* 21 (1953–4), pp. 81–106. For an update and overview, see in particular Avi J. Cohen and G. C. Harcourt, "Retrospectives: Whatever Happened to the Cambridge Capital Theory Controversies?", *Journal of Economic Perspectives* 17 (2003), pp. 199–214.

22. See Piketty, *Capital*, pp. 230–32. James K. Galbraith pointed this out in his critical but well-informed review article, "Kapital for the Twenty-First Century?", pp. 1–7.

23. Paul A. Samuelson, "A Summing Up", *Quarterly Journal of Economics* 80 (1966), pp. 568–83.

24. See, for example, Andrés Lazzarini's very careful analysis in the recent symposium on the issues involved, "Some Unsettled Issues in a Second Phase of the Cambridge–Cambridge Controversy", *Review of Radical Political Economics* 47 (2015), pp. 256–73.

25. See Irving Fisher, *The Theory of Interest* (New York: Macmillan, 1930); Harcourt, *Some Cambridge Controversies*, p. 161.

26. Joan Robinson, "Solow on the Rate of Return", *Economic Journal* 74 (1964), pp. 410–17.

27. Luigi Pasinetti, "Switches of Technique and the 'Rate of Return' in Capital Theory", *Economic Journal* 79 (1969), pp. 508–31; Luigi Pasinetti, "Again on Capital Theory and Solow's 'Rate of Return'", *Economic Journal* 80 (1970), pp. 428–31.

28. Amit Bhaduri, "On the Significance of Recent Controversies on Capital Theory", *Economic Journal* 79 (1969), pp. 532–9.

29. Anwar Shaikh, "Laws of Production and Laws of Algebra: The Humbug Production Function", *Review of Economics and Statistics* 54 (1974), pp. 115–20.

30. R. M. Solow, "Technical Change and the Aggregate Production Function", *Review of Economics and Statistics* 39 (1957), pp. 312–20.

31. Jesus Felipe and John S. L. McCombie, *The Aggregate Production Function and the Measurement of Technical Change: "Not Even Wrong"* (Cheltenham: Edward Elgar, 2013).

32. Jean-Baptiste Say argued that since products were bought with the revenues generated by the production process, production and consumption would always match, whether in the short or the long run; there could, therefore, be no crises associated with a shortfall of consumption. "Say's law" has, however, become known as the principle that "supply creates its own demand" (which is not quite the same idea).

33. Taylor, "Triumph of the Rentier?". For commentary on this see G. C. Harcourt, "Comment: Lance Taylor on Thomas Piketty's World as Seen Through the Eyes of Maynard Keynes and Luigi Pasinetti", *International Journal of Political Economy* 43(3) (2014), pp. 18–25; and Taylor's response, "Modeling Distribution and Growth: Replies to Garbellini and Wirkierman, Harcourt, and Nell", *International Journal of Political Economy* 43(3) (2014), pp. 44–54.

34. Michal Kalecki, "Political Aspects of Full Employment", *Political Quarterly* 14 (1943), pp. 322–31.

35. See T. Balogh, *The Irrelevance of Conventional Economics* (London: Weidenfeld & Nicolson, 1982), p. 77.

36. Edward J. Nell, "On the Causes of Growing Inequality: Piketty, Pasinetti and Taylor", *International Journal of Political Economy* 43 (2014), pp. 26–34.

37. Piketty, "Putting Distribution Back at the Center of Economics".

38. Galbraith, "Kapital", p. 2.

39. Nell, "On the Causes of Growing Inequality", p. 27, argues that this is indeed the case.

40. Piero Sraffa, "Introduction" to David Ricardo, *On the Principles of Political Economy and Taxation, Works and Correspondence of David Ricardo,* Volume I, Piero Sraffa (ed.), with the collaboration of M. H. Dobb (Cambridge: Cambridge University Press, 1951), p. xxxi.

41. Piero Sraffa, *Production of Commodities by Means of Commodities: Prelude to a Critique of Economic Theory* (Cambridge: Cambridge University Press, 1960).

42. Piero Sraffa, "Production of Commodities: a comment", *Economic Journal* 72 (1972), p. 479.

43. G. C. Harcourt, "The Accountant in a Golden Age", *Oxford Economic Papers* 17 (1965), pp. 66–80.

44. F. M. Fisher and J. J. McGowan, "On the Misuse of Accounting Rates of Return to Infer Monopoly Profits", *American Economic Review* 73 (1983), pp. 82–97.

3

INEQUALITY

Keith Tribe

Rising inequality in the distribution of income in advanced economies became a widely debated issue in the wake of the financial crisis that began in 2008. The Occupy movement and demonstrations in leading global financial centres against the concentrated wealth of "the one per cent" reflected a widespread feeling that the bankers and financiers whose activities had prompted the crisis not only failed to accept any responsibility, they also suffered little from its effects, since troubled financial institutions across the world were propped up by national governments and their taxpayers. In this context, the novelty of Thomas Piketty's *Capital in the Twenty-First Century* lay in his argument that an increasing polarization in the distribution of wealth and incomes was not simply associated with the wave of financial market liberalization that had taken place since the 1990s, culminating, but not ending, in the crash of 2008; but was instead part of a much longer-term, and global, trend. He presented his findings as a revision of the "Kuznets curve": the idea that while industrialization in the nineteenth century had been characterized by increasing income inequality, during the first two-thirds of the twentieth century polarization had diminished, a sequence of events represented by an inverted U-shaped curve of income distribution over time.[1]

Further, Piketty's prime focus appeared to be on wealth rather than income, broadening the base of his analysis. The broad aggregates that he deploys conceal a great deal: who the holders of great wealth are, how those people came by their wealth, and of what that wealth consists; the range of incomes around the median, and their distribution by race, age and gender; the differing ways in which households are poor, and the differing costs of being poor between countries in terms of access to clean water, housing, health care and education. All the same, a focus on the existing distribution of wealth and income within a national economy as part of a long-run trend is a start, and the interest that Piketty's book aroused demonstrated the extent of public concern.

Modern economists have generally paid relatively little attention to wealth, inequality and distribution; Piketty has moved these concerns up the public agenda, but his work is nonetheless rooted in research and publication by economists reaching back to the 1960s. Tony Atkinson published his major survey of the problem of income inequality in 2015,[2] but his important paper on measurement appeared almost fifty years ago in the *Journal of Economic Theory*.[3] Jan Pen published his well-known book *Income Distribution* in 1971, representing incomes in terms of human height and visualizing the distribution of incomes as a "parade of dwarfs (and a few giants)" that passes an observer within the space of an hour, and where only in the last few seconds do the colossal figures of the truly rich appear.[4] Amartya Sen published his initial economic analysis of inequality in 1973.[5] And before all of these, Henry Phelps Brown had published a survey of incomes in France, Germany, Sweden, Britain and the US for the period 1860–1960: a long-term study of the very same countries on which Piketty bases his analysis.[6] Along a different dimension, John Roemer points to the publication of Rawls's *Theory of Justice* in 1971 as a turning point in the discussion of distributive justice.[7] Nonetheless, where economists, including Piketty, have turned their attention to these issues, they have, naturally enough, focused on economic inequality, generally avoiding any wider discussion of the forms and social impact of inequality. The difficulty that follows from this is that, as with Piketty, framing the problem of inequality in strictly economic terms prompts a search for economic remedies, such as the global tax that Piketty advocates. Whether economic inequality might be better addressed by measures other than those directed to the distribution of income or wealth is not something that such writings generally consider.

In any case, some would argue that income distribution is not a matter that should be of central concern for economists, since remuneration is a reflection of market valuation, and where labour markets are efficient incomes are differentiated appropriately.[8] If it is pointed out that in 2016 a London tube driver earns twice as much as a junior doctor, who also works many more hours, then the response would be to point either to the detrimental effect of trade unions on labour markets or to the expectation that in some remote future a junior doctor might expect to be paid rather more.[9] But the story of tube drivers and hospital staff is also the story of executive pay; in both private and public sectors managerial and executive pay has ballooned in the past couple of decades while median incomes have remained stagnant. Efficient markets seem to apply only to the low paid, not to the high, and the inequity of this is obvious, if not to some economists.

Furthermore, while the use of deciles to characterize the distributional range of wealth or incomes facilitates comparison, this approach also involves significant loss of texture and detail. What counts as "wealth" at any one time in any one society will differ considerably from top to bottom; and this difference will create variations in the market value of whatever is counted as "wealth" and the degree to which it can be passed on to succeeding generations. Thus, the new "patrimonial capitalism" that Piketty has in view is more complex than it might at first appear. As far as income inequality goes, a focus upon income deciles obscures the composition of incomes and their relation to the existence of poverty: whether income is regular, or discontinuous, whether unemployment is compensated by welfare payments, the conditions upon which such payments are received, the different issues of youth unemployment and of redundancy, and the availability of pension schemes, whether state or private.

Like Piketty, Atkinson talks of *reducing* inequality,[10] and generally means by this fiscal mechanisms for the more equal distribution of current net incomes. This is, however, a very restricted perspective upon the general problem of inequality. When, in *The Spirit Level*, Wilkinson and Pickett list the "costs of inequality" – mental illness, low levels of life expectancy, obesity, teenage pregnancy, crime, limited social mobility – one could ask whether these markers of inequality are open to modification simply through the redistribution of income; whether, in fact, the causation might run more from these factors to income distribution rather than the other way around.[11] If we step back from the question of economic inequality to the way in which economic inequality is linked to broader issues of social equality, it becomes possible to move discussion beyond the issues of income distribution, complex and indeterminate as they already are. Furthermore, there is an unargued assumption running through much of the economic literature on inequality that it is a "bad thing", so that, *prima facie*, reducing it must be a "good thing". This unargued presumption invites the counterclaim that inequality is inevitable, and that a rising tide lifts all boats; that the unequal distribution of rewards promotes economic growth that, in the end, benefits both rich and poor alike. The aim of reducing inequality is certainly laudable, but there are very many ways in which this could be done, and particular policy measures might well create new (perhaps less critical) inequalities while fixing specific problems.

Moving away from income inequality to the larger question of the distribution of wealth, as Piketty does, greatly complicates issues of measurement, while at the same time failing to address this issue of quite *which sorts* of inequality are thought to be either undesirable or harmful. His perspective retains that blurring of inequality and difference that remains unaddressed in the modern literature. While there is a liberal adherence to the advantages of social and cultural diversity, the corollary to diversity is difference, and liberal discourse is far less comfortable talking about difference than it is about diversity. There is, consequently, a certain hollowness in discussing the "reduction" of inequality on the one hand without on the other hand acknowledging that without difference, there would be no diversity.

SOCIAL DIFFERENTIATION AND INEQUALITY

Stepping back from modern discussion to an older literature can help clarify this, for much modern debate simply repeats positions more clearly established long ago, but since neglected. We could do a great deal worse than first consider how Adam Smith argued about markets, wealth and inequality, and then consider what inequality has meant for past populations. For another problem with a reliance upon long runs of data on income distribution is that the existence of inequality has had different implications at different points in these time series. Being in the bottom 10 per cent of the income distribution in Britain one hundred years ago was a very different thing to being in the bottom 10 per cent today. As we shall see, as recently as one hundred years ago large areas of British towns and cities resembled the favelas and shanty towns of today. The shift from landed wealth to finance and property has itself been associated with major social changes. What economic inequality implies therefore shifts over time, and the longer the time period taken, the less useful is the distribution of income or wealth *in itself* as an indicator of economic welfare, social conditions and political structure.

Adam Smith wrote in 1776 about the *nature* and *causes* of the wealth of nations, and in making this distinction he meant something quite specific. The first was the "annual labour of every nation": broadly, economic activity or what we today know as gross domestic product. The more economic activity there was, the more wealthy a nation was, since national wealth was the aggregate of economic activity.[12] "Causes" were, by contrast, rooted in the human motivation to action, activity being directed to the acquisition of "necessaries and conveniences". Here again Smith is being quite precise in his use of language, for he was of the view that while "necessaries" were relatively easily acquired in a commercial society, the luxury goods that were "conveniences" absorbed the greater part of human effort: the striving for happiness through the emulation of others. Such striving, he suggested, did not actually make individuals any happier, but it did create wealthy nations. Furthermore, in a commercial society,

> the whole labour of society is so great, that all are often abundantly supplied, and a workman, even of the lowest and poorest order, if he is frugal and industrious, may enjoy a greater share of the necessaries and conveniences of life than it is possible for any savage to acquire.[13]

Smith thus identified a social mechanism that could account for the existence of both wealthy and poor nations. He believed that in the most primitive societies, based upon hunting and gathering, almost all activity was devoted to the meeting of immediate needs; while as societies moved through pastoral and agricultural stages to modern commercial societies, they became steadily more wealthy, because an increasing amount of time was available for the production and consumption of "conveniences".[14] As Istvan Hont emphasized, this conception of social progress was shared by Scottish writers of this period, and produced some sort of explanation of the distinction of rich from poor societies, underscoring too the benefits thought to accrue to all of those living in a commercial society compared with their contemporaries in less-developed societies.[15]

The relative wealth of commercial societies depended upon the degree of elaboration of the division of labour, which was limited only by the "extent of the market". Specialization of human activity increased the productivity of human labour, and it was the potential of this increase of labour productivity that lay at the heart of Smith's book. As individuals directed their efforts to increasingly specialized activity, they correspondingly relied more and more on the labour of others to supply all the necessaries, conveniences and amusements of human life, every man being "rich or poor according to the degree in which he can afford to enjoy" them.[16] The division of labour rested upon economic differentiation and specialization; individuals became part of networks of exchange that supplied them with their various wants. A wealthy society was therefore one in which the division of labour was well advanced, with a high degree of differentiation between individuals by activity, and a reliance for their needs on the efforts of others with whom they never came into direct contact. From this grew a natural inequality in occupations; and certainly, in the kind of society that Smith had in view, the social inequality in occupations created an inequality in incomes. In the hands of Malthus and Ricardo, social differentiation by income was converted into the wage-fund doctrine: that there was a fixed sum available for the remuneration of labour, and that any increase in numbers of workers would reduce the wages of each individual; or, correspondingly, that any increase in incomes would require a reduction in the number of workers. Inequality in the distribution of incomes became a "natural law" of political economy.

These are of course old arguments, but they do articulate a clear vision of the relation of economic activity to income inequality that has echoed down to the present,[17] and it is a vision that originated in societies much less egalitarian than ours. By the late nineteenth century the idea that there was a fixed sum available for the wage-workers who made up the great majority of the population had been replaced by the idea that the market for labour was like any other market, and that wage rates were governed by the interaction of supply and demand. Low wages in this account were the outcome of low skills, where the strength and endurance of one worker was much the same as that of another. Trade unions were formed in Britain to exert some bargaining power in these kinds of labour markets, but these organizations first emerged among skilled workers. It was not until the 1880s and 1890s in Britain that agitation began related to the low and irregular incomes of casual unskilled workers. The urban concentration of the British population also meant that social and economic disparities were obvious to all. As Charles Booth's poverty maps show, at the end of the nineteenth century rich and poor lived in close proximity to each other;[18] while in Seebohm Rowntree's mapping of York's slum, working-class and middle-class districts, the slum areas are concentrated around the central business area.[19] Social and economic inequality was written into the social geography of the city, and into the physical condition of its poorest inhabitants.[20] Rowntree records that of the 3,000 men who volunteered for the army during the years 1897–1901 in York, Leeds and Sheffield, 950 (or 26.5 per cent) were rejected outright and 760 (29 per cent) were accepted conditional upon their meeting the standards once they had completed basic training. Of those presenting themselves, 55.5 per cent thus failed the physical standard in some way. He also notes what the basic physical standards for the infantry were at that time: a minimum height of 5 feet 3 inches (160 centimetres), a minimum chest size of 33 inches (84 centimetres) and a minimum weight of 8 stones 3 pounds (52 kilogrammes).[21]

Rowntree's study of poverty in York was the first concise analysis in Britain of the way in which poverty was linked to employment, housing, household structure and income, demonstrating the connection between income inequality and welfare. He had taken his inspiration from Charles Booth's work on the life of the London working class, the first volume of Booth's survey appearing in 1889, with further parts being consolidated into nine volumes in the second edition of 1892–97. Determined to study one single provincial town in detail, Rowntree selected his native city of York, which in 1899 had around 15,000 houses and a population of 75,812. He set about recording the condition of every household dependent on waged income: house-to-house surveys were completed in 1899, the resulting notebooks then forming the basis for an evaluation of living conditions that was more concise than Booth's volumes, and which also set the analytical standard for later social surveys, such as the *Social Survey of Merseyside* in the 1930s.[22] Rowntree built upon the classification of families developed by Booth, dividing them among seven classes from A to G, where A represented the lower end: a family income of under 18 shillings a week for a "moderate" family of a mother, a father and two to four children.[23] Since family income here includes that from lodgers, who were counted as members of the family, the basic unit of study was the household, rather than a family unit as such.

Rowntree sought to establish a measure for poverty in York, and to determine how far existing poverty might result from insufficient income, or might instead arise, at least in part, from improvidence. He therefore distinguished between primary poverty, where total income was insufficient to obtain the minimum needed to maintain mere physical efficiency; and secondary poverty, where income would be sufficient to maintain physical efficiency were it not for some other expenditure, either useful or wasteful, that prevented this. The criterion of physical efficiency thus determined a "poverty line" (see Figure 3.1),[24] below which the balance of household income and expenditure was insufficient to maintain basic physical needs. Central to his analysis was the use of food budgets, recording the typical weekly food consumption of the household, determining the outlay necessary to acquire it, and evaluating consumption patterns in terms of calorific requirements.[25] By using as a standard the cost and calorific value of meals provided in the municipal workhouse, Rowntree was able to shed light on typical household diets. The calorific requirements of different kinds of work for men, those for women and those for children of various ages were also estimated using studies conducted in the US and Scotland, the latter in part being based on prisoners engaged in a "moderately active day's work" (the activity was stonebreaking).[26] Here and elsewhere, Rowntree emphasizes that basic nutritional provision was far better in prisons and workhouses than for the average labourer in York.[27]

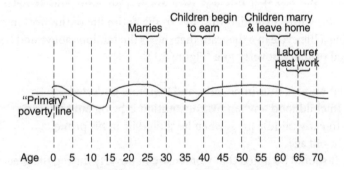

Figure 3.1. Poverty over the life cycle.
(*Source*: Seebohm Rowntree, *Poverty: A Study in Town Life*, p. 137.)

By recording rents, clothing and food budgets, and matching income to expenditure, Rowntree concluded that 1,465 families, or 7,230 persons, lived in primary poverty, making up 15.46 per cent of the wage-earning class and 9.91 per cent of the total population. For the poorest group, Class A (under 18 shillings per week income), 51 summaries are printed: for example, number 33 read "Labourer. Married. Four rooms. Six children. Filthy to extreme. This house shares one closet with another, and one water-tap with five others.

Rent 3s. 6d."[28] Class A includes only 4.2 per cent of the working-class population, and 2.6 per cent of the total population; on the other hand, Class D (income
over 30 shillings a week for a "moderate family") represents about one-third of
the total population, and half of the working-class population. This social class
is not in poverty and is described as "that section of our population upon which
the social and industrial development of England largely depends, and is the
one which will always exercise the most important influence in bringing about
the social elevation of those in the poorer classes".[29] The brief notes for this class
distinguish households from those in Class A principally through three factors:
regular employment, more rooms and a general cleanliness. There are, however,
several instances recorded of multiple households sharing a closet and a water
tap.[30] By contrast, the precariousness of life in a Class B household (income
between 18 and 21 shillings per week) was evident in the heavy use of the pawn-
shop: "Some families pawn their Sunday clothes regularly every Monday, and
redeem them as regularly on the following Saturday night when the week's wages
have been received."[31]

Rowntree also observes that once children begin to earn money many of these
Class B households will rise into a higher class, "possibly to sink back again,
however, when their children marry and leave home".[32] This draws attention to
another feature of his analysis of poverty: that it is treated as a dynamic, lifetime phenomenon. In his book on pauperism Charles Booth had already drawn
attention to the fact that this was very much a phenomenon associated with
old age;[33] Rowntree extended this idea to the entire life of the working classes,
presenting a life cycle in a diagram that shows fluctuations above and below the
horizontal primary poverty line (Figure 3.1):

> A labourer is thus in poverty, and therefore underfed –
> a) In childhood – when his constitution is being built up.
> b) In early middle life – when he should be in his prime.
> c) In old age.
> … It should be noted that women are in poverty during the greater
> part of the period that they are bearing children.[34]

Class C was an intermediary class related to this lifetime cycle: with a household income between 21 and 30 shillings, some of these households were still in
poverty, although those at the higher end of the distribution might live under
conditions not dissimilar to those of Class D. Importantly, this single class made
up 33.6 per cent of the working-class population and 20.7 per cent of the total
population; so when added to the numbers in social classes A and B, this means
that in 1900 more than 25 per cent of York's total population was either living
in a condition of poverty or was at risk of sinking into it.

DISTRIBUTION AND A DEMOCRATIC ORDER

This dynamic perspective upon questions of inequality was taken up by R. H. Tawney in his 1929 Halley Stewart lectures, published under the title "Equality" in 1931. The arguments he advanced about the assumptions governing modern conceptions of equality and inequality have lost little of their lucidity and relevance. He does not, as might be assumed, deny the natural fact of human inequality; rather, he contrasts the natural differences between human beings with those differences that are converted into inequalities. In his third chapter, "Inequality and Social Structure", he writes:

> So to criticize inequality and to desire equality is not, as is some-
> times suggested, to cherish the romantic illusion that men are equal
> in character and intelligence. It is to hold that, while their natural
> endowments differ profoundly, it is the mark of a civilized society to
> aim at eliminating such inequalities as have their source, not in indi-
> vidual differences, but in its own organization, and that individual
> differences, which are a source of social energy, are more likely to
> ripen and find expression if social inequalities are, as far as practi-
> cable, diminished.[35]

The greatest obstacle to the realization of greater equality was then described by Tawney as the "habit of mind" that thinks it natural, even desirable, that the community should be divided by "sharp differences of economic status, of environment, of education and culture and habit of life", and defending the social institutions and economic arrangements that "emphasized and enhanced" these differences. In approaching these issues Tawney drew extensively on recent estimates by Arthur Bowley and Josiah Stamp of the national income, which for 1924 concluded that 76 per cent of the occupied population were wage-earners, 14 per cent salaried, 6 per cent independent workers and 4 per cent employers, farmers or in the professions.[36] The way in which this was also a proxy for the distribution of income and wealth was pointed up by Tawney's comparison with the employment structure of France, where, for example, peasant proprietors outnumbered agricultural labourers by almost two to one, while in England the (much smaller) rural population was almost overwhelmingly made up of wage workers. This comparison enables Tawney to shift attention to the distribution of property, suggesting that, while in Britain Friendly Societies and other mutual institutions collectively held significant sums in the form of workers' savings, by comparison with property held by other sections of the population the amount owned was "impressive by its smallness rather than by its magnitude". And he goes on to note that an appreciable number of Englishmen were almost proper-tyless, with assets that probably do not equal "the value of the kit that they took into battle at Paschendaele or on the Somme."[37]

Drawing upon estimates of the accumulated savings of small investors made for Britain in 1925 by Caradog Jones and Carr-Saunders, Tawney then sketches some international comparisons before concluding that the distribution of property, where "two-thirds of the wealth is owned by one per cent of the population ... gives a peculiar and distinctive stamp to the social structure of England".[38] There is also a sharpness to the distinction between those who direct economic activity and those who carry out what they are directed to do: "the concentration of economic authority ... [being] of the essence of the modern industrial system", and lending the English social system its distinctive hierarchical form. Developing his argument through a discussion of health and education, Tawney then considers the limited pool from which political leaders are drawn, treating this as the third expression of the hierarchical character of English society. He notes at this point that there is unfortunately no word for the type of society that combines the institutional forms of political democracy with sharp economic and social divisions.[39] The US had enjoyed 200 years of agricultural, manufacturing and commercial development, but Tawney quotes De Tocqueville's warning that

> if ever aristocracy and permanent inequality of social conditions were to infiltrate the world once again, it is predictable that this [a new industrial aristocracy] is the door by which they would enter.[40]

Tawney maintains that in such a hierarchical society great contrasts of wealth and power do not promote the values of civilization, but thwart them; they are not a mark of civilization, but of its imperfection.

Not only does the existence of social inequality diminish the potential of a society, but Tawney also argues against the idea that social mobility is an adequate solution to the losses that he identifies. The possibility open to some of advancing from the bottom of society to the top cannot substitute for the existence of practical equality, nor does it eliminate existing disparities of income and social condition. By itself, social mobility is no solution to the existence of hierarchy and inequality, since opportunities to rise in this way are open only to the few.[41] The arguments put forward here by Tawney were taken up some thirty years later by Michael Young, but given a dystopian and satirical twist by imagining a future in which society had indeed become precisely sorted by merit, where those at the bottom knew that they belonged at the bottom, while the remainder of the population was allocated by aptitude to their position in the social scale:

The axiom of modern thought is that people are unequal, and the ensuing moral injunction that they should be accorded a station in life related to their capacities. By dint of a long struggle, society has at last been prevailed upon to conform: the mentally superior have been raised to the top and the mentally inferior lowered to the bottom.[42]

Young coined the name "meritocracy" for this kind of society, perhaps finding the term that had eluded Tawney for a form of democracy in which differences in aptitude are directly translated into social status.

In so doing, Young sketched a society whose complete fulfilment can only be achieved "by giving free rein to well-trained imagination and organized intelligence". The book is presented as a work of historical sociology charting an alternative and heroic trajectory for the rise of a system dedicated to educating the talented to rule and training the remainder for their respective stations in life. This trajectory is constructed from genuine sources for the first half of the twentieth century and from invented ones for subsequent developments: modern society (from the perspective of 2034) has emerged from the domination of an aristocracy of birth, and is now ruled by an aristocracy of talent. This was not rule by the people, but rule by the *cleverest* people; "not an aristocracy of birth, not a plutocracy of wealth, but a true meritocracy of talent".[43]

The (fictional) author writes in the context of protest from the lower orders, who, having hitherto accepted the positions allotted to them, were now in revolt. The book in fact purports to be printed from a manuscript written by an author killed in 2034 at a Mayday rally organized to promote a new People's Charter "with its echoes from the past in the quotations from the now long-forgotten Tawney and Cole, William Morris and John Ball",[44] the result of collaboration between women's organizations and dissident technicians. It is this resurgence of discontent over inequality that baffles the late author; for, he supposes,

> Civilization does not depend upon the stolid mass, the *homme moyen sensuel*, but upon the creative minority, the innovator who with one stroke can save the labour of 10,000, the brilliant few who cannot look without wonder, the restless élite who have made mutation a social, as well as a biological, fact.[45]

Rhetorically at least, the dystopian future that Young so gleefully sketched in the 1950s has already come to pass. This is the narrative of bankers, the "creative classes", and of Silicon Valley.[46]

At the time that Young was writing, Labour Party policy advocated the replacement of selective grammar schools by non-selective comprehensive schools; among the individuals thanked in Young's acknowledgements is Tony Crosland, who later became Labour Education Minister (1965–67) and was a famously vigorous opponent of grammar schools and selection by ability.[47] Using official reports and contemporary writings, Young presents an alternative history of English secondary education in which, by the 1980s, the comprehensive school experiment had failed, Britain's energy needs were entirely met by atomic energy, European unification had taken place, and fully selective schooling was the norm.[48] Education became a lifelong engagement: by the later 1990s, in this story, constant testing ensured precise selection, moving individuals up or down the occupational scale as they proceeded through their lives.

Young's book predates, but anticipates, the association of education, social mobility and human capital that has become embedded in modern policy. Importantly, he points out that a society in which social mobility is predicated upon "investment" in formal education – and a subsequent allocation to occupation and income by educational certification – can turn into a new kind of feudalism. He turned the dystopias of Yevgeny Zamyatin, George Orwell and Aldous Huxley into a plausible narrative of social development based on social selection through educational attainment. Ironically, of course, the "unpleasant term" that he coined to describe this dystopia, "meritocracy", is today always used positively, as an apparently natural corollary of a properly democratic society in which social advancement is based on personal merit. However, the concept of meritocracy presumes a mechanism allocating individuals to occupation, and so to income. Criticism of economic inequality today – that the financial privileges enjoyed by the select few are not only excessive, but undeserved – can imply endorsement of "meritocratic" principles: that there is in fact an appropriate differentiation of income according to talent and merit, that unequal incomes should properly reflect the natural inequality of talent – the very same implication that Young skewered in his book. The arguments that Tawney and Young made against inegalitarian societies were not, however, primarily concerned with the distribution of income but with the broader manner in which societies secured for their members the means to a worthwhile life. Conflating inequality with economic inequality implies that these means are purely financial: that the mere possession of adequate personal income and wealth will secure a worthwhile life.

The emphasis by Young on the role of the educational system as an instrument for social mobility is also evident in Mike Savage's *Social Class in the 21st Century*, the most recent account of Britain's class structure. This both synthesizes social survey findings (the online Great British Class Survey) and also devotes two chapters to social mobility: the first demonstrating the limited reach of recent mobility and the second examining the "universities and meritocracy".[49] Savage examines the social origins of those at the top and bottom of British society by occupation and concludes, first, that a very small number of those in the uppermost strata had not originated there; and, second, that this finding is mirrored in the social origins of the "precariat",[50] the majority of those at the bottom end of society having been born there, with little downward mobility into that group.[51] This points up the weakness in Piketty's focus on the top- to middle-income deciles,[52] rather than the overall income range, plus the lack of any sense of the dynamics of income distribution: it is simply assumed that "the one per cent" is a more or less static group accumulating a greater share of national income and wealth. Savage's data for Britain suggests that this assumption is probably true enough, but he links it to a more dynamic conception of access to and distribution of wealth.

The general conclusion reached by Savage is that origins – whether social or geographic – still mark an individual for life, and this has a great influence on the social distance any one person is able to travel within society. Advantages and disadvantages of birth persist; social mobility is indeed greater than it was, but chiefly among intermediate strata, with the highest and lowest remaining relatively self-contained. This story is replicated in the university system: where there once were universities, teacher training colleges, schools of nursing, technical colleges, polytechnics and various vocational establishments, there are now just "universities", which, despite the all-embracing name, are now differentiated by status and provision in much the same way that the previous structure of higher-education institutions had been. Young's dystopian vision is realized here more in rhetorical than actual terms; the prospect of upward social mobility through the acquisition of a university degree that prevailed for a short period in the middle of the twentieth century is, for most of today's students, turning into a reality in which the possession of a university degree secures, at best, the chance of regular, if shifting, employment. Substantial financial "investment" by students in their education turns out to be more a payment for entry into the labour market than a means of acquiring relevant skills. A university degree has by default become a necessary, but not sufficient, condition for any kind of income security, rather than a means for economic advancement.

INEQUALITY AND WELFARE

The focus of modern economists on the measurement of economic inequality is necessary if one is to be able to identify, standardize, render comparable over time and between regions, inequalities in the distribution of income. But as already noted, the assumption also prevails that once identified in this way, the most appropriate policies for the moderation of inequality are presumed to be fiscal: that taxes and subsidies acting directly on the distribution of income are the most effective remedy for any undesirable inequalities in that distribution.[53] Here again, clarity on this issue is best gained by returning to an older literature that was rather better at identifying theoretical problems and developing constructive responses than is usual in modern economic literature. The relevant analytical apparatus for such remedies was initially developed in the early 1900s by A. C. Pigou as a new welfare economics, but there is no index entry for Pigou in either Atkinson's *Inequality* or, for that matter, Piketty's *Capital in the Twenty-First Century*.

The shortcomings of treating inequality simply as income inequality, rather than treating it as the point of departure for an evaluation of welfare, are also evident from Anthony Atkinson's initial point of reference: Hugh Dalton's 1920 article on the measurement of income inequality.[54] Dalton opened here with the kind of bland assumption for which economists have long been notorious:

> It is generally agreed that, other things being equal, a consider-
> able reduction in the inequality of incomes found in most modern
> communities would be desirable.[55]

Although Dalton then suggests that there is a connection between the distribution of income and the total amount of economic welfare, he immediately nullifies this connection in a second assumption, presuming that "the relation of income to economic welfare is the same for all members of the community, and that, for each individual, marginal economic welfare diminishes as income increases."[56] The "problem of inequality" is, however, that the relation of income to economic welfare is *not* the same for all members of the community: a problem first raised by Henry Sidgwick and then developed by Pigou into the foundations of welfare economics. True enough, Dalton's second assumption was formalized and lent authority during the 1930s into the principle that interpersonal comparisons of utility could not be made, but the flaw in this principle was always to confuse a problem of measurement with one of condition. The difficulty of establishing a metric for interpersonal comparisons quickly led economists to presume (as did Dalton) that interpersonal differences could be treated, for analytical purposes, as non-existent.

Pigou's *Economics of Welfare* was, like Dalton's article, published in 1920; but instead of being sidetracked like Dalton by problems of measurement, Pigou took up the distributional aspects of the "problem of inequality". He built on the work of Henry Sidgwick, who had noted that the difficulties of comparing wealth over time or across space founder on the lack of a common measure of value, and that earlier writers had responded to this problem by imputing differences in utilities to differences in the qualities of commodities. John Stuart Mill had retained the Ricardian solution that utility should be treated as the sole measure of value: a man is rich or poor according to the necessaries and luxuries he can command; and if he can get two sacks instead of one, he gets double the quantity of riches, double the quantity of utility. Sidgwick objected:

> But surely any man who got two sacks of corn where he had only counted on one would willingly exchange a great part of the second for things which he would not take in exchange for an equal part of the first: if such an exchange is out of the question, though he might find a use for the second sack it will certainly not be as useful as the first.[57]

And he goes on:

> In fact, as Jevons has admirably explained, the variations in the relative market values of different articles express and correspond to variations in the comparative estimates formed by people in general, not of the *total* utilities of the amounts purchased of such articles, but of their *final* utilities.[58]

Following on from this idea, Sidgwick then made the point that a given commodity is "more useful when bought by the poor, because the poor have fewer luxuries and therefore get more enjoyment out of what they have".[59] This raises the awkward point that, if we measure wealth simply by its utility, then the amount of "wealth" in a given country will be altered by the way in which it is distributed among the population.

In his earlier book *Wealth and Welfare* Pigou had generalized the point raised by Sidgwick:

> If we assume all members of the community to be of similar temperament, and if these members are only two in number, it is easily shown that any transference from the richer to the poorer of the two, since it enables more intense wants to be satisfied at the expense of less intense wants, must increase the aggregate sum of satisfaction.[60]

But it was not only interpersonal transfers that might enhance the welfare of the community. The welfare of the community as a whole was also likely to be augmented if economic fluctuations were minimized. A steady increase in the size of the "national dividend" (what we know as GDP) was preferable to a sequence of booms and busts. The core of Pigou's argument as presented in 1912 in fact centred on the size and distribution of the national dividend: that (1) an increase in the size of the national dividend will probably increase economic welfare; (2) an increase in the share accruing to the poor will probably increase economic welfare; and (3) "diminution in the variability of the national dividend" will probably increase economic welfare.[61]

When Pigou augmented his *Wealth and Welfare* and turned it into *The Economics of Welfare*, one of the most significant additions was Part IV, "The National Dividend and Government Finance", which was quite probably prompted by the way in which the problems of public finance during the First World War had drawn attention to the issue that when a government increases taxes, it also alters the incidence of taxation.[62] This section of his book provided the foundation for all future thinking on the relationship between the incidence of taxation and the impact of changes in taxation on national income; but the question of distribution was dealt with separately, in the following part. Much of this recapitulated material on transfers from the "relatively rich" to the "relatively poor", ending with a chapter discussing "A National Minimum Standard of Real Income" that began, as had the corresponding chapter in *Wealth and Welfare*, from the point that establishing a national minimum might well reduce total national income while at the same time increasing the aggregate real income of the "relatively poor".[63]

The sophistication and detail of Pigou's analysis of welfare and inequality was smothered by later criticism that drastically simplified the issues he had raised and discarded the approach that he had taken.[64] The real value of reconsidering these original approaches to incomes and inequality can also be seen in the work of another economist who barely registers in modern discussion: Henry Phelps Brown. Like Pigou, Phelps Brown had a strong interest in labour relations, publishing a pioneering work of history and analysis in 1965 that forms a complement to Pigou's own *Principles and Methods of Industrial Peace* (1905), an early work that was later integrated into Part III of *Economics of Welfare* as "The National Dividend and Labour". In his *Growth of British Industrial Relations* Phelps Brown deals with the period that immediately followed the publication of Pigou's *Principles and Methods of Industrial Peace*, from the election of a reforming Liberal government in 1906 up to the outbreak of war in 1914, examining the role of unionization and labour disputes in the improved remuneration of wage labour, which at that time made up 75 per cent of the labour force.[65] His later *Inequality of Pay* (1977) deals with contemporary inequalities, drawing together material on occupations and differentials from many sources and investigating the various arguments advanced for the existence of such differentials. There are chapters on gender discrimination and race discrimination, on social class and intergenerational mobility, on the relation of social class to ability and education, and on variations in earnings in the same occupation. Phelps Brown's attention is fixed upon the detail of differentiation, not upon the conversion of statistical representations of differentiation into broad and abstract generalizations that then fail to illuminate the everyday lived reality of inequality.

This is especially clear in the way that he constructs his analysis of incomes over the period 1860–1960 in Britain, the US, Germany, France and Sweden. His focus is on wages: pay for work done or hours worked and distinct from the salaried workers' annual pay contract. Over the course of the nineteenth and twentieth centuries salaries only emerged as a significant share of remuneration during the 1920s, when the rule of thumb that wages formed 75 per cent of all remuneration began to break down; in addition, Phelps Brown notes the lack of data for salaries before this period. Here again, attention to the detail of the way in which individuals receive their incomes reveals discontinuities that are suppressed in the construction of long series of income data. His consolidated figures for average annual pay per employee date from the 1950s, and not before, implying that such estimates cannot be reliably projected back before that time.[66] And although Phelps Brown's prime attention here is on real increases in average income in developing industrial economies, and not on the distribution of income among the working population, the book teems with observations on working lives and living conditions that add considerably to our understanding of the relationship between income and inequality. For as Pigou pointed out, it was not only the distribution of income that affected the welfare of a population, but the overall amount of national income, together with the degree to which it fluctuated.

Tawney's emphasis on the kind of civilization in which we want to live has lost none of its pertinence. He accepted the natural fact of inequality as difference: between young and old, worker and employer, man and woman. But while he considered that such differences existed on many dimensions, he made the case that the inequalities that should concern us are those that are created and consolidated by social forces, and handed down through the inheritance of life chances. It was the mark of a civilized society to reduce and eliminate such differences. In seeking here to understand quite how, as societies grow wealthier, structural inequalities become greater rather than smaller, we might well draw upon the more radical implications of Adam Smith's view of commercial society: that the motor of social wealth is the human desire for "conveniences", for the "baubles and trinkets" possessed by others, the social power of envy and vanity.[67] The "rich lists" of today fit four-square into this perspective: that the very rich of today are more to be pitied for their vain pursuit of wealth than envied for the acquisition of that which makes them no more complete or happy.

The real problem is then not so much the fact that the 1 per cent are accumulating ever greater amounts of wealth; rather, that such accumulation is linked to the private appropriation of social wealth. Further, the consolidation of their power inflicts policies on the rest of society that impoverish the environment and social circumstances in which we all live.[68] The Panama Papers have shown that many of the very rich practice tax avoidance and evasion on an industrial scale;[69] but increasing higher rates of income taxation to make the tax system more progressive is not likely to alter this problem significantly. Western European fiscal systems do generally effect a redistribution from richer to poorer, and so the scope for fiscal solutions to inequality is limited. More important, in policy terms, would be to ensure that the contribution that the rich and the well-off already make to public finances is used to increase social wealth rather than, as is increasingly the case, public funds and assets being diverted for private ends, subsidizing private industry and commerce through outsourcing and privatization, contributing to a bloated financial sector driven by the economics of the rentier. It is commonplace today to bemoan the level of redistributive transfer payments made in industrial societies, presuming that the bulk of such payments are for "welfare", when in fact pension entitlements weigh heaviest on the public purse. While transfers from young to old – from those in work to those enjoying a prolonged retirement – are an increasing burden for all modern states, the financialization of the public domain increasingly recycles the taxes paid by the rich back into their own pockets. In the process, the finances of modern states increasingly resemble those of France under the *ancien régime*;[70] and the increasing gulf between the political class and voters has a similar precedent.

Notes for Chapter 3

1. Simon Kuznets presented this argument in his 1954 Presidential Address to the American Economic Association, published as "Economic Growth and Income Inequality", *American Economic Review* 45 (1955), pp. 1–28. Kuznets is quite explicit here (*Ibid.*, p. 18) that his observation concerning increasing income inequality in early industrialization is a working assumption, since he has no data for this period; the data that he discussed in his Presidential Address covers the period 1913–48 which, placed together with the presumed trend of the nineteenth century, creates the inverted U-curve that later became associated with his argument. Piketty presents data for the nineteenth century that supports the hypothesis of rising inequality, but argues that the twentieth-century downward slope identified by Kuznets inflected after the middle of the century, since when income inequality has been rising again.

2. Anthony B. Atkinson, *Inequality: What Can be Done?* (Cambridge, MA: Harvard University Press, 2015).

3. Anthony B. Atkinson, "On the Measurement of Inequality", *Journal of Economic Theory* 2 (1970), pp. 244–63.

4. Jan Pen, *Income Distribution* (London: Allen Lane, 1971), pp. 48ff.

5. Amartya Sen, *On Economic Inequality* (Oxford: Oxford University Press, 1973).

6. E. H. Phelps Brown, with Margaret H. Browne, *A Century of Pay: The Course of Pay and Production in France, Germany, Sweden, the United Kingdom, and the United States of America, 1860–1960* (London: Macmillan, 1968).

7. John E. Roemer, "Equality: Its Justification, Nature, and Domain", in *The Oxford Handbook of Economic Inequality,* Wiemer Salverda, Brian Nolan and Timothy M. Smeeding (eds) (Oxford: Oxford University Press, 2009), p. 25.

8. A prominent example being Robert Lucas, "The Industrial Revolution: Past and Future: 2003 Annual Report Essay", *The Region* (2004), www.minneapolisfed.org/publications/the-region/the-industrial-revolution-past-and-future (accessed 18 March 2016): "The potential for improving the lives of poor people by finding different ways of distributing current production is nothing compared to the apparently limitless potential of increasing production."

9. In early 2016, a London tube driver was reported as earning £49,673, with the lowest paid staff on about £30,000 (Conor Sullivan, "Union Deal Clears Way for Night Tube", *Financial Times,* 3 February 2016); junior doctors started on £23,000 and with additional pay for "unsociable hours" might earn slightly more than £30,000 (John Murray Brown, "Why Are Junior Doctors on Strike?", *Financial Times,* 12 January 2016).

10. Atkinson, *Inequality*, pp. 11–12.

11. Richard Wilkinson and Kate Pickett, *The Spirit Level: Why More Equal Societies Almost Always Do Better* (London: Allen Lane, 2009), Part Two. Wilkinson and Pickett do discuss issues of causality (pp. 187–92); their principal remedies concern the plugging of tax loopholes, and the development of workplace democracy (pp. 248–56).

12. Smith qualifies this argument by making a distinction between productive and unproductive labour, an important step in his argument but one that we do not need to consider here.

13. Adam Smith, *An Inquiry into the Nature and Causes of the Wealth of Nations*, R. H. Campbell, A. S. Skinner and W. B. Todd (eds) (Oxford: Oxford University Press, 1976), "Introduction and Plan of the Work", paragraph 4.

14. Here we should disregard what we know today, that hunter-gatherers in fact spend little time on the direct acquisition of food and materials, and that a reliance of societies upon agricultural production involved a sharp increase in the amount of work required to provide their basic needs.

15. See Istvan Hont, "The 'Rich Country–Poor Country' Debate in Scottish Classical Political Economy", in *Wealth and Virtue: The Shaping of Political Economy in the Scottish Enlightenment,* Istvan Hont and Michael Ignatieff (eds) (Cambridge: Cambridge University Press, 1983), pp. 271–315.

16. *Wealth of Nations*, I.v.1.

17. Indeed, this obsolete idea of a "wage fund" still exists in populist discourse regarding immigrants who "take our jobs".

18. To search Booth's poverty map see http://booth.lse.ac.uk/cgi-bin/do.pl?sub=view_boo th_and_barth&args=531000,180400,6,large,5 (accessed 21 March 2016).

19. B. Seebohm Rowntree, *Poverty: A Study in Town Life* (London: Macmillan, 1901), foldout map opposite title page.

20. General William Booth's *In Darkest England and the Way Out* (London: International Headquarters of the Salvation Army, 1890) deliberately played on the contemporary conception of "darkest Africa", describing "the darkness" of the "submerged tenth" in terms of homelessness and unemployment.

21. *Ibid.*, p. 217. The limitations of today's standard body mass indicator are demonstrated by the fact that this minimum for an 18-year-old male comes out at 20.3, and so well within the "healthy weight" range.

22. D. Caradog Jones (ed.), *The Social Survey of Merseyside*, three volumes (Liverpool: Liverpool University Press, 1934). The first volume included the results of a housing survey that recorded significant overcrowding, and also analysed household budgets to establish how many families lacked an income sufficient for adequate food and clothing, both aspects having been systematically introduced in Rowntree's study of York.

23. As he notes, in the 1891 census the average household size in England and Wales was just under five persons: Rowntree, *Poverty*, p. 28, fn. 3.

24. The title of Chapter IV. Since his "poverty line" is linked here to a lifetime profile, Rowntree implicitly anticipates aspects of the permanent income hypothesis and Becker's emphasis on the life cycle.

25. Detailed diaries for thirty-five families were kept, although in the course of the study standardization of the results reduced the total used to eighteen, of which fifteen were for three consecutive weeks or more (*Ibid.*, p. 224). In the circumstances, this was a great success: Elizabeth Bott's influential study *Family and Social Network* (London: Tavistock, 1957) was based on the records of only twenty families (p. 14).

26. Rowntree, *Poverty*, p. 94. For the discussion of daily calorific requirements, see pp. 226ff. There is now an extensive literature on nutrition and physical well-being in Britain during the eighteenth and nineteenth centuries: for a modern discussion of human calorific requirements in historical context see David Meredith and Deborah Oxley, "Food and Fodder: Feeding England 1700–1900", *Past & Present* 222 (2014), pp. 192ff.

27. See the chart facing p. 258 for the energy value and protein requirement of York labourers where family earnings were less than 26 shillings a week; American labourers; and the meals provided in prisons and workhouses.

28. Rowntree, *Poverty*, p. 36.

29. *Ibid.*, p. 79.

30. *Ibid.*, pp. 48–53.

31. *Ibid.*, p. 59.

32. *Loc. cit.*

33. Charles Booth, *Pauperism: A Picture and Endowment of Old Age: An Argument* (London: Macmillan, 1892); this was based on case studies from the London borough of Stepney recorded over a period of thirteen years.

34. Rowntree, *Poverty*, p. 137.

35. R. H. Tawney, *Equality* (London: Allen & Unwin, 1931), p. 63.

36. *Ibid.*, p. 78, citing A. L. Bowley and J. C. Stamp, *The National Income 1924* (Oxford: Oxford University Press, 1927), p. 12. Bowley conceived his work on social statistics as a direct continuation of Booth and Rowntree, and in the later 1920s contributed to the *New Survey of London Life and Labour*, nine volumes, H. Llewellyn Smith (ed.) (London: P. S. King, 1930–35).

37. *Ibid.*, p. 81.

38. *Ibid.*, p. 82.

39. *Ibid.*, p. 98.

40. Alexis de Tocqueville, *Democracy in America* (London: Penguin, 2003), p. 648.

41. Tawney, *Equality*, p. 147.

42. Michael Young, *The Rise of the Meritocracy 1870–2033* (Harmondsworth: Penguin, 1961 [original 1958]), p. 116.

43. *Ibid.*, p. 21. Here there is a footnote: "The origin of this unpleasant term, like that of 'equality of opportunity', is obscure. It seems to have been first generally used in the [nineteen]sixties of the last century in small-circulation journals attached to the Labour Party, and gained wide currency much later on." This is then an instance of Young's fictional reconstruction of a past that had not yet happened.

44. *Ibid.*, p. 187.

45. *Ibid.*, p. 15.

46. Young's book is littered with witty and prescient aperçus, such as: "As men became more like machines, machines became more like men, and when machines were built to mimic people, the ventriloquist at last understood himself." *Ibid.*, pp. 73–4.

47. Young writes with tongue firmly in cheek: "From the moment that Sir Anthony Crosland was persuaded that the battle for national survival would be won or lost in the 'A' streams all the way from nursery to grammar school, the money began to flow." *Ibid.*, p. 61. Crosland, who died in 1977, was never given a knighthood.

48. *Ibid.*, p. 46.

49. Chapters 6 and 7 of Mike Savage, *Social Class in the 21st Century* (London: Penguin, 2015). Chapter 8, the third in the part devoted to social mobility, deals with geography as a marker of inequality.

50. Estimated as 15 per cent of the population; Savage, *Social Class*, p. 333.

51. Table 6.1 "Family of Origin" and the GBCS's "Seven Classes", *idem.*, p. 195. Note that Rowntree placed emphasis upon the danger for those who lived just out of poverty of falling into it.

52. As noted by Soskice, "*Capital in the Twenty-First Century*", p. 654.

53. Atkinson presents an extensive range of measures that go beyond direct fiscal action, including employment policy, a sovereign wealth fund, a form of basic income,

and reform of social insurance; see "Proposals to Reduce the Extent of Inequality", *Inequality*, pp. 237–9.

54. Atkinson, *Inequality*, pp. 12 ff. The centrality of his article, rather than Dalton's *Some Aspects of the Inequality of Incomes in Modern Communities* (London: George Routledge & Sons, 1920), is emphasized in the introduction to its reprinted version: Anthony B. Atkinson and Andrea Brandolini, "Unveiling the Ethics behind Inequality Measurement: Dalton's Contribution to Economics", *Economic Journal* 125 (2015), pp. 209–34.

55. Hugh Dalton, "The Measurement of the Inequality of Incomes", *Economic Journal* 30 (1920), p. 348.

56. *Ibid.*, p. 349.

57. Sidgwick, *Principles of Political Economy*, 3rd edn (London: Macmillan, 1901), p. 81. In the first edition (1883, p. 74) the same point was made, but with respect to a harvest that was twice as big; the additional amount therefore not having the same utility as the amount equivalent to the previous year. The clarifying passage regarding the two sacks of corn was later inserted immediately preceding this passage, which was retained.

58. Sidgwick, *Principles of Political Economy* (London: Macmillan, 1883), pp. 74–5.

59. *Ibid.*, p. 76.

60. A. C. Pigou, *Wealth and Welfare* (London: Macmillan, 1912), p. 24. *Wealth and Welfare* was later revised and supplemented as *Economics of Welfare* (London: Macmillan, 1920).

61. Pigou, *Wealth and Welfare*, pp. 32, 66. Pigou remarked that the older political economy had conceived "distribution" to be among factors of production (land, labour, capital); whereas he was concerned with distribution among individuals. Living as he did in a society in which 75 per cent of the working population were paid a weekly wage, he proposed to get around this problem by treating the wage-earning classes collectively as "the poor", whose prime factor is labour. Wages are paid according to a fixed daily or weekly rate for a fixed period of work, or for a fixed amount of work; salaries are paid by the month and quoted as an annual payment for a broadly defined range of functions.

62. "Pigouvian taxes" as understood by the modern economist are means of compensating for positive or negative externalities, another conception originally introduced by Sidgwick in 1883; as such, they are taxes primarily designed to have specific economic effects rather than raise revenue, and so could also be generally assimilated to economic measures that are designed to reduce poverty.

63. Pigou, *Economics of Welfare*, Part V, Chapter XII, §1.

64. Influential in the misrepresentation and relegation of Pigou's approach was John Hicks's "The Foundations of Welfare Economics" [1939], reprinted in his *Wealth and Welfare: Collected Essays on Economic Theory*, Volume 1 (Oxford: Oxford University Press, 1981), pp. 59–77.

65. E. H. Phelps Brown, *The Growth of British Industrial Relations: A Study from the Standpoint of 1906–14* (London: Macmillan, 1965).

66. Phelps Brown with Browne, *A Century of Pay*, Table 26, pp. 274–5.

67. As formulated by Istvan Hont in his introductory essay with Michael Ignatieff, "Needs and Justice in the Wealth of Nations: An Introductory Essay", in Hont and Ignatieff, *Wealth and Virtue*, pp. 8–12.

68. See the points made in Chapter 13 by Prasannan Parthasarathi, pp. 240–44.

69. For a summary see Edward Luttwak, "Hidden Costs. The Panama Papers – A Radically New Explanation of Rising Inequality", *Times Literary Supplement*, 19/26 August 2016, pp. 10–11.

70. See J. F. Bosher, *French Finances 1770–1795: From Business to Bureaucracy* (Cambridge: Cambridge University Press, 1970), especially Chapter 5, "Private Enterprise in Public Finance", and pp. 19–20: "Until then [1789] the financial administration was characterized by what historians are inclined to call 'corruption', as though it were the moral turpitude of individuals, but which was a normal feature of the system and is better described as private enterprise."

4

MODELS, MONEY AND HOUSING

Avner Offer

Piketty's *Capital* is a stupendous achievement. It lays out a majestic panorama of the rise and fall and rise again of the wealthy over two centuries in several countries. It has a bearing on some unexpected questions. For example, I have a scholarly interest in nineteenth-century French landscape painting. During that period, more than 2,000 paintings on average were exhibited every year in the Paris salon, and similar numbers were rejected.[1] The best of these have become part of humanity's heritage; millions look at them in museums and reproductions abound. But how did they come into being? Who paid for them? Piketty shows that the French elite were immensely wealthy. The rich were numerous enough to sustain the hopes and expectations of thousands of artisan painters, and the pinnacle achievements of a few of them. Like other enduring assets of humanity, this art was created in response to the tastes and the buying power of the rich.

Piketty's prime achievement is a rich statistical description of the inequality of income and wealth in France, the US and Britain over two centuries. But something is lost as well. His focus is on the top 10 per cent, 1 per cent and 0.1 per cent, and in his story these are the only ones that count. The rest are written out and denied historical agency. During the past few decades, social invisibility has been lifted by the academic study of history from below. Inadvertently, in pursuit of a quantitative handle on the rich, Piketty has restored a history from above. This exclusive focus on the wealthy also imparts an explanatory bias: the waxing and waning of elite wealth cannot be explained entirely by observing the rich. That, however, is what Piketty attempts to do.

THE MODEL

The core concept is a purported historical regularity, namely that over the long run, $r > g$, where r is the prevailing business interest rate and g is the rate of economic growth. That in itself, if it were true, would be a simple mechanism for concentrating income and wealth. It does not require anything else. Borrowers would be paying more to service their debt every year than the growth of output as a whole. This microeconomic fact (it is intuitively plausible much of the time) has a macroeconomic consequence: namely, a shift in the share of income, and consequently of wealth, towards creditors. Casual observation tends to agree with Piketty: for two decades following the late 1980s – the time of the "Great Moderation" (though not always in the inflationary period before) – banks charged higher interest rates than the economic growth rate. It was not always thus: Japan's high post-war growth took place in the context of low interest rates (and Japan has remained relatively egalitarian). The implication of debt service rising faster than economic growth is a growing financialization of the economy, which is also consistent with long-term trends. Business, which depends on borrowing, tends to achieve a higher rate of return than economic growth per head. Otherwise, growth could not be sustained. What keeps the level of economic growth per head below prevailing interest rates is its being averaged statistically over ordinary households, whose income is more reliably tethered to the rate of growth, while not necessarily behind it, as it has been in the US during the last four decades.

Piketty could have stopped with this empirical observation, if that is what it is. For a credentialed economist that would not be sufficient. Neoclassical analysis usually implies methodological individualism and macroeconomic equilibrium.[2] Piketty feels obliged to make use of the standard tool kit, and he applies a modified Cobb–Douglas production function. In this model, output is produced by two factors: capital and labour. They are substitutes for each other: it is possible (up to a point) to maintain output levels by reducing labour input and increasing capital input, or vice versa. Each factor (labour, capital) is paid according to its marginal product, i.e. the output of the final unit of input, whether that is an hour of labour or a unit of machinery. Piketty imputes an elasticity of substitution greater than one: with the quantity of labour kept constant, every additional unit of capital increases the return to capital. This is actually inconsistent with the standard assumption of constant returns to scale and with the other standard assumption of diminishing returns, but (perhaps more realistically) it assumes rising technological productivity by means of technical innovation.

This growth model is subject to several more standard assumptions. The two factors are homogeneous (all workers are the same, capital is uniform and seamless). There is no money, no government, no natural resources (e.g. no land). It is open to the usual criticism that no such world can ever exist. Since Piketty does not push the analysis much further, there is not much point in dwelling on other shortcomings.[3] An elasticity of substitution greater than one may not be warranted by the evidence.[4]

A fundamental problem is raised by Piketty's core notion of capital, which provides the title for the book. The term capital has two meanings, as a requisite of production and as a store of wealth. For historical statistics, Piketty uses the store of wealth concept. The wealth distributions he describes are made up largely of financial claims. He inserts the very same data into the production function, where they become the capital factor of production. But the concepts are not the same and are not consistent with each other.[5] The wealth concept, derived from the national accounts, is not suitable for inserting into the production function. The substitution cannot work except under the most heroic assumptions. So why is this model required? It is supposed to explain how capital can increase its share of output. But that is not an explanation, it is a premise. The excess growth of capital revenue over labour revenue that may arise in production is not the same as the excess return to creditors over economic growth per head. Piketty provides no evidence that redistribution either towards the wealthy or away from them has anything to do with the economic productivity of capital.

If the model is meant as a prediction, it fails for much of the time, from the 1920s up to the 1980s, which is 60 per cent of the twentieth century. During this period the income and wealth shares of the wealthiest were declining. But it is not prediction, it is a tendency. It is what would happen if other things remained equal. And maybe tendencies is all that economic explanation can deliver. John Stuart Mill wrote that economics cannot predict, it can only identify tendencies. This view has been revived in recent decades by the philosophers of science and economics Nancy Cartwright and Daniel Hausman.[6] Cartwright even applies this stricture to physics. The tendencies are offset by countervailing and confounding factors, and hence are impossible to test. They are derived by deduction. Piketty has no theory or empirical account of confounders, and his offsetting factors are not articulated in any detail. It is not clear whether the outcomes he lays out should be attributed to the model or to the interferences. So his explanation is weak. He has no theory of declining inequality, which was the experience over most of the twentieth century.

There is, however, an alternative explanation available for falling inequality, which is social democracy. It does not conform to the neoclassical idea of what economic theory should look like. It does not invoke self-interested individuals engaging in market exchanges that scale up to equilibrium. The political challenge of social democracy was largely responsible for the reversal of inequality in the period between the 1920s and the 1980s. Rising taxes under social democracy acted to depress asset values. Social democracy rejected the neoclassical models that Piketty prefers. Hence he has no plausible account as to why the mechanism he invokes was reversed for such a long period of time.[7] In fact, the income share of the wealthy was reduced by political action, in defiance of the wealthy, which falls beyond Piketty's explanatory framework.

Piketty admits that the production function model cannot suffice. To explain changes in factor shares Piketty introduces bargaining and taxation. He sometimes says that he does not actually believe in factors being paid their marginal output, but does that with a wink.[8] Piketty is not a true believer but a neoclassical card carrier, expected, as in the old Soviet Union, to acknowledge the faith from time to time. What he does is pick and mix. His theory is a hybrid, with elements that contradict each other. Perfect competition, an underlying premise of growth theory, is not consistent with either bargaining or taxation. There is no bargaining in perfect competition, and no government (and hence no taxation) in standard growth theory. Instead, Piketty's conceptual mechanism has something for everyone. Not quite, however: it leaves out social democracy, which arguably provides the best explanation, a historical one, for the countervailing tendencies that undermine his predictions.

His approach is not unreasonable, however, it is just inconsistent. What Piketty betrays, perhaps without meaning to, is a deeper methodological problem in economics. The internal contradictions of his model require a certain agnosticism. Such offhand inconsistency is also shown by the Nobel Prize committee, which has three times handed out its awards, on single occasions, to pairs of economists whose doctrines were at odds with one another. Eight Nobel-winning economists have expressed disbelief in the core doctrines in the course of their Nobel lectures, and three others have expressed reservations on other occasions. It is a way of coping with the fact that economic theory does not add up.[9]

The historical context is the failure of the general equilibrium project. This was an attempt to establish a general model of economic activity based on the twin premises of equilibrium and optimality (no goods left unsold). This premise appeared to have been bolted down for good in the 1950s as the two theorems of welfare economics (Arrow–Debreu general equilibrium): namely, (1) that every general equilibrium is a Pareto optimum and (2) that every Pareto optimum can be produced by a general equilibrium. But this soon ran into trouble even in theory, especially in the so-called Sonnenschein–Mantel–Debreu conditions, which showed that individual preferences could not scale up to a unique equilibrium.[10] In response, the younger generation of economists eventually turned their backs on high theory, and top journal publications are currently dominated by empirical work in the form of laboratory experiments, field experiments and so-called natural experiments, i.e. the lessons of history.[11] Piketty's work also falls into that category, without showing complete awareness of its limitations. He tries to learn the lessons of history while clinging to neoclassical theory.

The narrative skips casually from one methodological position to another. For example, he condemns the controlled experiments carried out by economists in laboratory settings as a scientistic illusion: they "often lead to a neglect of history or the fact that historical experience remains our principal source of knowledge".[12] That statement is hardly consistent with the role of the production function in his own account. In other words, for all the descriptive appeal of his historical tapestry, Piketty does not tell a consistent causal story.

His glory is measurement: those time series extending over two centuries, tracing the ebb and flow of the wealthy. These data have an alluring precision. What do they signify? A flow of income is denominated in legal tender, and can be converted into consumption goods at will. Income is supposed to be liquid and instantly available. Wealth is a more nebulous measure: in the discourse of economics, it measures the current accounting value of future income flows. This value is thus as accurate as our knowledge of the future: in other words, not accurate at all. Piketty uses a "mark to market" concept: namely, what the assets in question would have fetched in current markets. But only a small fraction of wealth is realized at any given time, so the value of wealth is conditional on its not being realized. The revenue flows on which these valuations depend are what has been disclosed to the tax authorities. They constitute a lower bound. Currently, vast amounts of wealth are sheltered and shielded from tax collectors. A minimal estimate is about 8 per cent of household financial assets, but other estimates are three to four times higher.[13] The value of wealth is not as solid as an iron bar, or even a gold coin. It is contingent primarily on two factors: the first is the interest rate. With the revenue flow constant, a rising interest rate will automatically depress property values. Something like this took place in Britain during the Edwardian period, when a rise in interest rates depreciated real estate values by about 40 per cent in less than a decade, and had a similar effect on government bonds, both of which are essentially fixed-income assets.[14] When interest rates are volatile, asset values are volatile too. When interest rates come down, as they did after 1870 in Europe, property values go up automatically. The second factor that influences property values is taxation. In the latter part of the nineteenth century, taxation was already moving up, exacerbated in the 1900s by rising interest rates. The relative decline of wealth after 1920 can be attributed primarily to the rise in taxation due to rising proletarian bargaining power, as expressed in social democratic priorities. Interest rates were also high in the 1920s.[15] Piketty does not delve deeply into why this rise in equality took place. But he acknowledges this interpretation implicitly in his proposal for a global tax on wealth, as the only policy intervention that could undermine the immutable dominance of interest rates over economic growth.

What are the uses of a wealth that is nebulous in value and cannot be realized en masse? The first is a secure command of the means of existence. Not only subsistence but also comfort and ease. Not only comfort and ease, but also commanding the service of others, the ability to call on their care without having to reciprocate.[16] Not only to call on their care, but also to extract a deference that is itself a source of well-being. Wealth signifies a secure expectation of access to entitlements in the future, thus reducing the anxiety and insecurity that give rise to pervasive ill-being among those less privileged in competitive market societies.[17] Finally, wealth also confers social and political power, the ability to defend privilege and to pursue self-interest in the public domain.

Being wealthy is not only a state, but also an occupation. The entrepreneurial, managerial or professional rich are engaged during working hours with maintaining their wealth and extending it. Indeed, from the point of view of microeconomics, their work has no other purpose. Piketty makes a valuable distinction between entrepreneurial and patrimonial wealth. The descendants of the wealthy still need to strive to keep their wealth intact, but they also have the luxury of choosing how to spend their time. Wealth, then, is a nebulous cluster of options and opportunities. Measures of wealth, like the one that Piketty uses, can be seen as an index of these possibilities. Because they are measurable, they are also monitored anxiously by the wealthy. But they are not precise.

RESURGENT INEQUALITY

Since the mechanisms that Piketty puts forward are tendencies rather than laws, they are not much good for prediction. Here is some counterfactual history: had inequality not soared again after 1980, we would say that social democracy had won. History could have continued on its previous course. So the resurgence of inequality since the 1970s is crucial for the model's credibility. Much of the criticism that Piketty has attracted has focused on this period. Many critics say that it has something to do with housing wealth. Here is my version of this criticism: it contains a money story, and a housing story.

A money story

Piketty's neoclassical model contains no money. He makes the standard neoclassical assumption that money is neutral, that it is a mere veil for the real economy. This is an odd position to take for a book about capital, in which saving is so central. It is reminiscent of the gold standard world that existed in the second part of the nineteenth century, in which the unit of value appeared to be fixed in terms of gold, and could therefore be ignored. Price stability was maintained by the use of a metallic convertible money, and sound money underpinned the stability of wealth. This perspective suggests a monetary interpretation of

Piketty: in the nineteenth century price stability was achieved by externalizing risk and transmitting shocks to the rest of society, in the form of unemployment and a sequence of surges and slumps. This was possible in the absence of democracy, when society was governed for the benefit of the rich. Externalizing the shocks of financial and economic instability built up domestic pressures for more democracy, and international tensions that gave rise to the First World War.[18] In consequence, inter-war and post-war welfare states gave a lower priority to price stability, in order to contain economic and social risk. This process began between the wars and culminated in withdrawal from the gold standard. After 1945 it drove a gradually rising inflation, in conditions of full employment, leading to the final demise of monetary gold in 1971 and the end of the Bretton Woods fixed exchange rate system. During a decade of high inflation in the 1970s, the New Right recaptured the initiative. It restored the primacy of price stability and strove again to externalize social risk away from the wealthy and towards the rest of society, by prioritizing low retail price inflation, cutting taxes, implementing austerity and cutting social insurance payouts. The retail price stability achieved during this period earned it the rubric of "The Great Moderation". Suppressing inflation, interest rates and taxes was sufficient by itself to push up asset values, and to increase inequality sharply. In the UK, in the course of the Thatcher years between 1979 and 1991, the Gini coefficient rose some 40 per cent, from around 0.25 to around 0.35, and stabilized thereafter.[19]

From the early 1980s, asset prices started their long inflation, and rose much faster than economic growth. On the face of it, this is a vindication of Piketty. But the declining interest rates of this period are not entirely consistent with his story. With a shift from fixed to floating exchange rates, the monetary authorities (central bankers and finance ministers) thought they could allow market forces to determine interest rates. That was based on the assumption that money is priced like other commodities, in response to demand and supply; as if the gold standard still existed. In reality, however, and under the gold standard as well, money was redefined in a succession of innovations devised to circumvent the quantity constraints of commodity money. Banknotes served this purpose in the nineteenth century, followed by bank deposits and cheques as means of payment. The quantity theory of money, which was in vogue during the 1970s under the name of monetarism, relied on the money supply being contained by means of central bank reserves.

An alternative view, which has been in existence since at least the middle of the nineteenth century but was given a new impetus by monetarism, is endogenous money theory.[20] In standard textbook theory, lending is taken out of deposits.[21] In endogenous monetary theory it is the other way round: deposits are created by lending. The supply of credit is elastic, and responds to the demand for borrowing, and to the lenders' appetite for profit and risk. Before 1971, this

appetite was curbed by quantitative ceilings on lending, imposed by the authorities in order to support productive investment and the exchange rate.[22] By the
1980s these credit restrictions had been lifted in most advanced countries.

A housing story

Housing became an attractive asset for both lenders and borrowers. In Britain,
for example, commercial banks were allowed to provide residential mortgages
in the early 1980s: an activity previously restricted to building societies. Unlike
building societies, which acted as genuine financial intermediaries and funded
loans entirely out of savers' deposits, banks were able to create money by the
mere act of lending.

For banks, housing became the ideal asset. Collateral is literally built in.
Demand for housing rises with income, as with a normal good, and sometimes rises more than proportionally to income: housing is both a subsistence
good and a status good. It is impossible to opt out of housing competition,
and housing constitutes the largest item of consumer expenditure.[23] In the UK
supply was reduced in 1981 by the introduction of a subsidized right to buy for
tenants of public housing, while the houses sold were not replaced. People will
compete for scarce housing to the limits of their credit. Housing also benefits
from large tax privileges. The imputed rental income on the asset is not taxed
(such taxation was abolished in Britain in 1963); mortgage interest received
relief for many years (and continues to do so in the US). There is no capital gains
tax on a person's first residence, local government property taxation is regressive,
and inheritance tax is low or non-existent. The income released from taxation is
available to pay for debt service.

For borrowers, debt service came out of consumption and out of leisure
forgone. As the cost increased, borrowers (and renters as well) could also hold
the cost down by relocating to smaller premises. Debt service also held out the
prospect of rising property values: debt service paid off and property values rose.
Aggregate housing wealth grew faster than aggregate debt, mostly because active
borrowers drove up the value of all property including the growing proportion of houses no longer encumbered by debt.[24] The consequence was a tenfold
expansion of lending in relation to national income starting from the 1970s
onwards.[25] Although well above half of this lending was secured on real property, it is not clear that most of it took the form of residential (and related retail
development) mortgages. Aggregate banking sector balance sheets are ambig-
uous about this. A better guide is probably the rise in house values. Taking an
average of fourteen advanced countries, in contrast with previous periods, where
income growth and house prices tended to move together, "in the final decades
of the twentieth century, house price growth outpaced income growth by a

substantial margin".[26] The overwhelming share of post-1980 increase in capital to income ratios arose out of sharp increases in housing wealth. Post-1980s inequality would not have risen otherwise.[27] Creditors had the secure collateral, borrowers the rising asset. But assets were driven up by lending and could only increase as long as lending continued. Debt service required an increasing share of household income. This shifted income from consumers to lenders, dried up consumer demand and ultimately reduced employment and economic activity. Funds accumulating with lenders created a "savings glut", combined with under-consumption for borrowers. This eventually led to financial collapse.

None of this was intended initially. It was the unintended consequence of easy credit, which rested on unwarranted premises: namely, that a free market in money was self-regulating and self-limiting. Once the process began, however, it attracted bipartisan social and political support across the political spectrum. Property windfalls looked like a free lunch. They undermined the social democratic settlement and seemed set to achieve its promise of economic security by other means: namely, through nest egg property ownership. It is striking that the property windfall economy is actually driven by Piketty's formula of $r > g$. The share of finance rises faster than the share of labour. But this cannot go on for ever. When finance has captured everything and labour income has gone down to nothing, the process must stop. Indeed, it has to stop much sooner, and it came to a temporary halt in 2008, although it has since resumed, so another crisis is likely. Piketty does not expound on this mechanism. It is in the spirit not of his production function, but of his $r > g$ formula.

This analysis also suggests more effective remedies than those he puts forward. Piketty's only suggestion was a global tax on wealth. It had to be global because capital is mobile. It is utopian because no global fiscal authority exists. In contrast, the real estate interpretation suggests easier remedies. Unlike finance, housing cannot walk away and is readily taxed. Even easier and more effective would be to place a lid on credit. Housing wealth levels are driven by the flow of credit. Quantity limits on credit were standard policy before the 1970s, they can be implemented by any government on its own, they are difficult to evade, and they can gradually bring the tendencies towards inequality under control. Even if there are innate tendencies towards concentration, they have been offset for long periods by norms, politics and policies, without any manifest harm being done to prosperity. That said, even if Piketty is open to criticism, he merits the highest praise for placing wealth and inequality so firmly back on the agenda.

Notes for Chapter 4

1. Diana Greenwald, "Painting the Provincial: A Statistical Analysis of Rural Imagery at the Paris Salons, 1831–81", MPhil. Thesis, University of Oxford (2014), pp. 1, 45.

2. Avner Offer and Gabriel Söderberg, *The Nobel Factor: The Prize in Economics, Social Democracy and the Market Turn* (Princeton, NJ: Princeton University Press, 2016), p. 3.

3. Offer and Söderberg, *Nobel Factor*, Chapter 1.

4. Carlos Obregon, "Piketty is Wrong", MPRA Paper 64593 (Munich, 2015), pp. 12–14.

5. See pp. 19–21 of Yanis Varoufakis, "Egalitarianism's Latest Foe", *Real-World Economics Review* 69 (October 2014), pp. 18–35.

6. Nancy Cartwright, *Nature's Capacities and Their Measurement* (Oxford: Oxford University Press, 1994); Daniel M. Hausman, *The Inexact and Separate Science of Economics* (Cambridge: Cambridge University Press, 1992).

7. Offer and Söderberg, *Nobel Factor*, pp. 4–8, 149–50.

8. Thomas Piketty, *Capital in the Twenty-First Century* (Cambridge, MA: Harvard University Press, 2014), p. 331.

9. Offer and Söderberg, *Nobel Factor*, pp. 259–63.

10. Alan P. Kirman, "Whom or What Does the Representative Individual Represent?", *Journal of Economic Perspectives* 6(2) (1992), pp. 117–36; S. A. T. Rizvi, "The Sonnenschein–Mantel–Debreu Results after Thirty Years", *History of Political Economy: Agreement on Demand: Consumer Theory in the Twentieth Century*, Volume 38, Supplement (2006).

11. Offer and Söderberg, *Nobel Factor*, pp. 55–56; Roger Backhouse and Béatrice Cherrier, "Becoming Applied: The Transformation of Economics after 1970", University of Birmingham, Department of Economics, Discussion Paper 14-11 (2014); Joshua D. Angrist and Jorn-Steffen Pischke, "The Credibility Revolution in Empirical Economics: How Better Research Design is Taking the Con out of Econometrics", *Journal of Economic Perspectives* 24(2) (2010), pp. 3–30; David Card, Stefano DellaVigna and Ulrike Malmendier, "The Role of Theory in Field Experiments", *Journal of Economic Perspectives* 25(3) (2011), pp. 39–62.

12. Piketty, *Capital*, p. 575.

13. Gabriel Zucman, *The Hidden Wealth of Nations: The Scourge of Tax Havens* (Chicago, IL: University of Chicago Press, 2015); Nicholas Shaxson, *Treasure Islands: Tax Havens and the Men Who Stole the World* (London: Vintage, 2011); James S. Henry, "The Price of Offshore Revisited: New Estimates for 'Missing' Global Private Wealth, Income, Inequality, and Lost Taxes", Working Paper, Tax Justice Network (Chesham, 2012).

14. Avner Offer, *Property and Politics, 1870–1914: Landownership, Law, Ideology and Urban Development in England* (Cambridge: Cambridge University Press, 1981), Chapter 17; Avner Offer, "Empire and Social Reform: British Overseas Investment and Domestic Politics 1908–1914", *Historical Journal* 26 (1983), pp. 130–33. In retrospect, this rise in interest rates seems to be the main reason for the Edwardian property slump and the decline in UK government bonds (Consols), although it was less clear to me when writing about it at the time.

15. Sidney Homer and Richard Eugene Sylla, *A History of Interest Rates*, 3rd edn (New Brunswick, NJ: Rutgers University Press, 1991), Table 76, p. 555.

16. Avner Offer, "The Economy of Obligation: Incomplete Contracts and the Cost of the Welfare State", University of Oxford, Discussion Paper in Economic and Social History 103 (Oxford, 2012), pp. 5–6.

17. Avner Offer, *The Challenge of Affluence: Self-Control and Well-Being in the United States and Britain Since 1950* (Oxford: Oxford University Press, 2006); A. Offer, R. Pechey and S. Ulijaszek, "Obesity under Affluence Varies by Welfare Regimes: The Effect of Fast Food, Insecurity, and Inequality", *Economics and Human Biology* 8(3) (2010), pp. 297–308.

18. Avner Offer, *The First World War: An Agrarian Interpretation* (Oxford: Oxford University Press, 1989).

19. Offer, *Challenge of Affluence*, Figure 12.1, p. 272.

20. Joseph A. Schumpeter, *History of Economic Analysis*, Elizabeth Boody Schumpeter (ed.) (New York: Oxford University Press, 1954), pp. 1110–17; L. Randall Wray, *Modern Money Theory: A Primer on Macroeconomics for Sovereign Monetary Systems* (Basingstoke: Palgrave Macmillan, 2012); Basil J. Moore, *Horizontalists and Verticalists: The Macroeconomics of Credit Money* (Cambridge: Cambridge University Press, 1988); Thomas I. Palley, "Horizontalists, Verticalists, and Structuralists: The Theory of Endogenous Money Reassessed", Institut für Makroökonomie und Konjunktur forschung (IMK), Working Paper 121 (Düsseldorf, June 2013); Josh Ryan-Collins, Tony Greenham and Richard Werner, *Where Does Money Come From? A Guide to the UK Monetary and Banking System*, 2nd edn (London: New Economics Foundation, 2014); Richard A. Werner, "A Lost Century in Economics: Three Theories of Banking and the Conclusive Evidence", *International Review of Financial Analysis* 46 (2016), pp. 361–79.

21. Frederic S. Mishkin, *The Economics of Money, Banking, and Financial Markets*, 8th edn (Boston, MA: Pearson, 2007), pp. 219, 230–31.

22. Eric Monnet, "The Diversity in National Monetary and Credit Policies in Western Europe under the Bretton Woods System", in *Les Banques Centrales et Les États. Banques Centrales et Construction de L'État-Nation (XIXe et XXe Siècle) [Central Banks and Nation States (19th and 20th Century)]* (Paris, forthcoming).

23. Avner Offer,"Consumption and Affluence", in *Cambridge Economic History of Modern Britain*, Roderick Floud, Jane Humphries and Paul Johnson (eds), Volume 2, pp. 205–28 (Cambridge: Cambridge University Press, 2014): see pp. 215–17 specifically.

24. Jacob Isaksen, Paul Lassenius Kramp, Louise Funch Sørensen and Søren Vester Sørensen, "Household Balance Sheets and Debt: An International Country Study", *Danmarks Nationalbank Monetary Review*, 4th Quarter, Part 1 (2011).

25. Andrew G. Haldane, "Banking on the State", *BIS Review*, No. 139 (October 2009), pp. 1–20, Charts 1, 14.

26. Thomas Steger, Katharina Knoll and Moritz Schularick, "No Price Like Home: Global House Prices, 1870–2012", Verein für Socialpolitik, Beiträge zur Jahrestagung des Vereins für Socialpolitik 2015: "Ökonomische Entwicklung – Theorie und Politik", Session: Housing and the Macroeconomy, No. C06-V2 (2015).

27. Odran Bonnet, Pierre-Henri Bono, Guillaume Chapelle and Etienne Wasmer, "Does Housing Capital Contribute to Inequality? A Comment on Thomas Piketty's *Capital in the 21st Century*", Sciences Po, Sciences Po Economics Discussion Paper 2014-07 (Paris, 17 April 2014); Guillaume Allègre and Xavier Timbeau, "Does Housing Wealth Contribute to Wealth Inequality? A Tale of Two New Yorks", OFCE Briefing Paper 9 (8 January 2015).

PART II

PIKETTY IN WESTERN NATIONAL CONTEXTS

5

FRENCH IDIOSYNCRACIES

Gauthier Lanot

In his book *Capital in the Twenty-First Century* Thomas Piketty deploys three sources of evidence: first, aggregate data deduced from national accounts; second, sources related to the distribution of income; and third, evidence concerning the distribution of wealth in the population. In his treatment of income distribution in France, the latter two sources are related to the specifics of tax collection over the last two centuries, and the organized and careful recording of the data in simple and informative tables that can be analysed with a view to drawing aggregate conclusions.

From Piketty's work two conclusions are clear and undisputed: relative to the inequality experienced in the second half of the nineteenth century, wealth and income inequality were reduced substantially after the Second World War, following the destruction of assets caused by the war. This reduction in both forms of inequality persisted for the next thirty years or so. Piketty focuses on inequality at the top of the income or wealth distribution because these are characterized best in the sources he uses. However, since the 1980s inequality has increased in both dimensions and Piketty's prediction is that, in the future, it will resemble the inequality that characterized the distribution of income and wealth in the last part of the nineteenth century.

What happens in the first half of the twentieth century is outlined using aggregate evidence drawn from the national accounts, using reconstructed data for the years before 1950, and reporting a measure of aggregate return on capital. This evidence has been the source of some criticism, mostly because of the aggregate nature of the measurement that national accounts provide, and because of the difficulty in accounting for the differences between the three types of measurement in Piketty's work: income, wealth and capital.

The book does, however, provide a framework for relating these three concepts and supporting the main predictions that are made. The analysis favours the accumulation channel, whereby the value of today's total output is divided between labour income, capital income and investment (into physical capital). This in turn determines tomorrow's production. In this styl-ized world, capital income is the return obtained from owning shares on the production side, and we can think of these shares as wealth. In the absence of alternative assets in which to invest, households will hold their savings in capital, and wealth can therefore be identified with capital. The "real world" is, of course, more complicated: there are many forms of investment, some of which, like housing, are only indirectly related to productive capital. Piketty evaluates the (average) rate of return on capital from the ratio between income attributable to capital and the capital stock used for production, and not from observed returns on financial markets. This is of course consistent with the use of national accounts. Piketty's measurements are therefore rela-tively unaffected by inflation,[1] as long as inflation affects output price and the price of capital goods in a similar fashion.[2] Piketty's third law relies on the regularity $r > g$ and leads to an unpleasant prognosis: wealth will concentrate in the hands of the few. The mechanism is apparently straightforward, if r is large relative to the economy's growth rate (g), then a larger share of output has to be allocated to the payment of the rental price of capital, and the share allocated to all other inputs must decrease. This last implication means, in particular, that the share of output allocated to the payment of labour will decrease. Hence, the "third law" suggests that the dynamic of wealth accu-mulation is important for the distribution of income. So if $r > g$ always holds, and if the difference is large enough (more than that which the usual models would suggest is possible), then workers will capture proportionally less of the overall output. If workers cannot or do not save much, the owners of capital will capture almost all the gains from production and pass them on to their children. According to Piketty, this could happen in the relatively short term, say within the next few generations if r remains large. This is not a posi-tive development for the population's welfare. But there are feasible tools to modify the dynamic in order to preserve the distributional gains that were obtained in the first thirty years after the Second World War.

In the French case, however, the evidence is conflicted: on the one hand, many demographic and institutional aspects, particularly involving the regula-tion of the labour market, are very specific to France; while on the other hand, the overall evolution that Piketty describes does not make France a significant outlier relative to other countries. This last point is in fact one of the major strengths of Piketty's argument. Despite its idiosyncrasies, the development of the French economy over the last two centuries has followed a path that, while specific (characterized by a relatively larger reliance on agriculture earlier on, a relative absence of notable extractable resources since the 1970s, and delayed industrial development), is not that exceptional by international standards.[3] The institutions that determine some aspects of this development are also no doubt specific to France; however, based on Piketty's description of the main macroeconomic facts, the roles these institutions played are not sufficient, at first glance, to explain differences or similarities between the evolution of the French economy and those of other countries.

In this chapter, after reviewing the key findings concerning inequality, I single out two specificities of the French economy that qualify both Piketty's aggregate findings and his predictions for the future developmental path for inequality applied both to France and to other countries. I review the joint evolution of France's demography and those institutions related to the tax system, together with the French pension system. I then turn my attention to the interactions between the regulated labour market and technological progress, and the past and present difficulties of seeking to reform the first so that benefit can be derived from the second.

THE MEASUREMENT OF INEQUALITY IN
CAPITAL IN THE TWENTY-FIRST CENTURY

There are two sources of evidence for the long-run distribution of income and wealth among the French population. This information results from an enormous effort of collection, description and analysis that Piketty (with the help of several researchers) presented in his earlier book, *Les hauts revenus en France au XXe siècle*. In this work he describes in detail the evolution of income distribution among high-income (fiscal) households in France, and the redistributional impact of the various changes made to the fiscal system in the course of the twentieth century.[4]

The data on which the distributional analysis is based come from tables that count the number of households in a given taxable income bracket as well as the total taxable income declared within each interval. This form of data has been available, often annually, since 1910. The Second World War delayed, but did not stop, the tax authorities from eventually filing and describing its main work. Such data do not always exist with the same frequency for other countries over this entire period,[5] so the French data serves as a benchmark. Based on this data source, Piketty's *Les hauts revenue en France* provides a description of the evolution of the upper deciles and percentiles of the income distribution and thereby contributes to the factual grounding of much of the French evidence presented in *Capital in the Twenty-First Century*. In approaching this source of data his methodological choices are clear-cut: he focuses on the higher deciles and percentiles and does not engage in the use of "econometrics".[6] He does not propose an econometric model that would account for the correlations that are observed in the data, but instead describes overall patterns, suggesting and arguing for some particular associations. While this is at odds with the method-ology that empirical economists would deem more appropriate in other fields, this approach has the advantage of limiting the role of methodological choices in the conclusions he obtains.

The focus on the higher percentiles is justified by the rough stability in the distribution of wages over the second part of the twentieth century in France. Indeed the ratios of the tenth, fiftieth and ninetieth percentiles to the average wage are almost constant: "10% of salaried workers earn less than 50% of the annual average wage, 40% earn between 50% and 80% of the average wage and the next 40% earn between 80% and 160% of the average wage, the last 10% earn more than 160% of the average wage".[7]

The main finding is the initial collapse in the incomes of the very richest fiscal households, the last 0.01 per cent, from 1920 to 1945, and their slow but fairly continuous recovery since then. By 1990 the share of income of the richest fiscal households reaches a level comparable to that last seen in 1900–1910. This is well above the average income that the same fiscal households would have enjoyed before the 1929 crisis. The international comparisons that Piketty presents in *Capital in the Twenty-First Century* suggest that people in the top percentile of incomes experienced a decrease in their share of total income until 1980–90. In the US, the UK, Canada and Australia, however, the share of the top percentile began to increase noticeably, while in Continental Europe and Japan the top percentile of income as a share of total income has not increased in the same fashion, if at all.[8] On the face of it, the fate of the first percentile in Japan and in France is similar, with a share between 8 per cent and 9 per cent of total income in 2010, compared with a share of 18 per cent in the US and 14 per cent in the UK.

These are large numbers, indicating significant inequalities, and Piketty provides possible explanations for their existence. We can find such explanations in most labour economics textbooks: super managers, superstars, entrepreneurs selling a product that costs little at the margin and can be sold at a higher price to a large market – all of them benefiting from an ability to collect high rents, so that they end up capturing between 10 per cent and 20 per cent of annual output. This feature only becomes sharper as one concentrates on higher fractions of the upper centile: these fractions of the population have captured a growing share of annual output over the last twenty years or so.

The second source of data that Piketty describes at length arises from the administration of inheritance (the sum of bequests and gifts, i.e. the total value of all assets of the deceased at the time of death).[9] These have been recorded since the early nineteenth century so that inheritance taxes could be collected and the transmission of property rights organized. Here he focuses on the sum of all assets declared at the time of death to the tax authorities. Continuous records of such information have existed since the period following the Revolution, although not as frequently in recent years as in the case of income taxation; this permits detailed description of the top decile and the top percentile of the distribution of wealth in France.

Piketty relies on the randomness of death (in the population) and the relentless nature of the tax administration for his description of the distribution of wealth among the population. The estimates are likely to be biased, in particular among the very rich (in that case downwards, since households with large fortunes are able to plan and optimize the composition of their portfolios in ways that are difficult to track or value effectively). However, the change in the concentration of wealth among the first decile and percentile tells Piketty's story: for the first half of the twentieth century the concentration at the top decreased dramatically, while since 1945 it has recovered continuously, so that by the start of the twenty-first century the concentrations (at the top) are similar to what they were at the start of the twentieth century.

Based on these findings, Piketty's analysis shows that the concentration of wealth and taxable income has increased over the last half century in France, and elsewhere in the Western world as well. He shows, furthermore, that the proportion of aggregate wealth that is inherited every year has increased since the 1950s, and that as a percentage of national income, bequests and gifts amounted to slightly more than 4 per cent in 1950 but had grown to 12 per cent by 2000. Finally, he predicts that, depending on the difference between r and g, the proportion of bequests and gifts in national income could once again reach 20 per cent, a proportion that had characterized the period between the late nineteenth century and early twentieth century in France. If this path is followed, it is then likely that inherited wealth will make up more than 80 per cent of total wealth by 2050.

Although it is difficult to document in general, there are reasons to think that the return to capital is not identical for all agents in the economy[10] and may reflect economic rents and/or market power. Piketty argues for a broad-based tax on wealth with no exceptions, with the objective of regulating wealth inequality, opposing the accumulation of large fortunes held by the few. A necessary condition for the efficacy of wealth taxation is the ability to record wealth in all its forms wherever and however it is held. Piketty therefore suggests that wealth taxation would contribute to the regulation of capitalism, since it would make it harder to hide gains that reflect the exercise of some market power. Information transparency may have further advantages, particularly in recording and eventually limiting operations that are detrimental to the stability of the banking and financial systems but that may be very beneficial to a few. Given the recent history of the financial system it is difficult to argue against such objectives.

A COMPLEX DEMOGRAPHIC AND INSTITUTIONAL HISTORY

The demography of France has passed through many distinct regimes since 1800. The population rose from 30 million in 1810 to 40 million by 1900. In the first half of the twentieth century the two world wars inflicted major shocks on the structure of the population, so that after the Second World War the total population of France was roughly the same as it had been at the start of the century (effectively zero population growth over fifty years). There was a French baby boom between 1945 and 1965, with the number of children per woman increasing sharply, peaking at around 3 in 1947 and not falling below 2.7 until after 1965.[11] Furthermore, the working population has increased substantially since 1950, increasing at a rate of 0.5 per cent per year over the period: the total working population reached 25.7 million in 2007, against 19.4 million in 1949.

During the twentieth century the structure of employment in France was transformed: while 30 per cent of total employment was involved in agricultural work at the start of the century, by the end of the century that proportion was ten times smaller. As for most developed countries, the structure of production changed dramatically over the period: starting from a mix of agricultural and industrial production, the current output mix has, since the 1980s, been dominated by services. Over time, the resources available for French aggregate production changed: the resources extracted from mining in metropolitan France and from its colonies either became uneconomical to exploit, were exhausted or were no longer controlled directly by French interests. Hence, while mining, quarrying and manufacturing employed 4.5 million workers (full-time equivalent) in 1949 and peaked at about 5.3 million workers in 1974, the number has since declined (more or less) continuously, to less than 2.9 million in 2014. Self-employment has also fallen dramatically. In the agricultural sector, 91 per cent of the working population were employees in 2007; the equivalent figures for 1949 and 1900 are 64 per cent and 50 per cent, respectively.[12]

Associated with the transition away from agricultural activities, the distribution of the population across the territory has also altered dramatically. While in 1901 about 60 per cent of the population lived in rural areas (this figure was still above 45 per cent at the end of the Second World War), by 2010 the proportion was less than 22 per cent. A larger population now lives in a more concentrated fashion in "urban" areas.[13]

The population of France had aged earlier than in most other European countries, driven by a fall in fertility early on[14] and then by increases in life expectancy. Hence, while 8 per cent of the French population was over 60 in 1790, Sweden only reached this level around 1860 and the UK only around 1910. The 9 per cent level was reached in France after the First World War; the UK and

Germany reached this level in the 1940s.[15] Over the second half of the twentieth century the French population grew by about 20 million; nevertheless, the ageing of the population has not really abated over the long run, and the proportion of those over 65 increased from 11 per cent in 1950 to 17 per cent in 2010.

In response to this early ageing, financial institutions adapted early and the first pension systems appeared in France soon after the Revolution. Civil servants and the military were the first to be covered by a publicly funded scheme that required thirty years of contributions for a benefit worth one-quarter of a person's final salary.[16] This scheme started as a fully funded system but suffered from chronic underfunding and soon required direct public funding. By the middle of the nineteenth century it was transformed into a pay-as-you-go system of redistribution. In the private sector the difficulty of balancing the level of contribution on the part of workers and firms and the level of benefits meant that, eventually, only a minority of the population contributed. Hautcoeur and Le Quéré estimate that only about 7 million out of 18 million employees contributed in 1912, and in 1930 only 20 per cent of those older than 60 benefited from a private pension. Finally, while many mutual societies offered pensions by the 1900s, these pensions were not usually large enough to finance inactive retirement. Work therefore remained a common way to finance living costs during old age among poorer households; increasingly so, in fact, through the nineteenth century.[17] The current public and private pension system, based on transfers as its main distributional mechanism, was organized only after the end of the Second World War.[18]

The state is obviously not absent from the development of the French economy. Since the Second World War the large share of French GDP that is collected from direct and indirect taxes pays for a broad set of services (education, health, employment of civil servants, welfare transfers), and in particular finances social security expenditure, including pension payments. Over time, the share in GDP of tax on income and profits in France has increased, from 5.9 per cent in 1965 to 10.9 per cent in 2013, while for both Germany and the UK that share was above 10 per cent for the entire period. The taxation of income and profits, including payroll tax, amounted to 12.5 per cent of GDP in 2013.[19] The increase in public spending over time is directly related to the ageing of the population during the last fifty years, and to the increase in unemployment. In 1947 social security expenditure amounted to less than 10 per cent of GDP and central state expenditure approached 30 per cent of GDP; since the mid 1980s social security spending has claimed a larger share of GDP than central state expenditure, and aggregated total public spending currently represents more than 50 per cent of GDP.[20]

Taxation of different sources of income to finance public spending has evolved over time. To simplify, the early Revolutionary effort (1790–98) focused on the reform of taxation, seeking to create several forms of direct taxation on income. A range of taxes were applied to (i) income from land and dwellings (*contribution foncière*), (ii) income from financial assets (*contribution mobilière*), (iii) benefits from trade and production (*contribution des patentes*), and (iv) overall income (*contribution des portes et fenêtres*).[21] Indirect taxation only reappeared with the Second Empire in the middle of the nineteenth century. These various forms of taxation applied to all citizens and income levels and were assessed in simple ways (for example, the number of doors and windows and their sizes determined the amount owed). Earnings and pension income were not taxed directly. Direct income taxation became less important during the nineteenth century, and by the 1870s indirect taxation represented 50 per cent of total tax income. Over the twentieth century direct taxation of the different sources of income was reformed several times (1917, 1948, 1959, 1990), introducing and modifying the form of taxation of labour income, the taxation of benefits and the taxation of wealth, and in each case changing the basis for taxation. Since 1914 the income tax system has contained a progressive component that has assumed many forms over time (between 1919 and 1935 there were twenty-five tax brackets, there were five in 1946 and nine in 1949, there were eight or nine brackets between 1949 and 1974 and fourteen in 1983; there are five in 2016).

These reforms have sought to equalize taxation of different forms of income while simultaneously personalizing the forms of taxation applied to the various types of taxpayers. Since 1948 the income of married couples has been taxed jointly; furthermore, the size of the household contributes to the determination of the marginal tax rate that applies to the overall household income. The system is obviously more generous to households with spouses that have unequal incomes, and to households with more children. While this gain is capped, in practice it means that it is the relatively rich households who have benefited. In 1991 an additional form of income taxation, the "*contribution sociale généralisée*" (CSG),[22] bearing on all forms of income, labour and capital was introduced to reform the collection of social security contributions. This particular income tax is proportional (its rate has increased over time, from 1.1 per cent to between 6.2 per cent and 8 per cent in 2015) and applies to individuals, not to households. Because the tax base of the CSG is wider than the tax base of the income tax system, the CSG collects almost twice as much revenue. The overall consequence of this stream of reforms is that taxation in France is complex, with many exceptions that apply to specific categories of taxpayer.[23] Moreover, while the income tax system applied to households has, since 1914, contained a progressive component, overall taxation is regressive (taking into account the taxation of all forms of income and consumption): in 2010 an individual among the richest 1 per cent pays proportionally less tax than any individual belonging to the poorest 99 per cent.[24]

The decision to introduce a pension system transferring resources from those in work to those who no longer work means that public finances have to absorb substantial variations in spending when the size of the retired population increases relative to the size of the active population. In a demographic steady state, and assuming that all generations enjoy the same lifespan, the distribution mechanism can remain solvent: the active population can pay for the pensions of the retired, and the implicit rate of return in such a system is the growth rate of the population (adjusted for any productivity growth).

Over the last century the age composition of the population has changed. The size of the active population has decreased relative to the size of the dependent population more or less continuously. In 1902 the population aged between 20 and 65 in France reached 22.1 million, while the population aged 65 or more amounted to 3.3 million; in 1948 we find 24.13 million and 4.6 million, respectively; and in 2000 we find 34.38 million and 9.43 million. These figures imply theoretical dependency ratios of 6.8, 5.2 and 3.6 actives per inactive. By 2040 it is projected[25] that there may be 18 million people aged over 65 living in France against a population of 36.7 million aged between 20 and 65. These figures lead to a dependency ratio that at best reaches 2. The observed dependency ratio has been less than 2.5 since the 1980s and may, according to the projections, fall to 1.5 by 2040. Since the pension system relies on transfers between generations of unequal relative sizes, the future financial shortfalls are to be reduced by reforms that change the relationship between eligibility criteria and pension entitlements. Because such reforms cannot be quickly introduced (especially if the necessary changes are substantial), the remaining gap between pension payments and the resources of the pension system will have to be bridged through higher transfers from younger generations to older ones.[26] Since institutional choices have long-run consequences, the state remains a necessary presence in many markets so that the development of inequality might be moderated.

INEQUALITY AND TECHNOLOGICAL PROGRESS

Piketty presents several arguments in seeking to explain the evolution of income inequality. First, an increase in the number of employees in a "super-manager" position, who negotiate or extract large rewards relative to a median or an average worker thanks to their dominant managerial position.

Second, the exploitation of network externalities that help the creation of "global stars" (in sport, the arts, entertainment, literature, etc.) The world market is much larger in absolute terms today than it was at the start of the twentieth century,[27] and much larger absolute surpluses can be generated.[28] It is not clear, however, how much of the increased concentration of incomes and wealth in

France can be attributed solely to the growth of international trade, or to the network interactions that arise from the use of the internet.

Third, technological progress provides a set of possible explanations for the evolution of inequalities. Piketty dismisses out of hand this class of explanation as a source of the increase in inequality at the top. Technological progress explains changes in productivity. However, Piketty argues that the productivity of those who have been the main beneficiaries of the increase in wealth concentration may not have changed that dramatically (relative to anyone else), and this does not therefore explain why concentration of wealth remains high in the face of significant adverse events that should reduce it.[29]

Any firm attempting to pay as low a wage as possible for its workers will face competing firms that will find it profitable to pay slightly more to attract the same workers. Hence, *prima facie,* it is unlikely that earnings are permanently below a worker's productivity. How far below productivity a firm could pay will depend on the particular form of competition in the labour market. If the labour market is very fluid, i.e. if a generic worker is aware of the opportunities that are available in other firms, then earnings will track productivity closely. If, instead, the labour market is thin, i.e. workers only receive rare offers from competing firms, then the gap between earnings and productivity can be quite wide. This of course reflects the market power that firms have over workers. In the case of managers, pay is not necessarily determined by a process that solely reflects a manager's marginal productivity. It may take the form of a delayed reward for past achievements, for example if managers are selected from a pool of candidates using a tournament contest (e.g. best sales, or best results), or it might reflect both the lack of competition to obtain a job and a superior ability to negotiate on the part of the successful candidate relative to the hiring firm. In this latter case, pay would reflect the ability of the candidate to secure a job, not her ability to perform the particular managerial job she is hired for. Hence, any explanation of the increase in income concentration based on changes in the profile of productivities in the population appears tautological.

However, a form of this kind of explanation, based on the idea that automation has recently changed the supply and demand for labour across skill and occupation groups, provides an argument that is not tautological. Automation can in some cases replace jobs that are repetitive, for example some types of form filling or simple administrative tasks, while on the other hand there are tasks that require attention to specific features that would be hard or expensive to program, or would require expensive additional capital investment. For example, hairdressing or personal care cannot be easily or cheaply automated. Thus we have a form of technological progress biased in favour of either the very creative task or the very specific and complex one. This process is seen as providing an explanation of the "hollowing out of the wage distribution", whereby workers in jobs that can be automated have seen their jobs disappear, or their wages fall relative to those of workers in jobs that cannot be automated.

The process is therefore sometimes called "job polarization": jobs requiring skills usually associated with the middle deciles of the earnings distribution have disappeared, and the relative wage of remaining workers has decreased relative to lower-skilled workers. There is evidence for this hypothesis from US data,[30] and European evidence appears to support the idea that a similar process is also at work in Europe.[31] This process hurts employment mostly in occupations that are part of the middle deciles of the earnings distribution, while (relatively) benefiting the occupations that are part of the lower and higher deciles of the wage distribution.

The share of routine jobs in France and Germany fell from more than 45 per cent in 1992 to around 35 per cent of all jobs in 2008.[32] In 1992 the proportion of jobs involving abstract tasks was almost identical in France and Germany (about 33 per cent; 35 per cent in the US), whereas in 2008 it was slightly above 40 per cent for Germany and the US and below 40 per cent in France. The proportion of manual non-routine tasks is larger in France and the US (about 25 per cent in 2008) than it is in Germany (around 22 per cent). This evolution is obviously important when it comes to the distribution of income over the last twenty years or so. Albertini and his co-authors have suggested that the interactions between labour market institutions and the form of technological change had unpleasant consequences for the employment structure in France. Technological progress contributed to job losses that were limited by the increase in the supply of skilled workers. It is therefore the interaction between labour market institutions and the process of technological change that appears to explain these adverse effects. US employment benefited from technological progress, thanks to the flexibility of its labour market. This explanation is only indirect, and arises from the analysis of a particular model of the labour market and of particular forms of interactions between production and the labour market. However, the analysis suggests that more disaggregated processes in the labour market, at the job/occupation level, can contribute to the long-term evolution of inequality.

Labour market institutions and their transformation over the last century are mostly absent from Piketty's central discussion of the evolution of inequality in France. In fact, markets are largely absent from Piketty's account of inequalities altogether, since his focus is on the accumulation of wealth and its distribution. While he includes housing in wealth, for example, the way in which housing wealth accumulates is not linked to the structure of housing markets but to the inheritance of property and the wealth that it confers on particular social groups. Piketty's focus is clearly on the inequality at the top, where market mechanisms do not obviously bear that directly upon the accumulation of wealth.

The dysfunction of the labour market is mostly felt at the bottom of the income/ earnings distribution. I will in conclusion consider this aspect of inequality, since it provides an alternative perspective on the generation of income and wealth disparities.

LABOUR MARKET INSTITUTIONS AND THE CREATION OF INEQUALITY

Labour laws in France are regularly amended or reformed. Since 1990 there have been additions or modifications in most years.[33] These relatively frequent changes alternate between the updating of previous legislation, for example extending or modifying the rules that determine the representation of workers in private firms, and major modifications of the conditions of work, for example the reduction of working time to 39 hours in 1982 and then to 35 hours in 1998 (taking effect in 2000). Workers in France enjoy substantial employment protection. Labour unions, industry organizations and the state are regularly engaged in negotiations concerning pay and conditions more generally. One of the main features of these specific institutional arrangements since 1950 has been a hierarchy of negotiated "rights".[34] National collective agreements (*conventions collectives nationales*) can add to the requirements of labour laws and set the pay and conditions of work at the level of a branch, a firm or a region. National collective agreements then provide a minimum set of work conditions to all workers and firms covered by them. Local negotiations can improve on these rights, but they cannot restrict them. A small number of labour unions and industrial associations are mandated by law to represent the interests of workers and firms in negotiations. The minister in charge of labour affairs can then extend the resulting collective agreements to firms that were not represented, and to the workers of those firms. Hence while the rate of unionization of French workers is small, 8 per cent in 2000, more than 90 per cent of workers are covered by collective agreements.[35]

The modern French labour market is best described as dual: since the 1980s a growing proportion of (mostly young) workers with limited education have undergone short-term and infrequent spells of activity while older and/or better-educated workers monopolize long-term work contracts. Long-term contracts (known as *contrats à durées indeterminées* (CDIs)) provide workers with better representation, negotiation rights and greater legal protection. By contrast, short-term contracts (either interim contracts obtained through temporary work agencies, or *contrats à durées determinées* (CDDs) directly offered by firms) do not. Neither interim contracts nor CDDs are supposed to be offered to replace long-term contracts. Since 1982 the proportion of temporary contracts in the competitive part of the French labour market[36] has increased, from about 5 per cent in 1982 to 12–13 per cent from 2000 onwards.[37] Over that period most hires have taken the form of short-term contracts (more than 90 per cent of the total). Furthermore, it is the (very) short-term contracts (of less than a month) that have increased the most (from 25 per cent to about 40 per cent since 2000).

The multiple reforms to French labour laws since 1981 have therefore introduced substantial flexibility in the labour market. However, these reforms mostly concern workers aged between 15 and 24 (only 50 per cent of young workers had a CDI in 2012, compared with 90 per cent of workers aged between 25 and 49) and unskilled workers (about one-third of whom are employed on short-term contracts). Overall, about 90 per cent of workers aged between 30 and 50 are employed on a CDI contract. There are likely to be stark differences in the rate of employment over the life cycle of young compared with older French workers, in particular relative to their UK or US counterparts: they participate significantly less in the labour market.[38] This pattern, therefore, makes French workers from more recent generations less able to contribute to the funding of the health and pension benefits they might need to claim later in life. The life cycle labour market participation profile reported by Blundell will ultimately have real welfare consequences. Young workers who are currently weakly attached to the labour market are likely to see their entitlement to pension benefits fall since they will have contributed less. In the future, they will need to extend the length of their working lives beyond that of current generations. The labour market and its dysfunction are likely to be the source of changes to the distribution of income below the top centiles or decile.

This short description of the way in which the French labour market functions must be contrasted with Piketty's observation that over the last forty years or so the share of labour in total income in France has decreased slightly, after a steady increase from 1945 to the mid 1970s; while the share of very well-paid employees has increased significantly. In reality, the explanation for the high unemployment rate among young and unqualified workers is simply that their labour costs are too high given their productivity. In addition, firms have been able to invest in technologies that render some forms of unskilled work no longer necessary.

REFORMS AND INEQUALITY

In early 2016 the French government set out once more to reform the set of laws that regulate the labour market in France. The process of reform is supposed to conclude with a complete overhaul of labour law by the end of 2018. Youth unemployment and the lack of stable employment prospects for many workers in France justify the current flow of proposed reforms currently being considered, which aim to modernize labour laws in order both to protect all workers and to provide contractual certainty to firms (in particular when it comes to firing costs), to overhaul labour laws and adapt them to a changing labour market, to decrease the number of special cases, and to simplify the law that applies to small firms (with fewer than twenty employees).[39]

The public reaction to the reform is symptomatic of the perceptions of the role of the state in the labour market in France. The aim to simplify and bring fluidity to the labour market is supported by the associations that represent firms but rejected by most labour unions and by student and school associations for more or less the same reasons. Firms claim that workers' rights impose too many constraints on firms, and therefore increase the opportunity cost of hiring younger workers. As a result such rights contribute to a high unemployment rate. Younger workers demand protection against the excessive insecurity inflicted by the prevailing short-term contracts.

Past reforms, by right- and left-leaning governments, have introduced a variety of schemes designed to support the hiring of young workers, the hiring of old workers and the hiring of young and old workers together. Firms receive support to hire apprentices, to employ low-paid workers or to retrain unqualified workers. Nonetheless, part of the workforce is convinced that firms (in general) take advantage of the subsidies while reorganizing their workforce in such a way that youth unemployment remains high (20 per cent and more), particularly for those with limited training. For the current left-wing government, as for most governments since the 1990s, the prospects are not good. French workers will no doubt demonstrate their annoyance with the new law, while firms' representatives will try hard to extract technical exceptions and further subsidies in exchange for promises of future hires. The consequences of a failure to reform the labour market are worrying: without reforms, the labour market in France does not appear able to deliver a more equal distribution of labour income over a lifetime. A regulatory framework designed to protect the working population from the excesses of the market is currently hurting some of its potential members as much, or more, than the market would.

In *Capital in the Twenty-First Century* Piketty does not make the labour market key to his analysis, despite the great number of labour reforms and the importance of state regulation in France. Labour market regulation in France is clearly playing an increasing role in determining the distribution of income: it limits the chances of younger workers finding secure employment and adds to the costs of unemployment benefit and so to the costs of public finance, while also reducing the capacity of younger workers to contribute to their future pension needs. When added to the changing demographic profile of the French population, this will place severe strain on any capacity for redistribution from young to old and from those in work to those out of work or no longer working. This is therefore a significant element in the growth of income inequality in France, even though legislative effort is bent towards employment protection.

This particular feature of the French case is central to Piketty's analysis. He suggests instead a reform to the system of taxation of all forms of income, making the system more broad based, and more progressive rather than regressive at high income levels, as is currently the case. His objective is obviously not to modify directly the operational characteristics of the labour market (its ability to allocate jobs to workers efficiently) in general, but to allow the sharing of gains from aggregate activity among the population. This raises an important question about the reform of a modern welfare state: is it better to redesign the tax system (to include a more systematic wealth tax, to tax incomes in a more progressive fashion) or to reform the labour market (by making it more flexible and allowing for a more fluid allocation of resources) when the overall objective is to limit the extent of inequalities, support growth and increase the welfare of the population?

Piketty suggests that fiscal reform directed at a more equal distribution of income and wealth is more pressing in the medium to long term than reforms to the idiosyncratic French labour market. He argues in several places that the beneficiaries of inequality tend to suffer from illusions about the role of skill and hard work in their own good fortune. Once such rich individuals have the means to decide on the main objectives of national economic policy, they are very unlikely to agree to a reform that would harm their wealth or their capital. It may well be a great deal more effective or feasible to seek regulatory reforms involving the labour market and its institutions before the conditions of the nineteenth century reassert themselves.

Notes for Chapter 5

1. But see James Poterba, "The Rate of Return to Corporate Capital and Factor Shares: New Estimates Using Revised National Income Accounts and Capital Stock Data", *Carnegie–Rochester Conference Series on Public Policy* 48 (1998), pp. 211–46, for a discussion of the importance of the ratio of output price to the price of capital goods.

2. The capital losses that arose from the events of the first half of the twentieth century (illustrated in Figure 4.5, p. 147, in *Capital*) are therefore not accounted for in the returns. Figure 4.5 for β, Figure 6.4 for r and Figure 6.8 for α provide a consistent account of the evolution of the main quantities.

3. See Jean-Pierre Dormois, *The French Economy in the Twentieth Century* (Cambridge: Cambridge University Press, 2004). This discussion of French exceptionalism is not new; the changing views on French economic growth in the nineteenth century are

discussed in detail by Francois Crouzet, "The Historiography of French Economic Growth in the Nineteenth Century", *Economic History Review* 56(2) (May 2003), pp. 215–42. In his blog, Brad Delong notes that France is not a unique source of puzzles since there is "an earlier large puzzle in the production function, the twentieth-century retardation of the British economy".

4. Thomas Piketty, *Les hauts revenus en France au XXe siècle: inégalités et redistributions, 1901–1998* (Paris: Bernard Grasset, 2001). This is another weighty contribution. In the edition I have in front of me the main text contains more than 500 pages (more densely printed than the English translation of *Capital*), and added to this there are another 220 pages of appendices (printed in a smaller font), containing mostly data and notes on the data sources and on the text.

5. See Anthony B. Atkinson and Thomas Piketty (eds), *Top Incomes over the Twentieth Century: A Contrast between Continental European and English-Speaking Countries* (Oxford: Oxford University Press, 2007).

6. The determination of the exact characteristics of the percentiles is nevertheless the result of statistical work based on the raw data. For the higher percentiles he focuses on the description of the tails of the distribution, based on the characteristics of the best-fitting Pareto distribution.

7. See Piketty, *Les hauts revenus en France*, p. 213.

8. Piketty, *Capital*, Figure 9.3.

9. See Annex J in his *Les hauts revenus en France* for a discussion of the data from 1902 and 1994, and for a more detailed account, see Piketty "On the Long-Run Evolution of Inheritance: France 1820–2050", *Quarterly Journal of Economics* 126(3) (2011), pp. 1071–131.

10. Piketty provides us with one example where this is the case: the returns on the capital endowments of some US universities range between 6 per cent and 10 per cent, and increase with the size of the endowment.

11. See Gilles Pison, "France and the United Kingdom: Demographic Stability on the Continent and Stop-and-Go across the Channel", *Population et Societies* 520 (March 2015). In comparison, the fertility rate in the UK peaked first in 1947, with a rate equal to 2.7 children per woman, but in 1951 it was back at 2.1. French and British fertility rates peaked again in 1964 at the same level: around 2.9 children per woman.

12. See Gerard Bouvier and Charles Pilarski, "Soixante ans d'économie française: des mutations structurelles profondes", *Insee Première* 1201 (July 2008).

13. These changes occurred because of migration from the countryside to the towns, and from the reclassification of some areas from rural to urban. Furthermore, the map of France changed over time: for example, as result of territories lost and then recovered in Alsace and Lorraine from 1871 to 1919. Finally, the definition of an urban area altered as well. The numbers are therefore to be taken as orders of magnitude rather than precise quantities. See www.ined.fr/fichier/s_rubrique/21879/popu.frm.1846.1999. fr.xls for a history of the French population from 1846 to 1999 in metropolitan France.

14. Among women born between 1831 and 1840 there were 3.5 children on average per woman in France and almost 5 in England; the same numbers for the women born between 1891 and 1900 were about 2 for French women and less than 2.5 for English

women; for a more extensive discussion see Timothy W. Guinnane, "The Historical Fertility Transition: A Guide for Economists", *Journal of Economic Literature* 49 (2011), pp. 589–614.

15. See Joëlle Gaymu, *Le Vieillissement Démographique et les Personnes Agées en France*, International Institute on Ageing (Malta: United Nations, 1993); Jerôme Bourdieu and Lionel Kesztenbaum ("Comment vivre dans un monde vieillissant? Les personnes âgées en France, 1800–1940", LEA Working Paper 0601 (Paris: ENS, January 2006)) suggest even higher rates for France in 1900 based on the 3,000 families of the TRA survey.

16. For a more exhaustive discussion see Pierre-Cyrille Hautcoeur and Françoise Le Quéré, "Vieillissement, épargne et système financier: l'expérience française au XIXe siècle", Contribution au groupe de travail "Aspects financiers du viellissement de la population" du Conseil National du Crédit et du Titre (June 2000); Bourdieu and Kesztenbaum, "Comment vivre"; and Antoine Bozio, "Réformes des retraites: estimations sur données françaises", Doctoral Thesis (Paris: EHESS, 2006).

17. Bourdieu and Kesztenbaum estimate that about 33 per cent declared a non-agricultural activity between 1800 and 1829, while between 1880 and 1910 about 47 per cent made the same declaration. Between 1910 and 1940 this falls to 37 per cent.

18. See Bozio "Réformes des retraites" for more details.

19. It was 11.7 per cent in the UK and 11.3 per cent in Germany in 2013, while taxation of property amounted to 3.8 per cent of GDP (4 per cent in the UK and 0.9 per cent for Germany); see OECD, *Revenue Statistics 2015* (Paris 2015).

20. In 2011 transfers accounted for 42.6 per cent of public spending, while central services accounted for 31.8 per cent, and spending on health and education amounted to 25.5 per cent (see Projet de Loi de Finances pour 2013, Rapport sur la Dépense Publique et son Évolution, Ministère Délégué Chargé du Budget, Paris 2013, for more details).

21. See, for example, Conseil des Impôts, *L'impôt sur le revenu, Onzième rapport au président de la république*, Journal Officiel: Paris No. 4153 (1990).

22. An additional tax, the *contribution à la réduction de la dette sociale* (CRDS), which applies proportionally to the gross income of any individual domiciled in France, was added in 1996 with the aim of reducing the deficit on social security. Its rate is constant at 0.5 per cent.

23. See C. Landais, T. Piketty and E. Saez, *Pour une révolution fiscale, un impôt sur le revenu pour le XXIème siècle* (Le Seuil/République des Idées, January 2011).

24. See Landais, Piketty and Saez, *Pour une révolution fiscale*.

25. Nathalie Blanpain and Olivier Chardon, "Projections de population à l'horizon 2060: un tiers de la population âgé de plus de 60 ans", *Insee Premiere* 1320 (Octobre 2010).

26. Akiko Suwa-Eisenmann, Jérôme Bourdieu, Antoine Bommier and Stéphane Zuber analyse the transfers between generations in terms of pensions and education spending (Akiko Suwa-Eisenmann, Jérôme Bourdieu, Antoine Bommier and Stéphane Zuber, "Le développement des transferts publics d'éducation et d'assurance vieillesse par génération en France, 1850–2000", *Économie et Prévision* 180(4) (2007), pp. 1–17). They calculate that the net transfers from the young to the old were substantial for the generations born before 1935: that is, the first generations to benefit from the system. For the generations born after that date they calculate that because of the increase in education

spending after the war, the net transfer is negative, but less than 2.5 per cent of their lifetime income. These results are of course sensitive to many technical assumptions, e.g. concerning the discount rate or concerning the evolution of future benefits.

27. Hence when purchasing the latest novel by a successful author, even using the electronic version, I pay a price that is not related to the relative scarcity of the input needed to produce it: at the margin it does not cost much for the distributor to accept my credit card payment and send me a copy of the book's file, a fraction of a dollar/euro/pound at best. The quoted price that I will pay, however, is usually comparable (half to two-thirds) to the price of the print version of the book. Printed versions of successful authors outside of copyright, such that competition is likely to apply to the supply and pricing of these books, can be found at much lower cost, perhaps a few euros/dollars/pounds, while the latest production of a successful author will be priced about five to ten times higher. Authors and their publishers are of course monopolists for the production of their books, i.e. any other book will be a distant substitute, and they are able to charge a premium price. For example, although Piketty notes the similarities in the economic background that supports the respective plots of novels by Jane Austen and Honoré de Balzac, the novels are not perfect substitutes.

28. Bradford DeLong, "Estimates of World GDP, One Million BC–Present", posted in 1998, http://delong.typepad.com/print/20061012_LRWGDP.pdf (accessed 21 March 2016), reports a world GDP measure that is less than three times larger in 1940 than it was in 1900, but that was ten times larger in 2000 than it was in 1950. These are of course rough estimates, subjected to several assumptions so as to obtain a final number; but the orders of magnitude are eloquent about the size of the possible rents that can be extracted.

29. Productivity has a clear definition in the context of an abstract model that explains how the quantity or the value of output relates to some input. Marginal or average productivity can be easily described. Empirically, it can be harder to decide: labour economists would take the view that earnings mostly reflect the productivity of workers involved in industry or services.

30. David Autor, Frank Levy and Richard Murnane, "The Skill Content of Recent Technological Change: An Empirical Exploration", *Quarterly Journal of Economics* 118(4) (2003), pp. 1279–333; David Autor and David Dorn, "The Growth of Low-Skill Service Jobs and the Polarization of the US Labor Market", *American Economic Review* 103(5) (2013), pp. 1553–97.

31. Maarten Goos, Alan Manning and Anna Salomons, "Job Polarization in Europe", *American Economic Review* 99(2) (2009), pp. 58–63; for Europe, see Steve Macintosh, "Hollowing Out and the Future of the Labour Market", Department for Business Innovation and Skills Research Paper 134 (October 2013), p. 49, for a review with a UK policy focus.

32. See Julien Albertini, Jean Olivier Hairault, Francois Langot and Thepthida Sopraseuth, "Aggregate Employment, Job Polarisation and Inequalities: A Transatlantic Perspective", Mimeo, Humboldt University, Berlin (2015).

33. For a chronology of labour laws in France since 1791 see www.vie-publique.fr/poli tiques-publiques/regulation-relations-travail/chronologie. Economists are regularly involved in suggesting avenues for reform of the institutions: see, for example, Olivier Blanchard and Jean Tirole, *Protection de l'emploi et procédures de licenciement*, Rapport

au Conseil d'analyse économique (Paris: La Documentation Française, 2003); or Pierre Cahuc and Francis Kramarz, *De la précarité à la mobilité: vers une Sécurité sociale professionnelle*, Rapport au ministre de l'Économie, des Finances et de l'Industrie et au ministre de l'Emploi, du Travail et de la Cohésion sociale (Paris: La Documentation Française, 2005). Francis Kramarz ("Pourquoi est-il nécessaire de flexibiliser le marché du travail français?", *Regards croisés sur l'économie 2013/1* (No. 13), pp. 252–62) vents some of the frustrations that professional economists providing advice feel when they are ignored.

34. This is another aspect where French legislators are active. See www.vie-publique.fr/politiques-publiques/regulation-relations-travail/chronologie/ for a description of the chronology of laws regulating labour relations since 1791.

35. See Marine Cheuvreux and Corinne Darmaillacq, "La syndicalisation en France: paradoxes, enjeux et perspectives", Direction générale du Trésor, Lettre TRÉSOR-ÉCO, No. 129 (May 2014) for a factual discussion of the main features of unionization in France.

36. Outside the public sector; about 25 per cent of all salaried workers were working in the public sector in 2012.

37. Muriel Barlet, Claude Minni, Samuel Ettouati, Jean Finot and Xavier Paraire, "Entre 2000 et 2012, Forte Hausse des Embauches en Contrats Temporaires", *Dares Analyses* 56 (July 2014).

38. Richard Blundell, "How Responsive Is the Labor Market to Tax Policy?", *IZA World of Labour*, doi:10.15185/izawol.2 (May 2014).

39. Ministère du Travail, de l'Emploi, de la Formation Professionnelle et du Dialogue Social, "Simplifier, Négocier, Sécuriser: un code du Travail pour le XXIème siècle", Dossier de Presse (4 November 2015).

6

FACT OR FICTION? COMPLEXITIES
OF ECONOMIC INEQUALITY IN
TWENTIETH-CENTURY GERMANY

Jan-Otmar Hesse

What kind of a free market liberal society was Germany on the eve of the First World War? Robert Martin, a retired civil servant who had worked in the Ministry of the Interior, earned his keep by assembling detailed information from German tax statistics in his twenty-volume series *Yearbook of German Millionaires*. The collection included named individuals possessing a fortune worth more than a million marks, also giving their addresses. Since the annual publication was "bought as well as studied with the greatest care by the well-to-do, not only in Germany but in the whole world", Martin claimed that it was also "the most effective advertisement for the millionaires".[1] Martin also stated that the 10,000 individuals included in the new edition on the Rhineland (the western centre of heavy industry in Prussia) had been very helpful in improving the quality of the data by voluntarily submitting additional material, making it very likely that its coverage was complete. Even the emperor could be included, although he paid no tax in Prussia: his annual income exceeded the next wealthiest individual by 3 million marks, but he was not the wealthiest millionaire. That spot went to Bertha Krupp, recorded with a fortune of 283 million marks. Luxury and private wealth were apparently popular topics in those days, and nobody seems to have worried that thieves and conmen might also make use of the publication.

Thanks to Thomas Piketty and his team – among whom Fabien Dell assumed responsibility for the German component – we are all now aware that industrialized societies suffered from serious, and in many cases increasing, economic inequality at the end of the nineteenth century. Private wealth[2] reached a level six times the national income around 1910.[3] A fortune of a million marks was 800 times the average income of employees, making the 10,000 millionaires of Martin's yearbook a much more exclusive group than the 892,000 euro-millionaires in Germany today. Private wealth of a million euros today equals only thirty times the average annual income. However, Bertha Krupp's wealth in 1913 was 0.56 per cent of national income, while the fortune of the richest Germans today, the BMW-owning family the Quandts, is 0.87 per cent of current German GDP.[4] But what do all these figures tell us about the trajectory of economic inequality in Germany, and the evolution of German capitalism?

The following account will re-emphasize the fact that economic history must treat its historical source material with care, for this material can easily be transformed into pure fiction if the methods of data collection and statistical adjustment ignore the complexities of history. Even if the overall Piketty story of a secular reversal of the Kuznets curve since the 1970s largely holds for German history, closer consideration of the causes and consequences might lead us to completely different conclusions. We cannot engage in an exhaustive review of the Piketty data for Germany here, for that would take years.[5] We will focus instead upon four examples in Piketty's treatment of Germany statistics that need challenging.

(1) A careful consideration of the complicated history of income and wealth-taxes in Germany shows that, due to frequent regime changes, the production of straightforward data series is very difficult.

(2) The impact of two hyperinflations and a sovereign debt crisis on the accumulation of wealth will be discussed in greater detail.

(3) German citizens rely on pay-as-you-go state pensions as an instrument for future wealth accumulation; while this is treated only as income by Piketty, I will argue that this has to be treated as wealth, especially when it comes to cross-country comparisons.

(4) Housing also seems to be an asset with idiosyncratic features in Germany compared with other countries.

The chapter will start off with a summary of Piketty's findings with respect to German history, and a consideration of how these fit into the broader picture of a long tradition of domestic inequality research.

PIKETTY'S RESULTS IN THE LIGHT OF GERMAN INEQUALITY RESEARCH

From the 1960s to the 1980s economic inequality through German history was a much-debated issue, with detailed literature focused on nineteenth-century inequality in particular.[6] As in other countries, and perhaps paradoxically, scholarly interest on the part of economic historians was at its greatest when income inequality reached its lowest twentieth-century level, receding when inequality started rising. After the 1980s the topic was more or less left to sociologists, who focused on recent developments and used survey data on household incomes, instead of the tax data that is the main source for the Piketty group. Indeed, the success in Germany of *Capital in the Twenty-First Century* is in part a result of the fact that German economic historians abandoned the field of inequality research in the 1990s, and ceased working on reliable data series for twentieth-century Germany.

Data on economic inequality in Germany is available for the Imperial period before the First World War, but it has discontinuities and is only at the level of federal states. At the end of the nineteenth century personal income taxes were introduced by the federal states, which also collected data on incomes and on wealth. The German central government only collected revenue from various duties and "lived at the expense of the federal states", as Bismarck's famous statement has it. Progressive individual income tax was first introduced in Prussia in 1891, and Prussia also introduced a tax on wealth two years later. However, just as with the former class-based flat-rate taxes, these were applied only to incomes above 900 marks a year (which was a little below an average worker's annual income). In other federal states income tax was introduced only later: Bavaria followed, but not until 1910.[7] Taking into account the fact that the available data records self-assessed higher incomes only, the German literature of the 1970s already supported the Piketty findings: income inequality in Prussia (and the same was in general true for the rest of Germany) increased towards the end of the nineteenth century. The top percentile's share of income rose from 15 per cent to 19 per cent between 1875 and 1900, with some decrease afterwards.[8] The capital wealth of the top percentile accounted for nearly 50 per cent of the total in Prussia, which remained unchanged until the years before 1914, when there was a moderate decline.[9] However, contemporary observers considered it to be "democratic capitalism", because private wealth consisted of a large number of small fortunes that were used to increase the monthly income of the employed upper classes, as opposed to the "financial oligarchy" then prominent in France, where large fortunes were said to have been more concentrated.[10] Contemporary German evidence does not precisely translate into figures showing a similar distribution of wealth to that in France, except perhaps for the remarkable increase in wealth of the top percentile between 1890 and 1900 (from 50 per cent to 60 per cent).

Piketty's account supports the established data and knowledge of German economic inequality before the First World War, but the issue becomes much more complicated for the forty-year period following the war. Dell and Piketty deserve praise for having assembled the first reliable statistical analysis of economic inequality covering that very interesting, but also complicated, period of German history. The share of the top 1 per cent of all income recipients fell from its long-time high of 22 per cent (reached during the wartime industrial boom) to 11 per cent in the 1920s. It was the devastating impact of the war that turned the distributional structure of modern capitalism upside down, so the often-repeated story of Piketty goes. The First World War in particular interrupted the trend of increasing income inequality, but it resumed in the 1970s once there had been recovery from the long-term effects of war and depression. However, in the case of Germany the mechanism operated differently to the way it did in other European countries. Whereas in England and France the war had been financed by foreign capital, Germany had had to rely mainly on the domestic capital market; the debt was eliminated by high levels of inflation that started during the war and ended with the hyperinflation of 1922 and 1923.[11] The general effect of the war – the massive destruction of capital assets – was similar in all countries, but the distributional effects on wealth and income should have been different, especially between France and Germany, as we will see below (in the section titled "The Distributional Effects of Hyperinflation"). However, measured in raw figures, the countries experienced a similar decline in their national wealth. The capital to income ratio in Germany (Piketty's β) shrank from 600 per cent before the war to only 300 per cent after it,[12] and the capital share of the top 1 per cent shrank from 45 per cent to only 25 per cent in 1925.[13]

While such inequality measures fell more rapidly in Germany than in other Western countries, they show a remarkable resurgence in the 1930s, resulting from a combination of the criminal racial expropriation of the Jews and the Nazi armaments boom. The top percentile's income (down to 11 per cent after the First World War) jumped to a level of about 16 per cent in Germany shortly before the Second World War: about the level towards which it had been declining in the US and Great Britain.[14] In contrast, wealth inequality in Germany apparently remained unchanged: a stable share of around 25 per cent of the wealth was in the hands of the top percentile, still 10 per cent below the rate in France.[15] The effects of both hyperinflation and the Great Depression indicate a very particular trajectory for German income and wealth distribution through the first half of the twentieth century, which is far from surprising if we keep in mind the political "age of extremes". We will discuss below whether the country's history should make it exempt from the "general laws of capitalism", or instead presents a distinctive example of capitalism's varieties.

For Germans, the Second World War ended similarly to the First, with hidden hyperinflation that eventually devalued savings with another Currency Reform in 1948. Real capital had certainly been destroyed. But there is now a consensus that industrial capital was not as heavily hit by the bombing as one would have expected and, thanks to the high level of investment in armament programmes, capital stock was still at a higher level in 1948 than it had been in 1936.[16] This was not true of private wealth. The Currency Reform devalued savings by 93.5 per cent. This was the main mechanism behind the shrinkage of private wealth. National wealth in total bottomed out at the country's lowest level of 2.2 times GDP in 1950. The top percentile's share in the total wealth of the country fell to a very low 12.5 per cent: a figure never reached by other countries in either continental Europe or Britain or North America. However, within a few years it recovered to 17 per cent and levelled off at around 15 per cent for most of the period until the 1980s (though this was still below the European average).[17] Income inequality, by contrast, showed a pattern similar to that in the other countries of "continental Europe": it fell to a level of 12 per cent for the top percentile, where it stayed, more or less, for the rest of the twentieth century, without experiencing the remarkable resurgence to 16 per cent that countries driven by "neoliberal revolutions" experienced. However, the trajectory also differs. Germany's "economic miracle" of the 1950s was less equitable in its impact: contemporaries recall that it was first experienced by the top income earners and only later trickled down to the average German in the 1970s, such that until the 1960s there was a temporary increase in the share of income taken by top earners.[18] The arrival of a mass-consumption society was delayed in Germany until the 1970s.

To detect the reversal of the Kuznets curve in Germany we must turn our attention away from the top percentile of income receivers. Only the top decile shows a trajectory in Germany similar to that in other wealthy countries, although it is much less marked than in the UK and the US. The top decile increased its share of all incomes from 31 per cent to 36 per cent between the 1970s and the 2000s.[19] This modest reversal of the long-term trend was often discussed among German sociologists well before Piketty. They also used data on secondary income distribution – surveys of the "real available income of households" – to detect a more severe threat to German society. Data of this kind reflect the bottom income receivers more accurately than Piketty's analysis, because those on low incomes often do not reach the minimum threshold of taxable income and are therefore not included in tax statistics. The "adjusted available net income" of the top 10 per cent of German households accounted for 2.88 times that of the bottom 10 per cent in 1973, and had risen to 3.28 times by 1998.[20] In 2008 the multiple reached 3.5. Also, the Gini coefficient increased from a low of 0.25 in 1973 to 0.27 in 1998 according to official survey data, or from 0.255 in 2000 to 0.288 in 2005 according to the panel data of the German Institute for Economic Research. Because of the German "job market miracle", the Gini coefficient of income concentration stagnated between 2005 and 2012. Inequality seems not to have risen further during recent years.[21] According to OECD Gini figures, income inequality in Germany is significantly below the level in Japan (0.329), the UK (0.345) and the US (0.378).

The general methodological problems of using Gini coefficients are widely discussed by Piketty;[22] and it is also surprising how the measure still dominates statistical analysis, especially in work produced by the OECD. Closer attention to distribution tables may shed more light on recent German developments that are distinct from those in other countries and are not limited to small deviations of Gini coefficients. In Germany it was not so much the rise of top incomes that drove increasing income inequality over the last few decades but that the incomes of the lowest income decile really collapsed. While the inflation-adjusted market income of the top decile increased by "only" a little more than 15 per cent between 1991 and 2011, the bottom decile lost 60 per cent of the purchasing power of its income: a drastic consequence of, firstly, fast-rising unemployment after reunification and, secondly, the creation of a low-wage sector in Germany during the era of the Social Democrat/Green Party coalition that implemented neoliberal labour market reforms. If we compare inflation-adjusted net equivalent household incomes (including social benefits!), the bottom decile is still below the purchasing power it had some twenty-five years ago, while the top decile has increased its income by about 20 per cent. Recent increases in economic inequality in Germany seem to have been much more a story of impoverishment at the bottom end of the income pyramid than of the production of very high incomes at the top.

Since the publication of Piketty's book an increasingly politicized debate in Germany has oscillated between two empirical findings. On the one hand, most measures of domestic income distribution identify Germany as one of the most just and equitable countries, so that Piketty's claim that there was a looming threat of increasing social instability lacked empirical support and was accordingly criticized from both left and right.[23] On the other hand, inequalities of wealth began to increase rapidly, apparently mainly as a result of the liberalization of capital markets; this seems to have accelerated after the financial crisis, rather than being tempered by it. However, the rapid increase in large fortunes fuelled by general asset-price inflation and an expanding generation of heirs hiding their wealth in international tax havens has not so far translated into major income increases, except among the very rich 0.1 per cent of those receiving income.[24] Because empirical data on income and material wealth present a much less dramatic picture than in the US or the UK, debates on inequality in Germany focus much more on inequality of opportunity: inequalities in the access to education, in respect of gender, health and the risk of becoming unemployed.[25] Therefore, even after Piketty the perspective on income inequality in Germany remains largely dependent on political attitudes and has still not become a topic of objective academic debate.

FOUR EMPIRICAL CHALLENGES TO THE PIKETTY RESULTS

The labyrinthine paths of German tax legislation

Availability of comparable data is the main condition for reaching any conclusion about the long-term development of income inequality. Data of this kind have been produced by the emerging nation states of Western Europe and the US since they introduced personal income tax around the end of the nineteenth century. Legislation on personal income tax can therefore be considered a "watershed in historical study of income distribution".[26] However, the peculiarities of different forms of taxation and the detail of tax law translated into very varied tax structures, rendering direct comparison between states more or less impossible. A particular problem is the fact that for many years income tax was levied only on higher-income groups, while the majority of those earning incomes paid instead a variety of indirect taxes. At a time when the share of state expenditure was less than 15 per cent of GDP, and state budgets were significantly augmented by income from state enterprises (especially agriculture and forestry), administrations were reluctant to open up personal incomes to taxation. To begin with, those owing tax under Prussian income tax laws equalled only 22 per cent of the population, leading Franz Kraus to the conclusion that international comparisons of income distribution are only possible for the top 10 per cent of those receiving income before the First World War, and for the top 50 per cent thereafter.[27] International comparison in this respect also includes a comparison between individual German states, because – as already noted – taxation had been the prerogative of individual states in Germany and not of the central imperial authority before Matthias Erzberger's 1920 financial reform during the Weimar Republic. Before this first national tax law, states had even engaged in tax competition, the differences encompassing not only tax rates but also schedules and structures.[28] However, in all cases, the coverage of the tax system, the number of income classes and of progressive bands of taxation determined the quality and density of the data generated regarding income distribution: the available data do not therefore in themselves directly reflect income distribution.

The differences are even larger in the taxation of wealth: a second important source of taxation introduced in the 1890s. The Prussian "supplementary tax law" taxed all capital wealth from 1893, including housing and real estate above 6000 marks, applying a progressive rate starting at 0.05 per cent; but in 1895 it included no more than 3.7 per cent of the Prussian population.[29] Moreover, while the Prussian law included all forms of real estate, Saxony's wealth tax, for example, applied only to monetary and capital wealth. In Prussia the taxable value of real estate was estimated as twenty-five times the annual rent, whereas in Lippe or Hesse the tax was based directly on the income stream.[30] The definition of "wealth" differed greatly between states, as did the rules governing the estimation of capital value. Even more than the different definitions of "income", wealth tax legislation in individual states produced different and not necessarily comparable national figures for wealth distribution.[31]

The situation became even more complicated when, in 1913, the central authority, the "Reich", joined the group of bodies collecting direct tax. With the introduction of the *Wehrbeitrag* (a one-off capital levy for the defence budget), the central authority established its own wealth tax for fortunes of more than 10,000 marks. The revenue was intended as a contribution to armaments expenditure and accounted for almost half of the Reich budget (which was, of course, small compared with the budgets of the federal states). However, the collection of wealth taxes was disrupted by the war. Several new taxes had been introduced before 1920, targeting "war profits" (the *Kriegsgewinnsteuer* of 1916) and imposing a "Reich emergency levy" (the *Reichsnotopfer* of 1919). A final wealth tax was introduced by the Reich government in 1922 but was first applied only in 1925, following the currency stabilization, taxing private wealth above 5,000 Reichsmarks (or 30,000 Reichsmarks for individuals without additional income) with a rate starting at 0.5 per cent. Because income taxes now became the most important source of income for the Reich budget, wealth tax peaked at no more than 4 per cent of all public revenues and never became an important source of public finance.[32] Thus, during the period before 1920, German legislation on the taxation of both income and wealth changed so frequently and applied so many different rules for determining property values and minimum income requirements that it is difficult, if not impossible, to extract reliable data series on income and wealth distribution from this moving data-generation machine. The data itself can, however, be taken as historical evidence of changing attitudes among politicians seeking to counter tendencies of increasing inequality.[33]

A similar attitude, shared by German politicians and members of the Allied occupation regime, was much more successful after the Second World War. Again, the losses of the war had had an uneven impact upon German households. The authorities therefore introduced various laws to redistribute the losses from the war and the post-war years. The *Lastenausgleichsgesetz* (an act decreeing the transfer of compensation payments, hence "burden sharing") of 1952, and the previous regulations, imposed a wealth tax on different forms of monetary and real estate wealth and distributed its revenues to those displaced from the former eastern Germany, who had had to abandon their property, as well as to households that had lost their savings in the Currency Reform of 1948. In total, the law redistributed 127 billion marks between 1952 and 1985, of which roughly 37 per cent came from wealth taxes, the remainder being taken from the general government budget. In its early years, the volume of annual redistribution represented almost 2.5 per cent of West German GDP.[34] No less than 2.7 billion Deutschmarks were redistributed by the act during its peak year in 1954. Compensation payments declined afterwards, and from the mid 1960s revenue from the conventional wealth tax exceeded the revenues from compensatory transfers. Wealth taxes peaked at 0.5 per cent of GDP in the late 1960s and declined to half that amount before the end of the century, when they were abolished. They therefore never represented a prominent source of state revenue in Germany.[35] The availability of data made no contribution to greater transparency regarding wealth accumulation in Germany (an important argument of Pikkety for the introduction of wealth taxes), nor did revenues from wealth taxes have any effect on state budgets.

The distributional effects of hyperinflation

The two world wars were by far the most severe shocks for the distribution of income and wealth in Germany, as they were in other countries. According to Piketty, the First World War in particular initiated a series of redistributive policies that inhibited the increase of wealth and the decrease of remuneration to labour typical of modern capitalism. Only at the end of the twentieth century did these issues resurface. In the case of Germany we have some contrary indication of the effects of economic processes following the wars. For the time being this evidence should be treated with the greatest care, since it does not come from new research. It draws attention to a conflict between the Piketty results and some older findings from German literature that has not so far been discussed. Two economic turning points in German economic history are the focus here: the hyperinflation of 1922/23 and the Currency Reform of 1948.

As in France and Britain, the First World War halved the capital to income ratio (Piketty's β) in Germany to a low of 300 per cent.[36] We have seen that this was not so much because of any real destruction of capital, loss of territory or foreign wealth, but was instead because of several parallel wealth taxes in combination with a hidden, and later open, and rapid depreciation of the currency. Large private holdings of war bonds and other savings had been most severely affected by the inflation. At first sight it therefore seems plausible that the inflation led to a general adjustment in German holdings of wealth. According to Fabien Dell's figures, the destruction of capital assets went hand in hand with increasing wealth equality. The share of the top 1 per cent of wealth owners in the total of national wealth shrank from 45 per cent before the war to only 25 per cent in 1925.[37]

However, this is in contrast with other source material, which may be less reliable since it originates from politicized contemporary debates but is worth considering, nonetheless. The Berlin social scientist Franz Eulenburg, for example, claimed as early as 1924 that inflation would have increased wealth inequality in Germany. According to his estimates (made on the basis of income tax data), income from wealth (i.e. Piketty's α) accounted for 30 per cent of national income before the war, with income from employment accounting for

70 per cent. After the hyperinflation the proportions would have been in the order of 15 per cent and 85 per cent, respectively.[38] But Eulenburg thought that, while income from wealth had shrunk as a proportion of all income, this nonetheless represented an increase in inequality. During the course of the inflation, the very rich invested in real capital by raising additional credit for which they "paid" with what turned out to be worthless money. In contrast, those among the upper classes who invested in state bonds and who were not indebted lost their wealth, as did the outright owners of houses who lived from rental income that did not adjust fast enough to counteract inflation. Though Eulenburg's figure of a 15 per cent share of capital income fits exactly into the first Piketty equation ($\alpha = r * \beta$), and assuming that the rate of return on capital remained unchanged at 5 per cent during the inflation, his conclusion is quite different.[39] The hypothesis of increasing wealth inequality during the German hyperinflation matches other results as well. Paul Jostock's figures from the 1960s are based on data from the tax on wealth. If 221 individuals out of 10,000 had a fortune of more than 26,400 marks in 1913, the corresponding number of inflation-adjusted fortunes was 74 in 1928.[40] It seems as if the diminished wealth of the German people after the hyperinflation was distributed increasingly unequally. Germany experienced an uneven redistribution of war losses.

It is surprising that the redistributive effect of the German hyperinflation was not raised in Piketty's book, for it would have served as an interesting case study, and the data are readily available in Dell's dissertation.[41] Why did Piketty not dig deeper into that issue? In the case of France during the "chaos of the interwar years", he gave a convincing explanation for the expansion of the top-income decile that was matched by the decline of the top percentile, both linked to the marked price deflation in France between 1929 and 1936.[42] It appears that both income and wealth distribution are influenced by movements in currency values, and German economic history would have been the perfect "natural experiment" to study this.

Given the chaos of the years immediately following 1945, a reconstruction of the redistributional effect of the German Currency Reform of 1948 is more difficult. Furthermore, the process was so dynamic that monthly income distribution data would be needed to show up what was happening. The Currency Reform in fact consisted of several laws enacted by the three Western Military Governments, although the most important, the *Umstellungsgesetz* (the law governing currency conversion), was imposed a week after the introduction of the new currency and was a real shock for German savers. Savings became converted from Reichsmark to Deutschmark at the rate of 10:1. Small savings suffered especially, because every citizen got a flat rate payment (a *Kopf-Pauschale*) of 60 Deutschmarks that was deemed to be compensation for lost savings. This meant that all Germans with savings of less than 600 Reichsmarks (which would have been about a quarter of a worker's annual income in 1935) ended up in the same situation as Germans without savings. The second shock hit the remaining asset holders three months later, when the *Festkontengesetz* (relating to blocked accounts) was imposed, annulling 70 per cent of remaining savings. Within a year, total money savings held by all households fell to an average of 6.5 per cent of their original value. By contrast, houseowners and holders of other capital assets experienced almost no devaluation of their assets, and were only rarely affected by the subsequent compensation that imposed a small tax to be paid over a period of twenty years. Companies listed on the stock exchange were able to retain 96 per cent of their asset value, and following a rapid rise in asset prices over subsequent years stockholders benefited greatly. While the Currency Reform did have a levelling impact on the incomes of broad classes of Germans, it must also have had, if only temporarily, a disproportionately negative effect on wealth and the corresponding income streams; by the end of 1948 this represented a threat to social peace in Germany.[43] Rapidly rising incomes from early 1949 seem to have moderated that effect, highlighting Germany as a prominent example of what Albert O. Hirschman once called the "tunnel effect": a society will tolerate increasing inequality when citizens have reason to think that the income increase of a neighbour will translate into their own income increasing in the near future.[44] These two episodes show that structures of economic inequality can undergo short-term changes during economic crises, and that the experience might give rise to long-lasting social effects. Temporary fluctuations in measures of inequality should therefore be better integrated into analysis.

The lessons that historians of economic inequality can take from these two episodes are as follows. First, the specific manner in which losses in social welfare are distributed is relevant to the corresponding distributional outcome. Lacking any effective way for its impact to be moderated through redistribution, the hyperinflation of the early 1920s proved devastating. Germans were left with a strong sense of injustice that fuelled political radicalization, and resulted in a sensitivity to any kind of inflationary episode that has persisted right up to the present. By contrast, the Currency Reform is remembered as an instance of far-reaching economic democratization, although during its first months and years it was quite definitely not viewed in this way. Redistributive measures were only hesitatingly imposed once economic growth had returned. We can therefore also learn from both episodes that the chronology, time frame and short-term cycle of movements in inequality should not be neglected.

Varieties of welfare capitalism

After the fall of the Berlin Wall, political scientists, economists and historians engaged in debate on the "varieties of capitalism", seeking the fine differences between different types of market economies that appeared to have triumphed over socialism. Following the Second World War, "capitalism" took a variety of forms, there being a clear distinction between the "liberal market economies" of the UK and the US and the "coordinated market economies" of continental Europe and Scandinavia.[45] Although the arguments of the later 1990s did not pay attention to inequality, Piketty largely adopted its categories to organize his comparative framework. However, he did not pay great attention to differences in the nature of welfare states in those countries that were the subject of intensive discussion, despite these differences affecting the national forms of wealth accumulation, especially when different types of pension provision are involved.[46] If we consider accumulation not in the conventional sense of capital accumulation as a strategy for profit-maximizing investment in production processes but as a strategy to maximize consumer income streams in the present as well as in the future, then retirement savings have to be taken into account.[47] There are, however, large differences in the ways in which societies organize their collective provision for retirement. All countries have a mix of private and public insurance. Legally enforced public provision for old age has long covered most employees in Germany. The system was changed into a pay-as-you-go system in 1957, granting pensions to thousands of widows and other individuals who had suffered as a result of the war and lacked private savings. Following the baby boom of the 1960s, the birth rate in Germany went into decline from 1970 onwards, which, when coupled with increasing life expectancy, means that the numbers of retirees has increased faster than the number of employees. While 18.6 million contributors to old-age insurance paid for 7.2 million retirees in 1962, 36.2 million were contributing to the support of 16.8 pensioners by 2013.[48] All employees whose gross annual income is below a defined level (currently 72,600 euros a year) are obliged to contribute to statutory retirement insurance, which at present accounts for 18.7 per cent of their gross income. Piketty had to decide how this kind of wealth accumulation should be dealt with; it consists not of capital assets, housing or life insurance, as in many other countries without mandatory pension insurance, but of claims against a public system of retirement funding. This does not retain or invest contributions made by future retirees but simply transfers them to current retirees. Piketty opted to treat all pension payments as income, with the result that the claims accumulated in their lifetimes by German lower- and medium-income groups were ignored despite being part of their wealth accumulation.[49] Because claims against the system increased much more rapidly than the pensions transferred, this decision certainly distorts the analysis for Germany. Germany would probably be shown to have a more equal wealth distribution if this particular form of capital wealth were counted together with the one that partially compensates high-income earners and the self-employed for their not being included in the public pension system. Furthermore, Piketty's choice diminishes the validity of cross-country comparisons, which is a vital aim of his contribution since he is interested in capitalism's fundamental laws.

The issue gets even more complicated when we include pension claims against the state that civil servants acquire during their employment. The German category of "civil servant" extends far beyond state administrators to include most German school teachers and university professors; a German civil servant is guaranteed a lifetime employment contract by the state and is not covered by the public pension scheme, but is eligible to receive a direct non-contributory pension from the state calculated as a proportion of final salary. As with the pensions of other employees, these pension rights could be considered to be a form of wealth accumulation, and this would then provide a better benchmark for comparison with the labour markets of other countries. Today, Germany's public administration is reduced to only 1.6 million civil servants because of the privatization of Deutsche Bundesbahn and the postal service, but this is still a significant number of employees with pension rights. The current total number of state pensioners is 1.2 million. However, while pensioners' income is easy to include in historical research on income inequality, the claims of current civil servants against the state pension system are not as easy to relate to wealth inequality. It is estimated that the current value of future pension claims in Germany is around 4 trillion euros, representing almost a third of the figure for total private wealth.[50] If we included these pension claims in our consideration of wealth distribution, it would tend to revise it in the direction of greater equality, and this revised assessment would perhaps provide a better basis for comparison with countries in which mandatory pension insurance does not account for such a large proportion of pension provision.

There is a second argument here: we might expect that households in countries with a robust mandatory retirement payment system would reduce their voluntary private saving: saving rates in these countries would then appear to be lower in comparison with other countries lacking such a system. But interestingly enough, net saving rates in France and Germany oscillate around 10 per cent, and are therefore significantly higher than in the US and in Britain, where saving rates dropped to 5 per cent, and even became temporarily negative in Britain, shortly before the financial meltdown. Germans mainly put their money in bank savings accounts, ignoring the low interest rates, while Americans profited directly from asset-price booms; German savings were referred to as "stupid German money" and a body of literature has developed around the "German saving puzzle".[51] Together with the pension issue, this might remind us of the fact that national habits and traditions apparently play a role in the nature and the particular structure of a country's wealth.

The nature of German house price inflation

An important criticism of Piketty's arguments was raised comparatively late in debate over his work when a young MIT scholar drew the public's attention to the fact that the rapid increase in wealth in the last thirty years might simply be driven by house price inflation.[52] There has been considerable research in recent years seeking to quantify this point, which has I think now been broadly accepted. While the large fortunes of the late nineteenth century consisted of land, manufacturing capital and other assets, house ownership accounts for an important proportion of household wealth today. Adam Smith would have objected to including wealth from home ownership in estimates of capital, as Piketty does, especially when the owners live in their houses:

> The stock that is laid out in a house, if it is to be the dwelling-house
> of the proprietor, ceases from that moment to serve in the function
> of a capital, or to afford any revenue to its owner. A dwelling-house,
> as such, contributes nothing to the revenue of its inhabitant; and
> though it is, no doubt, extremely useful to him, it is as his cloaths
> and household furniture are useful to him, which, however, make a
> part of his expense, and not of his revenue.[53]

In the case of owner-occupied dwellings, Piketty's "wealth" is therefore nothing more than an accountant's profit that does not materialize for the home-owner so long as he or she does not sell the property, or request an extension of his or her mortgage in exchange for a higher valuation.

It is hard to say whether this finding undermines the entire wealth-inequality argument, or only touches upon its size and thus the extent of the Kuznets curve reversal. Since house and asset-price inflation have different trajectories in different countries, and since home ownership is at different levels, the house-price argument definitely demands more careful inter-country comparison. German housing prices and, more so, land prices have not increased as fast as in other countries, as recent research by Katharina Knoll, Moritz Schularick and Thomas Steger reveals.[54] For a price level of 1990 = 100, house prices in the UK, for example, did not exceed an index of 50 before the 1970s; subsequently, the rate of increase accelerated, and prices almost doubled between 1990 and the pre-crisis years.[55] For the US, prices increased faster and reached 100 after the Second World War, then jumped to 150 in the two decades before the 2008 crash. By contrast, in Germany prices reached the 1990 index of 100 before the First World War, then declined dramatically in the inter-war years to 30 per cent of the pre-war level, recovering between the Second World War and the 1970s, but then falling below the 1990 level after reunification. Only recently have prices begun to increase again.

The research is certainly inadequate, and suffers from the difficulty of defining the good in question, as the authors admit. But it does highlight the differences between developments in different countries regarding the production of dwellings, and does indicate the very particular situation in Germany. Due to the rapid growth in population, and especially large-scale internal migration from East to West, Germany started with an undersupply of housing before the First World War, which interrupted the building of new dwellings. To deal with the subsequent scarcity, the Weimar Republic chose to heavily regulate the housing market and imposed a tax on rental incomes that was intended to be used to build dwellings. Rents were also regulated. During the Second World War, urban destruction severely increased the housing shortage, and housing remained regulated until the 1970s, especially in the big cities. City landlords could not freely choose to whom they rented, but until 1968 had to let to households referred to them by the local housing administration.[56] This long period of strict regulation (from 1919 until the 1960s) is responsible not only for the comparatively moderate increase in house prices in Germany but also for a relatively low home ownership rate. Even after the recent period of convergence, still only 52.5 per cent of German households live in their own dwelling today (2014), in contrast to, for example, Norway (84.4 per cent), Spain (78.8 per cent) and Great Britain (64.4 per cent).[57] While a more moderate increase in house prices in Germany explains a good deal of the country's lower wealth-to-income ratio (Piketty's β) – as Piketty himself explained – the lower home ownership rate suggests that a higher proportion of this wealth is held for the purpose of profit, in the sense of Adam Smith, which partly devalues Piketty's prior argument.

CONCLUSION: ON THE PIKETTY OPPORTUNITY FOR GERMANY

Thomas Piketty's book and the tremendous amount of work that he and his group have dedicated to the history of economic inequality in Germany deserve, from the perspective of German economic history, the highest praise: in recent decades historical research has neglected a very important aspect of the evolution of modern industrial society. Furthermore, their work exemplifies how historical research in general, and economic history in particular, can actively participate in today's most important political debates. In times of shrinking state budgets for the humanities and the social sciences, this is not a minor achievement. However, I do not so far see many signs that German economic historians are willing to respond to the opportunity that Piketty presents. Only the work of Moritz Schularick and others on housing shows any sign of developing a new direction for empirical research.

The reticence of German economic historians with respect to economic inequality can be explained in two ways. On the one hand, we really struggle with the fact that over the past few decades inequality research in economic and social history has been completely incapacitated by the multiple "cultural turns" of many neighbouring disciplines claiming a stake in historical research. Specialists in the very basic techniques of inequality analysis are currently hard to find. I am inclined to say that the Piketty opportunity becomes a Piketty necessity in respect of the training of researchers in inequality, who are currently involved in economics and development studies and are neither interested in nor capable of dealing with historical data. On the other hand, the reticence of economic historians can be explained by Piketty's strong focus on economic theory. Though he does actively seek to dispel the idea that he is in thrall to any idea of economic determinism,[58] his claim to have formulated "fundamental laws of capitalism" and his idea that redistribution policies are "reactions" to "external shocks" still creates doubt. This corresponds with the misconception among economic historians (and also the public at large) that Piketty's work already is historical research, a stance with which I would disagree. It lacks critical discussion of competing source material and a familiarity with specialized historical literature.

Nonetheless, the debate can trigger and highlight the very strength of historical research. Piketty took the ball to economic historians and loudly invited them to play. This is the genuine opportunity that Piketty presents, not the proliferation of unchangeable empirical results. From the ongoing German debate I see, in particular, four fields in which economic historians can contribute with our own research, from which the subject can profit with respect to social relevance.

Firstly, German social scientists are actively engaged in arguments over the relation of rising economic inequality to the rate of economic growth.[59] From a historical perspective it could be argued that rising inequality retards growth, since global economic growth was strongest in the 1950s and 1960s, when economic inequality was falling very fast, by all measures, and without any doubt. Economic history might be the ideal field for an empirical test of the connection between inequality and growth.

Secondly, as the case of Germany shows most prominently, economic inequality is greatly affected by inflation. Discussion around Piketty's work has not touched on this so far, but there is certainly an opportunity to do so. This would probably reveal that short-term processes might be relevant for changes in the distributional structure of wealth as well as income, enriching both the debate and the political conclusions that could be drawn.

Thirdly, there is a technical opportunity that Piketty opens up that has not so far been the topic of much discussion. Since his method rests on relative income and wealth measures at a particular point in time, he avoids the deficiencies arising out of the need to deflate and harmonize data that is commonplace in the analysis of historical records. Deflation and indexization are the most brutal way of dealing with historical statistics: transforming them into purely fictional figures that are nonetheless described as "real", which they are not. The way in which Piketty uses distribution tables can brilliantly circumvent these issues while nevertheless producing long historical time series.

Fourthly, if we agree that the historical story that Piketty tells is less straight-forward and much more complex – as I suggest for the example of Germany – we are then obliged to contribute to the debate with corrected figures, the broadening of the empirical base, and the general enrichment of the source material. This can only be achieved in the near future by economic historians, who therefore bear great responsibility for improving the quality of debate. I consider this to be an opportunity, rather than a burden.

Notes for Chapter 6

1. Rudolf Martin, *Jahrbuch des Vermögens und Einkommens der Millionäre in der Rheinprovinz* (Berlin: Verlag Rudolf Martin, 1913), p. IV.

2. For reasons explained in the section "The Nature of German House Price Inflation", I have great reservations concerning Piketty's merger of the concepts of capital and wealth. Here I will use the expression "wealth" in the sense of "private household wealth", including monetary assets, capital assets and housing (i.e. Piketty's notion of "capital"); as opposed to "capital", which I use only for what is known as "productive capital", meaning capital assets linked to production processes.

3. Thomas Piketty, *Capital in the Twenty-First Century* (Cambridge, MA: Harvard University Press, 2014), p. 145.

4. According to *Manager-Magazin*, 6 October 2015, Stefan Quandt and his sister Susanne Klatten together have a fortune worth 26.5 billion euros, compared with German GDP of 3,025 billion euros. The corresponding figures for Krupp were 283 million marks in relation to a net domestic product of 50 billion marks. *Bevölkerung und Wirtschaft* 1972, p. 260, using the territory included in 1937 borders.

5. This is especially important for detailed discussion of the data used by the group. A more critical discussion of the ever-defective source material is just one of the important tasks for economic historians. Another task concerns the way in which different currencies were deflated and converted into euro values in most of the material. How these procedures affected the results that were gained requires careful assessment.

6. Maybe the most detailed work resulting from this research is a little-known article by Franz Kraus, "Historical Development of Income Inequality in Western Europe and the United States", in *The Development of Welfare States in Europe and America*, Peter Flora and Arnold J. Heidenheimer (eds) (New Brunswick, NJ: Transaction, 1981), pp. 187–238.

7. Wolfgang Zorn, "Staatliche Wirtschafts- und Sozialpolitik und öffentliche Finanzen 1800–1970", in *Handbuch der Deutschen Wirtschaftsgeschichte und Sozialgeschichte*, Band 2 Hermann Aubin *et al.* (eds) (Munich: Kett-Cotta, 1976), p. 183.

8. J. Heinz Müller and Siegfried Geisenberger, *Die Einkommensstruktur in verschiedenen deutschen Ländern 1874–1913* (Berlin: Duncker & Humblot, 1972), p. 39. In his PhD thesis Fabien Dell compares his results with those of Müller and Geisenberger: Fabian Dell, "L'Allemagne Inégale. Inégalités de revenus et de patrimoine en Allemagne, dynamique d'accumulation du capital et taxation de Bismarck á Schröder 1870–2005" (Paris, 2008), p. 49.

9. Dell, "L'Allemagne Inégale", p. 96.

10. Franz Eulenburg, "Die Sozialen Wirkungen der Währungsverhältnisse", *Jahrbücher für Nationalökonomie und Statistik*, Band 122 (1924), pp. 748–94, especially pp. 790ff.

11. Albrecht Ritschl, "The Pity of Peace: Germany's Economy at War, 1914–1918 and Beyond", in *The Economics of World War I*, Stephen N. Broadberry and Mark Harrison (eds) (Cambridge: Cambridge University Press, 2005), pp. 41–76; Gerald D. Feldman, *The Great Disorder: Politics, Economics and Society in the German Inflation, 1914–1924* (New York: Oxford University Press, 1996).

12. Piketty, *Capital*, p. 147.

13. Dell, "L'Allemagne Inégale", p. 137.

14. Piketty, *Capital*, pp. 316f.

15. Dell, "L'Allemagne Inégale", p. 136; Piketty, *Capital*, p. 340.

16. Werner Abelshauser, *Deutsche Wirtschaftsgeschichte seit 1945* (Munich: Beck, 2004), p. 70f.

17. Piketty, *Capital*, p. 340, highlights a figure of 35 per cent for France in 1950, dropping to 20 per cent in the 1970s. Dell, "L'Allemagne Inégale", p. 184.

18. Taken from Fabian Dell, "Top Incomes in Germany Throughout the Twentieth Century, 1891–1998", in *Top Incomes over the Twentieth Century: A Contrast between Continental European and English-Speaking Countries*, Anthony B. Atkinson and Thomas Piketty (eds) (Oxford: Oxford University Press, 2007), p. 379, comparing "the top percentile within the top decile".

19. Piketty, *Capital*, p. 323.

20. Stefan Hradil, *Die Sozialstruktur Deutschlands im Internationalen Vergleich* (Opladen: VS Verlag, 2004), p. 205. The "net equivalent household income" adjusts the household income to household size and structure. It is usually presented in the modified OECD definition, weighting the principal income receiver as 1, the next adult and children as 0.5 and children below 14 as 0.3. See also Markus Grabka, Jan Goebel and Carsten Schröder, "Income Inequality Remains High in Germany", *DIW Bulletin* 25 (2015), pp. 331ff.

21. Data for 1973–98 from Hradil, *Sozialstruktur*, p. 205, and for 2005 onwards from Grabka, Goebel and Schröder, "Income Inequality", pp. 325–39, especially Box 2, p. 329.

22. Piketty, *Capital*, p. 266. The main problem is – to cut a long statistical story short – that different distributional structures may lead to the same Gini coefficients.

23. "Wirtschaftsweiser Bofinger wirft Piketty schwere Fehler vor", *Der Spiegel*, 1 June 2014; Thomas Mayer, "Die wahre Ursache der Ungleichheit. Warum Piketty falschliegt", FAZ (Blog), 27 September 2014. For an overview of the debate see also Julian Bank, "Die Piketty-Rezeption in Deutschland", in *Thomas Piketty und die Verteilungsfrage: Analysen, Bewertungen und wirtschaftspolitische Implikationen für Deutschland*, Peter Bofinger *et al.* (eds) (SE Publishing, 2015), pp. 9–37.

24. See OECD, *Divided We Stand: Inequality Keeps Rising* (Paris: OECD, 2011), p. 39.

25. Marcel Fratzscher, *Verteilungskampf. Warum Deutschland immer ungleicher wird* (Berlin: Hanser, 2016). Claiming to be a strong argument for a less "economic" concept of inequality: Hartmut Kaelble, "Abmilderung der sozialen Ungleichheit? Das westliche Europa während des Wirtschaftsbooms der 1950er bis 1970er Jahre", *Geschichte und Gesellschaft* 40 (2014), pp. 591–609.

26. Franz Kraus, "Historical Development of Income Inequality in Western Europe and the United States", in *The Development of Welfare States*, P. Flora and A. J. Heidenheimer (eds), pp. 187–238, especially p. 190.

27. Kraus, "Historical Development", p. 192.

28. K. Häuser, "Abriß der geschichtlichen Entwicklung der öffentlichen Finanzwirtschaft" [1952], in *Handbuch der Finanzwissenschaft*, Auflage 3, Band 1 (1977), pp. 4–52.

29. Eckart Schremmer, *Steuern und Staatsfinanzen während der Industrialisierung Europas* (Berlin: Springer, 1994), p. 155.

30. Examples taken from E. Baltes, "Die deutschen Vermögenssteuern", *Finanzarchiv* 32(2) (1915), pp. 199–317.

31. W. Gerloff, "Der Staatshaushalt und das Finanzsystem Deutschlands", in *Handbuch der Finanzwissenschaft*, Auflage 1, Band 3 (1929), pp. 1–67.

32. Stefan Bach *et al.* (DIW), *Modelle für die Vermögensbesteuerung von natürlichen Personen und Kapitalgesellschaften (im Auftrag der Grünen/Bündnis 90)* (Berlin: DIW, 2004), p. 11.

33. "The attempt of the SPD to return to the status quo ante by dint of tax policy failed": Konrad Roesler, *Die Finanzpolitik des Deutschen Reiches im Ersten Weltkrieg* (Berlin: Duncker & Humblot, 1967), p. 176. For the different tax laws see also Fritz Terhalle, "Geschichte der deutschen öffentlichen Finanzwirtschaft vom Beginn des 19. Jahrhunderts bis zum Schlusse des zweiten Weltkrieges", in *Handbuch der Finanzwissenschaft*, Auflage 2, Band 1 (1952), pp. 274–327.

34. Stefan Bach, "Persönliche Vermögenssteuern in Deutschland", in *Thomas Piketty und die Verteilungsfrage*, Bofinger *et al.* (eds), pp. 193–241, especially p. 204.

35. *Bevölkerung und Wirtschaft* 1972, p. 239; Lutz Wiegand, *Der Lastenausgleich in der Bundesrepublik Deutschland 1949 bis 1985* (Frankfurt: Peter Lang, 1992), for figures referred to in the text, see pp. 198, 356f.

36. Piketty, *Capital*, p. 147.

37. Dell, "L'Allemagne Inégale", p. 137.

38. Eulenburg, "Die Sozialen Wirkungen der Währungsverhältnisse", p. 788.

39. The "rate of return on capital" is a very ill-defined category. Piketty himself often uses interest rates to illustrate his claim that *r* remained above 5 per cent throughout

most of human history, without clarifying the difference between *i* and *r* (see Piketty, *Capital*, pp. 353–58, and footnote 16, p. 613). For the inter-war period in Germany it is, however, rather improbable that *r* remained at 5 per cent, since different categories of interest rates peaked in the early 1920s and were still around 9 per cent in 1925. See Richard Tilly, *Geld und Kredit in der Wirtschaftsgeschichte* (Stuttgart: Steiner, 2003); also his "Geld und Kredit", in *Deutschland in Daten*, Thomas Rahlf (ed.) (Bonn: Bundeszentrale für politische Bildung, 2015), p. 222.

40. Knut Borchardt, "Die Erfahrungen mit Inflationen in Deutschland" [1972], in *Wachstum, Krisen – Handlungsspielräume der Wirtschaftspolitik: Studien zur Wirtschaftsgeschichte des 19. und 20. Jahrhundert*, K. Borchardt (ed.) (Göttingen: Vandenhoeck & Ruprecht, 1982), p. 160.

41. Dell, "L'Allemagne Inégale".

42. Piketty, *Capital*, pp. 284–7.

43. Christoph Buchheim, "Die Währungsreform 1948 in Westdeutschland", *Vierteljahreshefte für Zeitgeschichte* 36 (1988), pp. 189–231.

44. Albert Hirschmann, "The Changing Tolerance for Income Inequality in the Course of Economic Development", *Quarterly Journal of Economics* 87(4) (1973), pp. 544–66.

45. Peter Hall and David Soskice (eds), *Varieties of Capitalism: The Institutional Foundations of Comparative Advantage* (Oxford: Oxford University Press, 2001); Bob Hanacké (ed.), *Debating Varieties of Capitalism: A Reader* (Oxford: Oxford University Press, 2009).

46. See Ylva Hasselberg and Henry Ohlsson in this volume: Chapter 7.

47. For discussion, see Alexander M. Ring, *Die Verteilung der Vermögen in der Bundesrepublik Deutschland: Analyse und politische Schlußfolgerung* (Frankfurt: Peter Lang, 2000), pp. 51ff.

48. *Statistik der Deutschen Rentenversicherung: Rentenstatistik in Zahlen 2015* (Berlin: Deutsche Rentenversicherung Bund, 2015), p. 31.

49. Piketty, *Capital*, pp. 255, 602.

50. This is, however, only a very rough estimate, without any indication of how the figure was gained. See Hanno Beck and Aloys Prinz, *Staatsverschuldung: Ursachen, Folgen, Auswege* (Munich: Beck, 2011), pp. 43–51.

51. Axel Börsch-Supan, Micaela Coppola, Lothar Essig, Angelika Eymann and Daniel Schunk, *The German SAVE Study: Design and Results*, 2nd edn (Mannheim: MEA, 2009).

52. Matthew Rognlie, "Deciphering the Fall and Rises in the Net Capital Share", Brookings Papers on Economic Activity, March 2015.

53. Adam Smith, *An Inquiry into the Nature and Causes of the Wealth of Nations* [1776/1784], R. H. Campbell, A. S. Skinner and W. B. Todd (eds), Book 2, Chapter 1 (Oxford: Oxford University Press, 1976), p. 281.

54. Katharina Knoll, Moritz Schularick and Thomas Steger, "No Price like Home: Global House Prices, 1870–2012", CEPR Discussion Paper 10166 (revised April 2015).

55. See Jim Tomlinson's contribution to this book (pp. 173–74) for a discussion of the UK housing market. Following deregulation in the early 1970s, UK house prices increased

very rapidly, while from 1988 to 1996 the housing market was in recession, with static or falling prices.

56. Karl Christian Führer, *Mieter, Hausbesitzer, Staat und Wohnungsmarkt: Wohnungsmangel und Wohnungszwangswirtschaft in Deutschland 1914–1960* (Stuttgart: Steiner, 1995).

57. Eurostat Press Release 204/2015, 23 November 2015.

58. Thomas Piketty, "Putting Distribution Back at the Centre of Economics: Reflections on *Capital in the Twenty-First Century*", *Journal of Economic Perspectives* 29 (2015), pp. 67–88, especially p. 69.

59. Frederico Cingano, "Trends in Income Inequality and Its Impact on Economic Growth", OECD Social, Employment and Migration Working Paper 163 (2014); Johannes Pennekamp, "Schadet Ungleichheit dem Wachstum wirklich?", *Frankfurter Allgemeine Sonntagszeitung*, 20 February 2016.

7

COLLECTIVE WEALTH FORMATION: CONFLICT AND COMPROMISE IN SWEDEN, 1950–2000

Ylva Hasselberg and Henry Ohlsson

A quick glance at the curves describing income and wealth inequality or the capital/income ratio is enough to show that politics is ubiquitous and that economic and political changes are inextricably intertwined and must be studied together.[1]

Starting out from Thomas Piketty's *Capital in the Twenty-First Century*, this chapter will look at the problem of increasing inequality in wealth and income in Sweden from a historical perspective.[2] We have two theses, which can be stated as follows. First, the period 1950–*c.*1995 in Sweden can be characterized as a period in which individual wealth formation was challenged by collective wealth formation, in the form of public pension reserve funds and also in the form of so-called wage-earner funds. Occupational pension funds also increased considerably. An aspect of this development that is relevant for Piketty's general thesis is that *collective wealth formation* can be construed as an alternative to wealth taxation and progressive income taxation when it comes to altering the balance between labour and capital.[3] However, this possibility is not open to Piketty since he defines pension payments as income[4] and refrains from tackling the issue of how the source of this income in accumulated wealth pension payments might be dealt with. Suppose that the labour share of value-added decreases. Our claim is that the higher the share of collective wealth in total wealth, the lower will be the increase in inequality from the decreased labour share. This is simply because collective wealth is more equally distributed than individual wealth.

Our second claim is that the process of collective wealth formation in Sweden has in essence rested on a political process, and that ideological conflict between labour and capital in Sweden has manifested itself in these issues. Collective wealth has been fundamentally controversial, and this is so because the distribution of wealth is closely linked to the distribution of power. Power as a central aspect of wealth, i.e. the question of control as an aspect of ownership, is not very explicit in Piketty's great work. We will discuss the political issues related to collective wealth formation later. Starting out from the two major turning points that can be traced in Swedish twentieth-century wealth formation, we are going to discuss (a) the introduction of the general supplementary pension during the 1950s and (b) wage-earner funds, which were first discussed in the 1970s, then activated in the 1980s, and finally abolished at the beginning of the 1990s.

PIKETTY, TAXES AND INEQUALITY

The overarching problem in *Capital in the Twenty-First Century* is the fact that the diminishing ratio between wealth and income has, since 1980, resumed its upward trajectory. This is a result in the aggregate, but it follows that inequality has increased, since wealth is more unequally distributed than income. The problem can and should be construed as both a scientific and a political one. What, then, is to be done about it? In this chapter we will discuss how the problem of wealth inequality can and should be handled. We will do this by means of historical analysis, and we will try to prove that there have been conscious attempts to deal with the issue, both as a problem of inequality and as a problem of *power*. We believe that the aspect of power is largely invisible in Piketty's book. We offer no conclusion as to why this is so, and simply point out that the concept of power is seldom employed as an analytical tool by economists.

The two questions Piketty poses in Part IV of his book are as follows.
(1) What is the role of government in the accumulation and distribution of wealth in the twenty-first century?
(2) What kind of social state is most suitable for the future?[5]

The second question is hopelessly broad, and therefore hard to answer. "What kind of social state ...?" is a question that can be answered in a wide variety of ways, with only imagination limiting the possibilities. The first question is the one that Piketty really answers. His first and foremost answer is that the role of the government in the accumulation and distribution of wealth is to put more emphasis on the progressive taxation of wealth. Progressive income taxation was an effective tool in the twentieth century, during the period when the wealth–income ratio was at its lowest point; today, progressive taxation of wealth is potentially a better tool to tackle inequality, especially in relation to extreme wealth.[6] Wealth also affects the taxation of capital income, since this income is generated by wealth. Income taxes have become regressive at the top of the income distribution, as a result of capital income being largely free from progressive taxation.[7] Furthermore, the distribution of resources that can be effected by one individual becomes even more unbalanced as a result of the increasing importance of inherited wealth. Inheritance is less heavily taxed than income. The rising wealth–income ratio also means that substantial revenue can be gained even with a moderate level of taxation, albeit with a steeply progressive system. For Europe Piketty suggests annual tax rates of 0 per cent for fortunes less than 1 million euros, 1 per cent between 1 million and 5 million euros, and 2 per cent above 5 million euros.[8]

What, then, is the rationale behind the demand for progressive taxation of individual wealth? What is to be achieved with this tool? Piketty mentions four reasons for the progressive taxation of wealth:

(1) redistribution of means through the social state;
(2) the introduction of norms and regulations that will have a *performative* function in relation to the formation of capital;[9]
(3) increased transparency; and
(4) increased legitimacy of the globalized economy.

The overarching goals of progressive taxation of wealth are (a) to inject new blood into the social state, so that it can continue to fulfil its functions in a globalized economy, and (b) to redistribute resources, not from the wealthy to the poor but from the very wealthy to everyone else. The redistributional character of the social state is central to Piketty's argument. By introducing a new framework for economic activity, such economic activity can also be affected. Piketty does not clearly state what the potential effects would be, but it might be supposed that the progressive taxation of wealth would channel resources into more economic activity of a kind linked to tax avoidance. Defining norms and regulations would both presuppose and give rise to more transparency simply in terms of who owns what and where, in order for it to function satisfactorily. All in all, the first three consequences mentioned above would, Piketty argues, lead to increased legitimacy and more popular acceptance of a globalized economy. It would also supposedly lead to a more stable role in this globalized economy for the social state: a twentieth-century invention that has never, Piketty points out, been invested with more power than at present.

The crucial question now is whether progressive wealth taxation is the only method for reaching these goals? We argue that it is not. We also argue that there is historical evidence, in the case of Sweden, that bears witness to the effectiveness of another method: namely, the formation of *collective wealth*.

THE DEFINITION OF WEALTH

This leads us to the question of how we define *wealth*, and especially how we define *collective wealth*. The reader will by now have noticed that we do not employ Piketty's concept of capital, prefering the concept of wealth. This is partly to do with the factual differences between a small open economy (e.g. Sweden, our empirical case) and an economy based on a large domestic market (e.g. the US and France). In a small open economy the difference between the wealth of the population and the capital stock of the country may be substantial, as some of the wealth is held as foreign assets and some of the capital is provided by foreign wealth holders. Employing the concept of wealth enables us to avoid problems related to the conflation of capital and wealth, such as importing neoclassical growth models that incorporate only productive capital, that disregard public wealth and public investment, and that convey inappropriate assumptions about the definition of wealth.[10]

What, then, do we mean by collective wealth? Hypothetically, all wealth that is not owned by individuals is collective. All assets owned by the public sector can be included in collective wealth. Public wealth is, hypothetically, positively affected by progressive wealth taxation since this increases the tax revenue of the state. But collective wealth goes beyond the public sector. Occupational pension funds and life insurance wealth are also examples of collective wealth.

Historically, ownership has been much more complicated and *layered* than is generally assumed today.[11] This is still true to some extent, although some historical forms of collective ownership have become more unusual in industrial society (common land being a typical example). We tend to think of ownership in a sense that is normally associated with the ownership of chattel goods. If you own a chair, you have the right to paint it, sit on it or make a fire with it. You can give it away or just put it in the street for someone else to pick up. The last action may not be strictly legal but in many cities it is more or less accepted. But if you own a patch of land, for practical reasons you cannot put it out on the street, and you certainly cannot do whatever you want with it. In Sweden the things you cannot do with a patch of land, at least without permission, include building a house on it, fencing it in, planting it in its entirety with trees (if it is not already woodland, in which case you can), and disposing of environmental waste on it. On the other hand, in Sweden people in general may have rights relating to *your* land that would in many other countries be reserved for the owner, such as picking berries or mushrooms, according to the *allemansrätt*.[12] This is just one example from Sweden today, and it tells a story of ownership being not only subject to historical change but also dependent on the specific laws and cultural practices of a country. Ownership of land is circumscribed and has always been so. And though land is a particular case (one of the three goods that were thought to be *fictive* goods by Karl Polanyi[13]), ownership is in many instances circumscribed both by law and by custom. You can own a dog but you are not entitled to beat it to death; you can own a flower pot but if it falls from a window sill and kills someone, you are responsible for it. This problem is also relevant for the issue of collective wealth. What can you, as an individual, do with 1 million Swedish Krona in bills? What can you, as an individual, do with your public pension rights?

What we can take from this discussion is that it may not, in practice, be easy to define what is actually individual wealth and what is collective wealth. At least four aspects of ownership have to be considered: (1) disposition or use, (2) any benefit or profit flowing from ownership, (3) actual judicial ownership and (4) responsibility for something, or power over it. Time must also be taken into account. What is individually owned wealth at one point in time is already at that point invested with the rights of the next generation in terms of inheritance.

We define collective wealth as wealth that is (with certain exceptions) owned, disposed of and the responsibility of a collective in an institutionalized form, but where the capital income generated by it is individual. This may seem an overcomplicated definition, but it has the advantage of making the aspect of *power* visible, and also acknowledges the difference between capital income from individual wealth and capital income from collective wealth. Piketty argues for progressive wealth taxation as a method of redistributing material assets, giving the social state more money to spend on health care, education, pensions and the like, and for these benefits to be distributed to and shared by all. We argue that collective wealth distributes both resources and power more evenly, and that it does so independently of whether it is generated in the public or private sector.

By taking this standpoint we consciously place ourselves within the Ricardian/Marxian tradition that is one of the two analytical traditions with which Piketty's work can be associated. The contradictory nature of his intellectual inheritance – the other tradition being conventional neoclassical growth models – has been analysed by Harcourt and Tribe in Chapter 2. The attempted merger of the two traditions leads to the conflation of concepts and measurements of wealth and capital.[14] We leave the issue of capital formation and the assumptions connected to the productivity of labour and capital out of our analysis, instead concentrating on the effects that power relationships and political bargaining have on the composition of *wealth*, and, in the end, on equality. This does not mean that we are not interested in the issue of the balance between capital and labour. We find the recent article by Karabarbounis and Neiman on the global decline of the labour share of value-added very interesting.[15] As Erik Bengtsson has shown for Sweden, there is a strong correlation between the capital share and the top percentile's share of total income, leading to the conclusion that labour shares and capital shares are good indicators of the level of inequality in a society.[16] We address these indicators more indirectly, through the introduction of a definition of wealth that allows us to identify a type of wealth directly related to labour income (pensions) and, through our focus on labour and capital, to political force involved in the distribution and redistribution of wealth.

INDIVIDUAL AND COLLECTIVE WEALTH IN SWEDEN, 1950–95

We begin with a quick look at the overall development of wealth in Sweden. How does the Swedish case fit with Piketty's general thesis? The answer to that is that it fits very well. In a number of papers, Daniel Waldenström, Jesper Roine and Henry Ohlsson have explored the composition of wealth in Sweden between 1800 and 2010.[17] The ratio of private wealth to national income can be shown to have gone from roughly 300 per cent in 1870 to almost 450 per cent in the 1910s, before declining steadily from around 1920 – after a brief inflation-driven slump at the time of the First World War – to 1980, eventually going below pre-industrial levels. After 1990 the private wealth to income ratio rose sharply, and at present it is back at the level of the 1910s.[18]

Two forms of collective wealth introduced during this period in Sweden were the public pension reserve funds of 1959 and the wage-earner funds of 1983. Both were the result of political reforms to which we will return. The public pension reserve funds stopped increasing rapidly around the turn of the millennium when the annual pension payments from the funds were increased to the levels of the annual contributions (see Figure 7.1). The wage-earner funds were abolished in 1994, with funds being transferred to a number of new foundations with the aim of funding research and development.

The underlying hypothesis is that collective wealth, or rather the capital income generated by collective wealth, is more equally distributed than the capital income generated by individual wealth. The consequence of this would be that the higher the share of collective wealth in total wealth, the less would be any decrease in total wealth caused by shifts in the labour share. In other words, our hypothesis is that collective wealth, e.g. in the form of pension capital or wage-earner funds, will have acted (1) to increase total wealth accumulation, as all wage-earners contributed through contributions based on their labour income; (2) as a lever for economic equality, through the distribution of capital income in the form of pensions to wage-earners, thus adding to their ability to accumulate wealth as well as to their share of total wealth; and (3) as a lever for the distribution of power, since the creation of funds means that wage-earners, through their representatives and jointly with employers, manage a greater share of the total wealth of society. These hypotheses can of course neither be verified nor falsified by an investigation into the share of collective wealth in total wealth. However, what the result of such an investigation can do is suggest ways of dealing with increased inequality other than taxation of wealth and capital income.

Let us now look at the numbers. What interests us is the share of collective wealth in total wealth in Sweden, and its development over time. There are some methodological problems with a comparison between the private and public sectors here.[19] The question is whether to compare collective wealth generated in publicly owned and managed funds with gross or net individual wealth? For the sake of clarity we shall do both, starting with the comparison between gross individual financial assets and collective financial assets in both sectors. In Figure 7.1 we compare collective financial assets generated within the private and public sectors with total financial assets. The full comparison is only available from 1950 onwards, as no data are available for the public sector before that year.

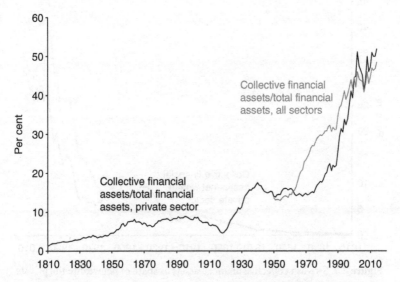

Figure 7.1. Swedish collective financial assets as share of total financial assets: the private sector separately and the private and public sectors taken together. (*Source*: calculated from the Swedish National Wealth Database (SNWD), 1810–2014 (www.uueconomics.se/danielw/SNWD.htm).)

The first thing to note is that collective wealth in the private sector, consisting of life insurance, property insurance, premium pensions (funded) and occupational pensions (funded), had a relatively stable share of total financial assets in the private sector through the nineteenth century, its share growing faster from a few years before 1920. The explanation for this could

possibly be the exclusion of life insurance from the taxation of wealth introduced in 1910, with the steep rise in the curve thus signalling tax avoidance.
This, however, remains speculation. In the growth years following the Second
World War the share of collective wealth in the total wealth of the private
sector stabilized at around 15 per cent, growing quickly again from the late
1970s onwards. The second period of growth can be characterized as the
period when wealth accumulation in occupational pension funds became
considerable.

The introduction of public pension reserve funds in 1959 can easily be seen
in the steep rise in the share of total collective financial assets from the late
1950s onwards. After the early 1960s the share of collective financial assets in
the public sector grew noticeably until the early 1990s. The gap between the two
curves, constituting the effect of introducing publicly managed collective wealth,
is at its largest point around 1985.

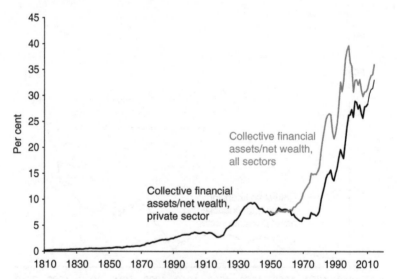

Figure 7.2. Swedish collective financial assets as share of net wealth: the private
sector separately and the private and public sectors taken together.
(*Source*: calculated from the SNWD.)

It is striking that the value of total collective financial assets today is as large
as the value of total individual financial assets. And this is the case regardless
of whether we look at the private sector separately or at the private and public
sectors taken together.

Let us now compare collective financial assets with total net wealth, adding
financial assets and real assets together and subtracting debts (see Figure 7.2).
This gives an alternative picture of the relationship between individual and

collective wealth in Sweden, and also a more realistic picture of the potential of collective wealth as a lever for economic equality.

As can be seen from the figure, when comparing collective financial assets with net wealth, the trends are similar to those in Figure 7.1. The introduction of public pension reserve funds is clearly visible in the development of total collective financial assets in relation to total net wealth from around 1960, and, just as in Figure 7.1, the stagnation of, or even downturn in, net wealth in the private sector increases the effect of public collective wealth, creating a gap that starts to diminish from around 1980. In net value, however, the effect is more durable, shrinking but not disappearing totally after 2000.

If we compare the value of total collective financial assets to the value of total net wealth instead of to the value of total financial assets, it is still the case that collective wealth has become considerable. The value of collective financial assets now corresponds to about a third of total net wealth.

COLLECTIVE WEALTH IN THE OECD: A COMPARISON

It is difficult to find comparable cross-country wealth data. Ambitious attempts to put together such data sets do exist: the Luxemburg Wealth Study,[20] the World Wealth and Income Database (WWID)[21] and the Global Wealth Reports published by Credit Suisse,[22] for example. The problem is, however, that these databases do not cover collective wealth, such as pension wealth. Instead the focus is on individual wealth.

It is possible, though, to use collective pension wealth data published by the OECD to get an idea of cross-country differences in collective wealth. Combining the information on private sector collective pension wealth recorded in one OECD report[23] with the information on public sector pension wealth reported in another[24] we produce a comparison of eleven OECD countries in Figure 7.3 (the data is incomplete for the UK). Collective pension wealth is here related to GDP.

It is, admittedly, a restriction that we cannot report measures of total collective wealth. And it should also be said that the OECD data do not provide complete coverage of all public pension reserve funds. The data presented in the figure should, therefore, be considered as lower estimates. Still, the cross-country differences are so considerable that we can argue, even if the data are not exact, that qualitative conclusions can be drawn.

The countries can be classified into three groups: Nordic countries, Anglo-Saxon countries and Latin countries. Denmark has the highest share of collective pension wealth. This is because occupational pension funds are considerable in Denmark. Norway has its Oil Revenue Fund, plus a great deal of collective pension wealth. Collective pension wealth is lower in Sweden than in the other two Nordic countries but still corresponds to 100 per cent of GDP.

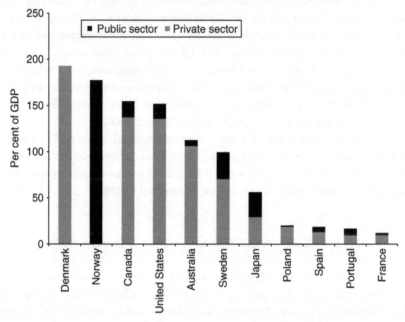

Figure 7.3. Collective pension wealth as share of GDP in 2014: private and public sectors. (*Source*: calculated from OECD data.)

There is also considerable collective pension wealth in Anglo-Saxon countries: around 150 per cent of GDP in Canada and the US; somewhat less in Australia. This wealth is almost exclusively in the private sector. This would seemingly point towards the more egalitarian nature of the Anglo-Saxon countries, but we instead argue that it points back to the issue of power. What is the difference, exactly, between collective wealth formed under public control and collective wealth formed within private companies?

Collective pension wealth in the Latin countries is much lower: 12 per cent of GDP in France and only a few percentage points more in Spain and Portugal. Pensions in these countries are not paid from previously accumulated funds. Instead, the pension systems are based on the pay-as-you-go principle, where the working-age generations pay the pensions of the retired generations. An important implication of this is that the income distributions in France, Portugal and Spain are much more sensitive to shifts in labour (or capital) shares of value-added than the income distributions in the Nordic and Anglo-Saxon countries. One can only speculate how the low share of collective (pension) wealth in France has affected Piketty's analysis and policy conclusions.

To summarize, collective wealth has undoubtedly had a substantial effect on the accumulation of wealth in Sweden since the late nineteenth century, institutionalization in itself pointing towards a shift in the distribution of power from individuals to institutions. More specifically, the constitution of total wealth has been strongly affected by the introduction of publicly managed collective wealth, particularly during the period c.1960–90. The international comparison demonstrates very clearly that taking France as a starting point for the analysis – as Piketty to a large extent does – runs the risk of downplaying collective wealth as a method for redistributing wealth. The international comparison also points to the importance of the institutional and political setting within which collective wealth is formed.

Providing that our assumptions regarding the effects of collective wealth on the distribution of total wealth are correct, it must be concluded that the Swedish political system during this period generated two reforms that affected, or were meant to affect, the distribution of wealth in the direction of more equality. Let us now turn to these two reforms and see if we can detect conscious support for, or opposition to, equality in wealth in the political negotiations that preceded them. Another question is, of course, related to the success of the public pension reserve funds, and the relative lack of success of the wage-earner funds.

THE POLITICS OF COLLECTIVE WEALTH: ATP

The history of the general supplementary pension (*Allmän Tilläggs Pension* (ATP)) dates back to the 1940s. A public pension reform had been introduced through a parliamentary vote in 1913 but the pension was very low and had to be treated as a supplement to individual savings. In the 1940s the Social Democrats were in power and social reforms were on the agenda. The majority of workers did not have access to pension benefits other than a public pension, while white collar occupations and civil servants were, in many cases, entitled to a pension through their employers. In 1944 a motion to investigate the issue of a general supplementary pension was proposed and a public committee was set up.[25] It issued its report in 1950, and one of its conclusions became central to later developments of the issue. A fundamental problem was ensuring that the purchasing power of pensioners would grow at the same pace as the purchasing power of wage-earners. To stabilize the value of pensions the connection between individual contributions to the pension system and benefits received had to be severed. What is now known as a pay-as-you-go system – meaning that the pensions paid out in any one year were to be taken from contributions made in the course of that year – was proposed. This would make it easy to adjust pensions to compensate pensioners for inflation, as well as for a general rise in the standard of living.[26] One might add that it also severed the tie between contributions and some kind of ownership or contracted right to the contributions that had been paid. Furthermore, the report concluded that the supplementary pension had to be mandatory for all wage-earners.

The conclusions of the report were not welcomed. A new committee was set up in 1951. The Swedish Trade Union Confederation, closely allied with the Social Democratic Party, watched developments closely. So did the Swedish Employers' Confederation. In 1954 the employers made their own proposal, based on a voluntary principle. They suggested, furthermore, that funds were to be company based, so that the security of pensions could be combined with wealth accumulation: wealth that was to be exempt from taxation. Private business would consequently retain control over pension funds, and employees would retain their individual entitlements to their pension contributions.[27] Pensions would never cease to be individual wealth. The less overt political motive for the supplementary pension was the accumulation of wealth, to be transformed into capital, in funds controlled and administered by the public. The minister for finance, Per-Edvin Sköld, stated this explicitly: the pension funds could and would be used to invest in growth and to stabilize the economy, to considerable effect.[28] The implication was that funds could and would be used as a tool for Keynesian countercyclical policy.

In 1955 the second pensions committee presented its report. The relative unity of the first committee on the principal issues had dissolved. The Social Democrats, backed by the trade unions, retained the earlier standpoint, while the Conservative Party members of the committee instead wanted to develop the general pension and abolish the proposed link between labour income and supplementary pension. The employers wanted the issue to be transferred from the political system to labour-market negotiations, which would be more in line with the Swedish model.[29] A third committee, the so-called *pensionsberedning*, consisting of representatives from "all four democratic parties" but excluding the communists, was quickly put together in January 1956 in the hope that it would negotiate a solution. It did not. The Liberal Party now joined forces with the Conservative Party, demanding observance of the voluntary principle and that the pensions issue be settled by negotiations between employers and workers. The Farmers' Party, in coalition with the Social Democrats, hesitated. The scene was set for perhaps the most dramatic series of events in Swedish twentieth-century politics: the ATP battle.

The 1956 election result was not a good one for the Social Democratic Party, but it was far worse for its coalition partner, the Farmers' Party. The two parties lost seven parliamentary seats between them, making the coalition very fragile, while the Social Democratic Party lost its overall parliamentary majority. In February 1957 the *pensionsberedning* delivered its report. No consensus has been reached but a majority of the committee had prepared a definite proposal: the supplementary pension was to be mandatory for all employees, and the total pension was to be fixed at a minimum of 65 per cent of the mean income for the fifteen consecutive years with the highest earnings. Pensions were to be indexed to inflation, and contributions were to be made by employers. Neither the Farmers nor the Liberals nor the Conservatives on the committee were in agreement with this. In the election campaign of 1956 Liberals and Conservatives had demanded a referendum on the supplementary pension. The government had blocked this, arguing that there had to be a report and a proposal before there was anything that could be voted on. In the spring of 1957 the government had to agree to a referendum being held in October that year. The ATP referendum became one of only five to be held in Sweden up to the present day. It ended with a slender victory for the Social Democratic proposal, following a very hard-fought campaign with accusations of foul play on all sides.

It would seem that the government had now secured the support necessary for the reform, but in reality it had not. The Farmers' Party left the coalition in October 1957 and the government had to resign. A Social Democratic minority government was formed. If the pension bill was to pass into law, support from the opposition had to be gained. In the meantime, the government had in April 1957 appointed a committee – led by the governor of the Riksbank, Per Åsbrink – to solve the question of how the pension funds were to be managed in practice. One of Sweden's leading bankers, Tore Browaldh, was also appointed to the committee, along with the Stockholm School economist Erik Lundberg and trade union representative Rudolf Meidner, the architect of the future wage-earner funds, which we will come to later. The committee made a suggestion about how the pension funds might be administered through the construction of three public pension reserve funds. There was now, therefore, a concrete proposal for three publicly governed funds that would, given the enormous sums, rapidly become a source of power in Swedish economic life.[30]

Negotiations to finalize the proposed pension reforms continued into early 1958. The main protagonists were the prime minister, Tage Erlander, and the leader of the Liberal Party, Bertil Ohlin. The opposition wanted funds to be managed by private insurance companies, plus exit rights for individual employees after a certain number of mandatory years of pension payments, as well as a right for unions and employers to negotiate other terms through collective agreement. Taken together, in our view these suggestions would have annihilated the core characteristic of the reforms: the gradual accumulation of collective wealth. Neither the government nor the Swedish Trade Union Confederation was prepared to compromise on these issues, and negotiations therefore broke down once more. In April 1958 the proposal was voted down in the second chamber of the parliament, and Erlander immediately dissolved parliament, appealing to the country. The new election was a disaster for the Liberal Party, but since both the Conservatives and the Farmers gained more votes, there was now parliamentary deadlock, with 115 votes for the pension reform and 115 votes against it in the second chamber. The pension reforms had now caused two elections and a referendum, and it seemed they would continue to cause trouble.

The final talks between Ohlin and Erlander in the autumn of 1958 were more interesting, because they explicitly and accurately identified the crucial problem: *capital formation*. Ohlin demanded guarantees against the *concentration of power* that the public pension reserve funds would create, and he did not see regulation as being a sufficient safeguard. The only way that concentration of power and the threat of socialization could be avoided was if funds were managed privately, and distributed across many companies. Ohlin maintained, again and again, that while he did not doubt that social security was the prime motive for the proposition, he was still afraid that the public pension reserve funds would provide a basis for *societal capital direction (samhällelig kapitaldirigering)*.[31] When the government made a formal demand that negotiations be opened, Ohlin went on the radio to tell the Swedish people that the answer was no.

The ATP battle culminated with a drama and a personal tragedy in January 1959. The Liberal member of parliament Ture Königsson of Gothenburg decided to follow his conscience and abstain from voting, so that the opposition now only had 114 votes against 115. For this he was ostracized by his fellow Liberals and his political career was finished. He was not re-elected in the election of 1960.[32] But the ATP battle was finally over and the new pension system came into existence in May 1959.

THE POLITICS OF COLLECTIVE WEALTH: WAGE-EARNER FUNDS

As can be seen from the discussion of the ATP battle, the indirect threat of socialization was a point of difficulty. There were no direct plans for socialization at the time, and in fact Swedish social democracy had long since abandoned socialization in favour of a planned economy. Still, economic democracy was central to social democracy and this had been so since the early days of the first social democratic government. The 1918 ministry of Hjalmar Branting instituted a committee on industrial democracy in 1920. In its 1923 report, Ernst Wigforss – who later became minister of finance (1925–6, 1932–6, 1936–49) and was one of the leading twentieth-century ideologists of Swedish social democracy – stated that "democracy cannot stop at the factory door". Inherited wealth was the foundation for a small group of people who took decisions that concerned the lives of thousands of workers. This was simply undemocratic.[33] The 1923 report suggested a law on worker's councils that would give such councils consultative powers only, but this proposal was not passed into law. A similar reform was passed in 1948, and it had by then become acceptable to the Swedish Employers' Confederation. After that, economic democracy as an overt political issue disappeared from the political agenda for more than twenty-five years.[34]

It reappeared in 1976. By then the first oil crisis had hit Sweden hard, and economic stagnation had set in. This was coupled with rising inflation, leading to what became known as stagflation. One of the striking similarities between the public pension reserve funds and the proposed wage-earner funds was the aim to use funds as a tool for countercyclical policy; they were, according to sociologist Walter Korpi, to be one of the main tools for "an alternative policy to meet the crisis".[35] The alternative policy would not primarily demand sacrifices from wage-earners, but instead utilize wage-earner funds to hinder the growth of inequality, balancing the potential slowing down of salary increases and, at the same time, generating capital for investment. The fundamental rationality of wage-earner funds rested not on economic stagnation, however, but on the relationship between wages and profit. The labour movement had successfully launched a wages policy built on solidarity with low-paid workers, with the aim of bringing their wages to the same level as the rest of the workers' collective. One of the cornerstones of this policy was the idea that it would be better to force low-profit companies that could not afford to pay the prevailing wage rate out of business, since they were economically inefficient. To fight inflation financial policy was to be restrictive while labour market policy was active, especially in terms of easing the movement of labour from declining parts of the labour market to those that were expanding. The policy has been summarized as "a non-inflationary full employment policy".[36] There was, however, a negative side effect of the levelling out of wages, since highly efficient and profitable companies could pay less in wages than they could afford. This would lead to excess profits, and it was these excess profits that, according to the labour movement, should now be tapped.[37]

In 1973 the board of the Swedish Trade Union Confederation set up a committee to investigate the possibility of establishing trade and other funds that might exploit profits and workers' savings. One of the committee members was Rudolf Meidner, who had been a member of the committee that had designed the public pension reserve funds, and who had furthermore been engaged in the issue of general wages policy, along with the young Social Democrat Anna Hedborg and the student of economics Gunnar Fond. They began their work in 1974.[38] The committee interpreted its mission thus: (1) to strengthen solidaristic wages policy through a cut in excess profits; (2) to strengthen the influence of wage-earners on the management of business; and (3) to break the trend of accumulation of individual wealth and capital. Points (2) and (3) concern power and economic democracy rather than wage policy, and point (3) addresses exactly the same issue as *Capital in the Twenty-First Century*, and also relies on a critique of uneven wealth distribution together with a critique of the uneven ownership of working capital.[39]

This emerging of economic democracy in Sweden was not at the time unique from a European perspective. The debate was especially intense in West Germany, and developments there were closely followed by the committee. The background in West Germany was very different to that in Sweden, though, mainly because of business conditions in post-war West Germany. The reconstruction of German industry had relied on restrictive wages policies and a high degree of internal financing, leading to a highly uneven reconstruction of wealth. This was the prime problem addressed in the German context, and there was little or no interest in the problem of wage-earner influence on wages policy.[40] The German counterpart to the Swedish Trade Union Confederation, the DGB (*Deutscher Gewerkschaftsbund*), had in 1972 suggested that wage-earners should, as a collective, be given a share in the wealth accumulated by private enterprise. Between 4 per cent and 15 per cent of profits were to be placed in regional funds, for which wage-earners were to be given certificates. The proposal was never realized, however: it remained controversial in parts of the labour movement, as well as in the Social Democratic Party.[41]

The final report came in 1976.[42] It proposed the creation of wage-earner funds to which private business enterprise would by law be obliged to pay 20 per cent of untaxed profits, not directly but through the issue of shares linked to wage-earner funds.[43] Wage-earner funds would thus gradually become major owners of private enterprises. Only companies with more than 50 or 100 employees would be included in the system, and the preferred model was industry-based and not regional.[44] The report stressed that the main task of the wage-earner funds would not be to strengthen the influence of workers in their own workplace. Neither was it to be seen as a transfer of initiative in economic policy from the political system to the funds. Economic policy should be decided by the elected government and by parliament. What the wage-earner funds would actually accomplish was to democratize decisions that were taken within a company, but which in reality concerned the company's relationship with society at large. In short, wage-earner funds "would make it possible to take democratic decisions on investments that concerned what should be produced and where".[45] Direct power would be exercised by wage-earner funds through the right to elect representatives to company boards; indirect power would be exercised through the investment of returns in education, research and development.[46]

A notable aspect of the proposed design – and a central one in this context – was its direct relation to the public pension reserve funds. The report explicitly stated that the problematic reduction in public saving experienced during the early 1970s was to be addressed by increasing the payments to the public pension reserve funds; their role was thus to regain the balance between public and private saving. Wage-earner funds should instead be used to alter the structure of ownership in favour of employees. They were not primarily for wealth formation aimed at investment; they could be used to facilitate capital formation, but it was not their main goal.[47] A central conclusion is, therefore, that the original proposal for wage-earner funds, which bore the stamp of Rudolf Meidner, should be seen as the second step in a conscious process of constructing collective wealth, and that public pension reserve funds and wage-earner funds were given complementary roles in this vision.

The Social Democrats lost the 1976 election and the need was felt to anchor the wage-earner funds more firmly in the whole of the labour movement. A new committee with delegates from both the Swedish Trade Union Confederation and the Social Democrats produced a compromise proposition that foregrounded the need for capital formation and downplayed economic democracy. The Social Democrat Congress of 1978 could not agree on the issue and referred it for further investigation. The third committee, led by Kjell-Olof Feldt (who later became minister of finance), placed more emphasis on capital formation and integrated wage-earner funds into the system of public pension reserve funds. In addition, according to the new proposal there would be no takeover of shares; payments to the wage-earner funds would be made in cash. This much less radical proposal was accepted by both the Swedish Trade Union Confederation Congress and the Social Democratic Congress of 1981, and a year after the Social Democrats won the 1982 election a wage-earner funds bill was passed. The funds were announced to be on trial, and the trial was to last for seven years.

In the meantime, for private business and the Conservative and Liberal parties, wage-earner funds had become emblematic of all that was considered to be a problem in Swedish politics: an issue that could possibly be used as a lever to mobilize non-socialist parties and organizations, and challenge the success of the Swedish labour movement. A formidable U-turn was performed by the employers in 1980; having been mildly sympathetic to the wage-earner funds and ready to discuss technicalities, they now emphatically rejected them. The shift can be attributed to a change in the leadership of the Swedish Employers' Confederation.[48] It now took centre stage in a formidable emergent protest movement, culminating in the *4 October Movement* of 1983. For the first time in Swedish history business representatives organized mass demonstrations and waved banners. The opposition was fierce and widespread. The wage-earner funds were in existence for eight years before being dissolved in 1991. The opposition had made it their foremost pledge to electors to abolish them if they won the election, so they did. The wealth was transferred to the pension system and to a number of foundations whose main purpose was research and development. The initial proposal had, however, been to transfer the money directly to Swedish savers through the so-called *allemansfonder*.[49] Wage-earner funds never had the impact of public pension reserve funds on wealth accumulation. They existed too briefly. We have included them here because analysis of the events strengthens the hypothesis that the formation of collective wealth was what was at stake, both regarding ATP and wage-earner funds; and it was a fundamentally controversial political issue.

CONCLUSION

We start our concluding remarks by returning to the four tasks of progressive taxation of individual wealth presented by Piketty: redistribution, introduction of norms and regulations that are performative, increased transparency, and increased legitimacy of the globalized economy. We argue that the formation of collective wealth in Sweden contributed, or had the opportunity to contribute, to the first three of these:

- the numbers have quite convincingly demonstrated that there was an actual redistribution of wealth – the collective wealth share of total wealth increased considerably at the expense of the individual wealth share;
- collective wealth has, in terms of institutionalization, contributed to new organizations, new regulations and new norms in financial markets; and
- collective wealth has been managed by representatives of a large number of the people and these representatives have been accountable.

How the institutionalization of collective wealth has in practice affected the totality of financial regulation and practice is a question that will have to be dealt with elsewhere.

What were the motives and countermotives for the two political reforms in question? The motives were in both cases clearly related to capital formation, seen from the perspective of Keynesian economic policy. The public pension reserve funds were thought to be a potential source of fiscal policy and public investment in an era of stable growth and low unemployment. The contributions to collective wealth formation were directly related to labour income, and the pensions to be received were related to the same income. However, in the meantime, wage-earners could benefit from taking part of the return on wealth from the economy at large through the funds. The wage-earner funds, which were initially conceived during the first oil crisis, were to be the foundation of an alternative crisis policy that did not shift the balance of power unfavourably, i.e. to industry. Latterly, the motive of capital formation was foregrounded in an effort to gain support for the reform, and direct economic democracy was pushed into the background.

Likewise, the formation of collective capital was the prime motivation of opposition to the reforms. The constitution of large publicly managed funds was a threat in itself, because it meant a shift in power. In 1959 the Liberal leader Bertil Ohlin concluded that the temptation for economic *dirigisme* would be too strong once such funds came into existence. In the case of wage-earner funds, private wealth would be acquired for the purpose of creating funds that would have direct power to influence the use of the same individual wealth in terms of policy and investment. All the alternatives formulated by the Liberals, by the Conservative Party and by the Swedish Employers' Confederation, regardless of whether they concerned public pension reserve funds or wage-earner funds, had as their core assumption that funds would be *individually owned*, not collectively owned. The shift of power was therefore as important an argument for and against collective wealth as the shift of wealth.

There are many differences between the two cases. Both the political context and the economic context were fundamentally different: the late 1950s was a peak period in the Swedish economy, as well as in the supremacy of social democratic welfare capitalism; the early 1970s was a period of economic crisis and of growing criticism of the public sector. A third difference relates to the distribution of power that resulted: the public pension reserve funds were and still are governed according to the Swedish model, with representatives from both employers and employees; the wage-earner funds were at the disposal of the public sector and trade unions, with little oversight or influence from industry. But perhaps the most striking difference pertains to what Harcourt and Tribe refer to in Chapter 2 as the difference between a political economy of sustained full employment and a political economy where the ruling class no longer tolerates the transfer of economic, political and social power, reinstating unemployment as a means of coming to terms with the problem.[50] Returning to Piketty's general conclusions, and asking ourselves exactly how a causal relationship involving the changing ratio between wealth and income over time should be construed, we can therefore justifiably enquire whether the slowdown in growth has indeed brought about a return to inequality, or if it is perhaps instead the case that the return to inequality has been caused by changes in politics and power relations?

Lastly, we would like to address a specific question in relation to the central results of Thomas Piketty. What will happen if the labour share of value-added continues to decrease? Can collective wealth be a form of (equality) insurance in such a situation, through – in the Swedish case – its close relationship to previous labour income? And, if we are right on this, can we guarantee that wealth taxes are used for the same purpose? In the first case, the institutional structure has binding consequences; in the second case, the outcome is entirely a matter of political negotiation.

Notes for Chapter 7

1. Thomas Piketty, *Capital in the Twenty-First Century* (Cambridge, MA: Harvard University Press, 2014), p. 577.

2. We would like to thank Martin Daunton for organizing the Philomathia Symposium, "Wealth, Inheritance and Inequality", 13–14 April 2015, Moeller Centre, Churchill College, Cambridge, where some of the ideas in this chapter were presented and discussed. The views expressed are solely the responsibility of the authors and should not be interpreted as reflecting the views of Sveriges Riksbank.

3. Piketty's *Capital* uses the terms capital and wealth as synonyms. This is correct for closed economies, whereas it is an approximation for open economies. Wealth accumulates through savings, while capital accumulates through investment. In most cases wealth is channelled through financial markets to allow investment and capital accumulation.

4. Piketty, *Capital*, pp. 205, 602. See also the parallel discussion of pensions as wealth in the chapter by Hesse in this volume: Chapter 6.

5. Piketty, *Capital*, pp. 471–72.

6. *Ibid.*, p. 473.

7. This also applies for income taxation in the Nordic countries. The dual income tax systems in the Nordic countries combine progressive taxation of labour income with proportional taxation of capital income.

8. Piketty, *Capital*, p. 528.

9. *Ibid.*, p. 518–21.

10. See Chapter 2 in this volume, by Harcourt and Tribe.

11. Two influential Swedish studies that have broadened our understanding of ownership, especially land ownership, in pre-industrial Sweden are Christer Winberg, *Grenverket: Studier rörande jord, släktskapssystem och ståndsprivilegier* (Stockholm: Institutet för rättshistorisk forskning, 1985) and Maria Ågren, *Jord och gäld: Social skiktning och rättslig konflikt I södra Dalarna ca 1650–1850* (Uppsala: Acta Universitatis Upsaliensis, 1992).

12. The Instrument of Government of Sweden (SFS, 1974) 152; The Environmental Code of Sweden (SFS, 1998) 808, Chapters 2 and 7.

13. Karl Polanyi, *The Great Transformation* (New York: Farrar & Rinehart, 1944).

14. See Harcourt and Tribe, pp. 14–16 in this volume.

15. Loukas Karabarbounis and Brent Neiman, "The Global Decline of the Labor Share", *Quarterly Journal of Economics* 129 (2014), pp. 61–103.

16. Erik Bengtsson, "Labour's Share in Twentieth-Century Sweden: A Reinterpretation", *Scandinavian Economic History Review* 62 (2014), pp. 295–96.

17. Daniel Waldenström has prepared the Swedish National Wealth Database (SNWD), 1810–2014. The database is presented in Waldenström, "The National Wealth of Sweden, 1810–2014", *Scandinavian Economic History Review* 64 (2016), pp. 36–54, and is used to calculate wealth–income ratios in his "Wealth–Income Ratios in a Small, Late-Industrializing, Welfare-State Economy: Sweden, 1810–2010", Working Paper 2015:4 (Department of Economics, Uppsala University, 2015). The database can be downloaded from www.uueconomics.se/danielw/SNWD.htm (we use version 1.2). The long-run changes in the concentration of wealth in Sweden are discussed in Henry Ohlsson, Jesper Roine and Daniel Waldenström, "Long-Run Changes in the Concentration of Wealth: An Overview of Recent Findings", in *Personal Wealth from a Global Perspective*, J. B. Davies (ed.) (Oxford: Oxford University Press, 2008); Henry Ohlsson, Jesper Roine and Daniel Waldenström, "Inherited Wealth over the Path of Development: Sweden, 1810–2010", Working Paper 2014:7 (Department of Economics, Uppsala University); Roine and Waldenström, "Wealth Concentration over the Path of Development: Sweden, 1873–2006", *Scandinavian Journal of Economics* 111 (2009), pp. 151–87; Jesper Roine and Daniel Waldenström, "Long Run Trends in the Distribution of Income and Wealth", in *Handbook of Income Distribution*, A. Atkinson and F. Bourguignon (eds), Volume 2A (Amsterdam: Elsevier, 2015).

18. Waldenström, "National Wealth of Sweden", pp. 41–2. Waldenström relies on the definition of two forms of wealth: public (or government) wealth and private wealth. In this he basically follows Piketty. Certain problems arise from this definition when it comes to defining pension wealth. Waldenström notes its importance, but places unfunded (defined-benefit) private pension entitlements outside the main wealth concept, while including funded private pensions saving unequivocally in private wealth. The practice of excluding unfunded pension entitlements from the analysis of wealth adheres to the practice of the System of National Accounts of the United Nations, SNA 2008 (United Nations, 2009). Moreover, he does not include the public pension reserve funds in funded pension wealth. Instead, these funds are included as public wealth in a more general sense.

19. It is true that the rates of return on collective wealth, such as pension and social insurance funds, may fluctuate substantially. But the same is true for the returns on individual wealth. With a higher share of collective wealth in total wealth, low income/low wealth people in general will get a share when returns are high. On the other hand, they will also be affected by low returns. But, in the long run, returns to wealth have on average been high, and can be expected to continue to be so. It is therefore in the interests of equality that the share of collective wealth in total wealth be high.

20. www.lisdatacenter.org/our-data/lws-database/.

21. www.wid.world/.

22. www.credit-suisse.com/je/en/about-us/research/research-institute/global-wealth-report.html.

23. *Pension Markets in Focus 2014* (Paris: OECD, 2014).

24. *Annual Survey of Large Pension Funds and Public Pension Reserve Funds 2014* (Paris: OECD, 2014).

25. Björn Molin, *Tjänstepensionsfrågan: En Studie i Svensk Partipolitik* (Gothenburg: Akademiförlaget, 1965), pp. 9–10.

26. Tage Erlander, *Tage Erlander 1955–1960* (Stockholm: Hjalmarson & Högberg, 1976), p. 131.

27. Molin, *Tjänstepensionsfrågan*, pp. 32–5.

28. Erlander, *Tage Erlander*, p. 135.

29. *Ibid.*, pp. 137–8.

30. The Swedish government's official investigations, *Promemoria med förslag om fondförvaltning m.m. i samband med en utbyggd pensionering* (1958:4).

31. Erlander, *Tage Erlander*, pp. 248–51.

32. Ture Königson, *ATP-striden: Ett tioårsminne* (Stockholm: Samhällsgemenskap, 1968).

33. Walter Korpi, *Från undersåte till medborgare: om fonder och ekonomisk demokrati* (Stockholm: Tiden, 1982), pp. 55 ff. The quote can be found on p. 56.

34. *Ibid.*, p. 17.

35. *Ibid.*, p. 14.

36. Rudolf Meidner, *Spelet om löntagarfonder* (Stockholm: Bokförlaget Atlas, 2005), p. 17.

37. *Ibid.*, pp. 17–38.

38. *Ibid.*, p. 34.

39. *Kollektiv kapitalbildning genom löntagarfonder: rapport till LO-kongressen 1976* (Stockholm: Prisma/Landsorganisationen i Sverige, 1976), pp. 34 ff.

40. Meidner, *Spelet om löntagarfonder*, pp. 51ff.

41. *Ibid.*, pp. 47–57.

42. *Ibid.*, pp. 65ff.

43. *Kollektiv kapitalbildning*, p. 17.

44. *Ibid.*, pp. 108 ff.

45. *Ibid.*, p. 87 (our translation).

46. *Ibid.* A flowchart of the construction can be found on pp. 114–15.

47. *Ibid.*, p. 127.

48. Erik Åsard, *Kampen om löntagarfonderna: Fondutredningen från samtal till sammanbrott* (Stockholm: Norstedt, 1985), pp. 102–22.

49. Swedish parliamentary records, government bill 1991/1992: 36.

50. See Harcourt and Tribe, p. 23 in this volume.

8

A CONFUSION OF CAPITAL IN
THE UNITED STATES

Mary A. O'Sullivan

The central issue addressed in Thomas Piketty's *Capital in the Twenty-First Century* is the historical relationship between capital accumulation and inequality. It has gained widespread recognition, even notoriety, for its claim that capitalism systematically breeds inequality. Piketty's authority in making that controversial claim derives from the extensive historical analysis that he offers of long-term trends in the accumulation of capital and the returns that it generates. Yet, even though these trends are of central importance in determining the plausibility of Piketty's central thesis, his measurement and interpretation of capital's role and rewards have received only limited attention.

In this chapter I present a critical analysis of the image that Piketty constructs of the history of capital in the US. The US economy, to its champions and its critics, is often seen as exemplifying all that is characteristic of capitalism. Therefore, if one is interested in learning about capital in capitalism, the history of the US is a promising source of insight. In my first section below I sketch the image that Piketty presents of historical trends in capital's role in US history and explain how he constructs it. He does so by departing from an approach to defining and measuring capital that has become standard in economics today, and that is why the image of capital that he presents for the US is a distinctive one.

The novelty of Piketty's treatment of capital raises the important question, which I address in my second section, of whether it makes conceptual sense. Specifically, is it consistent with the way he understands the economic role of capital and the rewards that accrue to it? In fact, *Capital* offers surprisingly little insofar as conceptualizing the economic role of capital is concerned, and, when it comes to understanding capital's rewards, the book largely piggybacks on the standard model from mainstream economics. Doing so creates an important incoherence in Piketty's work since the neoclassical theory of distribution is based on an entirely different concept of capital than the one he favours.

However, moving forward on the history of capital in the US will not be achieved by moving backward to a mainstream analysis of capital, even if it offers internal coherence, given that it has significant problems of its own.

What we need instead is an alternative vision of the economic role and rewards of capital. The history of economic thought is an important source of inspiration for any such alternative, but economists' debates on capital theory can take us only so far given their limited engagement with capital's empirical record. As I explain in my third section, economic history offers fertile ground for developing new ways of thinking about capital. Based on a limited review of several important features of capital's history in the US, I suggest a number of complexities that are ignored or misunderstood by existing approaches to capital. Taken together they imply the importance of an analysis of capital's role and rewards in the context of the evolving social organization of capitalism.

PIKETTY'S HISTORY OF US CAPITAL

To understand the importance of capital across economies and within these economies over time, Thomas Piketty estimates the significance of capital relative to an economy's total income to construct a measure of capital intensity that he describes as a "capital–income ratio". The historical patterns that he generates for the US present an image of capital in that country that has some similarities to Britain and France but that is highly distinctive in its own right. At the dawn of the new American republic, Piketty suggests that capital mattered much less than in the Old World, since land was more plentiful and, therefore, less valuable, and immigrants had not had enough time to accumulate much real estate or business capital. Between 1770 and 1810, capital hovered around 300 per cent of national income in the US, compared with more than 700 per cent in Britain and France.[1] Piketty does offer one qualification to this image that stems from recognizing slavery as a form of capital; from 1770 to 1860, the market value of slaves adds about 100 per cent of national income to measured US capital (Figure 8.1), and proportionately more if we focus on the American South.[2]

What that implies is that the Civil War, in ending the pernicious practice of holding human beings as chattels, reduces Piketty's measure of national capital. He also emphasizes the decline in the value of US farmland in the nineteenth century, a trend he also observes for Europe. Nevertheless, he points to an overall increase in the US capital stock by the end of the century, given the accumulation of a much larger stock of real estate and other domestic capital. By 1910, as a result, US capital had risen to nearly five times national income, compared with only three times in 1810, bringing it closer to, if still well below, British and

French capital–income ratios of about 6.5 times.[3] As Piketty concludes: "The United States had become capitalist, but wealth continued to have less influence than in Belle Epoque Europe, at least if we consider the vast US territory as a whole. If we limit our gaze to the East Coast, the gap is smaller still."[4]

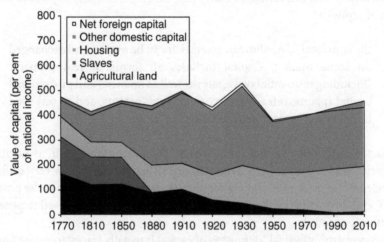

Figure 8.1. The composition of US capital, 1770–2010.
(*Source*: Piketty, *Capital*, Figure 4.10, p. 160.)

For the twentieth century, Piketty presents an image of turbulence, with the US capital–income ratio initially declining from 1910 to 1920 and then soaring to almost 500 per cent of national income by 1930. It then collapsed with the Great Depression and was still only 400 per cent in 1970, even if the decline was less dramatic than in European countries where the capital–output ratio dropped from approximately 700 per cent to 300 per cent or less during the same period. Since the 1970s, the US has witnessed the same rebound in capital as European countries, but, as Piketty notes, the U-shaped pattern in capital–income ratios in the twentieth century has been less strong in the US. Its capital rebounded as a share of national income by 2007 but then retreated sharply to just over 400 per cent by 2010, compared with a steadier 600–700 per cent in Europe.[5]

Piketty's definition of capital

There are many aspects of the image that Piketty presents of the history of capital in the US that invite questions. Certainly, the traces of a conventional under-standing of different phases of US economic history are not easy to discern within it. However, it would be impetuous to try to make economic sense of

Piketty's image without understanding the bases on which his estimates of capital are constructed. As Piketty himself notes, the question "What is capital?" is central to his investigation,[6] so it is only by understanding how he addresses it that we can hope to decipher the image of capital he presents for the US.

As is now well understood, Piketty proposes a particularly expansive definition of capital as

> the sum total of nonhuman assets that can be owned and exchanged on some market. Capital includes all forms of real property (including residential real estate) as well as financial and professional capital (plants, infrastructure, machinery, patents, and so on) used by firms and government agencies.[7]

In fact, Piketty uses "capital" and "wealth" interchangeably, as if, as he puts it himself, "they were perfectly synonymous".[8] That puts him on a very different wavelength to most of his fellow economists, who define capital as the physical stuff, and, in particular, the equipment and buildings, that are used to generate economic output.[9]

Economists' "physical" definition of capital is usually traced to Adam Smith's *The Wealth of Nations*, in which, as Edwin Cannan put it, "Instead of making the capital a sum of money which is to be invested, or which has been invested in certain things, Smith makes it the things themselves".[10] Yet, even as that concept of capital came to dominate in economics, it drew forceful criticism.[11] Thorstein Veblen emphasized just how much the physical meaning of capital departed from the monetary meaning that capitalists themselves assigned it.[12] Joseph Schumpeter also pointed out that the concept of capital had long had an essentially monetary meaning, "meaning either actual money, or claims to money, or some goods evaluated in money", and claimed that economists would have done well to stick with it:

> What a mass of confused, futile, and downright silly controversies it would have saved us, if economists had had the sense to stick to those monetary and accounting meanings of the term instead of trying to "deepen" them![13]

Nevertheless, it was a physical meaning of capital that prevailed in the economics mainstream, as we see in neoclassical growth theory, the primary branch of economics where the concept of capital is invoked today. For that reason, in reviewing Piketty's book, Robert Solow, one of the originators of growth theory, highlighted just how much it departs from the dominant concept of capital as a "factor of production".[14] And what that means is that Piketty's definition of capital generates an image of capital in the US that is quite different from one that a mainstream economist might construct.

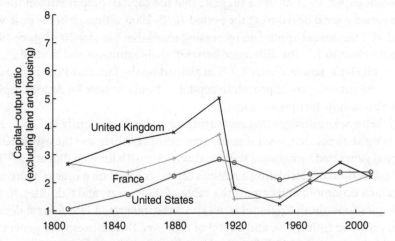

Figure 8.2. The capital–output ratio excluding land and housing.
(*Source*: Jones (2015).[15])

Residential capital is important in this regard since it plays a major role in driving Piketty's historical analysis but is excluded from most mainstream conceptions of "productive" capital. For the US, as Bonnet, Bono, Chapelle and Wasmer show, housing plays an important role in driving the increase in Piketty's capital–output ratio since 1950.[16] Important though it is, residential capital is not the only feature of Piketty's capital that distinguishes it from the conventional one, since his inclusion of land represents another contrast with most economists' focus on reproducible capital.[17] We can see the difference the distinctive character of Piketty's definition of capital makes, as Charles Jones shows, by using the French economist's data to construct a picture of reproducible, non-residential capital in the US, as depicted in Figure 8.2. As Jones observes, it is different from Piketty's image but it "corresponds much more closely to what we think of when we model physical capital in macro models".[18]

Piketty's measurement of capital

Even so, what we see in Figure 8.2 is still not what most economists would expect to observe for the capital–output ratio in US economic history. In a much-cited paper, Nicholas Kaldor claimed that a roughly stable capital–output ratio was one of six stylized facts that characterized economic growth in advanced economies over the long run.[19] Despite the widespread acceptance of that fact by many economists, little empirical work has been undertaken to determine whether it is true, as Jakob Madsen and Russell Smyth point out in a recent paper. Their analysis suggests that the capital–output ratio in the US has varied a good deal during the period 1870–2000, although in the post-war period it fluctuated around an increasing trend that has stabilized since 1980 at very close to 2.[20] The difference between their estimates and those derived from Piketty's data in Figure 8.2 is explained by the fact that Piketty departs from the mainstream approach to capital not only in how he defines capital but also in how he measures it.

Piketty acknowledges that measuring capital is "notoriously difficult", and he is right about that, even if many economists blithely use the estimates of capital generated by national statistical agencies with little qualification.[21] The oldest method of calculating a nation's capital is based on a census approach, in which economic units report the value of their assets and liabilities. In the US, questions about households' wealth were integrated into federal decennial censuses from 1850, and a total of nine wealth censuses were generated on this basis until 1922.[22] In principle, these censuses offer comprehensive coverage of wealth holdings in the US, but, as Stephen Hoenack explained, "The potential usefulness of the censuses of wealth for analysis has been shown to be limited because of the inaccuracies and unclear meaning of their estimates and the lack of an adequate categorisation for meaningful comparisons of the components of wealth."[23]

Thus, when the US wealth censuses were discontinued in 1922, there was good reason to develop alternative ways of measuring capital. In the inter-war period, interest in doing so was limited as estimates of national income took priority.[24] However, from the mid-twentieth century, a new method of measuring capital emerged, known as the perpetual inventory method (PIM). Developed by US economist Raymond Goldsmith, the PIM constructs the capital stock as a perpetual function of cumulated investment expenditures, adjusted for estimates of depreciation and changes in prices, on top of an estimated initial capital stock. The PIM quickly gained ground among national statistical agencies to become the standard approach to the measurement of capital.

It is largely as a result of the PIM's widespread application that estimates of capital stock by industry, sector and economy were generated for much of the twentieth century. As a result, the PIM is the foundation for the conventional estimates of the capital stock that mainstream economists employ. They may, in theory, speak of capital as a composite physical stock, but from the 1950s they increasingly relied on monetary estimates of capital in so-called growth accounting exercises. That such estimates were available reflected the widespread acceptance of the PIM as a legitimate basis for constructing estimates of the capital stock.[25]

However, in recent years, criticism of the PIM has exposed the host of heroic assumptions about depreciation and obsolescence on which it relies. For some economists, its deficiencies are sufficiently important to move back to census-based approaches to estimate market valuations of a nation's capital. Piketty is one such economist, proving both an articulate critic of the "pitfalls" of the PIM and an enthusiastic proponent of measuring capital at market valuations.[26] Still, calculating market prices for capital brings measurement challenges of its own. Estimates of house prices may be available based on census methods but that is not true of many important categories of assets. As Piketty himself acknowledges, "Whether we are speaking of a building or a company, a manufacturing firm or a service firm, it is always very difficult to set a price on capital."[27]

That difficulty provokes the question of how Piketty applies his principle of measurement in practice, notably to the business sector, given the difficulties of finding market prices for the machines and structures it uses in the production of goods and services. Rather than attempting the impossible challenge of trying to establish these assets' market valuations based on census-like procedures, Piketty makes an assumption that greatly simplifies his task. He assumes that the value of corporations' capital can be proxied by their stock market capitalizations and, specifically, household and other sectors' holdings of corporate equity.[28]

That assumption is a bold one given that the determinants of corporate stock prices have eluded the sustained efforts of financial economists to uncover them. Studying corporate valuations over long periods of time only deepens the mystery, since there are significant changes over time in the relationships between the values the stock market assigns to corporate stocks and corporations' earnings or the book value of their physical assets. Piketty acknowledges that using market valuations "introduces an element of arbitrariness (markets are often capricious)",[29] but he relies heavily on the dubious assumption that the stock market can be taken as a reasonable arbiter of the value of the corporate sector's capital.[30]

That means that his estimates of the corporate sector's capital differ from those that most economists propose. Specifically, the fact that stock market capitalizations have grown relative to the book value of their assets over the post-war period, albeit unevenly, as Figure 8.3 shows, means that Piketty's estimates of corporate capital are higher than the standard ones for recent periods. Thus, it contributes, along with rising market values of real estate, to Piketty's finding of a rising capital–income ratio in recent decades.[31] In contrast, as Bob Rowthorn explains, "conventional measures of this [capital–output] ratio indicate that it has been either stationary or has fallen in most advanced economies during the period in question". As Rowthorn notes, that suggests a rather different interpretation to Piketty's one, specifically: "The basic problem is not the over-accumulation of capital, but just the opposite. There has been too little real investment."[32]

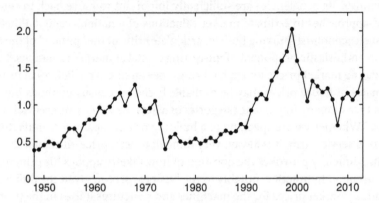

Figure 8.3. Ratio of total market value to the book value of equipment, structures and land, US corporate sector. (*Source*: Matthew Rognlie (2015), Figure 9.[33])

We might take issue with Piketty's reliance on market capitalization of corporate stock as a proxy for corporate capital, but it does simplify his measurement challenges for the period from 1945 to 2010. However, that is not true for earlier periods, given the limited availability of estimates of corporate valuations and the diminishing economic importance of corporations in the US economy as we go backward, especially into the nineteenth century. What then does Piketty do as he moves back in time, indeed all the way back to 1770, to measure the capital employed in the US economy?

He resolves the problem by altering his methods and, specifically, by dispensing with the challenge of estimating the capital of the corporate, or even business, sector. Instead, he relies on more aggregated estimates of national wealth that come from a variety of sources and are calculated using diverse methods. For 1900 and 1912, for example, Piketty uses estimates generated by Raymond Goldsmith based on the perpetual inventory method rather than market valuations. For 1850, 1860 and 1880, in contrast, he employs estimates of household wealth from the decennial wealth censuses. These data were intended to approximate market valuations but, as I noted, they suffered from all kinds of problems and were deemed especially deficient for estimating the value of physical capital used by the business sector. In acknowledgement of these difficulties, Piketty increases the estimates of household wealth he finds there by a flat rate, although he does not explain the rationale for setting that rate at 20 per cent or why, given changes in the census methodology, it should be applied as a flat rate to all years.[34]

CONCEPTUALIZING CAPITAL'S ROLE AND REWARDS

Having understood something about the way that Piketty defines and measures capital, there are several grounds on which we might take issue with the image of capital that he presents for the US. Undoubtedly, the easiest target is the way he handles historical data to measure capital. Certainly there seem to be grounds for questioning what he does given his (debatable) choices with regard to selecting proxies for market valuations of capital, his willingness to combine sources that use disparate methodologies and his manipulation of the data to smooth their differences.[35]

More fundamentally, it might seem tempting to challenge Piketty on the legitimacy of his concept of capital, given the extent to which it departs from standard usage of the term in economics today. However, the mere fact that Piketty is unconventional in conceptualizing capital does not make him wrong. After all, as we have seen, he is not the only scholar in the history of economic thought to challenge the notion that capital can be understood as the physical stuff used in production.[36] Whether Piketty's concept of capital is legitimate or otherwise depends on how he uses it, or, more precisely, on how it fits into his theory of capital's economic role and rewards.

That observation is, of course, just as true for mainstream economists, but they have shown a marked lack of interest in critical discussion of the conceptual foundations that underpin their own definition and measurement of capital. Raymond Goldsmith, a towering figure in the empirical analysis of capital, was unabashed in proclaiming that "my appetite for discussion of concepts is limited, and I feel they have for quite a while produced nothing that is new in this field".[37] Robert Solow also dismissed the importance of economic debates on capital theory by suggesting that they had endured for such a long time only because the central question they addressed was "badly posed".[38]

These economists' disdain for conceptual discussions of capital reflects their commitment to one particular way of understanding its economic role and rewards and their limited imagination in conceiving viable alternatives to it. The mainstream view is embedded in what is described as the "neoclassical" approach to growth and distribution, which can be summarized in three "parables" about capital's role and rewards. First, capital is a physical quantity that serves as a "factor of production" with a productive contribution that can be identified and measured independently of the contributions of other factors. Second, there are diminishing marginal returns to individual inputs, including capital, so that a greater quantity of capital leads to a lower marginal product of additional capital. Third, the return on capital is determined by the marginal productivity of aggregate capital as well as the relative scarcity of capital.[39]

These claims remain widely accepted in economics today, but they are just claims and, as such, far from self-evident.[40] Indeed, it is precisely for this reason that there has been scope in the history of economic thought for alternative interpretations of capital's role and rewards.[41] The question this observation begs is whether Piketty thinks of capital differently from the neoclassical approach. In a book that seeks to challenge the conventional wisdom on the relationships that link economic growth, the capital intensity of the economy and the return to capital, we might expect to find an extensive conceptual discussion that offers new ways of thinking about them. Yet, when we go looking for a theoretical discussion of capital in Piketty's book, the pickings are surprisingly slim.

Insofar as the economic role of capital is concerned, Piketty is adamant that we cannot understand it if we conceptualize it merely as a factor of production:

> Some definitions of "capital" hold that the term should apply only to those components of wealth directly employed in the production process. For instance, gold might be counted as part of wealth but not of capital, because gold is said to be useful only as a store of value. Once again, this limitation strikes me as neither desirable nor practical (because gold can be a factor of production, not only in the manufacture of jewelry but also in electronics and nanotechnology). Capital in all its forms has always played a dual role, as both a store of value and a factor of production. I therefore decided that it was simpler not to impose a rigid distinction between wealth and capital.[42]

Piketty clearly suggests the need for an alternative theory of capital that goes beyond the neoclassical theory of production to take account of capital's "dual role". Yet, he offers no guidance on how we might understand how capital functions in its financial role as a store of value and, specifically, on how it might interact with capital's productive role in the process of economic development. Moreover, even allowing for his claim that capital's productive role should not be everything in a theory of capital, it seems unreasonable to say nothing further on the matter. Yet, in an entire chapter devoted to "Growth: Illusions and Realities", Piketty speaks of technology, innovation and knowledge diffusion when he discusses the dynamics that foster economic growth and makes no mention at all of capital. Thus, although *Capital* clearly suggests the importance of an alternative theory of capital's economic role, it does not offer one.

Worse still, when we turn to Piketty's analysis of the rewards to capital, where he has more to say, his analysis hijacks a model from mainstream economics that is based on precisely the limited understanding of capital "directly employed in the productive process" that he criticizes. He evokes alternatives to the "simple economic models" that suggest that "the rate of return on capital should be exactly equal to the 'marginal productivity' of capital".[43] He alludes to a different, more "complex" and "realistic" approach, in which "the rate of return on capital also depends on the relative bargaining power of the various parties involved". But then he disappoints in opting for an analysis of capital's rewards that is remarkably close to a neoclassical line. Thus, he asserts that "the rate of return on capital is determined by the following two forces: technology (what is capital used for?), and second, the abundance of the capital stock (too much capital kills the return on capital)". Once he explains that "technology" means that "it is natural to expect that the marginal productivity of capital decreases as the stock of capital increases", the similarity with the neoclassical theory of capital's rewards becomes clear.[44]

These observations provoke the question of how Piketty's analysis of the rewards to capital could present a challenge to conventional wisdom if it is constructed on similar conceptual foundations. In fact, the controversy his book has stimulated stems from his empirical analysis and, specifically, the trends he identifies in capital's share of income, rather than from any theoretical innovation. Consistent with his expansive definition of capital, Piketty measures its income in broad terms to include "the various amounts of income from capital included in national accounts, regardless of legal classification (rent, profits, dividends, interest, royalties, etc., excluding interest on public debt and before taxes)".[45] On this basis, he observes that capital's net share of income has risen in the last several decades in developed economies, even as their capital–income ratios have increased.[46]

Piketty explains this empirical regularity not by challenging the neoclassical principle of a diminishing marginal productivity of capital but by suggesting that, in practice, it may diminish more slowly than most neoclassical economists believe: "The interesting question is therefore not whether the marginal productivity of capital decreases when the stock of capital increases (this is obvious) but rather how fast it decreases."[47] To answer this question, he suggests, we need to look to the character of the "production function" ("a mathematical formula reflecting the technological possibilities that exist in a given society") and, specifically, the elasticity of substitution that it specifies between capital and labour.[48] In this regard, Piketty takes issue with economists' reliance on the Cobb–Douglas production function, which assumes the elasticity of substitution to be exactly equal to one, due to its "inadequacy" for "studying evolutions over the very long run". Piketty suggests that "over a very long period of time, the elasticity of substitution between capital and labor seems to have been greater than one".[49]

In making this claim, Piketty has stirred up an empirical debate on the elasticity of substitution between capital and labour. However, that should not distract from the fact that his analysis of capital's rewards is based on a theory of distribution that is indistinguishable from the mainstream one. This suggests a major problem of conceptual incoherence at the heart of Piketty's analysis. He defines capital differently, and much more broadly, than neoclassical economists do, and yet he still uses the same theory of distribution, based on a much narrower understanding of capital, that they employ. Put differently, he extends the neoclassical parables of capital theory from their relatively narrow application to the physical assets used in production to the whole panoply of assets that he deems to constitute capital.

Unsurprisingly, some neoclassical economists have expressed discomfort with his doing so. They have voiced particular concern about his inclusion of housing on the grounds that it produces returns in a way that is quite different from capital used in the production of other goods and services. Thus, Matthew Rognlie argues that the recent rise in capital income from housing cannot be explained by the inherent productivity of the underlying physical assets; it is instead driven "in large part by artificial scarcity through land use regulation" and, one might add, an expanded global mortgage market.[50]

Much the same concern can be raised about Piketty's reliance on stock prices to estimate the market valuations of corporate assets. Doing so, he acknowledges, implies a rather different concept of corporate capital than the physical assets on which mainstream economists focus:

> The stock market value of a company often depends on its reputation and trademarks, its information systems and modes of organization, its investments, whether material or immaterial, for the purpose of making its products and services more visible and attractive, and so on. All of this is reflected in the price of common stock and other corporate financial assets and therefore in national wealth.[51]

Even if Piketty were right, that stock market capitalizations incorporate different components of corporate capital in such a rational and systematic fashion, he does not explain why the same parables that economists apply to thinking about physical capital might be expected to apply to "reputation" and "modes of organization".[52]

Yet, whatever the conceptual inconsistencies of Piketty's analysis, it does not necessarily follow that we should return to the mainstream vision of capital, since it confronts significant problems of its own. The conventional view may be clear on the importance of capital in its productive role but it suffers from weaknesses when incorporating capital into a theory of growth. It does so, as we have seen, based on a series of postulates about the way in which capital operates as a factor of production. These were derived, in the first instance, by classical economists from their observations about land and were extended much later, without further empirical scrutiny, to the machines and structures that neoclassical economists define as capital.[53]

Tellingly, when neoclassical economists at the forefront of this logical extension sought real-life examples to motivate their claims, they typically appealed to fables of orchards and the fruits of a bounteous nature rather than empirical evidence of capital's role in production. Little wonder, then, that Irving Fisher found himself accused of designing a theory in which "income streams, like mountain brooks, gush spontaneously from nature's hillsides".[54] He fought back in emphasizing that "the technique of production" was a central element in his analysis.[55] Still, he did not believe that a theory of capital's rewards needed "to launch itself upon a lengthy discussion of the productive process, division of labour, utilization of land, capital, and scientific management".[56]

Neoclassical economists have maintained much the same stance ever since, insisting their claims about capital are "natural" or "evident" without offering much evidence for them. As we have seen, Piketty adopts these unfortunate habits too, although he occasionally hints at the lack of empirical support for the neoclassical theory of capital. He notes, for example, that it is hard to know whether the rate of return on capital is higher or lower than the marginal productivity of capital "since this quantity is not always precisely measurable".[57]

Even more problematic than concerns about the empirical basis for claims of a diminishing marginal productivity of capital is the fact that economists often depend for their plausibility on technology being stable. Clearly there are no grounds for applying that assumption, or a theory of distribution that depends on it, to a long-run analysis. Yet, in the absence of a more suitable alternative, that is precisely what neoclassical economists do. As Robert Solow explained in a survey article on "The Neoclassical Theory of Growth and Distribution":

> Very little has been said in this survey about income distribution (in other words, about the determination of factor prices). That is because there is no special connection between the neoclassical model of growth and the determination of factor prices. The usual practice is to appeal to the same view of factor pricing that characterizes static neoclassical equilibrium theory.[58]

The illegitimacy of applying a static theory of distribution to a dynamic setting is obvious, but it is all the more flagrant given what neoclassical economists believe they have discovered over the last fifty years about the contributions of different factors of production to economic growth. Empirical research on growth is dominated by an approach that "decomposes" aggregate output into the contributions of different factors based on the Solow–Swan model of economic growth. In accounting for the rising labour productivity that has characterized the US and other advanced economies over the last two centuries, studies of growth accounting have shown that capital, as neoclassical economists define and measure it, does not take us far. The implication is that "something else" accounts for rising labour productivity: an unexplained residual that is usually labelled "total factor productivity" (TFP).

Table 8.1. Accounting for labour productivity growth,
US private domestic economy, 1800–1989 (in per cent per year).
(*Source:* Abramovitz and David (2000).[59])

	Output per man hour	Capital stock per man hour	Total factor productivity
1800–1855	0.39	0.19	0.20
1855–1890	1.06	0.69	0.37
1890–1927	2.00	0.51	1.49
1929–1966	2.52	0.43	2.09
1966–1989	1.23	0.57	0.66

The importance of this unexplained residual can be seen in the historical data shown in Table 8.1 for the US: it has been significant, relative to the measured contribution of capital, since the beginning of the nineteenth century. Moreover, its importance increased from the middle of the nineteenth century and, although capital's measured contribution also increased, from the late nineteenth century the increase of TFP was much greater. Indeed, TFP exceeded capital's measured contribution rather dramatically until the last quarter of the twentieth century, when TFP's significance diminished but continued to rival the estimated contribution of capital in accounting for growth.

However, even to speak of TFP in these terms, although descriptively efficient, is problematic given its lack of conceptual meaning. All it represents, as the term "residual" suggests, is what is left over after accounting for growth in terms of measured inputs whose productive contribution economists think they do understand. Although TFP is often interpreted as "technology", it is more properly seen, as Moses Abramovitz candidly admitted, as a measure of economists' ignorance about the sources of economic growth.[60]

The importance and persistence of this unexplained residual has led some economists to devise empirical strategies to eliminate it, many of which involve "improvements" in the measurement of capital.[61] Estimates of TFP are so sensitive to the way capital is measured, and the assumptions behind that measurement are so debatable, that there are limitless opportunities for these efforts.[62] Yet, the shadow that the residual casts over growth accounting suggests another interpretation, which is arguably more obvious but certainly more devastating: that the neoclassical theory of growth is not a terribly useful basis for understanding the productive role of capital in the economy.

Even some adepts of growth accounting have admitted as much, with Abramovitz proving especially critical in this regard. His initial concern with the residual, expressed more than half a century ago, was that "the Residual in its early primitive form was a cover for many sources of growth besides technological advance", so that "the Residual was really a grab-bag" for which growth theorists had no explanation. Decades later his concerns had gone much deeper, right to the core of growth theory's conceptualization of economic growth and, specifically, to "the notion that the several proximate sources of growth that it identifies operate independently of one another".[63] What that perspective ignores, Abramovitz argued, was the importance for economic growth of "the interdependence of what we have come to call the 'proximate sources' of growth".[64] Its continued influence meant that: "We know all too little about the interactions among our infamous 'proximate causes'. They constitute an area of ignorance even larger than the old primitive Residual."[65]

If the disappointments of growth accounting point to the limits of neoclassical growth theory for understanding capital's economic role, they also suggest serious concerns about a neoclassical theory of distribution applied to the long run. After all, if we cannot account for economic growth in terms of the productive contributions of capital and labour, we ought not to assume that the rewards of economic progress should be absorbed by payments to them. Yet, that is what neoclassical economists instinctively do when they analyse the distribution of economic rewards and, indeed, what Piketty does as well. At least to the extent that the "unexplained residual" reflects the deliberate efforts of some specific type or group of economic actors, we risk distributing the fruits of economic progress in ways that do not compensate those responsible for generating them. Indeed, as I argue below, that is exactly what has happened in the US corporate sector in recent decades.

CONFRONTING THE HISTORY OF US CAPITAL

The substantial shortcomings of the way in which both Piketty and neoclassical economists conceptualize the economics of capital can be seen as an invitation to develop an alternative vision of capital's role and rewards. The history of economic thought is an important source of inspiration for such alternatives, but economists' debates on capital theory can only take us so far, given their limited contact with the empirical characteristics of capitalist economies.[66] That problem can only be overcome to the extent that new thinking about capital's role and rewards is systematically grounded in what we know about capital from economic, business and financial history.

In this regard, the history of capital in the US offers inspiration for new ways of thinking about the role and rewards of capital. Even a limited review of several important features of the history of US capitalism, although it makes no claims to completeness, suggests a number of insights that are ignored or misunderstood in existing approaches to capital. Taken together, they underline the importance of an analysis of capital's role and rewards in the historical context of the evolving social organization of US capitalism.

The productive organization of US capital

The conventional approach to thinking about the role of capital in economics, as we have seen, is to emphasize its importance for the production of goods and services. From a neoclassical perspective, once the level of investment and, therefore, the capital intensity of an economy is established, its economic implications are determined by structural relationships that obtain between the aggregate amount of capital invested in the economy and its productivity. Thus, capitalists may differ in their propensity to invest, but they are bound by similar structural constraints insofar as the economic outcomes of their investments are concerned.

However, the history of US capitalism shows that the productive role of capital is determined not only by the amount of capital invested but also by how that capital is used. Moreover, since the utilization of capital is shaped by the organization of the process through which goods and services are produced, an analysis of the productivity of capital requires an understanding of the characteristics of that organization. And, because organizational characteristics vary across economic units as well as over time, we observe significant heterogeneity in the productivity with which they employed capital. Thus, the challenge of understanding the productive role of capital goes well beyond measuring the aggregate quantity of capital employed in a specific economy, sector or industry to include an analysis of how capital is used in different organizational contexts.

In the decades after the American Revolution, the importance of organization to the productivity of US capitalism was not immediately apparent, given the structure of the new republic's economy. Agriculture remained overwhelmingly dominant at the time, employing three-quarters of the nation's workforce in 1800, with trade representing a much less important, but still significant, sector.[67] Traditional economic units characterized the US economy at the time, with family farms dominating the organization of agricultural production, and sole proprietorships and partnerships elsewhere. These units expanded their output largely by employing more inputs, essentially labour, since capital requirements were modest in agricultural and mercantile activities in the early nineteenth century.[68]

The larger slave plantations in the South represented the main exception to these patterns given the relatively large scale of their workforce and invested capital. As Stanley Engerman noted, these plantations "had many of the characteristics of modern industrial firms, being described as 'a factory in the field'". Crucial to their profitability was the ability to use their capital productively; since a large proportion of that capital was represented by slaves themselves. The prices of slaves were determined by expectations of the output they could produce, merely investing in capital was no guarantee of generating profits from it.[69] Slave masters had to devise methods of making their slaves as productive as possible. In part, they accomplished this feat, as several recent books remind us, by devising unusually cruel forms of physical and psychological exploitation.[70] Yet, planters and their overseers also focused attention on the division and coordination of slaves' work to make their coercion as productive as possible.[71]

Until the middle of the nineteenth century, besides slave plantations, the only other economic units of any significant scale were to be found in the country's rapidly developing industrial sector. Although industry was of negligible importance in the early decades of the American republic, an indigenous process of industrialization got underway in the US from the 1810s. By 1860 the US industrial sector had grown to a substantial size, led by the expansion of textiles and footwear. However, until the Civil War, it was dominated by small-scale enterprises, characterized by limited workforces and capital requirements, with only a few exceptions in the textile industry.[72]

Productivity growth in early US industry was much less impressive than what was to come, but it was significant relative to historical alternatives. That provokes the question of how it was achieved, especially since capital requirements were not that high at the time. In this regard, Kenneth Sokoloff's microeconomic studies of productivity growth during early US industrialization offer some provocative results. Using data at the industry level, he claims that investment in fixed capital cannot account for most of the productivity gains recorded during this period. The capital invested in circulating or working capital was more important, he suggests, than that invested in equipment and structures. Yet, even allowing for working as well as fixed capital, most of the advance in labour productivity recorded in US manufacturing between 1820 and 1860 cannot be attributed to capital formation and ends up being classified as TFP. Having considered several possible explanations for this residual, Sokoloff suggests that it is explained by the changes in the organization and intensification of work that are emphasized in enterprise and industry studies of early industrialization.[73]

It is precisely that logic that is at the heart of Alfred D. Chandler's account of the organizational "revolution" that occurred in the US economy with the rise of big business. Although Chandler acknowledges that the organizational challenges that confronted plantations and early industrial companies seemed significant in the first half of the nineteenth century, he emphasizes just how limited they were compared with those associated with the "modern business enterprises" that emerged in the US economy from the 1850s.[74] These enterprises made their initial appearance not in the industrial sector but in transportation and communication, especially in the railroad sector. They emerged there, as Chandler explains, as a consequence of the unprecedented scale of railroads' capital requirements and the complexity of their production process.

In the presence of large capital commitments, railroad enterprises faced high fixed costs and needed to generate a large volume of traffic to turn a profit; however, handling that volume created major challenges, given the growing complexity of the tasks involved and the importance of coordinating them. The solution, as Chandler explains it, was the emergence of "managerial organisations" to divide and integrate the work of planning and coordinating the railroad business. The administrative tasks involved were so numerous, varied and complex that they were increasingly handled by men with special skills, who were hired and trained by the railroad. Moreover, the growing challenges of coordinating trains and the flow of rail traffic encouraged growing attention to lines of responsibility, communication and authority within railroad companies. Thus, it was railroad enterprises that were pioneers in the emergence of what Chandler describes as "modern management" in the US.[75]

Railroad managers focused growing attention on the organization of work within railroad enterprises, but they increasingly faced the problem of dealing with industrial organization too. The characteristics of railroads' investment meant that they all faced a similar imperative of increasing volume. Increasingly, these incentives led to price wars among carriers as they struggled to generate the business they needed to cover their fixed costs. Initially, US railroad enterprises attempted to limit the problem of ruinous competition through price agreements with their competitors; however, these proved to be of only limited efficacy, and rate wars continued to weigh heavily on railroads' profitability. A new solution to the challenge of controlling competition emerged with massive consolidation or "system-building", which extended throughout the railroad industry from the mid 1880s.[76] Soon the most aggressive system builders had grown to a gargantuan scale to dominate the US railroad industry.[77]

In other sectors of the US economy, the pressures for the emergence of managerial organization depended on the extent of capital investments required.

Thus, it was in the rapidly evolving US industrial sector in the decades after the Civil War that big business became prominent. That was because the transition to mass production involved increasing capital requirements, associated with growing vertical integration in the most rapidly developing industries of the time. It was there that managerial organization developed, giving rise to "modern industrial enterprises" that, like railroad enterprises, were concerned with utilizing the capital at their disposal as effectively as possible through a complex division and organization of work.

In emphasizing the significance of Chandler's insights into the organizational revolution in US capitalism, economic historian Alexander Field characterizes the modern business enterprise as a "capital-saving" innovation. As he explains, "the introduction and diffusion of what Alfred Chandler called modern business enterprise had a profound capital-saving impact on the American economy ... principally via increased speed of production and inventory turnover, which spread costs of holding capital over a larger volume of output".[78] Thus, far from taking capital intensity as a technological "given", enterprises could manage the relationship between capital and output to the extent that they could build organizations that were capable of planning and using capital more effectively.

US entrepreneurs and managers in capital-intensive activities understood this logic very well, as Andrew Carnegie's legendary "hard-driving" policies suggest. The results were evident in the performance of the blast furnaces, which year after year showed a dramatic increase in their productivity.[79] Hard-driving took its toll on the Carnegie Company's workforce but it also succeeded in wringing the maximum output from its capital.

Still, making profits in the US steel industry depended not just on driving machines and men as hard as possible to produce more output but also on producing products that could be sold at favourable prices. As in the railroad sector, ruinous competition became a problem as increasing capital investments induced steel enterprises to engage in price wars to generate enough volume to cover their fixed costs. The Carnegie Company proved effective at breaking out of this spiral by diversifying out of steel rails, where price competition was particularly intense, through product and process innovation that allowed it to move into structural steel. It was not, however, until the giant consolidation of the US steel industry, which gave rise to United States Steel, that price competition was brought under effective control in the US steel industry.[80]

We see a similar "capital-saving" logic at work in other US capital-intensive industries in which modern business enterprise emerged in the way that Chandler describes.[81] Indeed, the importance that large US industrial enterprises attached to using their capital intensively, rather than to capital intensity as such, was made very explicit at DuPont in the early 1910s. There, F. Donaldson Brown developed a simple formula that isolated the determinants of a business's return on capital and became the basis of a management tool that diffused throughout the US business sector. The "DuPont formula" (Return on Investment = (Profit/Sales) × (Sales/Assets)) made it clear that a company's return on investment (ROI) is driven by the efficiency with which a company uses its assets just as much as the profitability of its sales. The ratio used to measure a firm's efficiency in using its assets, usually described as "asset turnover", is an inversion of the capital–output ratio that economists use to measure capital intensity.

The managerial implications of the inversion were clear: the goal of capitalist enterprise was not just to invest in capital but to squeeze every possible dollar of profit out of it. Achieving this objective was far from straightforward, however, since it depended on building and running an organization that was capable of using capital as intensively as possible. Thus, when we measure asset turnover in, for example, the electrical equipment and automobile industries, we observe important and persistent differences across companies in how effective they were in using their capital.[82]

Table 8.2. "Hard-driving" capital in the US retail industry.
(Source: Walmart and Target Annual Reports (2010).)

In billions of dollars, unless specified, 2010	Walmart	Target
Sales	405.0	67.4
Total asset turnover	2.38	1.54
Fixed asset turnover		
Square footage of stores (millions)	603	234
$ of sales per square foot	672	288
Inventory turnover	12.2	8.9

The historical examples that I have offered are meant to be suggestive of the importance of organization in determining the productive role of capital. The fact that I have taken some of the most provocative ones from the industrial sector should not imply that the logic they illustrate is confined to that sector. On the contrary, it has just as much resonance for the trade, wholesale and retail industry that has become an exemplar of the post-industrial economy in the US and elsewhere. Indeed, what distinguishes Walmart, the industry giant in the US, is its overwhelming commitment to "hard-driving" its capital compared with its competitors. As a result, as Table 8.2 shows, Walmart significantly outperforms its closest US competitor, Target, in the utilization of both its fixed and working capital. If there is some "technological" logic that determines the relationship between the capital invested in the retail industry and the returns it ought to deliver, then Walmart spends an inordinate amount of time in studiously neglecting it.

There is certainly room for debate about the precise characteristics of the division and coordination of work that are important in determining the productivity of capital. Empirical analyses of slave plantations and early industrial companies focus on the organization of work in the field or the factory given the limited depth of their managerial hierarchies. In contrast, Chandler's work says nothing at all about the US factory floor or its Fordist principles, although other scholars have offered a corrective to his exclusive focus on managerial organization. Questions have been asked, too, about the continued relevance of the managerial organization that Chandler celebrated, given the dramatic changes in the way US corporations divide and coordinate work internally and with respect to subcontractors both in the US and internationally. Still, my concern here is not so much with the particular characteristics of business organization that might prove more or less effective at any moment in time but rather the general importance of organization in determining the efficiency with which capital is used.

There has been a temptation to claim that the importance of complex business organization in the US has receded in recent years with the diminution of former corporate giants. Even sober-minded scholars have heralded the demise of the corporation and the resurgence of the market in the US business sector.[83] However, recognition of the continued concentration of crucial economic variables, not least capital formation itself, shows just how misleading such claims can be. As a recent paper puts it: "This high concentration at the top of the distribution of capital spenders presents a challenge to the existing literature on corporate investment."[84] In fact, its observation that "the investment behaviour of the very largest corporations is distinct and important" represents a much broader challenge than the paper allows, since it confronts most economic analyses of the productive role of capital for their failure to grapple with complex organizations.

In response, economists must acknowledge that enterprises are not necessarily bound by homogeneous structural constraints insofar as the outcomes of their investments are concerned. As a result, it is not sufficient to look at the amount of investment they make to understand the productivity with which they employ it. Relatedly, the economic implications of variations in capital intensity over time, as measured by the standard K/Y ratio, cannot be fully understood from a macroeconomic level. A decline in measured capital intensity might signal a diminished role for capital in the production of goods and services, but it could just as easily occur because capital is being used more intensively. Indeed, that is precisely what we observe in certain key phases of the expansion of important industries in the US, such as the growth of the automobile industry during the 1920s.

The fallacy of productive factors and their rewards

There are a great number of empirical questions that remain to be answered about the historical role of capital in the production of goods and services. Yet, even the limited observations I have made based on the history of capital in US capitalism suggest significant problems with the standard way that many economists understand it. For them, the economic analysis of capital is limited to the determinants of its investment; what happens thereafter, as one textbook puts it, is not an economic question but "a purely technological question about the production function". What I have suggested instead is that the question is very much about economics and, specifically, about the way economic units organize themselves to generate a return on the investments they make. The economics of capital, therefore, must be studied in organizational or relational terms as much as in technical ones.[85]

The claim that the productive role of capital can be understood only in the context of the organizations that use it differs from the dominant view of capital as a "factor of production" since it implies that machines and structures cannot be thought of as inherently productive or unproductive. The Carnegie Company's blast furnaces were more productive than other steel companies' blast furnaces because the Carnegie Company had the organizational capacity to use them more intensively than its competitors. Replicating that capacity was much more difficult for a competitor than merely buying a similar machine.

A vision of economic progress based on factors of production may have made sense in an economy in which the distinct contributions of landowners, workers and capitalists seemed paramount. However, the emergence of large and complex organizations as central players in the most dynamic sectors of the economy gave some economists pause about its continued relevance. Certainly Alfred Marshall recognized the problem and even tried to deal with it by proposing a new factor of production called "organization". However, in doing so, he sought to bolster the conventional vision of the economic process by maintaining the illusion that capital's productive contribution could be separated from that of organization. The more recent emphasis on the "interdependence" of factors of production by Moses Abramovitz and other economists might seem to suggest an improvement in this regard. However, they tend to characterize such interdependence in a highly schematic way that abstracts from the fact that it is undertaken, to a large extent, by organizations established and operated precisely for the purpose of bringing capital together with other "factors of production" to make them work interdependently.

Fortunately, there have been economists interested in studying the implications of the rising importance of organization in capitalism. When Schumpeter launched his original attack on neoclassical economics for its neglect of innovation, he characterized the process that he deemed to be the "central fact of economic life" as dependent on the individual initiative and effort of the entrepreneur. However, his increasing attention to the dynamics of business and economic history led him to acknowledge that:

> the entrepreneurial function need not be embodied in a physical person and in particular in a single physical person … the entrepreneurial function may be and often is filled co-operatively. With the development of the largest-scale corporations this has evidently become of major importance: aptitudes that no single individual combines can thus be built into a corporate personality.[86]

Thus, "the large-scale establishment or unit of control" played a central role in bringing about "economic progress", and Schumpeter castigated neoclassical economists for casting it as an aberration in a well-functioning market economy. To the contrary, he argued, "it had come to be the most powerful engine of that progress and in particular of the long-run expansion of total output".[87] Capital, from his point of view, was "a necessary complement of entrepreneurial action" but fundamentally dependent for its productivity on the organizations that employed it.

Notwithstanding the originality of Schumpeter's insights, there is much research that remains to be done to understand how capital's role in the production of goods and services depends on the characteristics of the organizations that invest and use it.[88] Nevertheless, it is already clear that such a conceptualization of capital's role has crucial implications for understanding the economic origins of profit. Given the time and uncertainty involved in building complex organizations, there is no reason to expect that profits would come quickly or easily. But, once they appeared, they might endure for some time, given the challenges for competitors of replicating organizational capabilities. What this means for successful enterprises is that it is impossible to make a clear distinction between profits that accrue from their productive use of resources and those that stem from their market power, since they are so inextricably bound together.[89] It also implies that enterprises that have created highly productive organizations in the past may continue to enjoy profits even as their organizational capacities diminish.

Such a world is a far cry from the neoclassical ideal in which corporate organizations make only transitory profits. However, it seems much closer to the historical experience of an advanced economy such as the US, in which large and persistent corporate profits have long been a reality. Neoclassical economists have a hard time explaining how that came to be the case, and Piketty too lacks a theory of capital that could account for high and sustained profits in the corporate sector. He implicitly acknowledges such a limitation towards the end of his book when he says that he knows "virtually nothing" about exactly how Bill Gates became rich. He appeals to the standard economic explanation in suggesting that Bill Gates "profited from a virtual monopoly of operating systems (as have many other high-tech entrepreneurs in industries ranging from telecommunications to Facebook)", although that is like saying Einstein owed his success to his monopoly on the theory of relativity. However, Piketty also hints at something more analytically ambitious when he says: "I believe that Gates's contributions depended on the work of thousands of engineers and scientists doing basic research in electronics and computer science, without whom none of his innovations would have been possible." Had that statement come at the beginning of his book, it might have provided the basis for a rethinking of the productive role of capital, but on page 445 it is little more than a throwaway comment.

That corporations integrate capital in complex organizational processes to produce goods and services has implications not only for an economic analysis of the source of profits but also for their distribution. The neoclassical theory of distribution implies that actors receive economic rewards commensurate with their productive contributions. The mechanisms for establishing such a clear link between contribution and reward depend on strict technological conditions that cannot be expected to hold in an economy in which complex organizations predominate. And the even more fundamental assumption on which the neoclassical theory of distribution relies – that we can isolate capital's contribution to the production of goods and services – seems quite implausible. If capital depends for its productivity on the organization that uses it, then its productive contribution is inextricably bound up with it.

In their empirical analyses of distribution, many economists are perfectly willing to admit the problem of distinguishing between different types of productive contributions in the case of sole proprietorships and partnerships. Piketty follows their lead in this regard in acknowledging that the men and women who run these businesses are often both "owner" and "operator", so the payments they receive conflate rewards to labour and capital. However, he draws a sharp contrast, as many economists do, with "most private economic activity [which] today is organized around corporations or, more generally, joint-stock companies". On the books of these companies, Piketty suggests, "there is a clear distinction between remuneration of labor (wages, salaries, bonuses, and other payments to employees, including managers, who contribute labor to the company's activities) and remuneration of capital (dividends, interest, profits reinvested to increase the value of the firm's capital, etc.)".[90] In fact, whatever the accounting clarity associated with these income streams, nothing could be further from the truth insofar as their economic character is concerned. Even at the level of a particular corporate enterprise it is impossible to make any such "clear distinction", and it is fantastical to imagine it can be done at the level of the corporate economy. Indeed, that is precisely the gist of Piketty's musing about Gates's dependence on his "thousands of engineers and scientists", but the insight does not penetrate his analysis of capital's rewards in corporate organizations.

Precisely because of the complex economic relationship between effort and reward in such organizations, there is room for considerable bargaining about who gets what. That bargaining can take place at the level of the economy, the sector or industry as well as at the level of the enterprise itself and, as we know from research on "varieties of capitalism", it rests on institutional foundations that may differ across countries and change over time. Certainly, in the history of the US corporate economy bargaining over the fruits of corporate success has worked itself out in drastically different ways over time.

One way in which the organizational foundations of corporate success have been acknowledged in leading US corporations in the past is through the retention and reinvestment of their profits. In this way, the average employee, just as much as executives and shareholders, can derive future benefits from corporate success. However, that mechanism has broken down in recent decades, as US corporations have paid out more and more of their profits through dividend payouts and stock repurchases.[91]

That pattern developed through an unholy alliance of corporate executives and financial interests. Until the 1980s, the rewards that US corporate executives received for their efforts were tied closely to the fortunes of the organizations they managed and the other people who worked for them. In recent years, however, these links have been broken, as suggested by the dramatic increase in top managers' rewards, relative to those of production workers, in the US corporate economy.[92] Top managers of US corporations have reaped extravagant rewards in the form of bonuses and stock-based compensation largely for their cooperation in diverting the fruits of organizational success to shareholders.[93]

Interestingly, Piketty places a great deal of emphasis on the rise of the "super-manager" in his analysis of growing inequality in the US in the late twentieth century. Moreover, in a section called "The Illusion of Marginal Productivity" he rails against economists who justify these managers' outsized pay packages in terms of the standard neoclassical theory of distribution. Noting that "the vast majority of top earners are senior managers of large firms", he emphasizes that the notion of individual marginal productivity is impossible to define in such settings and "becomes something close to a pure ideological construct" to justify higher compensation. Despite his concerns about the illusion of marginal productivity as applied to labour, Piketty never challenges its relevance for thinking about capital's role and rewards. And, oddly enough, he makes no attempt to link "the takeoff of the super-managers" to the dynamics of capital in US capitalism.[94]

The financial organization of capital

To understand how these changes came about, an analysis of the historical distinctiveness and significance of recent trends towards "financialization" in the US economy is required. In analytical terms, that means we need to grapple with a historical reality in which capital is financial as well as productive. As we have seen, Piketty emphasizes that capital has such a dual identity, but, unfortunately, he does not propose an analysis of the financial, any more than the productive, dynamics of capital.[95]

There are other scholars who have underlined the importance of capital's dual role; these include Rudolf Hilferding and Hyman Minsky, who look at capital from an economic perspective, and Fernand Braudel and Giovanni Arrighi, who approach it from a historical one. These scholars conceive of the interaction between capital's financial and productive dynamics in distinct ways, but the general lesson we learn from their work is that the character of their interaction varies a great deal over time. Financial capital may facilitate the formation and utilization of productive capital, it may develop and profit from it, and it may feed upon it and even undermine it. What that implies is a need to study capital's financial dynamics in their own right and not just as ancillary to capital's productive role in the economy.

The financial dynamics of capital in the US economy go far beyond their relationship to the US corporate sector but, given the limited scope of this chapter, I will focus my remarks on the financialization of US corporations. The corporate form, by its very nature, creates the potential for financial and productive capital to be more autonomous of each other than is the case for other legal forms such as the sole proprietorship or the partnership. However, whether that potential is realized depends on the dynamics of the corporate, as well as the financial, sector.

In the history of the US, financial and productive capital began to develop some independence from each other through the separation of shareholding and control within the corporate sector as liquid markets for corporate stocks and bonds emerged in the financial sector. These developments did not occur spontaneously with the emergence of the corporate form as a legal option in the US. Instead, they followed the rise of big business, manifesting themselves initially in the railroad sector before spreading to the industrial sector, and even then taking decades to unfold. By the end of the nineteenth century, we can begin to speak of a separation of ownership and control in the US railroad corporation, although it was far from complete, and liquid markets for their securities. For industrial corporations, in contrast, it was not until the decade after the First World War that we observe the development of broad and deep markets for their stocks and bonds. A separation of ownership and control occurred much later than it did for US railroads, attracting a great deal of attention only from the 1920s, although it was far from definitive even then.[96]

As these developments occurred, we can increasingly distinguish between the dynamics of financial and productive capital in the US corporate sector. From the perspective of financial capital, at least from the First World War on, what that largely created was greater scope for financial speculation. Indeed, the trading of corporate stocks and bonds became, along with real estate speculation, the vibrant hub of a "financialized" economy in the 1920s. Yet, even as speculation in corporate securities exploded, it had little impact on the operation of the underlying corporations themselves. On the contrary, the dynamics of productive capital in the US corporate sector enjoyed increasing independence from financial capital as the 1920s unfolded.

Eventually, the speculative bubble burst, and productive capital in the US corporate sector gained even greater autonomy as the 1929 crash, and the onset of the Great Depression, generated significant regulatory restrictions on financial capital that lasted for several decades. It is during this period that we observe growing discomfort with the characterization of corporate managers as servants of financial capital. In 1932, Berle and Means emphasized how the corporate revolution had created centres of economic power on an unprecedented scale and, at the same time, led to an explosion of "the atom" of private property. Thus, they argued, economic power was increasingly concentrated in the hands of managers who were not owners, and property in the corporation was becoming a passive institution. From their perspective, private property no longer offered an adequate justification for the exercise of corporate control or the distribution of corporate profits.[97]

Instead, they claimed, there was a need to go beyond traditional economic and legal theory to develop concepts that were more appropriate to the new reality of the US corporate economy. In this regard, Berle and Means proposed that corporations be made responsible not just for dividends but for a much broader set of "claims of the community", including "fair wages" and "security to employees". To achieve these results, they deemed it necessary that corporate management develop into a "purely neutral technocracy". In the decades that followed, we do observe the development of a powerful "managerialist" ideology for the US corporation. As the editors of *Fortune* put it in 1951, "the manager is becoming a professional in the sense that like all professional men he has a responsibility to society as a whole".[98]

Yet, for all of the influence that US corporate managers exercised at this time, and the autonomy they enjoyed from financial interests, the acquiescence of corporate law to managerial control remained implicit. As Erber put it, "the managers have not succeeded, either through legislation or adjudication, to resolve their ambivalent, contradictory status of power without property". That left the legitimacy of managerial control vulnerable to challenge and, ultimately, to a concerted attack from scholars and pundits who were intent on reviving the philosophy that corporations should be run for the benefit of shareholders.[99]

The opening for that attack came as US corporations confronted major productive challenges beginning in the 1970s, in the face of an intensification of international competition in a wide range of industries. These competitive challenges demanded a response, but as US enterprises struggled with what was going on in the productive sphere, they discovered that the financial ground had shifted under their feet. Specifically, a transformation in how US households saved, as well as a concerted move towards financial deregulation, led to a major intensification of the pressures on US corporations to deliver higher and higher returns on their corporate stocks.

These pressures manifested themselves in a variety of ways, from battles for corporate control to institutional investor activism. Initially, many US corporate managers resisted the logic of "shareholder value", which they perceived as a challenge to their longstanding discretion in the corporate sphere. However, their opposition to shareholder value as the benchmark for corporate performance abated as executive pay packages became more and more dependent on stock compensation. Taken together, these pressures have dramatically remade the relationship between financial and productive capital in the US corporate sector.

The implications of this transformation remain to be fully understood, but the most important lines of inquiry focus on the implications of the "financialization" of the US corporation for the relationship between corporate profits and investments, often described as the profit–investment nexus.[100] Some scholars argue that financialization means that high US corporate profits can no longer be expected to translate into buoyant corporate investment, while others focus on its impact on the types, rather than magnitude, of investments that US corporations make.[101] There has been interest too in financialization as a spur to profit-making schemes by US corporations that require little productive investment at all. In this regard, the growing role of financial activities as a source of profits, even for industrial corporations, has drawn scholarly attention. So too the growing intensity of US corporations' efforts to evade taxes, reflected in their increased use of international tax havens in recent decades, is surely related to the pressures they face for ever-increasing financial returns.[102] Although there is much more to learn, it is already clear that to ignore the dynamics of financial capital is to overlook perhaps the most important trend in the role of capital in US capitalism over the last twenty-five years.

CONCLUSION

Thomas Piketty's *Capital in the Twenty-First Century* reopens fundamental questions about the role and rewards of capital that economists have never resolved. It does so by exploring the history of capital in capitalism and derives much of its credibility from the historical evidence it marshals in defence of its claims. In this chapter, I have sought to evaluate the basis for Piketty's arguments by considering them in light of the history of US capitalism.

I have argued that it is extremely difficult to make economic sense of Piketty's historical analysis of capital in the US in the nineteenth and twentieth centuries. That is only in part due to the distinctive choices he makes, compared with mainstream economists, in defining and measuring capital. Much more problematic, in fact, are the theoretical commitments he shares with them that preclude an understanding of capital's historical role and rewards in the US economy. Based on a discussion of several important features of US economic history, I have argued that such an understanding demands a historical analysis of capital, both productive and financial, in relation to the evolving social organization of capitalism in the US.

Notes for Chapter 8

1. Thomas Piketty, *Capital in the Twenty-First Century* (Cambridge, MA: Harvard University Press, 2014), pp. 128, 150.

2. Piketty, *Capital*, pp. 159–60. He acknowledges that both Britain and France incorporated major slave-based economies in the Caribbean as part of their empires in the late eighteenth century, but suggests that the share of slaves in the total wealth of these economies was much lower than in the US (p. 162).

3. *Ibid.*, p. 165.

4. *Ibid.*, p. 152.

5. *Ibid.*, pp. 150–55.

6. *Ibid.*, p. 46.

7. *Ibid.*

8. *Ibid.*, p. 47.

9. See Chapter 2 of this volume: Harcourt and Tribe, "Capital and Wealth".

10. E. Cannan, "Early History of the Term Capital", *Quarterly Journal of Economics* 35 (1921), p. 480.

11. G. M. Hodgson, "What is Capital? Economists and Sociologists Have Changed Its Meaning: Should It Be Changed Back?", *Cambridge Journal of Economics* 38 (2014), pp. 1063–86.

12. Thorstein Veblen, "Professor Clark's Economics", *Quarterly Journal of Economics* 22 (1908), pp. 147–95.

13. Joseph Schumpeter, *History of Economic Analysis* (Oxford: Oxford University Press, 1954), pp. 322–3.

14. Robert Solow, "Thomas Piketty Is Right: Everything You Need to Know About *Capital in the Twenty-First Century*", *New Republic*, 22 April 2014.

15. Charles Jones, "Pareto and Piketty: The Macroeconomics of Top Income and Wealth Inequality", *Journal of Economic Perspectives* 29 (2015), p. 41.

16. Odran Bonnet, Pierre-Henri Bono, Guillaume Chapelle and Etienne Wasmer, "Does Housing Capital Contribute to Inequality? A Comment on Thomas Piketty's *Capital in the 21st Century*", Sciences Po Economics Discussion Paper, 2014-07 (2014), p. 323.

17. Jones, "Pareto and Piketty", p. 41.

18. *Ibid.*; see also Keith Tribe, "Wealth and Inequality: Thomas Piketty's *Capital in the Twenty-First Century*", *Past & Present* 227 (2015), pp. 257–8.

19. Nicholas Kaldor, "Capital Accumulation and Economic Growth", in *The Theory of Capital*, F. A. Lutz and D. C. Hague (eds) (London: Macmillan, 1961).

20. Jakob Madsen, Vinod Mishra and Russell Smyth, "Is the Output–Capital Ratio Constant in the Very Long Run?", *The Manchester School* 80 (2012), p. 214. In contrast to Piketty, they estimate the capital stock using the perpetual inventory method.

21. Thomas Piketty and Gabriel Zucman, "Capital Is Back: Wealth–Income Ratios in Rich Countries, 1700–2010", Data Appendix (2013), p. 5 (http://piketty.pse.ens.fr/files/PikettyZucman2013Appendix.pdf).

22. 1850, 1860, 1870, 1880, 1890, 1900, 1904, 1912, 1922.

23. Stephen Hoenack, "Historical Censuses and Estimates of Wealth in the United States", in *Measuring the Nation's Wealth, Report to US Congress Joint Economic Committee*, John Kendrick (ed.) (Washington, DC: Joint Economic Committee, 1964), pp. 177–218.

24. André Vanoli, *Une histoire de la comptabilité nationale* (Paris: Éditions La Découverte, 2002), p. 304.

25. See, for example, *Measuring Capital: Measurement of Capital Stocks, Consumption of Fixed Capital and Capital Services* (Paris: OECD, 2001), pp. 43–62.

26. Piketty and Zucman, "Capital is Back", Appendix, pp. 7–10.

27. Piketty, *Capital*, p. 49.

28. *Ibid.*, p. 27.

29. *Ibid.*, p. 149.

30. Indeed, that assumption has implications for his estimates of capital beyond the corporate sector, since, as Piketty and Zucman explain, unlisted shares are valued "on the basis of observed market prices for comparable, publicly traded companies" (Piketty and Zucman, "Capital is Back", p. 1268).

31. Indeed, if one digs deeply enough, Piketty and Zucman offer an estimate of how important the difference is for the US for 2012, with their market valuation of real estate and corporate capital increasing the capital–income ratio by 76 per cent and 36 per cent of national income, respectively (*ibid.*, p. 33).

32. Robert Rowthorn, "A Note on Piketty's *Capital in the Twenty-First Century*", *Cambridge Journal of Economics* 38 (2014), pp. 1275–84.

33. Matthew Rognlie, "Deciphering the Fall and Rise in the Net Capital Share", Brookings Papers on Economic Activity, Conference Draft, 19–20 March 2015.

34. Piketty and Zucman, "Capital is Back", pp. 57, 62–3.

35. For a trenchant critique of similar practices with respect to historical sources and data on US inequality, see Richard Sutch, "The One-Percent across Two Centuries: A Replication of Thomas Piketty's Data on the Distribution of Wealth for the United States", Working Paper, 12 December 2015.

36. Hodgson, "What is Capital?", p. 1081.

37. Raymond Goldsmith, "'Comment' on Robert Gallman, 'The United States Capital Stock in the Nineteenth Century'", in *Long-Term Factors in American Economic Growth*, Stanley Engerman and Robert Gallman (eds) (Chicago, IL: University of Chicago Press, 1986), p. 207.

38. Robert Solow, *Capital Theory and the Rate of Return* (Amsterdam: North Holland, 1963), p. 10.

39. Paul Samuelson, "Parable and Realism in Capital Theory: The Surrogate Production Function", *Review of Economic Studies* 29 (1962), pp. 193–206.

40. As Schumpeter said with respect to the diminishing marginal productivity of capital: "we are asserting a fact and this imposes upon us the duty of factual verification" and "we have no logical right to reply that the challenged proposition is 'obvious'; and we are committing a definite error, if we call it 'evident'" (Schumpeter, *History of Economic Analysis*, p. 1037).

41. See, for example, Avi Cohen and G. C. Harcourt, "Retrospectives: Whatever Happened to the Cambridge Capital Theory Controversies?", *Journal of Economic Perspectives* 17 (2003), pp. 207–10.

42. Piketty, *Capital*, pp. 47–48.

43. *Ibid*, p. 212.

44. *Ibid.*, p. 215.

45. *Ibid.*, pp. 202–3.

46. *Ibid.*, p. 222; Piketty and Zucman, "Capital is Back".

47. Piketty, *Capital*, p. 216.

48. *Ibid.*, p. 216.

49. *Ibid*, pp. 220–1.

50. Matthew Rognlie, "A Note on Piketty and Diminishing Returns to Capital", Working Paper, 15 June 2014, pp. 16–18.

51. Piketty, *Capital*, p. 49.

52. Indeed, much of new growth theory was based on claims of increasing, rather than constant, returns to scale in such domains.

53. Luigi Pasinetti, "Critique of the Neoclassical Theory of Growth and Distribution", *BNL Quarterly Review* 215 (2000), pp. 383–431.

54. H. Seager, "The Impatience Theory of Interest", *American Economic Review* 2 (1912), p. 835.

55. Irving Fisher, "The Impatience Theory of Interest", *American Economic Review* 3 (1913), p. 610.

56. Irving Fisher, *The Theory of Interest* (New York: Macmillan, 1930), p. 473.

57. Piketty, *Capital*, p. 212.

58. Robert Solow, "A Neoclassical Theory of Growth and Distribution", *BNL Quarterly Review* 215 (2000), p. 349.

59. Moses Abramovitz and Paul David, "American Macroeconomic Growth in the Era of Knowledge-Based Progress: The Long-Run Perspective", in *The Cambridge Economic History of the United States, Volume 3: The Twentieth Century*, Stanley Engerman and Robert Gallman (eds) (Cambridge: Cambridge University Press, 2000), pp. 1–92.

60. Moses Abramovitz, "The Search for the Sources of Growth: Areas of Ignorance, Old and New", *Journal of Economic History* 53 (1993), pp. 217–43.

61. It has found expression largely in a debate about whether technological change is "embodied" in capital so that its benefits can be reaped through the investment of capital rather than being "disembodied" and showing up as total factor productivity.

62. Michael C. Burda and Battista Severgnini, "Solow Residuals without Capital Stocks", CEPR Discussion Paper 7990 (2009).

63. Abramovitz, "Search for the Sources of Growth", p. 220.

64. *Ibid.*, p. 236.

65. *Ibid.*, p. 237. The development of new growth theory can be seen as an acknowledgement of the theoretical limitations of old growth theory, even though it has achieved only limited success in overcoming them (Paul Krugman, "The New Growth Fizzle", *New York Times*, 18 August 2013).

66. Cohen and Harcourt, "Retrospectives", p. 209.

67. Robert Margo, "The Labor Force in the Nineteenth Century", in *The Cambridge Economic History of the United States, Volume 2: The Long Nineteenth Century*, Stanley Engerman and Robert Gallman (eds) (Cambridge: Cambridge University Press, 2000), pp. 207–43.

68. Rapid population growth in the US of more than 3 per cent per annum between 1800 and 1855 facilitated an increase in the overall size of the workforce, and there was also an annual increase of 0.48 per cent in manhours per capita over the same period (Abramovitz and David, "American Macroeconomic Growth in the Era of Knowledge-Based Progress", pp. 8, 14).

69. Stanley Engerman, "Slavery and Its Consequences for the South in the Nineteenth Century", in *The Cambridge Economic History of the United States, Volume 2*, Stanley Engerman and Robert Gallman (eds), pp. 329–66.

70. See, for example, Walter Johnson, *River of Dark Dreams: Slavery and Empire in the Cotton Kingdom* (Cambridge, MA: Harvard University Press, 2013) and Edward Baptist, *The Half Has Never Been Told: Slavery and the Making of American Capitalism* (New York: Basic Books, 2014).

71. Engerman, "Slavery", p. 342; Alfred D. Chandler, Jr, *The Visible Hand: The Managerial Revolution in American Business* (Cambridge, MA: Harvard University Press, 1977), p. 65.

72. Naomi Lamoreaux, "Entrepreneurship, Business Organization, and Economic Concentration", in *The Cambridge Economic History of the United States, Volume 2*, Stanley Engerman and Robert Gallman (eds), pp. 403–34.

73. Kenneth Sokoloff, "Productivity Growth in Manufacturing during Early Industrialization: Evidence from the American Northeast, 1820–1860", in Engerman and Gallman (eds), *Long-Term Factors*, pp. 679–729. For a summary and further development of the evidence to which Sokoloff refers, see William Lazonick, *Competitive Advantage on the Shop Floor* (Cambridge, MA: Harvard University Press, 1990).

74. Chandler, *The Visible Hand*, p. 64.

75. *Ibid.*, pp. 81–121.

76. *Ibid.*, Chapter 5, pp. 145ff.

77. By 1893 "the thirty-three railroad corporations with a capitalization of $100 million or more operated 69 per cent of the railroad mileage in the United States" (*ibid.*, p. 167).

78. Alexander Field, "Modern Business Enterprise as a Capital Saving Innovation", *Journal of Economic History* 47 (1987), pp. 473–85.

79. David Nasaw, *Andrew Carnegie* (London: Penguin, 2006), p. 400.

80. Naomi Lamoreaux, *The Great Merger Movement in American Business, 1895–1904* (Cambridge: Cambridge University Press, 1988).

81. For the US electrical equipment industry and the challenge of using working, as much as fixed, capital intensively, see Mary O'Sullivan, "Living with the US Financial System: The Experiences of GE and Westinghouse in the Last Century", *Business History Review* 80(4) (Winter 2006), pp. 621–55.

82. *Ibid.*

83. Richard Langlois, "The Vanishing Hand: The Changing Dynamics of Industrial Capitalism", *Industrial and Corporate Change* 12 (2003), pp. 351–85.

84. Gustavo Grullon, John Hund and James Weston, "Investment Concentration and the Importance of Cash Flow", Working Paper (2014). For similar data on the concentration of R&D spending, see Mark Hirschey, Hilla Skiba and M. Babajide Wintoki, "The Size, Concentration and Evolution of Corporate R&D Spending in U.S. Firms from 1976 to 2010: Evidence and Implications", *Journal of Corporate Finance* 18 (2012), pp. 496–518.

85. Amit Bhadhuri, "On the Significance of Recent Controversies on Capital Theory: A Marxian View", *Economic Journal* 79 (1969), pp. 532–9.

86. Joseph Schumpeter, "Economic Theory and Entrepreneurial History", in *Change and the Entrepreneur*, Research Center in Entrepreneurial History, Harvard University (Cambridge, MA: Harvard University Press, 1949), p. 71.

87. Joseph Schumpeter, *Capitalism, Socialism and Democracy* (New York: Harper, 1975), p. 106.

88. Especially since economists who recognize the importance of economic organization in theories of the firm, even those operating in a Schumpeterian tradition, tend to downplay the role of capital (Mary O'Sullivan, "Finance and Innovation", in *The Oxford Handbook of Innovation*, Jan Fagerberg, David Mowery and Richard Nelson (eds) (Oxford: Oxford University Press, 2005), pp. 240–65; Anthony M. Endres and David A. Harper, "The Kinetics of Capital Formation and Economic Organisation", *Cambridge Journal of Economics* 36 (2012), pp. 963–80.

89. Schumpeter, *Capitalism, Socialism and Democracy*, Chapter 8, pp. 87–106.

90. Piketty, *Capital*, p. 203. In fact, he uses the purportedly clear capital–labour split for the corporate economy as the basis for estimating one for sole proprietorships and partnerships.

91. Mary A. O'Sullivan, *Contests for Corporate Control: Corporate Governance and Economic Performance in the United States and Germany* (Oxford: Oxford University Press, 2000); William Lazonick and Mary A. O'Sullivan, "Maximizing Shareholder Value: A New Ideology for Corporate Governance", *Economy and Society* 29 (2000), pp. 13–35.

92. Carola Frydman and Raven Saks, "Executive Compensation: A New View from a Long-Term Perspective, 1936–2005", *Review of Financial Studies* 23(5) (2010), pp. 2099–138.

93. O'Sullivan, *Contests for Corporate Control*; Lazonick and O'Sullivan, "Maximizing Shareholder Value".

94. Piketty, *Capital*, pp. 330–33.

95. Tribe, "Wealth and Inequality", p. 262–3.

96. On the separation of ownership and control, see Brian Cheffins and Steven Bank, "Is Berle and Means Really a Myth?", *Business History Review* 83 (2009), pp. 443–74; on the development of securities markets, see Mary A. O'Sullivan, *Dividends of Development: Fits and Starts in the History of US Securities Markets, 1866–1922* (Oxford: Oxford University Press, 2016).

97. O'Sullivan, *Contests for Corporate Control*.

98. For a somewhat different interpretation of the same phenomenon, see James Burnham, *The Managerial Revolution: What Is Happening in the World* (New York: Day, 1941).

99. The following discussion is based on O'Sullivan, *Contests for Corporate Control*, and Lazonick and O'Sullivan, "Maximizing Shareholder Value".

100. United Nations Conference on Trade and Development, *Trade and Development Report* (Geneva, 1997).

101. Lazonick and O'Sullivan, "Maximizing Shareholder Value"; Julie Froud, Colin Haslam, Sukhdev Johal and Karel Williams, "Cars after Financialisation: A Case Study in Financial Underperformance, Constraints and Consequences", *Competition and Change* 6 (2002), pp. 13–41; Engelbert Stockhammer, "Shareholder Value Orientation and the Investment–Profit Puzzle", *Journal of Post-Keynesian Economics* 28 (2006), pp. 193–215; Will Milberg, "Shifting Resources and Uses of Profits: Sustaining US Financialization with Global Value Chains", *Economy and Society* 37 (2008), pp. 420–51; Will Milberg and Deborah Winkler, *Outsourcing Economics: Global*

Value Chains in Capitalist Development (Cambridge: Cambridge University Press, 2013); William Lazonick, "The Financialization of the US Corporation: What Has Been Lost, and How It Can Be Regained", *Seattle University Law Review* 36 (2013), pp. 857–909.

102. Gabriel Zucman, "Taxing Across Borders: Tracking Personal Wealth and Corporate Profits", *Journal of Economic Perspectives* 28 (2014), pp. 121–48.

9

DISTRIBUTIONAL POLITICS:
THE SEARCH FOR EQUALITY IN BRITAIN
SINCE THE FIRST WORLD WAR

Jim Tomlinson

In *Capital in the Twenty-First Century*, Thomas Piketty spends relatively little time discussing the politics and policies affecting inequality.[1] However, in a subsequent reflection on the debate his book has produced, he stresses the complexity of these issues and suggests that, in the book, "[he] may have devoted too much attention to progressive capital taxation and too little attention to a number of institutional evolutions that could prove equally important, such as the development of alternative forms of property arrangements and participatory governance".[2] In the spirit of Piketty, this chapter starts from the need to see the complex politics and policy relating to inequality as something that can only be understood historically. The focus is on the attempts to reduce economic and social inequality that have been a key characteristic of social democratic politics in Britain since the First World War.[3] This pursuit has had to take place in circumstances very much not of social democrats' choosing: conditions of war, depressions and enormous changes in economic structure. As Piketty stresses, "there have been many twists and turns and certainly no irrepressible, regular tendency towards a 'natural equilibrium'".[4] The pursuit of this goal rests on complicated ideological foundations, and there is a substantial literature that examines the relevant doctrinal history.[5] Inequality is complex and multidimensional, but this essay is restricted to "vertical" disparities in income and wealth, which have been an important, sometimes pre-eminent, component of that broader concern.

The focus here is on the shifting policy agendas that have accompanied this concern, seeing these shifts as based on interplay between doctrinal views and changing understandings of the forces affecting income and wealth distribution. Like all understandings of modern economic life, these have been grounded in a developing field of statistics: statistics that have both helped to shape and, in turn, been shaped by contemporary political and policy concerns.[6]

This chapter is divided into four sections. First, we discuss "classic social democracy"; this is grounded in the concept of equality articulated by R. H. Tawney, which has dominated our understanding of the period from the First World War down to the 1950s, including the construction of the "classic welfare state" in the 1940s. Second, we look at the challenges to egalitarian optimism that accompanied the post-war settlement, articulated from the late 1950s, which helped to shape the agenda at the height of social democracy's electoral success in the 1960s and early 1970s. Third, we discuss the responses to the crises of the 1970s, the rise of Thatcherism and the step-change towards greater inequality that followed in the 1980s, culminating in the policies of the New Labour period. The final section looks at the current position: "reducing inequality" has become a prominent feature of almost all mainstream rhetoric but the policy agenda that might achieve this goal remains very much open.

CLASSIC SOCIAL DEMOCRACY

In his classic text of 1931, Tawney suggested that there was widespread agreement that measures to reduce inequality were of three types:

> those, in the first place, such as the extension of social services and progressive taxation ... by securing that wealth which would otherwise have been spent by a minority is applied to purposes of common advantage ... those, in the second place, such as trade unions and industrial legislation, which ... soften inequalities of economic power ... those, in the third place, like the development of undertakings carried on as public services, or the co-operative movement, which ... transfer the direction of economic policy from the hands of capitalists and their agents to those of an authority responsible to society.[7]

He saw these measures as together constituting a "strategy of equality" (though he argued that we were not likely to get far with the first two unless the third was achieved).[8] Whether there ever really was a coherent British social democratic "strategy of equality" has subsequently been much disputed – a point that we return to below – but Tawney provides a useful initial typology for analysing the developing policy agenda.

As this quotation from Tawney makes clear, his notion of equality was not narrowly focused on economic distribution. Instead, it embraced the distribution of power; elsewhere in his book, he famously articulated a broader notion of equality as "fellowship".[9] But the concern here is with the narrower issues of income and wealth disparities. In this context, it was the first strand of Tawney's "strategy", social services and taxation, that was most directly relevant to the initial stage of Labour's policy development.

Taking "social services" to embrace all kinds of social welfare expenditure, both income transfers and provision of services in kind, these were indeed central to Labour's policy agenda right from the party's foundation. However, the aim of this provision was not normally articulated directly as the reduction of inequality, but rather the relief of poverty, the provision of a "national minimum" as the key first step in reducing income disparities. As regards social security, the broad trajectory of Labour's agenda was away from advocacy of a highly redistributive tax-funded system to the embrace of a Beveridge-style social insurance scheme with limited vertical (as opposed to life-cycle) redistribution. This system of National Insurance was inaugurated in 1911 but significantly extended in the 1940s. It was based on contributions from employers, employees and the state (contributions were at a flat rate until the 1960s). Such a system does have some impact on vertical distribution, but plainly the underlying ideology of social insurance was to emphasize worker contributions to funding their own benefits: a rejection of the "Santa Claus state".[10] So, the (vertically) redistributive consequences of the radical extension of the system were quite limited.

A similar broad point can be made about the expansion of tax-funded health and education spending. The purpose of these policies was not directly to equalize income but to equalize access to these services. Their impact on income distribution was not focused on at the time, and only later were the redistributive effects of the expansion of services in kind discussed among social democrats (see the next section). The most significant directly redistributive expenditure policy pursued by the Attlee government was food subsidies, but these were severely cut back in the late 1940s because of their cost and "market distorting" effects.[11] Also very important in this period was full employment; this significantly reduced inequalities consequent upon unemployment, which was a prominent feature of the 1930s.

The post-1945 Attlee government inherited a wartime fiscal regime that had raised overall taxation, in particular by lowering the income tax threshold. For the first time, income tax came to be paid by an average working-class wage-earner. This process was aided by the introduction of Pay As You Earn (PAYE) in 1940, which allowed direct deduction from wage packets. In office, the government was able to reduce overall taxation as wartime spending fell. It concentrated on raising the income tax threshold, in the belief that this was crucial for worker incentives, though there was evidence that popular opinion was more focused on indirect taxes. By the time this government left office, the bulk of tax paid by the working class took the form of indirect taxes, especially duties on alcohol and tobacco, along with highly regressive employee National Insurance. However, because these payments were initially flat rate, their contribution to total taxation was quite small (2–3 per cent of GDP, compared with over 6 per cent today). The distributional issues raised by this tax structure were little discussed in official circles.[12]

Wealth inequality was prioritized by many on the Left because of the belief that its distribution was especially unequal, and because that inequality was seen as little related to its owners' productive contribution to society. In particular, attention was focused on inherited wealth; here, Labour thinkers followed the tradition of their Radical Liberal predecessors in giving a great deal of attention to the design of wealth taxes, and especially to Estate Duty, introduced in a temporary form in 1889. (This was renamed Capital Transfer Tax in 1975 and known as Inheritance Tax from 1986.)[13]

The tax on estates (i.e. wealth held at time of death) was the nearest Britain came to a wealth tax. As wealth has never been taxed directly in Britain, the Estate Duty was for a long time the only official source for wealth statistics, but that source was not used to produce official distributional data until 1960.[14] Analysis before that date was all unofficial, and two authoritative authors remarked in 1961 that "despite the various attempts that have been made to discover the facts about the distribution of capital in Britain, the most striking aspect of the subject is the statistical darkness that surrounds it".[15]

In the 1940s there was no attempt to introduce a wealth tax to replace Estate Duty, with its limited redistributive impact. Hugh Dalton, Chancellor from 1945 to 1947, was previously an academic economist with a specialism in inequality and the tax system.[16] In office, he raised the duty, while his successor, Stafford Cripps, introduced a one-off "Special Contribution". This was instead of the Capital Levy that many on the Left advocated as a means of reducing the National Debt, as had happened after the First World War. In addition, although a transfer of economic power as promoted in Tawney's schema flowed from the Attlee government's nationalization programme, any direct impact on wealth ownership was negated by the generous compensation paid to previous owners.

The most distinctively social democratic tax innovation of the Attlee period was the differential taxation of distributed and undistributed profits. The low tax for the latter was intended to encourage corporate investment while discouraging the growth of non-wage incomes, especially in the context of restraints on the growth of wages through an incomes policy.[17] The best analysis of the equalizing effects of the Attlee government's policies suggested that the overall impact was considerable, but the size depended crucially on the distributive impact of government spending on health, education and other government services. This was conceptually much more difficult to deal with even than the effects of taxation and spending on social security.[18] Such analyses were mainly produced by academics, though the first official account came in 1949 (see the next section).

In his landmark "revisionist" text *The Future of Socialism*, Anthony Crosland made the scale of redistribution of income in the early 1950s compared with pre-war conditions a central part of his opposition to the idea that Britain was any longer a "capitalist" country. In his view, the scale of redistribution of income meant that a fundamental change had come about, achieved without the need for the widespread socialization advocated by "orthodox" Labourism.[19] But when he claimed that "further redistribution would make little difference to the standard of living of the masses", this related only to income.[20] He argued that the equality agenda should now focus on wealth alongside "social equality", with the latter to be brought about, for example, by radical reform of the school system. Importantly, Crosland's optimistic view of the redistributive effects of the post-war settlement did *not* assume that benefits in kind were redistributive; indeed, he explicitly repudiated this as both aim and outcome.[21]

The most innovative redistributive ideas produced by Labour in the 1950s linked pensions to broader issues of capital ownership and investment. The proposed system of National Superannuation would have combined higher, earnings-related contributory pensions with investment of the accumulated funds in the stock market. This, therefore, was a highly "socialist" proposal, with echoes of the famous Swedish Rehn–Meidner proposals for employee funds in the 1970s.[22] It was defeated by the mobilization of union members against both its redistributive aspects and the threat it posed to existing private occupational pensions.[23]

CHALLENGES TO EGALITARIAN OPTIMISM

Alongside the often-noted "rediscovery of poverty", from the end of the 1950s there arose challenges to the optimism about the redistributive impact of the post-war welfare state, linked especially to the work of Richard Titmuss. His *Essays on the Welfare State* showed how, alongside the "formal" welfare state, there had emerged an occupational welfare system and a fiscal one underpinned by tax breaks, both much less egalitarian than that "formal" structure.[24] In addition, his book *Income Distribution and Social Change* was a highly detailed critique of the statistical underpinnings of most serious commentary on the post-war distribution of income, based as these were on the data and analysis of the Board of Inland Revenue.[25] The Board had published data based on income tax returns from 1890, but only in the late 1940s did it publish an analysis of trends. It argued in 1948/9 that there had been "a very considerable redistribution in income since pre-war ... most marked in the case of net incomes after tax".[26] Titmuss showed how fragile this conclusion was, especially because of the incomplete coverage of the data, the basis of the aggregation of incomes (especially in the light of the rising number of working married women) and the disregard of wealth. In his view, the distributive consequences of post-war policies had been greatly exaggerated because people had been "mesmerised by the language of The Welfare State".[27] This pessimistic conclusion was derived from a critique of the data used by Crosland for his optimistic assessment of 1956; Crosland had cited work by Dudley Seers deploying the Inland Revenue figures.[28] Subsequent studies suggest there was significant overall income equalization across the war period, but this soon tailed off in the 1950s, with most of the changes down to the mid 1960s concentrated in the top half of the distribution.[29]

The public debate on the distributive impact of the welfare state was the background to the production of the first official data in the field; this was published by the Central Statistical Office (CSO) from 1962 and based on the Family Expenditure Survey (FES). The purpose of the FES was not directly to measure income distribution, but to provide expenditure data for the construction of the Cost of Living Index. Nevertheless, it provided material on those incomes below the tax threshold excluded from the Inland Revenue numbers, though conversely it was poorer at capturing higher incomes.[30]

Most innovative in the CSO analysis of the FES data was the first systematic attempt to value the distributive consequences of "payments in kind" by the welfare state, covering the National Health Service (NHS), state education and smaller items such as free school milk and meals. There were serious problems with this analysis, especially regarding how the value of such services to their recipients might be evaluated, and how the use of such services varied between households.[31] More broadly, this issue of how far health, education and other in-kind or heavily subsidized services should be treated as redistributive was to be much debated, and not only on the Left. It overlapped with the discussion of cash benefits, and how far cash benefits should be means tested or universal, with the latter on the face of it being a less redistributive mechanism. The Labour Party was very hostile towards means testing; this was grounded historically in a disgust at the operation of the inter-war household means test for the dole, which notoriously reduced the benefit of male "heads of household" if their children's incomes exceeded a low threshold. Practically, post-war social democrats had embraced universalism by treating National Insurance as the major basis for social security. They had also argued that universalism, with its connotation of equality of treatment, was in the long run the only way to provide well for the poor. In this view, services provided only for the poor would soon become "poor services", as the better-off, excluded from benefiting, would no longer be willing to pay taxes sufficient to assure adequate provision.[32] The same argument was applied to health, education and other in-kind services.

Debate about the redistributive effects of expenditure on these latter services was partly based on the difficulties of measuring levels of use by different social groups. But, much more broadly, it raised the question of the extent to which the (near) universalism of these services was in practice mostly to the benefit of the middle classes, a theme that understandably exercised many socialists as well as becoming an allegation made by right-wing critics of the welfare state. This argument can be traced back to the 1950s and was taken up by a number of analysts, including Titmuss.[33] It was put forward with particular force by Le Grand in 1982. When criticized, he defended his arguments and claimed that they were being taken up by policymakers, for example, in the reduction of mortgage interest relief on house purchases: this was inaugurated by *Conservative* governments, albeit continued by New Labour. However, the core services of schools, education and the NHS were untouched by these arguments, though it was the latter upon which Le Grand had initially focused his critique.[34]

While Titmuss's critique centred on tax-derived data, he was not primarily concerned with the impact of the tax system on income distribution, though he did assert that, especially as a result of the growth of tax allowances in combination with National Insurance contributions, "there appears to be little progression for most employed people with earned incomes under £2,000 a year".[35]

While the Attlee government was keen to maintain the very high tax rates it inherited in order to suppress consumption and transfer resources into investment and exports, there was growing belief in both official and ministerial circles that Britain had reached the limits of taxable capacity. In response, Labour set up the Royal Commission into the Taxation of Profits and Wealth. The argument that income tax had exhausted its capacity as an agent of redistribution was a major element that underpinned the advocacy of a lifetime expenditure tax: a progressive alternative by Labour's foremost expert on taxation, Nicholas Kaldor.[36] However, little was done. With declining revenues from company taxation, increasing receipts came from a sustained fall in the income tax threshold (especially by non-indexation for inflation), which brought the bulk of the working class, even those deemed to be "in poverty" by the social security rules, into the income tax system.[37] The effect of this was that income tax, historically thought to be a great engine of redistribution, was by the early 1970s a broadly proportional tax, with some limited progressive elements right at the top of the distribution.[38] Alongside this trend, National Insurance contributions, though graduated in part from 1961, retained a ceiling. They were therefore regressive in impact, a result strengthened by the declining share of the Treasury in funding National Insurance.[39]

The 1964 Labour government prioritized increasing economic growth as a route to higher social spending. As a minister put it in 1969, "our purpose in political life is to expand the social wage through large increases in public expenditure on education, health, housing and the social services".[40] But the aims of faster growth and higher social spending were perceived by many in the government to be at odds. This was due to the worry that direct taxes were already at heights at which they acted as a disincentive, while indirect taxes were known to be regressive. In the event, the biggest tax changes in the 1960s were the introduction of corporation and capital gains taxes, which were not intended primarily as major revenue earners.[41] As far as social spending is concerned, accounts of this government's record normally focus on the big cuts beginning in 1968 following devaluation. Despite this, the overall effects of tax and spend policies were mildly egalitarian, though without the sense that this was a goal clearly prioritized and pursued.[42]

Housing was a long-standing issue for the Left in Britain, with the extent of overcrowding bequeathed by the breakneck growth of Victorian industrial cities posing major challenges well into the twentieth century. In response came one of social democracy's major contributions to twentieth-century Britain: the creation of a huge publicly owned housing sector. Like many social democratic policies, this was not directly aimed at reducing inequality, but rather at reducing "squalor", as Beveridge had termed the condition of much housing in 1942. In the inter-war years, there was a widespread distributive battle between those who prioritized local housing construction with low rents and those who wanted to minimize the rate burden of such policies. In the post-war period, the distributive aspect took a new form. Rent subsidies became less of a *local* issue, as the funding switched to central government.[43]

The CSO/FES analysis of redistribution sought to take these housing subsidies into account in its assessment of the redistributive effects of public spending. However, it failed to take into account the other major form of housing subsidy, that of tax relief on mortgage interest.[44] (Home ownership was also favoured by the abolition of income tax on imputed rents ("Schedule A") in 1963, and the exemption from Capital Gains Tax.) The distributive consequences of these two types of public intervention were different, but the idea lurking behind many critiques from the Left that council house subsidies were for the working class and mortgage subsidies were for the middle class broke down as working-class home ownership expanded. By 1970, home ownership reached 50 per cent of households.[45]

This expansion mixed a wider ideological issue with direct distributional aspects. Traditionally, socialist discussion of wealth focused on inherited wealth, and wealth from the corporate sector, not housing; the distributive consequences of home ownership were not focused on.[46] While home ownership was promoted as part of a "property-owning democracy" by Conservatives, some on the Left saw the democratization of property, especially through housing, as a route to greater equality.[47] This was an idea associated with the "liberal socialist" tradition of such writers as James Meade (and, on a more philosophical plane, John Rawls).[48] Under Labour, in the 1960s, a small number of council houses were sold, but there was neither a strong national policy nor a clear ideological positioning on the issue of housing wealth. The wealth aspects of housing were to become more troubling for Labour when Thatcher privatized a significant proportion of the housing stock in the 1980s and did not allow local authorities to use the proceeds to replenish the stock.

In opposition, during the early 1970s, the Labour Party proposed raising the income tax threshold, increasing rates at the upper end of the income scale and bringing in a wealth tax.[49] But, by the middle of the decade, in the face of rapid inflation, the effective income tax threshold fell sharply, given the absence of indexation. This encouraged the Left to emphasize the limits of income tax as an instrument of egalitarianism, as well as the lack of progressivity of the overall tax system.[50]

This combination of traditional incentive and newly emphasized egalitarian lines of argument meant that income tax was no longer at the centre of distributional politics. While upon coming into power in 1974 Labour had put an unusually strong emphasis on redistribution, with taxation as a means to achieve this, the terms of debate and policy soon shifted.[51] The issue of the "social wage" mutated into bargaining over income tax cuts between government and unions in the context of the "Social Contract", with the government seeking wage restraint in return for concessions to trade unions. By the mid 1970s, in the face of an economic crisis, Labour was losing faith in income tax, and there was a marked shift towards expenditure taxes in the overall revenue mix; although *within* income tax, progressivity was sharpened.[52] As Whiting puts it, "the industrial worker had emerged as one of the conservative (i.e. constraining) influences upon Labour's tax policy through his inclusion in income tax at the standard rate".[53]

In power after 1974, Labour also dropped the party's proposal for a wealth tax. Estate Duty was replaced by Capital Transfer Tax, but this was not much more than a change of name. There was a strong sense that Labour had lost its way on tax policy, and the scope and sophistication of party debate can be adversely compared with that of the 1920s.[54]

Widely seen as the turning point for social democracy in Britain, the mid 1970s saw public spending constrained from 1975, a tightening that was reinforced in the run-up to the International Monetary Fund (IMF) loan of the following year; 1976/7 marked a long-run peak in the ratio of spending to GDP. In the short run, the incomes policies of the mid 1970s had a notable egalitarian effect on wage distribution, but this proved unsustainable. The broader egalitarian possibilities of capital-sharing, though advocated by some figures in the Labour Party, were not pursued: a similar story to that of the late 1950s.[55]

The 1970s were notable for the production of by far the most comprehensive official analysis on income and wealth distribution by a Royal Commission on the Distribution of Income and Wealth. This was set up by the Labour government but was quickly abolished by the Conservatives. While the Commission generated some data improvements, it had no evident effects on policy.[56] In this respect, it was akin to the Meade report, which reiterated many of the proposals of the "radical centre" for a shift to progressive taxes on consumption and a wealth tax, without having any significant impact.[57]

RESPONSES TO THE CRISES OF THE 1970S

The failure of Labour to grapple successfully with the (very large) challenges of pursuing egalitarian policies in the 1970s raises the question of how far their approach rested on a failure to take account of the changing social structure, as suggested by Daunton.[58] He notes in particular the troubles Labour had with the changing incidence and, hence, politics of income tax, as outlined above. Indeed, we can see here the establishment of a long-lived obsession with income tax rates in political debate, which is an obsession that has lasted to the present. The focus on these rates, underpinned by highly politicized annual (or more frequent) budgets, in which these rates were often emphasized, obscures both the limited role of income tax in total revenue (less than 30 per cent today) and the crucial role played in determining the distributive impact of the tax by the levels of allowances and thresholds.[59]

More broadly, in looking at the social changes within which the tax system operates, Atkinson's analysis of the shortcomings of approaches using the factoral distribution of income is very useful. He considers the pitfalls of emphasizing the distribution of factors of production, in the modern period essentially capital and labour.[60] This approach was very much the tradition in economics, stretching back to Malthus and Ricardo, but it also fitted with the Left's view about the fundamental societal division between capital and labour.[61] It was a common starting point for the Left's discussions of distributional issues, though one that had long been recognized as problematic.[62]

In the 1990s, Atkinson identified six problems with this approach. First, he highlighted the heterogeneity of incomes *within* factoral classes, and above all the size distribution of wages. Growing disparities within this distribution are clear from the 1970s, and they made a significant contribution to widening inequality in that decade. Second, he found evidence that this wage dispersion is heavily influenced by promoting "human capital" formation – the investment in skills and education available to workers – thus making access to this investment an important determinant of inequality.

A third aspect is the *diversity* of income sources available to individuals and households. These might include wages, interest and rent (this is especially important if imputed rent on owner-occupied housing is included). This means that, for example, changes in interest rates will have significant distributional consequences due to their impact on both savers and borrowers. (A striking case of this was in the era of ultra-low interest rates after 2008.) Greater longevity means reliance on non-wage income is inevitably increased, even for those whose working life has been spent as a wage-earner.[63]

This links to Atkinson's fourth point, the importance of "intervening institutions", which stand between the production side of the economy and household incomes. One of the most important of these is the pension fund, whose rise has, of course, reflected both the ageing of the population and the financialization of pensions. This rise is also linked to a major shift in the pattern of shareholding, away from individual capitalists to institutions. As noted above, Labour has made proposals to address this issue, most significantly in 1957, but nothing has come of these. Analytically, this change cuts across any simple labour/capital divide. Overseas holdings of British capital assets also increasingly complicate the story. Finally, and perhaps most obviously, the state budget cannot be simply slotted into a labour income/capital income dichotomy.

This analysis suggests that if we are concerned with inequality it is wrong to focus too much on factor shares. Until recently, this argument was bolstered by a belief in the *stability* of these shares, and therefore their inability to explain changes in inequality. But this story of stability has been strongly questioned by Piketty as well as by Atkinson's most recent writings. As a result, Atkinson argues that while there is no straightforward relationship between a falling wage share and rising inequality, empirically this link has operated and is part of the explanation for the inegalitarian trend since the 1970s.[64]

Revival of a concern with factoral shares is not helpful in considering the significance of housing for wealth distribution. Piketty conflates "wealth" (all assets) with "capital" (means of production), and while housing is a large part of the former, it is not part of the latter. So, discussion of the distributional aspects of housing, and how these might be addressed, does not sit easily with a strong emphasis on the capital share.

These analytical and political problems for the Left in thinking about income distribution were sharpened by the challenge of responding to the Thatcher government after 1979. This government seriously assaulted all three elements of Tawney's "strategy". Overall public expenditure did increase, but specific cuts were generally concentrated on the poorest, especially the unemployed, whose numbers grew sharply. In addition, the tax system was made much less progressive by reductions in higher income tax rates and large increases in VAT. Beyond that, trade unions were weakened and industrial regulation shifted in the direction of employers, while there was, of course, large-scale privatization both of council housing and nationalized industries. While the distributive consequences of some of these measures may be disputed, the overall pattern was starkly clear: a huge increase in inequality was the most unambiguous effect of the Thatcher government.[65] This step-change is summarized by the Gini coefficient, which went from 0.23 in 1978 to 0.34 in 1990 (an increase of 50 per cent).[66]

Why did inequality increase so starkly in the 1980s? Because, as Hills notes, "most of the factors determining income distribution were pushing in the same direction".[67] Taxation was radically reformed, with cuts to income tax rates and sharp increases in VAT and Excise Duties.[68] In addition, most benefits were increased in line with prices rather than incomes, at a time of significant inflation. Overall, Clark and Leicester calculate that tax and benefit changes contributed half of the total increase in inequality in the 1980s.[69]

The cuts in real benefit levels had an especially big impact because of the rise in unemployment, which rose to over three million by the mid-1980s (an effect only slightly mitigated by the shift of some older unemployed workers onto the higher rates of Disability Benefit). This was accompanied by the widening of the (male) earnings distribution. Between 1978 and 1992, "the 10th percentile wage did not change, never recovering the wages received in 1975, while the median grew by 35 per cent and the 90th percentile by over 50 per cent".[70]

Less well known than the above changes was the rise in self-employment, which doubled between 1979 and 1989 to reach almost one in eight of those in employment. This played a significant role in increasing inequality, as the range of earnings among the self-employed is considerably greater than among the employed. While we cannot say definitively why such a large rise took place, it seems highly likely that much of it was driven by the lack of job availability, for which, in many cases, self-employment was a poorly paid and insecure substitute.[71]

Almost the only exception to this pattern of increasing inequality was, importantly, wealth, where there was little evidence of change in the distribution of marketable wealth (i.e. excluding pension rights), although this followed a period of falling inequality.[72] This was mainly the effect of the spread of house ownership, though this did little for those at the bottom of the distribution.

As the parliamentary opposition between 1979 and 1997, Labour saw marked swings in policy and struggled to respond consistently to the Thatcher agenda and its consequences for inequality. The eventual emergence of New Labour meant a rhetorical emphasis on equality of *opportunity* and poverty reduction rather than on inequality *per se.*[73]

How did New Labour, in office after 1997, respond to the major attacks on "the strategy of equality" pursued by the Thatcher government? There was no reversal of the privatization of state-owned industry, and no initiatives on extending the ownership of capital in industry. Proposals along these lines were put forward as part of Will Hutton's "stakeholder capitalism", which aimed simultaneously to democratize the company, spread ownership and revive investment.[74] In the event, little came of this, though in the individualistic form of "asset-based welfare" it mutated into the Child Trust Fund, under which every child received a tax-funded sum at birth, added to by family contributions until the age of eighteen.[75]

On home ownership, the sale of council houses had undoubtedly put New Labour on the defensive. New Labour stressed its commitment to home ownership (although the government completed the abolition of Mortgage Interest Relief at Source (MIRAS), begun under the Conservatives). The overwhelming bulk of houses built between 1997 and 2010 were for private ownership; almost none (0.3 per cent) were for council ownership, and about 13 per cent were for housing associations. On trade unions, there was no significant going back to the status quo prior to 1979.[76] However, a national minimum wage was introduced for the first time (most industry-specific Wage Councils had been abolished in the 1980s).

Taxation policy was a hugely sensitive issue for New Labour because of the key role it had played in the defeat of 1992 and the victory of 1997. In 1997, the party made a commitment to stabilize income tax rates and not to raise the higher rate above 40 per cent.[77] However, some mildly redistributive "stealth tax" changes were introduced.

On benefits, Labour devoted a great deal of resources to reducing pensioner and child poverty, with considerable success. In this respect, along with the huge increases in education and health spending, New Labour can be seen as successfully pursuing a key part of Tawney's "strategy of equality". While the Gini coefficient rose slightly in the 2000s, this mainly reflected the growth in incomes right at the top of the distribution, while otherwise there was a movement to greater equality.[78] In the long run, arguably the most important feature of New Labour's social spending was the great expansion of in-work benefits, which I return to in the final section of this chapter.

In higher education, New Labour introduced student fees, which followed studies, especially by Nicholas Barr, who proposed a graduate tax on egalitarian grounds.[79] When the government did start to charge student fees (albeit under a different name), it was attacked by many on the Left. This was an interesting case for distributional politics, where a clearly egalitarian proposal was opposed by many on the Left as in contradiction with another principle: in this case, that of "free education", which in the university sector had led to a particularly regressive form of spending.

CONTEMPORARY POLICY OPTIONS

By 2015, attacks on growing inequality had become a staple of mainstream global policy debate. A striking symbol of this positioning is the paper prepared for the G20 meeting in September 2015, at which a joint contribution from the International Labour Organization (ILO), IMF, OECD and World Bank followed on from the previous G20 Leaders' Summit's commitment to "reduce inequality and poverty". These organizations endorsed a statement strongly supporting measures to reduce inequality because of its role in slowing growth as well as on account of its "corrosive effect on social and political cohesion".[80] A traditional concern of the Left has therefore become a mainstay of debate across the advanced capitalist world, not just in Britain, although the increase in inequality here is amongst the highest in the OECD world.

In addressing contemporary inequality, we can ask the following: what are the main dimensions of the problem, and which of these are new? One of the most striking trends is the rise of the "top 1 per cent", the working-rich, who have appropriated a large proportion of the recent rise in national income in Britain. Because of the "super-tax" introduced in 1908, we have much better long-run statistical data for top-income groups than for many other categories. These data show a fall in the share of the top 1 per cent from almost 20 per cent of national income to around 6 per cent between 1908 and 1978, but since then there has been a sharp reversal, with a rise to around 13 per cent by 2000 and with no sign of the trend slowing.[81]

While we have not quite achieved the "euthanasia of the rentier" embraced by Keynes, it is clear that the "idle rich" so strongly anathematized by early socialists have largely disappeared. But other changes in recent decades have worked against the hopes and expectations of mid-century reformers and socialists in ways that have exacerbated inequality. First, unemployment levels have increased significantly since the 1970s, with three major slumps, each pushing measured unemployment over the two million mark.[82] Alongside these cycles has come a rise in chronic unemployment. This has been partly hidden by the rise in incapacity benefit, which has acted to disguise the weakness of labour demand. Estimates of the "real" level of unemployment, making allowances for this disguise, suggest that even in the good times unemployment has been much higher than in the "golden age". Thus, for January 2007, just before the financial crisis, Beatty *et al.* calculate a rate of 7.2 per cent, measured as the sum of claimant levels (2.6 per cent), plus 1.8 per cent under the ILO measure ("actively seeking work") and 2.9 per cent for hidden unemployment among those on incapacity benefit.[83] Unemployment is also hidden by the rise in self-employment, which has shot up since 2009, just as it did in the 1980s, and probably with similar effects in increasing income inequality.

Alongside the rise in unemployment since the 1970s has come a deterioration in the relative income position of the unemployed. In the 1960s, unemployment pay was adjusted upwards, according to previous earnings levels, to encourage labour mobility. But the trend in unemployment pay relative to average incomes has been downwards since the 1980s, and this policy was reinforced under the Coalition.[84] So, since the "golden age", unemployment has become more prevalent and more painful when experienced.

Reducing unemployment has rightly played a large role in the Left's political concerns throughout the twentieth century. But a key underpinning for that concern – the belief that work is a route out of poverty – no longer holds, due to labour market polarization. The divergence in earnings, beginning in the 1960s, was especially evident from the end of the 1970s, and it has continued. The scale of this polarization makes it a key challenge to egalitarianism.[85] The long-run trend associated with structural change in twentieth-century Britain was towards higher demand for more skilled labour, and the supply of such labour has also risen. But there remain many poorly skilled (or redundantly skilled) workers that the pace of deindustrialization has left behind.

Of course, changes in demand for labour are a constant feature of a market economy, and as the major surveys of Britain at the beginning of the century (such as that of Seebohm Rowntree[86]) showed, many of those in work at that time earned only poverty wages. From the First World War down to the 1960s, there was a trend to wage equalization. Since that decade, many routine, middle-income jobs have been displaced by a more polarized labour market, with an expansion of jobs at the top end, which require non-routine cognitive skills, and also at the bottom end, which demand non-routine manual skills. While services have seen a "bifurcation" in the labour employed between the lowest and highest skilled and rewarded, manufacturing has seen a clear "up-skilling" taking place: the number of those employed in manufacturing with no formal qualifications fell from 26 per cent in 1993 to 8 per cent in 2013, while those with first degrees rose from 7 per cent to 16 per cent.[87]

The rapid growth in low-paid jobs in the service sector is suggested in the figures in Table 9.1, where "non-routine service" covers occupations such as care attendant; shop, restaurant and bar worker; hairdresser; and beautician.

Table 9.1. Growth rates of various occupational categories in the UK (1981–2008). (*Source*: Holmes and Mayhew (2012).[88])

Occupations	Growth rate 1981–2008 (percentage)
Professional	56.4
Managerial	56.7
Intermediate	56.6
Routine admin	–35.8
Routine manual	–50.4
Non-routine service	72.2
Non-routine manual	–4.3

As a result, "Wage inequality is significantly higher now than it was some thirty years ago. This is true for men and women, and is the case in both the upper and lower halves of the distribution."[89] Machin calculates the ratio at between the ninetieth and tenth percentiles for the period 1970–2009 and suggests that in those years this dispersion rose by approximately 50 per cent.[90]

We should note that almost all of the "non-routine service" jobs referred to in the table are disproportionately done by women, many on a part-time basis. As Connolly and Gregory put it:

> Women working full-time, who are increasingly the equal of men in education and qualifications, do rather different jobs from men, in different professions and in offices rather than factories, but at broadly the same occupational level. Women who work part-time, on the other hand, remain significantly less well-qualified, are under-represented in the higher-level occupations, and are concentrated into a relatively narrow range of lower-level jobs.[91]

The introduction of a national minimum wage was partly a response to this polarization. But even more important has been its mitigation by the expansion of in-work benefits, mainly tax credits and Housing Benefit. In this way, structural changes in the labour market have led to profound changes in the social security system. It is not only that these in-work benefits have come to greatly exceed payments made to the unemployed; the whole principle of post-war welfare has shifted. The classic mid-twentieth-century Beveridge analysis of the sources of poverty suggested that the problem fundamentally lay in "interruption to earnings" (by unemployment, sickness or age), along with large numbers of children, the latter to be addressed by "Family Allowances" (later,

Child Benefit).[92] While this analysis always misrepresented the labour market, not least in its barely qualified notion of the "male-breadwinner household", its fundamental idea that normally paid work would provide a route out of poverty has underpinned most modern understandings of how society works. What has changed in the period of deindustrialization has been the numbers earning very low wages and being supported by in-work benefits.

Evidence of these trends can be found in the rise of in-work poverty, a central feature of the post-industrial period. While in the industrial period employment did not guarantee an above-poverty income, most poverty was among non-workers (the sick and disabled, pensioners, single mothers) or those with unusually large families. Abel-Smith and Townsend showed that in 1960 about 40 per cent of households in poverty (those below 140 per cent of the then National Assistance level) had a working member. But overwhelmingly they also had a large number of children (four or more).[93] Recent work suggests that a majority of the poor are now members of households with at least one member in work: "As pensioner poverty is now at low levels, the rate of in-work poverty is the most distinctive characteristic of poverty today."[94]

Effectively we have moved towards a huge new "Speenhamland system" of "outdoor relief" for the employed; or, viewing the same thing from a different perspective, towards a system of large subsidies to employers. Such payments have mitigated but not cured the problem of poverty-level wages.[95] The original Speenhamland system was introduced in a parish of that name near Newbury in the south of England in 1795. Wages deemed to be below those sufficient for subsistence were subsidized through the Poor Law out of taxes (local poor rates). This system was not actually new, nor did it become universal, but it has been widely recognized as symbolizing the rejection of a crucial principle of liberal political economy: the principle that wages should be determined in a market and should not be subsidized out of the public purse.[96] Those hostile to Speenhamland argued that it created no incentives for the workers to maximize their wages, nor for employers to pay what was affordable to them. These perverse consequences were held up as the typical result of well-intentioned but misguided intervention in the labour market. Eventually, under the Poor Law Amendment Act of 1834, such subsidies were outlawed; relief went mainly to those confined to institutions ("indoor relief"); and liberal political economy was triumphant.

The reinvention of Speenhamland has come from a clash between neoliberal principles and the impact of deindustrialization on the labour market. A core belief of British neoliberals in the 1970s and 1980s was that unemployment was in large part the consequence of unemployment pay being too high relative to wages, thus providing an incentive to remain unemployed and not seek work.[97] From this premise, two policies followed: reducing unemployment pay (pursued from 1981), while simultaneously increasing "in-work" benefits. Initially, the latter were limited in scale and scope, but by 1991 the Conservatives were boasting about the expansion of Family Credit, "the most generous benefit ever available in Britain specifically targeted at families with a breadwinner in low paid employment."[98] Recipient numbers grew as the number of poorly paid jobs increased, while simultaneously the elimination of rent controls, the decline of social housing and the persistent rise in the real price of housing led to a parallel expansion in payments of Housing Benefits, much of which were paid to those in work. Under New Labour the increase in wage subsidies was much faster, as the government combined a continued belief in the importance of incentives for the unemployed with a serious desire to reduce poverty amongst the employed. Working Tax Credit and similar programmes became the fastest growing element of social security spending. By 2013/14, there were 2.5 million recipients of Working Tax Credits and expenditure of £6.3 billion; Housing Benefit cost over £23 billion and went to five million people, of whom at least half were in employment.[99]

Similarly unforeseen by mid-twentieth-century social democrats was the expansion of home ownership and its spread to large sections (but by no means all) of the working class. This has spread wealth significantly down the social scale, though it is still much more unevenly distributed than disposable income.[100] This spread has been accompanied by a major expansion of household debt, which has risen from the equivalent of 50 per cent of GDP in 1970 to 150 per cent today, so that "financialization" has been a key feature of Britain since the 1970s.[101] Paradoxically, the growth of home ownership, very much encouraged by, and used as a reason *for*, financial liberalization, is now in decline, reflecting the rising cost of housing. This has been driven in part by its continuing favourable tax treatment. The spread of housing wealth has been accompanied by rising real levels of rent, a form of tenure most common at the bottom of the income distribution.

To address these new patterns, do we need a "new egalitarianism"?[102] One of the key themes of proponents of this idea is that "the left's traditional distributive goals should be pursued not only through income redistribution or solidaristic wage policies, but through more concerted action to change the initial distribution of assets and productive endowments".[103] This is an important point, especially if "distribution of assets and productive endowments" goes beyond simply focusing on "education, education, education", with the implication that the supply of good jobs will automatically expand with the expansion of a skilled labour force. While few dispute the benefits of maximizing educational opportunities, the idea that potentially all jobs could become high skilled and high paid is a chimera. Polarization in the demand for labour is having profound effects. The expansion of in-work benefits has increasingly detached income from labour market status, and that is a process which would be accelerated by the introduction of a Basic or Citizen's Income. The same is true for Atkinson's proposal of a "Participation Income", where "participation" would be broadly defined as making a social contribution, "which for those of working-age could be fulfilled by full- or part-time waged employment or self-employment, by education, training, or an active job search, by home care for infant children or frail elderly people, or by regular voluntary work in a recognised association".[104]

Advocates of the "new egalitarianism", being New Labour thinkers, tend to exaggerate the novelty of the world we now live in; they are too dismissive of older social democratic policies. "Original incomes", prior to any tax or spending impact, have been becoming more unequal (with brief reversals) since the 1960s. But this does not mean abandoning, for example, higher income tax rates (Atkinson suggests a top rate of 65 per cent) or too readily accepting claims that health and education spending over-favour the middle classes.[105]

Indeed, underpinning Atkinson's proposals for reducing inequality is the belief that achieving this objective will require a wide range of policies that recognize the complexity of the forces at work: for example, in the case of housing, recognizing that reforms to make the taxation of housing progressive should be combined with action on pensions to make "buy-to-let" less appealing to retirees.[106] More broadly on wealth, he advocates the imposition of a lifetime capital receipts tax alongside a significant capital endowment for all citizens.

Piketty proposes "a progressive global tax on capital", but he describes this as "utopian". Even if it were achievable, it would be no "magic bullet" for reducing inequality. A strategy for that purpose today requires a combination of most of Tawney's suggested components as well as many others (including the closest we can get to a "progressive global tax on capital") to address the changes in economic and social structure that have occurred since he was writing.

Notes for Chapter 9

1. I am grateful to Ben Jackson, Pat Hudson and Keith Tribe for constructive comments on an earlier draft of this chapter.

2. Thomas Piketty, "Putting Distribution Back at the Center of Economics: Reflections on *Capital in the Twenty-First Century*", *Journal of Economic Perspectives* 29 (2015), p. 87.

3. "Social democratic" is treated as an appropriate characterization of the politics of the Labour Party from its beginnings up until the 1990s; with the dominance of New Labour, such a characterization can only be applied with great reservation. By contrast, Conservatives have with varying degrees of ideological enthusiasm repudiated such a goal: see Keith Joseph and Jonathan Sumption, *Equality* (London: John Murray, 1979); William Letwin (ed.), *Against Equality: Readings on Economic and Social Policy* (London: Macmillan, 1983).

4. Thomas Piketty, *Capital in the Twenty-First Century* (Cambridge, MA: Harvard University Press, 2014), p. 274.

5. Ben Jackson, *Equality and the British Left* (Manchester: Manchester University Press, 2007); Nicholas Ellison, *Egalitarian Thought and Labour Politics: Retreating Visions* (London: Routledge, 1994); Norman Dennis and Albert Halsey, *English Ethical Socialism: Thomas More to R. H. Tawney* (Oxford: Clarendon Press, 1988); Martin Francis, *Ideas and Politics under Labour, 1945–51* (Manchester: Manchester University Press, 1997).

6. For the interplay between statistics and policy on the related issue of poverty, see Ian Gazeley, *Poverty in Britain, 1900–1965* (Basingstoke: Palgrave Macmillan, 2003).

7. R. H. Tawney, *Equality* [1931], 5th edn with an introduction by Richard M. Titmuss (London: Allen & Unwin, 1964), p. 119.

8. *Ibid.*, p. 120.

9. Ellison, *Egalitarian Thought*, pp. 21–26.

10. Jose Harris, "Labour's Political and Social Thought", in *Labour's First Century,* Duncan Tanner, Pat Thane and Nick Tiratsoo (eds) (Cambridge: Cambridge University Press, 2000), pp. 8–45.

11. Jim Tomlinson, *Democratic Socialism and Economic Policy* (Cambridge: Cambridge University Press, 1997), pp. 218–9.

12. *Ibid.*, pp. 265–70.

13. In his *The Acquisitive Society* (1921), Tawney had made the case for "functional" private property, that is, related to productive effort, as opposed to "functionless" property, often acquired through inheritance.

14. *Royal Commission on the Distribution of Income and Wealth* (hereafter RCDIW), Report 1, Command 6171 (1975), Paragraph 186.

15. Cited in Anthony Atkinson, *Unequal Shares*, revised edn (Harmondsworth: Penguin, 1974), p. 9.

16. Hugh Dalton, *Some Aspects of the Inequality of Incomes in Modern Communities* (London: George Routledge & Son, 1920); a consolidated Estate Duty was first introduced in 1894.

17. Richard Whiting, *The Labour Party and Taxation* (Cambridge: Cambridge University Press, 2000); Martin Daunton, *Just Taxes: The Politics of Taxation in Britain 1914–1979* (Cambridge: Cambridge University Press, 2002).

18. Allan Carter, *The Redistribution of Income in Post-War Britain* (New Haven, CT: Yale University Press, 1955).

19. Anthony Crosland, *The Future of Socialism* (London: Jonathan Cape, 1956), pp. 51–3, 62.

20. *Ibid.*, p. 190. Crosland is clear that, in his view, concern for incentives "rules out any further major distribution of earned income by direct taxation", p. 298.

21. *Ibid.*, pp. 146–8.

22. See Chapter 7 in this volume, by Ylva Hasselberg and Henry Ohlsson.

23. H. Pemberton, "'What Matters is What Works': Labour's Journey from 'National Superannuation' to 'Personal Accounts'", *British Politics* 5 (2010), pp. 41–64.

24. Richard Titmuss, *Essays on the Welfare State* (London: Allen & Unwin, 1958).

25. Richard Titmuss, *Income Distribution and Social Change* (London: Allen & Unwin, 1963).

26. *Ibid.*, p. 25

27. *Ibid.*, p. 188. In his introduction to the 1964 edition of Tawney's *Equality* (p. 10), Titmuss had noted how "the simpler tools of measurement and analysis used by himself [i.e. Tawney] and others in the past were no longer adequate".

28. Dudley Seers, "The Levelling of Incomes", *Bulletin of the Oxford University Institute of Statistics* 12 (1950), pp. 271–98, cited by Crosland, *Future*, pp. 49, 51–2.

29. Anthony Atkinson, "The Distribution of Income in the UK and OECD Countries in the Twentieth Century", *Oxford Review of Economic Policy* 15 (1999), p. 60.

30. Frank Field, Molly Meacher and Chris Pond, *To Him Who Hath* (Harmondsworth: Penguin, 1977) pp. 185–7; RCDIW Report 1, Paragraphs 110–20.

31. RCDIW, Report 1, Paragraph 149; Field, Meacher and Pond, *To Him Who Hath*, pp. 192–8.

32. This debate: Thomas Marshall, *Citizenship and Social Class* (Cambridge: Cambridge University Press, 1950); Barbara Wootton, "The Labour Party and Social Services", *Political Quarterly* 24 (1953), pp. 55–67; Crosland, *Future*, pp. 140–48, 158–65; Titmuss, *Essays*, Chapter 2.

33. Barry Hindess, *Freedom, Equality and the Market: Arguments on Social Policy* (London: Routledge, 1987), p. 84.

34. Julian Le Grand, *The Strategy of Equality* (London: Allen & Unwin, 1982); M. Powell, "The Strategy of Equality Revisited", *Journal of Social Policy* 24 (1995), pp. 163–85; and Le Grand, "A Reply", *Journal of Social Policy* 24 (1995), pp. 187–91.

35. Titmuss, *Income Distribution*, pp. 197–8.

36. Nicholas Kaldor, *An Expenditure Tax* (London: Allen & Unwin, 1955).

37. Field, Meacher and Pond, *To Him Who Hath*, p. 32.

38. *Ibid.*, pp. 57–69.

39. *Ibid.*, pp. 76–84.

40. Joel Barnett, cited in Whiting, *Labour Party*, p. 210.

41. Whiting, *Labour Party*, pp. 159–72.

42. Michael Stewart, "The Distribution of Income", in *The Labour Government's Economic Record, 1964–1970*, Wilfred Beckerman (ed.) (London: Duckworth, 1972), pp. 75–117; Nicholas Bosanquet and Peter Townsend (eds), *Labour and Inequality: Sixteen Fabian Essays* (London: Fabian Society, 1972).

43. Daunton, *Just Taxes*, pp. 339–50.

44. Field, Meacher and Pond, *To Him Who Hath*, pp. 198–200.

45. Chris Hamnett and Jenny Seavers, "Home-ownership, Housing Wealth and Wealth Distribution in Britain", in *New Inequalities: The Changing Distribution of Income and Wealth in the UK*, John Hills (ed.) (Cambridge: Cambridge University Press, 1996), p. 350.

46. For example, Atkinson, *Unequal Shares*.

47. Martin Daunton, *A Property-owning Democracy? Housing in Britain* (London: Faber, 1987).

48. Ben Jackson, "Property-owning Democracy: A Short History", in *Property-owning Democracy: Rawls and Beyond*, Martin O'Neill and Thad Williamson (eds) (Chichester: Wiley, 2012), pp. 33–52; Ben Jackson, "Revisionism Reconsidered: 'Property-owning Democracy' in Post-War Britain", *Twentieth Century British History* 16 (2005), pp. 416–40.

49. Daunton, *Just Taxes*, p. 328.

50. Field, Meacher and Pond, *To Him Who Hath*, pp. 49–71.

51. Alan Gillie, "Redistribution", in *Labour's Economic Policies 1974–79*, Michael Artis and David Cobham (eds) (Manchester: Manchester University Press, 1991), pp. 229–47.

52. Whiting, *Labour Party*, pp. 216, 252.

53. *Ibid.*, p. 235. Income tax fell from its peak of 51 per cent of total revenue in 1975 to 38 per cent in 1979, before falling to 31 per cent by 1997: Ben Jackson and Robert Saunders (eds), *Making Thatcher's Britain* (Cambridge: Cambridge University Press, 2014), p. 275.

54. Daunton, *Just Taxes*, pp. 331–2; Whiting, *Labour Party*, pp. 238–9.

55. Whiting, *Labour Party*, pp. 217–19.

56. RCDIW, Report 8, Command 7679, pp. 237–8; Hills, *New Inequalities*, is an update of the Commission's work covering the period when the step change to greater inequality took place.

57. *The Structure and Reform of Direct Taxation*, Report of a Committee chaired by J. E. Meade focused on expenditure tax, like Kaldor's 1956 proposal.

58. Daunton, *Just Taxes*, pp. 331, 335–8.

59. This narrowing of debate about the tax system is very evident in Scotland, where the devolution of tax powers is almost wholly limited to income tax rates, giving the Scottish government very little room for manoeuvre.

60. Atkinson, "Seeking to Explain the Distribution of Income", in Hills, *New Inequalities*, pp. 19–48.

61. Atkinson, "Bringing Income Distribution in from the Cold", *Economic Journal* 107 (1997), pp. 297–321.

62. Dalton, *Some Aspects*; Stewart, "Distribution of Income", p. 78.

63. This, of course, is an important contributory factor to the "financialization" of the economy: Anthony B. Atkinson, *Inequality: What Can Be Done?* (Cambridge, MA: Harvard University Press, 2015), p. 71.

64. Atkinson, *Inequality*, pp. 68–70. For Marxist analysts of social democracy, factor shares are crucial: Andrew Glyn and Robert Sutcliffe, *British Capitalism, Workers and the Profits Squeeze* (Harmondsworth: Penguin, 1972).

65. Jackson and Saunders, *Making Thatcher's Britain*, pp. 15–16.

66. John Hills, Tom Sefton and Kitty Stewart (eds), *Towards a More Equal Society? Poverty, Inequality and Policy Since 1997* (Bristol: Policy Press, 2009), p. 3. This picture is robust for the use of other measures of inequality: Tom Clark and Andrew Leicester,

"Inequality and Two Decades of British Tax and Benefit Reforms", *Fiscal Studies* 25 (2004), p. 145.

67. Hills, "Introduction" to *New Inequalities*, p. 11.

68. Though it is over-simple to suggest every tax change made was inegalitarian; as well as rises in employers' National Insurance contributions, the Conservatives also notably cut MIRAS, the tax relief on mortgage payments.

69. Clark and Leicester, "Inequality"; this is against a benchmark of benefits rising in line with incomes.

70. Amanda Gosling, Stephen Machin and Costas Meghir, "What Has Happened to the Wages of Men Since 1966?", in Hills, *New Inequalities*, p. 136.

71. Nigel Meager, Gill Court and Janet Moralee, "Self-employment and the Distribution of Income", in Hills, *New Inequalities*, pp. 208–35; D. Blanchflower, "Self-employment in OECD Countries", National Bureau of Economic Research Working Paper 7486 (2000).

72. Hills, "Introduction" to *New Inequalities*, p. 13.

73. Richard Hill, *The Labour Party and Economic Strategy, 1979–1997* (Basingstoke: Palgrave Macmillan, 2001).

74. Will Hutton, *The State We're In* (London: Vintage, 1994).

75. Stuart White, "New Labour and the Politics of Ownership", in *Reassessing New Labour: Market, State and Society under Blair and Brown,* Patrick Diamond and Michael Kenny (eds) (Chichester: Wiley, 2011), pp. 140–51.

76. John Pencavel, "The Surprising Retreat of Union Britain", in *Seeking a Premier Economy: The Effects of British Economic Reforms, 1980–2000,* David Card, Richard Blundell and Richard Freeman (eds) (Chicago, IL: University of Chicago Press, 2004), pp. 181–232.

77. Whiting, *Labour Party*, pp. 259–61.

78. James Browne and David Phillips, *Tax and Benefit Reforms under Labour* (London: Institute for Fiscal Studies, 2008).

79. Nicholas Barr and Keith Shaw, *Income Contingent Student Loans: An Idea Whose Time Has Come* (Chichester: Wiley, 1991).

80. ILO/IMF/OECD/World Bank, "Income Inequality and Labour Income Share in G20 Countries: Trends, Impacts and Causes", prepared for the G20 Labour and Employment Ministers and Joint Meeting with Finance Ministers, Ankara, Turkey, 3–4 September 2015.

81. Anthony Atkinson, "Top Incomes in the UK over the Twentieth Century", *Journal of the Royal Statistical Society* A 168 (2005), pp. 325–43; Mike Savage and Karel Williams, "Elites: Remembered in Capitalism and Forgotten by Social Sciences", in *Remembering Elites,* Mike Savage and Karel Williams (eds) (Oxford: Blackwell, 2008), p. 11.

82. Tim Hatton and George Boyer, "Unemployment and the UK Labour Market Before, During and After the Golden Age", *European Review of Economic History* 9 (2005), pp. 35–60.

83. Christina Beatty, Steve Fothergill, Tony Gore and Ryan Powell, *The Real Rate of Unemployment 2007* (Sheffield: Sheffield Hallam University, 2007), p. 22.

84. Andrew Glyn, *Capitalism Unleashed: Finance, Globalization and Welfare* (Oxford: Oxford University Press, 2006), pp. 114–16; Nickell, "Fundamental Change", p. 724.

85. Stephen Machin, "Changes in UK Wage Inequality over the Last Forty Years", in *The Labour Market in Winter,* Paul Gregg and Jonathan Wadsworth (eds) (Oxford: Oxford University Press, 2011), p. 157; Maarten Goos and Andrew Manning, "Lousy and Lovely Jobs: the Rising Polarization of Work in Britain", *Review of Economics and Statistics* 89 (2007), pp. 118–33.

86. See the discussion of Rowntree's study of York in Keith Tribe's chapter on "Inequality", pp. 34–36.

87. Michael Hardie and Andrew Banks, "The Changing Shape of UK Manufacturing", London: Office for National Statistics (2014) (www.ons.gov.uk/ons/dcp171766_381512.pdf; accessed 27 April 2016).

88. Craig Holmes and Ken Mayhew, "The Changing Shape of the UK Job Market and Its Implications for the Bottom Half of Earners", Report, Resolution Foundation, London (2012), p. 5.

89. Machin, "Changes", p. 157.

90. *Ibid.*, pp. 157–8.

91. Sara Connolly and Mary Gregory, "Women and Work Since 1970", in *Work and Pay in Twentieth Century Britain,* Nicholas Crafts, Ian Gazeley and Andrew Newell (eds) (Oxford: Oxford University Press, 2007), p. 156.

92. Anthony Cutler, Karel Williams and John Williams, *Keynes, Beveridge and Beyond* (London: Routledge, 1986).

93. Brian Abel-Smith and Peter Townsend, *The Poor and the Poorest* (London: Bell, 1963), p. 49.

94. Joseph Rowntree Foundation, *Monitoring Poverty and Social Exclusion* (London: 2012), pp. 1–2.

95. Kevin Farnsworth, *Social Versus Corporate Welfare: Competing Needs and Interests Within the Welfare State* (London: Palgrave Macmillan, 2012).

96. Karl Polanyi, *The Great Transformation: The Political and Economic Origins of Our Time* (New York: Farrar & Reinhart, 1945), pp. 73–107.

97. Patrick Minford, *Unemployment: Cause and Cure* (Oxford: Blackwell, 1983).

98. Conservative Research Department, *The Minimum Wage: Labour's Axe on Jobs* (London, 1991), p. 10.

99. Andrew Hood and Laura Oakley, *A Survey of the GB Benefit System* (London: Institute for Fiscal Studies, 2014), p. 8.

100. Atkinson, *Inequality*, p. 161, suggests a Gini coefficient for housing wealth of around 56 per cent, while for income the figure is around 35 per cent.

101. Avner Offer, "The Market Turn: From Social Democracy to Market Liberalism", Economic History Society Tawney Lecture, April 2016, available at www.ehs.org.uk/multimedia/tawney-lecture-2016-the-market-turn-from-social-democracy-to-market-liberalism.

102. Anthony Giddens and Patrick Diamond (eds), *The New Egalitarianism* (Cambridge: Polity, 2005).

103. Patrick Diamond and Anthony Giddens, "The New Egalitarianism: Economic Inequality in the UK", in Giddens and Diamond, *The New Egalitarianism*, p. 107.

104. Atkinson, *Inequality*, p. 219; such ideas, with various names, have a long history in post-war Britain, and their advocates come from a range of ideological positions: see, for example, Wootton, "Labour Party", pp. 64–5.

105. Diamond and Giddens, "New Egalitarianism", pp. 118, 115.

106. Atkinson, *Inequality*, pp. 162–3. The comprehensive radicalism of Atkinson's proposals has similarities with the later work of James Meade, notably *The Intelligent Radical's Guide to Economic Policy* (London: Routledge, 1975) and *Agathopia: The Economics of Partnership* (Aberdeen: Aberdeen University Press, 1989); see Jackson, "Property-owning Democracy", pp. 44–8. Meade also foresaw increased polarization of the labour market: Martin O'Neill, "Piketty, Meade and Predistribution", http://crooked-timber.org/2015/12/17/piketty-meade-and-predistribution/ (accessed 27 April 2016).

PART III

PIKETTY: GLOBAL COMMENTARIES

10

LOOKING AT PIKETTY FROM
THE PERIPHERY

Luis Bértola

Thomas Piketty's *Capital in the Twenty-First Century* fully merits being the object of so much international attention and being the main topic of the present volume.[1] While a critical approach is needed, and while many weak points of the book, or even errors, are discussed in this volume, I cannot start this commentary without asserting my full agreement and concurrence with many points of departure adopted by Piketty.

THE APPROACH

The central question of the book is very relevant today across the globe. Is capitalism always leading, as Marx suggested, towards a steadily increasing concentration of wealth, income and power? Or, on the contrary, are the forces that counteract these trends likely to prevail, making capitalism compatible with democracy and the ideal of an egalitarian society, as the badly interpreted Kuznets curve suggests?

When tackling this question, Piketty adopts some points of view that awaken my enthusiasm: he makes an effort to present an innovative theoretical framework; he bases his conclusions on impressive empirical work, accumulated by large numbers of scholars and with an important degree of methodological ingenuity; and he shows serious commitment, involving himself in controversial policy recommendations that are certainly not likely to be acceptable in the eyes of powerful actors in the economy, in politics and in academia. In short, he offers a precise definition and description of the problem, a theoretical framework to approach and explain it, and some courageous policy recommendations.

The way in which Piketty understands what economic science is about is entirely accurate. Departing from an abstract definition of a perfectly functioning economy and discussing the way in which we should approach this abstract model, the strategy is to see how things really work, what the real trends are, and to try to explain them with a set of tools that largely surpass what is often considered as pure economics. This necessarily involves knowledge generated by other social sciences. Using these different sets of tools is the way in which relevant, penetrating and realistic theories, deeply rooted in historical contexts, can be constructed. Among the long list of so-called fundamental sources of growth and development presented by Adam Szirmai,[2] there are none that could be termed purely, or even largely, "economic": geography, institutions, the state, power, social classes, culture and more are not part of the core of what is commonly defined, and taught, as economics these days. Thus, Piketty's political economy approach recovers the best of the tradition of economics, and it does not get dazzled by the lights of supposedly more scientific modelling. I find it interesting to note how the so-called convergence/divergence debate has hitherto considered divergence as some kind of market failure. It has been seen as an exception and, most of the time, defined in terms of conditional convergence, occurring because various obstacles have interrupted the "normal" path of development. Once one controls for the many variables that might explain deviation from the expected result, divergence is assumed to disappear. This is amazing because the clearly dominant stylized fact of modern development, particularly since the Industrial Revolution, has been divergence in growth rates and per capita income levels globally. In spite of several strong criticisms, the economics profession, in most universities around the world, has mainly focused on more and more sophisticated elaborations of convergence models that often do not take into consideration critical qualitative aspects or other quantifiable variables, which are difficult to introduce in linear conceptualizations. Fortunately, other scholars, such as neo-institutionalists, evolutionaries, neo-Schumpeterians, neo-structuralists and others, fully accept divergence as the dominating stylized fact, and focus their studies on the different convergence and divergence trends and cycles in different parts of the globe and in different periods of time. Unfortunately, these approaches are still at the periphery of economics.

The relevance of the topics addressed by Piketty can hardly be overstated. Capitalism has shown itself to be well capable of improving the standard of living of the population. This is noticeable almost everywhere. Nevertheless, it is also clear that it produces and reproduces unacceptable inequalities, with an incredible concentration of wealth and political power, and the persistence, in many parts of the globe, of extreme poverty, exclusion, marginalization, coercive labour conditions and even slavery. One of the most revealing images of this situation is probably the massive contemporary immigration to Europe and the US, and the severe measures being taken to reduce and control such labour movements, at a time when free capital and commodity movements are prized as the path to development and higher growth. The power to impose free trade in manufactured goods and free capital movements contrasts with the exertion of that same power to reduce labour movements and to protect agricultural production in the developed world.

THE THEORY: A CONTEXT

Piketty's theory and conclusions about the prospects for the world economy and for future inequality trends are simple and clear. I will present them very briefly, as they can be found elsewhere in this volume. His first law of capitalism says that the share of capital profits in economic output depends on the interest rate and the wealth–income ratio. If the rate of return is given (say, 5 per cent, as he has measured it), then the income share of capital will depend on the wealth–income ratio. The second law says that, if a fixed savings rate is assumed, movements in inequality depend on the growth rate of the economy: the lower the growth rate, the higher the wealth–income ratio and share of capital profits in total income, and vice versa. On the basis of his assumptions and stylized facts, and based on different estimates of future growth rates worldwide in the decades to come, Piketty concludes that inequality will continue to rise unless counteracting political action is taken.

In order to discuss Piketty's contribution, it is important to place it within a more general framework: that of the relationship between growth and distribution in the world economy. Figure 10.1 presents a sketch of the main relationships that one needs to consider. Let us say that we have two kinds of country: more developed and less developed (A and B). Let us assume that there are two kinds of forces in action that determine the way in which growth impacts on distribution: pure economic forces on the one hand and social forces on the other, including power relations, institutions, culture and more. Let us also assume that these forces have an impact both on domestic distribution and on distribution between the two kinds of country. Let us further assume that distribution has an impact on growth at the domestic level as well as on relative growth between this pair of countries.

Piketty's approach mainly concentrates on the relations included in the oval. I do not mean that he completely forgets the other relations but, as we will see, his statements are mainly focused on this part of the story. And that is why I think his approach is severely limited. My purpose is not to completely disregard his theory, but I would like to make some criticisms of the way he approaches some of these relations as well as to present some ideas on how the inequality map can be completed.

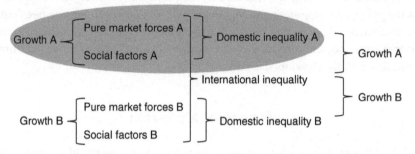

Figure 10.1. Distribution and growth in the world economy.

WHAT PIKETTY SAYS

Piketty can easily be placed in the Kuznetsian tradition that discusses the impact of growth on inequality. In the end, what he is saying is that, left to economic forces alone, the rate of growth determines the inequality outcome. He does not give us many ideas about how inequality impacts on growth. His concerns about inequality are mainly to do with social and political outcomes, and with ethical values. There is a large amount of literature discussing how inequality impacts on growth: through human capital, through the distribution of financial assets, through political instability, through aggregated demand, through the impact of heterogeneous consumption markets on innovation and economies of scale, through the creation of extractive institutions and more. These lines of research are very weak in his approach.

In discussing how growth impacts on inequality, he defends the interdisciplinary political economy approach. However, his work is not entirely consistent. Jan Bohlin, in his excellent review of *Capital in the Twenty-First Century* (unfortunately only published in Swedish),[3] very clearly shows how Piketty is weak when discussing the Cambridge debate and naively adopts the neoclassical approach to capital. As is well known, the European Cambridge view is that capital cannot be measured using its own technical unit; this is in contrast to labour, which can be measured in working hours. The only economically meaningful way to measure capital is by using its monetary value, as Piketty does. But that also means that the market value of capital is dependent on the income it generates. When profits rise among firms, their market value rises on the stock exchange. The same goes for the value of land if the income of landowners increases. This is probably the mechanism behind the remarkable long-run trend (around 5 per cent) in the rate of return on capital, documented by Piketty. Why the long-run rate of return on capital should fluctuate around 5 per cent is left unexplained by Picketty; however, it surely cannot be explained by the marginal productivity of "capital", since the market value of the latter, and thus its productivity, is causally dependent on the income stream it purportedly should explain.

What is really important is that there is an alternative way to approach the profit accruing to capital, not by quantifying it and estimating the average return to capital, but the other way round: by estimating the value of capital through the profits capitalists expect to gain. This profitability is not a pure market relation, but a social relation. The profit expected by capitalists is a social relation that rests upon the relation of forces in terms of market power as well as social and political power. The profit accruing to capital is itself a social relation. This is the approach followed not only by Marxists but also by post-Keynesians associated with the surplus approach, such as Piero Sraffa. The theoretical option chosen by Piketty is strange because the surplus approach seems to be much more in line with his general approach. However, by adopting the surplus approach the theory loses the deterministic outcome present in Piketty's predictions. His message suggests that if economic forces are left alone, the outcome will be a bad one. The problem is that there are no pure economic forces in the way in which the returns to capital are set. Continuing in this direction, the explanations of the different trends in income distribution may be better understood in terms of the social actors involved and the ways in which they organize and develop their bargaining forces. A highly industrialized society, with well-organized unions and a powerful social state, may give rise to a more equal society than one that is dominated by less organized service-sector workers within a globalized world, facing important outsourcing processes. Many other arguments along these lines may be mobilized to explain the trends found by Piketty.

WHAT PIKETTY DOES NOT SAY

So far I have mentioned that Piketty does not really pay much attention to the way in which inequality impacts on growth. There are in fact several issues that he does not deal with. Let us go back to Figure 10.1 and look more closely at the less developed world. How can we understand inequality trends there? In spite of his goodwill, Piketty's approach has been very Eurocentric. The data available, on the basis of which the main stylized facts are created, are largely from the most developed European countries, and many times we get the idea that the entire story of inequality is about the developed world. Of course, this is not what Piketty thinks. Nevertheless, he devoted less than five pages to inequality trends in emerging economies, without reaching any clear conclusions.[4]

The case of China is challenging. China has been growing very fast, with increasing inequality. Is this because the amount of capital has grown much faster than the rate of economic growth, or is it mainly due to a changing institutional environment? Or perhaps it is because of a huge technological spillover. The case of Latin America could validate the laws we are discussing, if we consider that South America is a continent that, in the long run, has been growing rather slowly and has maintained very high levels of inequality. In spite of many internal differences, Latin America has had structurally high inequality. No doubt these inequality levels must be related to particular economic, social and political circumstances, which have developed and transformed over the very long period of time since the European conquest. Nevertheless, if we look at the period since the 1870s, it is very difficult to find a law relating growth to inequality. We have witnessed several different patterns of growth alongside different patterns of inequality. We have long-run estimates for two Latin American countries: Chile[5] and Uruguay[6]. These two cases show, on the one hand, that the levels of inequality were steadily higher in Chile than in Uruguay. But, on the other hand, and in spite of that, both countries show a similar pattern. Instead of a Kuznets curve, we have a succession of periods of increasing and falling inequality, with some periods lasting several decades. In neither of the two countries is it possible to find a correlation between inequality trends and growth trends: periods of fast growth are found both with increasing and falling inequality, and the other way round. Moreover, inequality changes differ from crisis to crisis. What the authors of the studies on Chile and Uruguay agree on is that what matters are the patterns of economic development, which can only be understood using a political economy approach.

Piketty very briefly mentions the importance of the profits from natural resources for some less developed countries. It is difficult to overestimate the role played by this. As with other primary producers, Latin American countries have been subject to very high volatility in their growth rates, which can mainly be related to patterns of specialization based on a few families of products centred on primary production.[7] In spite of the existence of significant technological change and productivity growth, cyclical growth is mainly explained by the appearance and disappearence of huge profits from natural resources. The way in which these profits are distributed is at the core of political life in Latin America and the crises produced by the downward phase of the cycles have in most cases induced radical political changes. It is no accident that the current crisis of the Latin American economies after a decade of fast growth has been accompanied by extensive political changes. While many populist and Leftist movements in power fuelled the social agenda and were able to construct broad political alliances behind them, the fall of commodity prices made the distributive agreements unsustainable, including the distribution of bribes among politicians. These trends are not clearly related to the capital–output ratio, productivity growth or technological change. The prospects for income inequality in Latin America are very much tied up with how the profits from the natural resources are distributed, in a context in which, finally, democratic rule seems to have consolidated. These prospects also depend on whether Latin American countries will be able to change their pattern of development through changes in their productive structures and institutional environments and take advantage of the huge technological gap still in existence.

But this is not the whole story. What is also of great importance is how inequality has impacted on growth in Latin America. Some authors, such as Coatsworth,[8] have stressed that increasing inequality was a precondition for growth during the nineteenth century, which involved the privatization of land and the creation of a capitalist labour market. However, there is no doubt that the sequels of slavery and other forms of coercive labour have impacted upon Latin American social structures, leaving a legacy of limited access to political participation, significant backwardness in levels of education and very slow development of skill-based economic activities. Thus, the link between high inequality and distinctive patterns of development and specialization ended in a long-run trend of slow growth and limited structural change.

MIND THE GAP

It is somewhat confusing to see how the concepts of inequality and divergence are used almost as synonyms in Piketty's work. He is well aware of the work of Bourguignon and Morrison,[9] who adopted the global view by quantifying inequality "among world citizens", which is something that has also been done by Branko Milanovic in several books.[10] This approach explicitly considers and quantifies both domestic and international inequalities. Moreover, Milanovic likes to say that, in order to understand inequality nowadays, it is of more importance to know someone's nationality than their social class. However, this is not congruent with Piketty's work, because his whole discussion has been clearly dominated by inequality trends within the developed countries. Because of his approach, Piketty is missing the very important debate about convergence and divergence trends in the world economy that has been taking place in recent decades. This debate involves both empircal and theoretical questions of huge interest.

The bold lines of international relative growth are very clear: divergence has been the dominating stylized fact since the Industrial Revolution, even during the decades in which Piketty finds decreasing inequality in the developed countries due to high growth rates. The high growth rates of the Golden Age implied a huge increase in international inequality. This is very important, because the income of capital is a socioeconomic phenomenon that takes place within and between particular political units, with particular institutional features. As has been stressed many times, the fruits of productivity growth are not distributed as if markets worked perfectly; most of the time, distribution takes collusive forms. These collusive forms apply to the international arena in particular. However, in spite of growing inequality in both the developed world and China, the high growth rates of China and other emerging economies have produced, in recent decades, a slight reversal of the long-run inequality trend. Thus, when taking inequality worldwide into account, the stylized facts look quite different to those sketched by Piketty, and we need more analytical tools.

In order to simplify this discussion, let us consider that international divergence or convergence trends depend on factor accumulation and factor movements as well as on technological change. If factors move following the neoclassical diminishing marginal returns assumption, then we can expect a process of convergence. However, we have seen that the profits of capital involve social relations that may take different forms. Besides, the very concept of marginal diminishing returns to capital has been criticized from very different schools of thought, even the neoclassical, because of the existence of economies of scale and agglomeration. Even if these arguments may be used in favour of Piketty's assumptions of increased inequality (between countries), the logic is quite different and, if the social conditions are given, as the case of China is showing us, capital may move to the less developed regions and foster high growth rates there.

What about technological change as a source of growth? For the sake of simplicity, let us follow the model developed by Verspagen.[11] Technological change depends on R&D investment, some kind of supply of knowledge, and a demand-side technological change induced through the pattern of specialization, i.e. through the dynamic response of exports to the expansion of world demand. It can be assumed that in both cases developed countries have an advantage over less developed countries. The per capita GDP level is higher, and the shares of R&D investment in GDP are higher in developed countries than in developing ones. The pattern of specialization is much more favourable, as rich countries control the markets of fast-expanding sectors, inducing faster technological change. Thus, the expected outcome is one of international divergence and, thus, increasing world inequality. However, as endogenous growth theories have stressed, there exist counteracting mechanisms, such as technological spillovers. The wider the technological gap, the higher the potential growth rate of technological change of a less developed country. Technological spillovers may overcome the increasing gap produced by the two other components, thus generating a process of convergence. However, a very wide gap may imply that the less developed country has no social capabilities to make use of the gap; therefore, the divergent trend results in a steady process of polarization. There is plenty of space here for policy: increasing R&D investment, changing the patterns of specialization, developing social capabilities to take advantage of the gap, etc. A country may diverge if the gap is wide and social capabilities weak; a country may conditionally converge, using the gap, towards a point of equilibrium given by the relative position in terms of specialization and R&D investment; and a country may absolutely converge, or even forge ahead, if it takes leading positions in R&D investment and specialization.

In short, we can get quite different outcomes as a result of the interaction between different supply and demand forces. Different growth rates at the international level result in changing international inequalities, but these changing inequalities have a huge impact on growth prospects in different parts of the world. It is difficult to believe that increasing international inequality can be the best environment for increasing global growth rates. International coordination and cooperation is not only a way to reduce inequality within countries, but also a way to reduce inequality between countries and to stabilize and increase global growth.

Finally, a short note on technological change and economic growth. Technological change is not at the core of Piketty's theory, but technological change has been the driving force of capitalist development. Much of future development will depend on how our societies succeed in directing technological change in environmentally friendly ways as well as on the path that the new technological paradigm – based on information and communications technology, nanoscience and biotechnologies – follows across the world. We will face new challenges in measuring growth and well-being, and it will probably be difficult to compare growth rates between different periods, as the content of growth and development may differ. If we were just talking about how the less developed countries of today could make use of the still huge technological gap, we could be optimistic about a reduction in international inequalities. However, technology is specific to particular sectors and activities, and taking advantage of the gap will depend on many domestic transformations in the developing countries. The great problem we are facing is that the whole world economy needs a substantial change in the technological and social paradigm to take place in order to continue growing, so the developing countries have to converge towards an unknown. In a context in which technological change is at the core, the distributive outcomes of growth within and between countries is not predictable. Neither is the way in which distributional outcomes will impact on the pattern of technological change and the pace of economic growth.

In any case, my agreement with Piketty on this point is total: policy matters, politics and social relations are at the core of this, and the extent to which the world will be a better place to live in in the future depends upon both.

Notes for Chapter 10

1. I want to thank Jan Bohlin for instructive conversations and comments and corrections to the first draft of the manuscript. Thanks also to Jorge Álvarez and Javier Rodríguez Weber for reading and commenting on the first draft. And thanks to the editors of this volume for their comments and help with the editing.

2. Adam Szirmai, *Socio-Economic Development*, 2nd edn (Cambridge: Cambridge University Press, 2015). Szirmai is a professor at UNU-MERIT and Maastricht University.

3. Jan Bohlin, "Kapitalism och ojämlikhet: *Capital in the twenty-first century* av Thomas Piketty", *Historisk tidskrift* 134(4) (2014), pp. 686–97.

4. Thomas Piketty, *Capital in the Twenty-First Century* (Cambridge, MA: Harvard University Press, 2014), pp. 326–30.

5. Javier Rodríguez Weber, *Desarrollo y Desigualdad en Chile (1850–2009): Historia de su economía política* (Centro de Investigaciones Diego Barros Arana: Ediciones de la Dirección de Bibliotecas, Archivos y Museos, 2016).

6. Luis Bértola, "A 50 años de la curva de Kuznets: crecimiento económico y distribución del ingreso en Uruguay y otras economías de nuevo asentamiento desde 1870", *Investigaciones de Historia Económica* 3 (2005), pp. 135–76.

7. Luis Bértola and José Antonio Ocampo, *The Economic Development of Latin America Since Independence* (Oxford: Oxford University Press, 2012).

8. John H. Coatsworth, "Inequality, Institutions and Economic Growth in Latin America", *Journal of Latin American Studies* 40 (2008), pp. 545–69.

9. François Bourguignon and Christian Morrison, "Inequality among World Citizens: 1820–1992", *American Economic Review* 92(4) (2002), pp. 727–44.

10. Branko Milanovic, *Global Inequality: A New Approach for the Age of Globalization* (Cambridge, MA: Harvard University Press, 2016); Branko Milanovic, *The Haves and the Have-Nots: A Brief and Idiosyncratic History of Global Inequality* (New York: Basic Books, 2010); Branko Milanovic, *Worlds Apart: Measuring International and Global Inequality* (Princeton, NJ: Princeton University Press, 2005).

11. Bart Verspagen, *Uneven Growth Between Interdependent Economies: An Evolutionary View on Technology Gaps, Trade and Growth* (Aldershot: Avebury, 1993).

11

THE DIFFERENCES OF INEQUALITY IN AFRICA

Patrick Manning and Matt Drwenski

Piketty's main argument on the world's economies, in highly condensed form, is that the rate of return on capital r (annual corporate profits divided by the market value of capital stock) exceeds the rate of growth of domestic economies g (the average annual change in net national income). As a result, income for the wealthy grows so that inequality (measured by distribution of either income or wealth) continues to grow. Further, where formation of capital is through inheritance rather than saving, this inequality is reinforced. Piketty proposes a tax on capital as a way to redress the balance and limit inequality.

The African continent, while often neglected in economic studies, is a region of growing population and economic transformation, though not of impressive growth. The design of this chapter is to assume considerable validity in Piketty's assertions for the leading global economies, and to ask to what degree these assertions apply to Africa: to individual nations or to the continent as a whole. Is it the case that rates of profit in Africa exceed rates of economic growth? Is the level of inequality and the growth of inequality in Africa greater or lower than for leading economies? More generally, in what way does Africa contribute to global inequality?

We review the application of Piketty's thinking on Africa and emphasize three main points. First, African levels of inequality seem generally high, and the temporal shifts of inequality in the undercapitalized countries of the African tropics seem to differ significantly from major economies. Our initial analysis suggests that inequality in African nations has been higher than for the major world economies highlighted in Piketty's analysis and, in addition, that the shifting temporal patterns of inequality for most of Africa differ from patterns for leading economies. In many African economies, the peak of income inequality occurred around the 1960s, the very period of the lowest inequality in Europe and the US. Additionally, while inequality has risen in African economies from the 1990s, most African countries have avoided the rapid increase in income inequality that marked the economies in Piketty's analysis. We also note that the rate and timing of inequality for African economies is dispersed to a greater degree than for leading economies.

Second, for Africa, Piketty's calculations of income and wealth need to be adjusted to account for international transfers. Moving beyond GDP to consider the details of net national income, especially international transfers, brings increased precision to estimates of the rate of return and levels of inequality within many African domestic economies.[1] Outbound repatriation of profits reduces national income and lowers incremental additions to capital stock, thereby reducing top domestic incomes and overall inequality. Inbound remittance of wages adds to mid-level incomes and further mitigates inequality. Overall, accounting for transfers reduces estimates of African inequality.

Third, deficiencies in African data must be overcome to permit a full analysis. We have not found adequate estimates of African wealth or inheritance patterns. We thus restrict our analysis to income inequality, neglecting patterns of wealth and inheritance. Within the analysis of income inequality, we must still grapple with the deficiencies of survey data. The scarcity of African taxation data requires us to rely on survey data to estimate incomes: these estimates fluctuate with high volatility and, most importantly, underestimate the degree of inequality because of under-sampling among top incomes.[2] In addition, using Gini coefficients as a measure of inequality (whether with tax-based or survey-based income data) may give underestimates of inequality, especially at upper and lower limits. The deficiencies in African data bring both upward and downward biases, but overall, it appears that current data underestimate African inequality.

The discussion here takes place in four sections. The first two sections address readily available data on African colonial and national economies. First, we explore a range of income inequality measures for African economies from as early as 1910, and focus on the era from 1993 to 2012. With these calculations we estimate levels of African inequality, the timing of shifts in African inequality, the dispersion in African rates of inequality and the discrepancies caused by inadequate data. Second, we explore data on African capital investment from 1870 to 1935, which shows the sharp difference between the highly capitalized mining economy of southern Africa and the territories of tropical Africa.

The second half of the chapter addresses our concerns about, and revisions to, the estimates of African inequality. In the third section, we model two sorts of complication to Piketty's analysis through explicit accounting of international transfers: outbound repatriation of profits and inbound remittance of wages. Fourth, we develop estimates of rates and directions of inequality for African economies beginning in 1993, with attention to international transfers and their effect on growth and profitability. In a concluding section we emphasize the importance and the feasibility of developing better data for African economies, but we also emphasize the importance of extending studies of inequality from the current focus on income to the broader contours of social inequality.

AFRICAN INCOME INEQUALITY, 1950–2012

We find several distinctive patterns of African inequality, based on evidence drawn primarily from survey data. First, along with Latin America, Africa as a whole is estimated to have the highest level of income inequality today. It also appears to have been among the most unequal regions in the world in the last half of the twentieth century, and perhaps earlier as well.

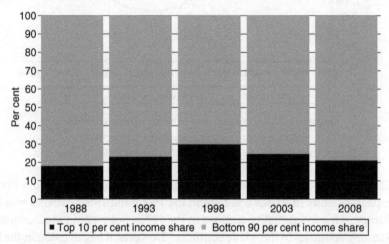

Figure 11.1. Total African top decile income share (1988, 1993, 1998, 2003, 2008). Includes aggregated figures for nations with two-thirds of the African population. (*Source:* Lakner–Milanovic World Panel Income Distribution database.)

Data from Milanovic's World Panel Income Distribution database on inequality (2008) shows that the top decile's share of total income in surveyed African nations was approximately 51 per cent, compared with Piketty's estimates of 45 per cent for the US and 37 per cent for Europe at that time.[3] Another breakdown of income distribution, shown in Figure 11.1 and also prepared by Milanovic, contrasts the top decile of continental African income, for five selected years, with the remaining 90 per cent. These five years of estimates show a decline in African income inequality after 1998 that contrasts with the contemporary upward trend in Europe and North America. The latter estimates of top-decile share of income are lower than in the previous case, since under-sampling for the top decile is more severe in this case.[4]

Figure 11.2 pursues this point, showing steady growth in African inequality from 1950 to 2008. It sums the inequality in mean GDP per capita among African nations, weighted by population. The same figure shows the global average of inequality calculated in the same way. Comparing the curves shows the relative level of African inequality and the distinctiveness of the African trajectory.

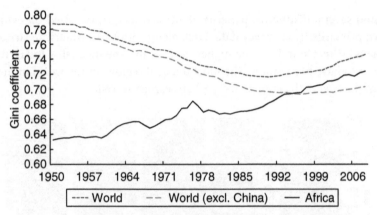

Figure 11.2. Gini coefficient of GDP for African economies,
weighted by population, with global comparators.
(*Source:* Angus Maddison project (http://bit.ly/1JoYD3B), 2013 version.)

The timing of change in African inequality differs substantially from that in Europe. Inequality in Africa was high in the 1950s and 1960s, when it was low in Europe. African inequality declined in the 1970s, both within most countries and among countries in the whole continent. However, it began rising in the late 1980s as it remained flat in continental Europe but increased in North America and Britain. Many African economies avoided the dramatic spike in income inequality in the major economies that started in the 1990s.

Piketty correctly emphasizes that global patterns of destruction and creation of capital, as in the world wars, tend to synchronize the timing of shifts in inequality. On the other hand, variant regional rates of growth, the presence or absence of mineral wealth, fluctuating prices of export commodities and regional or national-level crises can help to explain the lack of unifying trends in African economic inequality.[5]

As a supplementary point, the per capita national income of African countries diverged significantly during the post-independence period. Figure 11.3 shows the share of the top 10 per cent of incomes for West African economies, notably Senegal, Nigeria and Côte d'Ivoire: the period of the 1970s through the 1990s was a period of flat or declining inequality.[6] As scholars working for the World Income and Wealth Database have noted, these surveys consistently under-sample high incomes and understate the top echelon's share. While it is the case that many of these surveys are unreliable and rely on equally unreliable national accounts data, the broad trends and directions of the data from household surveys do match top-income data collected from tax records. Both groups of nations – those whose inequality patterns match the cycles of leading economies and those that do not – illustrate that the 1960s was a time of peak inequality in many African economies.

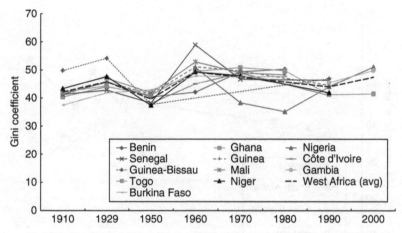

Figure 11.3. National Gini coefficients of income for West African nations with an unweighted average. (*Source:* Clio Infra.[7])

South Africa is an outlier in Figure 11.4 (p. 212), which indicates top income shares. It parallels the leading economies surveyed in *Capital in the Twenty-First Century*; the other African countries follow different temporal patterns. The variations in Gini coefficients for West Africa shown in Figure 11.3 illustrate the dispersion of African levels of inequality, in contrast with the consistency of inequality as found by Piketty for European economies.

To explore further the difference in inequality estimates based on survey data and tax-based data, Figure 11.5 presents both types of estimates for South Africa. South Africa is one of the few countries for which inequality can be estimated both from survey and tax-based data. In Figure 11.5, which graphs both survey and tax record estimates of the same measure of top-income shares, we can see that the survey data point for 1965 is significantly lower than the tax record data for the same period. The higher quality surveys from more recent years give numbers quite similar to those from tax data. The use of less reliable surveys to fill in gaps in other records and to approximate trends cannot be overlooked for nations with a paucity of available historical records. Figure 11.5 shows that South African survey-based estimates of the Gini coefficient of income inequality are more volatile than tax-based estimates. However, it is possible that both are capturing similar general trends in the evolution of national income inequality. Many of the surveys compiled in the global data sets on income inequality for African economies are labelled poor or unreliable, and many more show impossibly large fluctuations from year to year. Improved data are in preparation, but for now we must work with less reliable data from household surveys.[8]

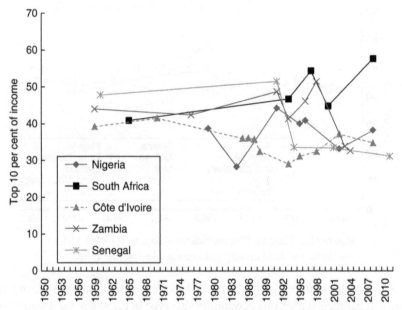

Figure 11.4. Top 10 per cent income shares in select African economies.
(*Source:* UNU–WIID survey data from Côte d'Ivoire,
South Africa, Zambia, Nigeria and Senegal.)

We can see that, despite the pitfalls of top-income data, shares of the top decile or top 1 per cent often follow patterns parallel to other measures of inequality, such as the Gini coefficient. The survey data from the United Nations University–World Income Inequality Database (UNU–WIID) follow a pattern similar to the tax record data collected by the WWID, as shown in Figure 11.6. More generally, African economies have the largest percentage of their populations living in poverty: 42.7 per cent were living on $1.90 or less a day in 2012, according to the World Bank. David Soskice notes Piketty's inattention to poverty and bottom incomes in general; this gap in the analysis is of special concern for African economies.[9]

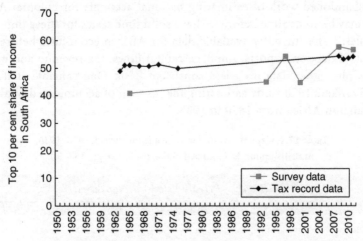

Figure 11.5. Comparison of tax record and survey data measuring
top 10 per cent share of income in South Africa.
(*Source:* UNU–WIID (surveys) and WWID (tax records).)

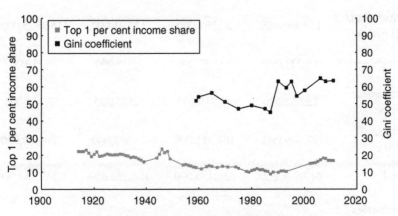

Figure 11.6. Top incomes for South Africa (left *y*-axis)
and Gini coefficients for South Africa (right *y*-axis).
(*Source:* World Bank Estimates (Gini) and WWID (top 1 per cent).)

CAPITAL AND INEQUALITY IN AFRICAN ECONOMIES, 1870–1935

Historical estimates of domestic product and domestic income in the years
before 1960, while estimated in some detail for South Africa, are almost
absent for most African economies.[10] Morten Jerven has returned to the

long-abandoned work of estimating national accounts for colonial Africa, but it may be some time before we have solid time series for these important variables.[11] The currently available data for African economies before 1960 consist of data on exports, imports, capital flows, tax revenue and expenditure, plus other data on a less consistent basis. One valuable analysis is S. H. Frankel's 1938 study estimating the "growth of accumulated wealth" in sub-Saharan Africa from 1870 to 1935.[12]

Table 11.1. Capital invested in Africa from abroad, 1870–1936, in British pounds. (*Source:* Frankel (note 12), pp. 158–9.)

	Public-listed capital	Private-listed capital	Non-listed capital (est.)	Total capital
Regions				
Southern Africa	285,802,000	311,547,000	59,735,000	657,084,000
British West Africa	50,871,000	60,430,000	5,429,000	116,730,000
British East/ NE Africa	112,163,000	30,569,000	13,791,000	156,523,000
French Africa	43,031,000	23,931,000	3,348,000	70,310,000
Portuguese Africa	18,532,000	42,710,000	5,390,000	66,732,000
Belgian Africa	97,509,000	167,311,000	15,559,000	280,379,000
Total	617,908,000	636,498,000	103,252,000	1,347,758,000
Territories				
Union of South Africa	224,089,000	250,835,000	47,547,000	522,471,000
Nigeria	34,721,000	36,790,000	3,576,000	75,087,000
Tanganyika & Zanzibar	31,340,000	15,841,000	4,718,000	51,899,000

Frankel showed that huge amounts of European capital flowed to South Africa from the 1870s for investment in the diamond mines of Kimberley.

These investments were highly profitable, and the profits were held dominantly in South Africa. As a result, when the gold mines expanded dramatically in the 1890s, they drew especially on the accumulated profits from diamonds to invest in gold, rather than expanding sharply the overseas investment in gold. The high profitability of gold mining continued for the first half of the twentieth century; the South African government taxed gold enterprises very heavily, investing the revenues especially in programmes of social support for the Afrikaner population, principally in rural areas.[13]

Frankel's estimate of aggregate overseas investment in sub-Saharan Africa (1870–1913) totalled £610 million, including £370 million for Southern Africa.[14] By 1935, this total had roughly doubled to £1,322 million for sub-Saharan Africa, with £523 million for the Union of South Africa alone. The deceleration of overseas investment in South Africa was in response to the early accumulation and high profitability of domestic South African capital. For sub-Saharan Africa as a whole, the annual net overseas investment averaged £7–8 million per year from 1870 to 1936.[15]

Table 11.1 shows a regional breakdown of aggregate overseas investment in sub-Saharan Africa. This is based on published records for government and public investment as well as on statements of private listed capital. For non-listed capital, notably that brought by immigrants to Africa, Frankel offered speculative estimates.

Frankel also provided estimates of funded debt, though only for British African territories, as shown in Table 11.2. For South Africa, he estimated that 90 per cent of funded debt was external; the figure would have been even higher for other territories. Interest rates on these debts ranged from 3 per cent to 5 per cent per year. While GDP figures are not yet available for African territories in the inter-war years, Frankel did calculate ratios of debt charges to the value of domestic exports, and to the value of territorial government revenue, for the years 1928–35. For Kenya, debt charges ranged from 16 per cent to 44 per cent of export value, and from 18 per cent to 34 per cent of revenue. For Nigeria, debt charges ranged from 8 per cent to 19 per cent of export value, and from 22 per cent to 33 per cent of revenue.[16]

Table 11.2: Funded debt of British African territories, in British pounds. (*Source:* Frankel (note 12), pp. 176–7.)

	Union of South Africa	Other British Africa
1925	209,310,000	63,699,000
1935	247,439,000	99,320,000

In sum, Frankel shows that South Africa received large amounts of overseas capital, especially during the mining boom before the First World War, and retained most profits to build a substantial domestic capital stock that has since fuelled growth in the domestic economy. Among African economies, South Africa has been closest by far to the pattern of leading economies. Unsurprisingly, South African income inequality in the rest of the twentieth century is much closer to the pattern in major economies outside of Africa. Tropical African territories, of much larger area and population, received smaller amounts of overseas capital. Even in the Belgian Congo, a site of relatively high investment, it is likely that large proportions of mining profits were repatriated. Teasing out the implications of these colonial-era patterns for the levels and timing of inequality in tropical Africa, however, remains a task for future research.

MODELLING INEQUALITY WITH ATTENTION TO TRANSFERS

Piketty, after initially expressing his interpretation in terms of r (rate of return on capital) and g (annual growth in national income), extends his argument by exploring the accounting identity $\alpha = r \times \beta$. In this identity, α is the share of income from capital in national income, β is the overall capital–income ratio and r remains the rate of return on capital. As noted earlier, the details of our analysis are not in terms of the GDP figures on which Piketty mainly relies, but rather in terms of net national income (NNI), in order to give attention to transfers. "National income", in this case, is net national income, after depreciation of capital, but adding and subtracting international transfers of income (T); overall capital at market rate is K.[17] As shown in the accompanying note, we find that important issues can be raised by breaking down the various international transfers of income to reveal big questions about inequality in the domestic economy.[18]

The result of this specification of transfers, for African and doubtless other economies, is that α decreases and β increases. Further, for the identity $\alpha = r \times \beta$ to remain in force, the decrease in α and the increase in β mean that r must decrease, and by a larger degree than the change in either α or β. The simple algebra of this exercise demonstrates that repatriation of profits must reduce the profitability of the domestic economy. The same algebraic statements indicate the effects of other types of African transfers on the shares of income and the capital–income ratio. The implications of these points for African inequality are substantial, as we will show below.

Now that we have derived the direction of the effects of transfers on African macroeconomies, we must inquire as to their magnitude. At this point, we are short of data, but we can offer a heuristic estimate to suggest that transfers can in fact be significant overall. Let us begin with the common figure for shares of income: 30 per cent profit and 70 per cent wages. Then, we can cautiously suggest that corporate profits are half of income from capital (15 per cent of national income), while rent and interest comprise the other half. If 60 per cent of corporate profits were repatriated, that would come to 9 per cent of NNI, enough to create a measurable reduction in overall domestic rates of return. Further, as we show in the next section, transfers from migrant workers commonly reach 3 per cent of GDP, and sometimes exceed that level. Our overall point is that, if the magnitude of some of these transfers becomes large enough, they can influence the value of all the variables in this analysis of economic growth and inequality.

A perhaps smaller, but still significant, issue in the African macroeconomics of growth and change is the consistent underestimation of domestic capital formation. This includes underestimation of African financial capital, but the issue focuses primarily on underestimation of investment in housing, land improvements, intermediate goods and human capital.[19] If capital stock is estimated as the full market value of in-country capital, but in-country income does not include departing repatriation of profit by either domestic or foreign investors, the level of r will be reduced. If the estimate of capital stock adds neglected small-scale domestic capital, the level of β increases and the level of r for the domestic economy will be reduced as a result.

In short, because of the significance of international transfers, calculations based simply on GDP may significantly distort the levels and distribution of African national incomes. For Piketty's analysis, the estimation of g is not difficult, in that annual estimates of NNI and interannual growth rates are calculated by individual countries and international organizations. But as with capital and investment, the calculation of national income and national product involve many options for transfers that can raise and lower the estimates for key variables. The rising importance of remittances from emigrant nationals adds to the nation's income and tends to balance any outflow of corporate profit. It is worthy of note that financial transactions are formally left outside of national income analysis, so that even "income" may mean a different thing when one is calculating r rather than calculating g. A few experiments with alternative possibilities show that the potential fluctuation of estimates for r is greater than that for g; the overall potential fluctuation in the ratio of r to g is greater than either taken alone.

This is the basic dilemma of investigating Piketty's theses for Africa. The need to account for international flows of capital, income and output makes it difficult to calculate rates of g and r for any individual nation and, further, basically makes it necessary to conduct the analysis for groups of nations rather than for any single nation. To know whether growth rates and profit rates in Africa are higher or lower than for other regions – that is, whether Africa is adding to global inequality or not – requires taking positions on the various ways of estimating r and g for Africa, finding relevant data and conducting the test.

AFRICAN INEQUALITY SINCE 1993: ACCOUNTING FOR TRANSFERS

Data from the World Bank Migration Remittance Project shows that twenty of Africa's fifty national units have incoming migrant remittance rates of over 3 per cent of GDP per year; for all of them, the outgoing remittance rates are far smaller and are commonly negligible. The African nations with relatively high incoming remittances are especially small countries, with populations under 2 million (Gambia: 21.2 per cent of GDP per year, Comoros: 20.2 per cent, Cabo Verde: 10.5 per cent and São Tomé: 8.0 per cent). However, also included are countries with populations of over 10 million, including Senegal (10.5 per cent), Mali (7.4 per cent), Egypt (6.5 per cent), Ghana (5.2 per cent), Madagascar (4.0 per cent), Nigeria (3.7 per cent), Uganda (3.3 per cent), Benin (3.2 per cent) and Burkina Faso (3.2 per cent), as well as two countries with a population of over 80 million: Egypt (6.5 per cent of GDP) and Nigeria (3.7 per cent).

Most remittances come from outside of Africa. There is also significant remittance among African countries, commonly with neighbouring countries. For Nigeria in 2014, $14.8 billion in remittances came from outside Africa out of a total of $20.8 billion in total remittances; for Senegal the equivalent figures were $1.1 billion out of $1.6 billion, and for Liberia they were $263 million out of $528 million. An exception was Lesotho, for which remittances came overwhelmingly from South Africa. Remittance streams, though poorly documented until recently, seem to be fairly stable for each country, though they vary significantly among countries. They add to national income and to the non-corporate sector of the national economy.

A 2014 study estimated large-scale African transfers, suggesting that a net $46 billion in corporate profit is transferred annually out of Africa, plus an additional $30 billion in illicit financial flows.[20] A 2015 *Wall Street Journal* article argued that, for US corporations in 2014, some 65 per cent of net profits in overseas enterprises were repatriated to the US.[21] For many economies, two-way repatriation of corporate profit would yield a small net flow. But African economies have not made substantial direct investments overseas, so the annual outflow of corporate profits is likely to be rather close to the net flow of corporate profits. In sum, this quick exploration suggests that the contribution of corporate profits to NNI in African economies is significantly reduced by transfers. As a result, the domestic rate of return on capital and the domestic share of capital in national income are each reduced measurably.

CONCLUSION

Piketty argues, in his projection for the future, that "Africa would be the only exception: in the central scenario ... the capital–income ratio is expected to be lower in Africa than in other continents throughout the twenty-first century (essentially because Africa is catching up economically much more slowly and its demographic transition is also delayed)".[22] Piketty's analysis is based on gross capital stock. However, if substantial repatriation of profits continues at the present rate, the size of African capital stock will be even smaller than he has shown. The pattern of substantial repatriation of profits has continued in Africa for over a century (with the exception of South Africa); changing that pattern will be difficult.[23]

We are left, then, with seemingly contradictory conclusions about African inequality and about African capital–income ratios. The empirical surveys of inequality appear to show that African inequality is relatively high, which would tend to suggest a high capital–income ratio. But the study of Africa's international transfers suggests that high levels of repatriation of profits remove a large stream of capital from African domestic economies, thereby reducing the domestic capital–income ratio. At this stage of our research, we are unable to resolve this contradiction. Instead, we make the argument that this contradiction makes African situations into a set of interesting outliers in the global economic system, and we call for more research into the details underlying these initial observations.

We have established a strong presumption that African levels of inequality, for the twentieth and twenty-first centuries, have been high on a world scale. We propose a comparison of African inequality with that of India and Indonesia. To take the comparison further, we would test the hypothesis that inequality and its shifts for those two national economies are intermediate between African economies, whose pattern they most closely resemble in the decades after independence, and those of Europe, whose pattern these economies have moved towards in the last three decades. What, then, is the practical social character of such inequality? What social description can be given to such inequality? For instance, are households separated into discrete strata and regional groupings at various levels of income, or are households of various incomes linked to each other in chains of dependence? One approach to answering such questions requires pursuing deeper economic analysis. For instance, while inequality surveys commonly identify subjects as equal members of households, the surveys can be expanded to analyse individuals within their households. This would make it possible to learn, for instance, whether female incomes have risen over time, thus lowering inequality. Another approach to the meaning of inequality is to consult the very large literatures in the sociology and anthropology of Africa, which can surely be linked to evidence on economic inequality to construct a picture of the character and functioning of these inegalitarian societies. The problem presents an opportunity for historians and economists to incorporate more local or micro-level information, as well as patterns of everyday living, into larger studies.

We favour not only deepening the economic analysis of inequality but also expanding the analysis beyond economic data to consider social, health and other dimensions of human inequality. While income and wealth reflect the most prominent dimensions of inequality, it is not necessarily the case that today's situation of massive economic inequality has its origin or its underlying motor in economic phenomena. That is, it might be that social prejudices and stratification have done much to initiate inequality, and that differential health conditions have reinforced inequalities in income. This is in addition to economic mechanisms expanding inequality, such as those identified by Piketty. Similar to Piketty's outlining of the broad forces of convergence and divergence in levels of economic inequality, scholars should seek to outline what forces, actions, state policies and historical inheritances drive other forms of non-economic inequality to either crosscut and bridge divisions of wealth and income, or reinforce and bolster economic strata. To explore this range of social and historical issues, our research group is building infrastructure and collecting data to create and to archive world-historical information on inequality and related phenomena.[24]

Notes for Chapter 11

1. Piketty gives a clear and early statement of the advantages of net national income over gross domestic product (GDP) for the study of income inequality (pp. 43–5), but in practice he uses GDP for his analysis and illustrations. Thomas Piketty, *Capital in the Twenty-First Century* (Cambridge, MA: Harvard University Press, 2014), pp. 60–1.

2. Anthony B. Atkinson, Thomas Piketty and Emmanuel Saez, "Top Incomes in the Long Run of History", *Journal of Economic Literature* 49 (2011), pp. 3–71. Additional complications of interest are that African economies, while they are and have long been thoroughly monetized, maintain significant boundaries among different market segments. Distinctions of rural versus urban and domestic versus international sectors of the economy make it difficult to come up with internationally comparable figures for national income, much less economic welfare. Small-scale domestic investment is typically underestimated or neglected for African economies.

3. The survey covers two-thirds of Africa's population. Branko Milanovic, 2008 update to the World Income Distribution (WYD) data set; Piketty, *Capital*, statistical appendix; Atkinson *et al.*, "Top Incomes in the Long Run".

4. While this survey only breaks down each of the sixteen countries surveyed into income percentiles, it most likely still under-samples the upper tail of the income distribution beyond the top 1 per cent. The estimates of Figure 11.1, while illustrative, lack the complete coverage of the continent needed for a comparison with other African data and with the major world economies. Christoph Lakner and Branko Milanovic (2013), "World Panel Income Distribution", in "Global Income Distribution: From the Fall of the Berlin Wall to the Great Recession", World Bank Policy Research Working Paper 6719 (Washington, DC: World Bank, 2013).

5. Piketty, *Capital*, pp. 146–50.

6. Based on surveys of varying-quality data compiled from the UNU–WIIDER project (www.wider.unu.edu/).

7. "Income Inequality" data set by Michalis Moatsis, Jan Luiten van Zanden, Joerg Baten, Peter Foldvari and Bas van Leeuwen, Clio-Infra (www.clio-infra.eu/datasets/search). The records are derived from surveys, historical reconstructions, and estimations.

8. In comparison to the US and the Western European economies, we have little compiled data on top incomes for African economies, although Tony Atkinson of the WWID is making remarkable progress on this front.

9. David Soskice, *"Capital in the Twenty-First Century*: A Critique", *British Journal of Sociology* 65 (2014), p. 651.

10. Exceptions are the important initial work of Phyllis Deane, focusing on what is now Zambia, and P. N. C. Okigbo for Nigeria. See Phyllis Deane, *The Measurement of Colonial National Incomes: An Experiment* (Cambridge: Cambridge University Press, 1948); Phyllis Deane, *Colonial Social Accounting* (Cambridge: Cambridge University Press, 1953); P. N. C. Okigbo, *Nigerian Public Finance* (Evanston, IL: Northwestern University Press, 1965).

11. Morten Jerven has embarked on work to create retrospective national accounts for the colonial era for some African countries. See also Morten Jerven, *Economic Growth and Measurement Reconsidered in Botswana, Kenya, Tanzania, and Zambia, 1965–1995* (Oxford: Oxford University Press, 2014).

12. Frankel drew on 1913 estimates of British overseas capital investment to 1913 by Sir George Paish, and added his own estimates for the period to 1935. See S. Herbert Frankel, *Capital Investment in Africa* (Oxford: Oxford University Press, 1938). The earlier works of Sir George Paish, published 1909–14, are reprinted in Mira Wilkins (ed.), *British Overseas Investments, 1907–1948* (New York: Arno Press, 1977).

13. Frankel, *Capital Investment*, pp. 52–148.

14. The remainder of aggregate overseas investment in Africa, 1870–1913, included £37 million for British West Africa, £30 million for British East Africa and Sudan, £40 million for the Belgian Congo, £85 million for German Africa and £25 million for French Africa. *Ibid.*, p. 150.

15. *Ibid.*, p. 151.

16. In addition, Gold Coast debt charges ranged from 5 per cent to 9 per cent of export value and from 18 per cent to 30 per cent of revenue; for Tanganyika, debt charges ranged from 4 per cent to 19 per cent of export value and from 8 per cent to 25 per cent of revenue. *Ibid.*, p. 182.

17. David Soskice notes that Piketty actually uses the standard neoclassical definition of capital in his estimates. Soskice, "*Capital in the Twenty-First Century*", p. 651.

18. In this discussion, we break down national income to reveal elements of wages, profits and transfers. We divide wages into domestic wages "$W(d)$" and wages of expatriates "$W(e)$." We divide profits into net business profits after depreciation "π", rents "R", and interest income "i". For net transfers, we identify four categories: repatriation of profits "$T(\pi)$"; remittances by migrants "$T(m)$", mostly low-paid; remittances by expatriate wage-earners "$T(e)$", mostly high-paid; and transfers by non-governmental or governmental international organizations "$T(n)$". We sum up these transfers as follows. Equation (1): $T = -T(\pi) + T(m) - T(e) + T(n)$. The signs of each term are assigned based on the expected value for African economies. That is, profit transfers are mainly out of the country and thus negative, migrant wage transfers are mostly into the country, transfers by expatriates are mainly out of the country, and transfers by NGOs are mostly into the country. Now we explore Piketty's $\alpha = r \times \beta$ identity to show how transfers in African economies can affect α (the share of income from capital in national income) and β (the capital–income ratio). Equation (2): $\alpha = [\pi - T(\pi) + R + i] / [W(d) + W(e) + \pi - T(\pi) + R + i + T(m) - T(e) + T(n)]$. Equation (3): $\beta = K / [W(d) + W(e) + \pi - T(\pi) + R + i + T(m) - T(e) + T(n)]$. Assuming, as shown, that transfers of profits $T(\pi)$ are negative, net domestic business profit now declines to $\pi - T(\pi)$.

19. To analyse this issue formally, one might use $K1$ as a term for capital stock at market value and $K2$ for the unlisted, small-scale domestic capital. If the sum of the two were used in place of $K1$ for calculations of income and growth, small but perhaps important differences would result.

20. "Honest Accounts? The True Story of Africa's Billion Dollar Losses" (www.franco phonie.org/IMG/pdf/honest-accounts_final-version.pdf). In response to these outflows of profits, Aarsnes and Pôyry suggest tax policies by which African countries could limit profit repatriation. Frian Aarsnes and Econ Pöyry, "The Taxation of Multinationals in Africa: Fiscal Competition and Profit Repatriation (Including Transfer Pricing)", OECD report (www.oecd.org/site/devaeo10/44276251.pdf).

21. Vipal Monga, "US Companies Bring More Foreign Profit Home", *Wall Street Journal*, 23 March 2015 (www.wsj.com/articles/u-s-companies-bring-more-foreign-profit-home -1427154070).

22. Piketty, *Capital*, p. 461.

23. *Ibid.*, Figure 12.5, p. 462.

24. Collaborative for Historical Information and Analysis (CHIA, http://chia.pitt.edu). This multidisciplinary, cross-institutional collaborative was created in 2011.

12

INCOME DISTRIBUTION IN PRE-WAR JAPAN

Tetsuji Okazaki

Increasing income inequality is one of the most serious problems in the contemporary world, and Japan is no exception. In this context, it is only natural that Thomas Piketty's *Capital in the Twenty-First Century* has attracted great interest from general audiences as well as from academia. His book is impressive because it is based on extensive research and a rich long-term data set for the major developed countries. This data set includes the research by Moriguchi and Saez,[1] who studied long-term change in the top income share in Japan. As these authors pointed out, there is a great deal of literature on the long-term development of income distribution patterns in Japan. In this chapter, I begin by surveying this literature, focusing on research into the pre-war period; this is unique, in that studies based on individual-level data exist for this period and, moreover, there is scope to extend these studies. Then, using the new data set, I explore the relationship between income and assets at the individual level in Japan during the pre-war period.

This chapter is organized as follows. The first two sections survey the literature, with the former looking at the functional income distribution and the latter focusing on the individual income distribution. The third section relates the individual distribution of income to the distribution of assets. The final section gives my concluding remarks.

THE FUNCTIONAL DISTRIBUTION OF INCOME

The functional distribution of income in Japan has been studied since the pre-war period,[2] but the systematic estimation of long-term economic statistics in the 1970s substantially improved income distribution estimates. The most important work on this issue is that by Minami and Ono,[3] who estimated the functional distribution of income in the private non-agricultural sector by industry, focusing on the manufacturing and mining industries ("M industry") and the service sector ("S industry").

Figure 12.1 shows the change in the capital share (capital income/total income) from 1906 to 1940, using data from Minami and Ono (1978a). While there was a procyclical fluctuation, a clear upward trend can be observed in the capital share, which rose from 0.39 in 1906 to 0.54 in 1940. This upward trend in Japan is noteworthy when compared with the downward trend of the capital share in Britain and France over the same period, as shown in Piketty's book. Further, the level of the capital share in Japan was substantially higher than that in Britain and France over the same period.

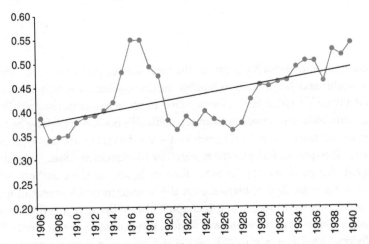

Figure 12.1. Change over time in the capital share in the non-agricultural sector. (*Source:* Minami and Ono (1978a).)

Combining the estimates of capital income by Minami and Ono (1978a) with the estimates of capital stock by Ohkawa *et al.*,[4] I decompose the capital share of the private M and S industries into the rate of return on capital (r) and the capital stock as a proportion of income (K/Y), following Piketty (Figure 12.2). That is,

$$\text{capital share} = (rK)/Y = r \times (K/Y),$$

where r denotes the rate of return on capital, K denotes the capital stock and Y denotes the total income.

There is no clear trend in r during the pre-war period in Japan, which is similar to the situation in Britain and France. However, K/Y exhibits an upward trend in Japan, whereas it exhibits a downward trend in Britain and France. In other words, the upward trend in K/Y was the major factor behind the upward trend of the capital share in Japan, which may reflect the fact that Japan was in an earlier stage of economic development and industrialization in this period compared with Britain or France.

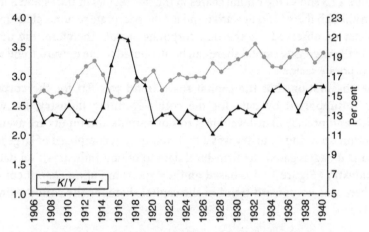

Figure 12.2. Components of the capital share (*K/Y*) and *r*.
(*Source:* Minami and Ono (1978a) and Ohkawa *et al.* (1966).[5])

Figure 12.3. Capital share in the corporate and non-corporate sectors.
(*Source:* Minami and Ono (1978a).)

It is interesting that Minami and Ono (1978a) estimated the income distribution by dividing each industry into corporate and non-corporate sectors. The
non-corporate sector refers to the sector composed of self-employed persons
and small, unincorporated firms. In the pre-war period, this sector accounted for
a substantial part of the Japanese economy. For instance, in 1906 and 1940, the
non-corporate sector's share in the total income of the M and S industries was
74.7 per cent and 53.1 per cent, respectively (Minami and Ono 1978a, p. 161).

Figure 12.3 shows the capital shares in the two sectors in the M and S industries. Although there is no upward trend for the corporate sector, a clear upward trend can be observed for the non-corporate sector. Therefore, the upward trend in the aggregate capital share can be attributed to the upward trend in the non-corporate sector.

The observation that the capital share trend was flat for the corporate sector is supported by data for the cotton-spinning industry, for which detailed and precise firm-level measures of outputs and inputs are available. The cotton-spinning industry was a typical industry, composed of large firms. Fujino *et al.* aggregated the firm-level data to obtain industry-level data for this industry.[6] Figure 12.4 is based on the data from Fujino *et al.* It confirms that there was no upward trend in the capital share for the cotton-spinning industry.

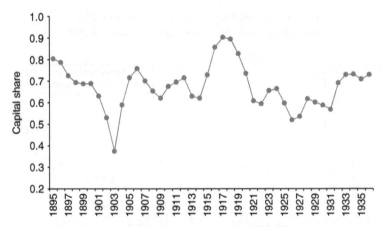

Figure 12.4. Capital share in the cotton-spinning industry.
(*Source:* Fujino *et al.* (1979).)

Minami and Ono (1978b) explain the upward trend in the capital share in the non-corporate sector using the unlimited labour supply model of Arthur Lewis.[7] Figure 12.5 summarizes the unlimited labour supply model and its implications for income distribution. The basic idea is that the non-corporate sector has excess labour for which the marginal productivity is lower than the wage in the early stages of economic development. This is because the marginal productivity of labour is lower than the minimum subsistence level. Given this, when economic development proceeds and labour moves from the non-corporate sector to the corporate sector, the marginal productivity of labour in the non-corporate sector rises, which, in turn, increases the capital share. Minami showed that the marginal productivity in the agricultural sector in Japan was indeed lower than the real wage before the 1960s.[8]

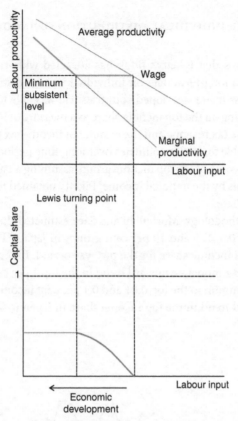

Figure 12.5. Lewis turning point and capital share of the non-corporate sector.

Table 12.1: The Lewis turning point in Japan.
(*Source:* Minami (2002), p. 215.)

	(1) Average productivity in agriculture (yen/person)	(2) Marginal productivity in agriculture (yen/person)	(3) Real wage in agriculture (yen/person)	(4) (3)/(2)
1900	130	22	108	4.9
1920	196	33	122	3.7
1938	238	70	118	1.7
1955	460,000	259,000	219,000	0.8
1970	1,142,000	642,000	495,000	0.8
1990	2,371,000	1,333,000	969,000	0.7

The pre-war productivity and wage are at the 1934–36 price, and the post-war productivity and price are at the 1990 price. The figures for 1900, 1920, 1970 and 1990 are seven-year moving averages, while those for 1938 and 1955 are five-year moving averages.

THE INDIVIDUAL DISTRIBUTION OF INCOME

One of the reasons that Piketty's book has attracted wide-ranging interest is that it is based on long-term data on individual income distributions that are comparable across major developed countries. He was able to undertake such research by focusing on the top income share as a measure of income inequality. As data on income tax revenue and the number of income tax payers by income bracket are available for major countries over long time periods, it was possible to estimate the income of the top income group, assuming a Pareto distribution. Then, dividing this by the national income, Piketty obtained long-term data on the top income share.

Using this methodology, Moriguchi and Saez estimated the income share of the top 0.01, 0.1, 0.5, 1, 5 and 10 per cent groups in Japan.[9] Figure 12.6 shows the top 1 per cent income share for the pre-war period. Except for a decline in the 1890s, there is a moderate upward trend in the top 1 per cent income share. This feature is common to the top 0.01 and 0.1 per cent income shares. In addition, the level and trend in the top income share in Japan is similar to those in France and the US.

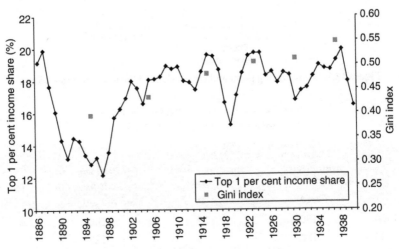

Figure 12.6. Indices of income inequality.
(*Source:* Minami (1996) and Moriguchi and Saez (2010).)

In the pre-war period, income taxes generally covered only a small portion of people because of high exemption points. As a result, only between 4 per cent and 13 per cent of households in Japan paid Class III income tax.[10] As mentioned above, Piketty chose a clever strategy to overcome this data limitation by assuming a Pareto distribution for income. For pre-war Japan, in addition to income tax data, another important data source for studying income distribution is available: the household tax (*kosu wari*) records.

The household tax was a local tax, introduced in 1878. The most distinctive feature of the household tax is that it covered almost all of the households in each city, town and village. Indeed, the percentage of households covered was higher than 90 per cent in most cases.[11] A further advantage is that the income in the household tax records includes interest on public and corporate bonds, which was not included in the Class III income tax records.[12] Until the 1910s, the amount of tax for each household was determined at the discretion of the authorities of each city, town and village; hence, the household tax records did not contain information on the income of each household. In 1921 and 1922, the Household Tax Act and the "Detailed Regulations for Enforcement" of that act were legislated. Following the change in the legal framework, the household tax records came to include detailed household-level information, including the names of the householders, their income, their income after exemptions, and their estates.[13] For these reasons, there are great advantages to using the household tax records, but there are also shortcomings. First, these records were made and preserved by individual cities, towns and villages, so it is not easy for researchers to collect them systematically. Second, thirteen large cities, including Tokyo, Osaka, Nagoya and Kyoto, did not impose the household tax.[14]

Minami and Ono collected the records of 210 cities, towns and villages. In his 1996 book, using this household tax data and other sources, Minami studied the long-term income distribution in Japan; in particular, he estimated a Gini index at the national level for 1923, 1930 and 1937. With respect to the high-income group (income above 1,500 yen), the index was calculated with the Class III income tax data, whereas for the group whose income was below 1,500 yen, the index was calculated with the household tax data. Then, the two indices were combined to obtain a Gini index at the national level. Although the income information from the household tax records has limitations, as mentioned above, Minami was able to present a retroactive estimation of the Gini index from the 1890s.

The result is shown in Figure 12.6. This indicates that the Gini index had an upward trend in pre-war Japan, which is consistent with the trend in the top 1 per cent income share, and that it reached 0.547 in 1937. This is substantially higher than the index in modern Japan and in other developed countries in the 1980s and 1990s. It should be noted that the estimated Gini index in pre-war Japan is based on income before redistribution. The Gini index before redistribution in modern Japan was 0.317 in 1989 and 0.326 in 1994. By comparison, it was 0.411 in the US in 1986, 0.428 in the UK in 1986, and 0.417 in France in 1984.[15]

As the literature surveyed indicates, pre-war Japanese society was characterized by large income inequalities, with the top income group including very wealthy people. Yazawa investigated the attributes of those wealthy people in 1936, using the 1937 issue of *Who's Who Japan (Nihon Shinshiroku)*.[16] *Who's Who Japan* contains individual-level information about noteworthy and rich individuals,[17] including their names, addresses, affiliations, Class III income tax and business profit tax. The 1937 issue provides information on 187,000 persons. A shortcoming of the source is that it covers only people who resided in major cities and their suburban counties. The areas covered in the 1937 issue are located in twenty-one of Japan's forty-seven prefectures. Using these data, Yazawa[18] examined the top 5,000 persons (0.013 per cent of the adult population) in terms of their Class III income tax and found three overlapping social groups. The first group consisted of 259 persons who founded and invested in asset holding companies, including the holding companies of the *zaibatsu* (very large business groups).[19] The second group consisted of ninety-eight nobles, and the third was composed of the eighty-eight National Diet members.[20]

THE RELATIONSHIP BETWEEN INCOME AND ASSETS AT THE INDIVIDUAL LEVEL

Although *Who's Who Japan* is a valuable source, it covers only the major cities and their suburban areas, as mentioned above. This means that it excludes the large landowners in rural areas. Therefore, other sources, including (a) "Zenkoku kinmanka obanzuke" (Ranking list of wealthy persons in Japan) and (b) "Zenkoku tagaku nouzeisha ichiran" (List of high taxpayers in Japan), are useful in gaining a picture of the wealthy class in Japanese society. Both sources were compiled by credit bureaus: (a) by Teikoku Koshinjo and (b) by Tokyo Shobunsham. Both lists cover all of the forty-seven prefectures and were published in 1933 by Kodan Kurabu. Information on the individual-level assets evaluated by the credit bureau is provided by (a), whereas (b) provides information on individual-level Class III income tax. From the Class III income tax data, I can calculate the Class III income. Using these two sources, I can match the income tax information with the asset information at the individual level.

Detailed investigations using these sources are left for future research but some basic observations are provided here. First, I examine the top 100 income earners (Table 12.2). The incomes reported here are calculated from the Class III income tax paid. The average income of this group was 388,201 yen, which is 1,218 times larger than the average income of the adult population in

1933.[21] The person with the largest income was Takakimi Mitsui, head of the Mitsui family and the president of Mitsui Gomei Kaisha (the holding company of Mitsui Zaibatsu). A total of fifty-two persons in the top 100 lived in Tokyo prefecture, with Osaka and Hyogo having the second and third largest concentrations of top-100 persons, respectively.

Table 12.2. Top 100 income earners by prefecture in 1933.
(*Source:* "Zenkoku tagaku nouzeisha ichiran", Economic Planning Agency (1965).)

	Number of top 100 income persons	Income			Average income/ (average income of the adult population in Japan)
		Average yen	Max yen	Min yen	
Total	100	388,201	1,820,695	202,226	1,218
Tokyo	52	444,051	1,820,695	207,434	1,393
Osaka	22	292,866	540,176	204,438	919
Hyogo	10	364,928	1,012,681	210,134	1,145
Aichi	4	367,956	554,331	276,018	1,154
Kyoto	2	351,830	433,930	269,730	1,104
Nigata	2	456,738	711,250	202,226	1,433
Hokkaido	2	341,568	401,894	281,242	1,072
Mie	1	231,402	231,402	231,402	726
Yamagata	1	238,350	238,350	238,350	748
Nara	1	684,835	684,835	684,835	2,149
Toyama	1	244,690	244,690	244,690	768
Fukui	1	249,618	249,618	249,618	783
Fukuoka	1	216,138	216,138	216,138	678

Second, Table 12.3 shows the basic statistics for the top 104 asset holders. As the asset data from source (a) are based on the evaluation of the credit bureau, the data are rounded. The average assets of the top 104 asset holders amounted to 58.48 million yen, which is 21,815 times more than the average assets of the adult population in 1930.[22] Compared with Table 12.2, we find that assets were much more concentrated than income, which is consistent with the data for France for the same era, as indicated in Piketty's book.

It is interesting to note how closely assets and income are correlated. Matching the list of top 100 income earners with the list of large asset holders (330 persons who owned assets of no less than five million yen in 1933), I find that 76 of the top 100 income earners had assets of no less than five million yen. In other words, most of the top 100 income earners were large asset holders at the same time. Figure 12.7 is a scatter diagram that indicates the correlation between assets and income. As the figure shows, there is a close correlation between assets and income, which suggests that the top 100 income earners were as wealthy as they were because they owned large assets.

Table 12.3. Top 104 asset holders by prefecture in 1933.
(*Source*: "Zenkoku kinmanka obanzuke", Economic Planning Agency (1976).)

| | Number of top 104 asset holders | Asset | | | Average asset/ (average asset/adult population in Japan in 1930) |
		Average ten thou- sand yen	Max ten thou- sand yen	Min ten thou- sand yen	
Total	104	5,848	45,000	1,200	21,815
Tokyo	58	7,700	45,000	1,200	28,724
Hyogo	13	5,169	30,000	1,200	19,283
Osaka	10	2,820	5,000	1,200	10,520
Aichi	5	2,180	400	1,200	8,132
Kyoto	3	2,933	4,000	1,300	10,942
Shiga	2	3,250	3,500	3,000	12,124
Nara	2	1,750	2,000	1,500	6,528
Nigata	2	5,000	8,000	2,000	18,652
Kanagawa	1	2,000	2,000	2,000	7,461
Gifu	1	1,500	1,500	1,500	5,596
Shimane	1	4,000	4,000	4,000	14,921
Chiba	1	3,000	3,000	3,000	11,191
Toyama	1	2,000	2,000	2,000	7,461
Hokkaido	1	5,000	5,000	5,000	18,652
Miyagi	1	3,000	3,000	3,000	11,191
Yamagata	1	3,000	3,000	3,000	11,191
Yamaguchi	1	3,000	3,000	3,000	11,191

A regression analysis provides additional evidence. We regress the income of each person on his or her assets. In this regression, we assume that assets are zero for those persons whose assets were less than five million yen. As shown in Table 12.4, even with this assumption, the coefficient for assets is positive and strongly significant, and the R^2 value is as large as 0.686. Thus, it can be inferred that a substantial part of the income of the top income group, very narrowly defined, was derived from their assets. That said, it should be noted that among the twenty-four persons who were in the top 100 income earners but were not in the list of large asset holders (i.e. they had assets of less than five million yen), we find famous, professional corporate executives, including Nagafumi Aruga (executive director of Mitsui Gomei Gaisha), Yunosuke Yasukawa (executive director of Mitsui & Co.) and Tamaki Makita (executive director of Mitsui Mining), which suggests that the salaries of these corporate executives were sufficiently high for them to be included in the top income earners even though they did not derive their large incomes from their assets.[23]

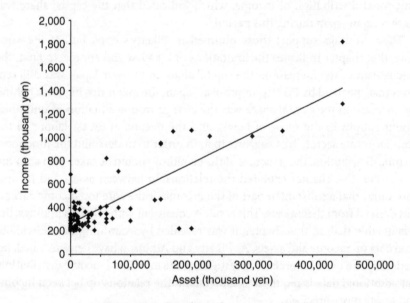

Figure 12.7. Correlation between assets and income for top 100 income earners in 1933.

Table 12.4. Assets as a determinant of income.
(Heteroscedasticity robust t-values are in parentheses.)

Dependent variable: income		
Asset	0.00258	(8.67)
Const.	265,667	(19.23)
Obs.	100	
R^2	0.686	

CONCLUDING REMARKS

Japan is an attractive field for conducting research on income distribution from a historical perspective, as rich sources of relevant information and data are available from the late nineteenth century to the present. Exploiting this advantage, many scholars have studied the historical evolution of income distribution in Japan. This chapter surveyed the literature on income distribution, focusing on research on the pre-war period. From the literature it has been established that pre-war Japanese society exhibited high income inequality, and that this inequality increased over time. This evidence is consistent with findings on the functional distribution of income, which indicated that the capital share was increasing in Japan during this period.

These findings support those outlined in Piketty's book but, at the same time, this chapter indicates the limitations of his view and approach. First, the mechanism of the increase in the capital share in pre-war Japan was different from that specified by Piketty. In pre-war Japan, the major driving force behind the increase in the capital share was the change from a situation of unlimited labour supply, in the sense of Lewis, and the decline of excess labour in the non-corporate sector. This suggests that, in order to understand the functional income distribution, the structure of the economy should be taken into account.

Further, this chapter explored the relationship between assets and income and found that a substantial part of the income of the core top income earners was derived from their assets. This result is consistent with Piketty's findings, but it is notable that, in this chapter, it was revealed by examining the individual-level data on income and assets. As Piketty and Atkinson have demonstrated, tax statistics are a useful source for investigating the individual income distribution, but additional data is required to understand the relationship between income and assets more precisely.

Notes for Chapter 12

1. C. Moriguchi and E. Saez, "The Evolution of Income Concentration in Japan, 1886–2005: Evidence from Income Tax Statistics", in *Top Incomes: A Global Perspective*, A. B. Atkinson and T. Piketty (eds) (Oxford: Oxford University Press, 2010), pp. 76–170.

2. S. Hijikata, *Kokumin Shotoku no Kosei* [Composition of National Income] (Tokyo: Nihon Hyoronsha, 1933); Y. Yamada, *Nihon Kokuin Shotoku Suikei Siryou* [Materials for Estimation of the Japanese National Income] (Tokyo: Toyo Keizai Shinposha, 1951).

3. R. Minami and A. Ono, "Yoso shotoku to bunpairitsu no suikei: Minkan hi-ichiji sangyo" [Estimation of factor income and factor share: private non-agricultural sector], *Keizai Kenkyu* 29(2) (1978a), pp. 143–69; R. Minami and A. Ono, "Bunpairisu

no susei to hendo" [Trends and cycles in factor share], *Keizai Kenkyu* 29(3) (1978b), pp. 230–42.

4. K. Ohkawa *et al.*, *Shihon Sutokku* [Capital Stock] (Tokyo: Toyo Keizai Shinposha, 1966).

5. We converted the nominal profit in Minami and Ono (1978a) to the profit at a 1934–6 constant price using the GNP deflater of Ohkawa *et al.*, *Kokumin Shotoku* [National Income] (Tokyo: Toyo Keizai Shinposha, 1974).

6. S. Fujino and A. Ono, *Sen'i Kogyo* [Textile Industry] (Tokyo: Toyo Keizai Shinposha, 1979).

7. W. A. Lewis, "Economic Development with Unlimited Supplies of Labour", *Manchester School of Economic and Social Studies* 22 (1954), pp. 139–91; J. C. Fei and G. Ranis, *Development of Labor Surplus Economy: Theory and Policy* (Homewood, IL: Irwin, 1964); R. Minami, *The Turning Point in Economic Development: Japan's Experience* (Tokyo: Kinokuniya, 1973); H. Yoshikawa, "Rodo bunpairitsu to Nihon keizai no Seicho, Junkan" [Labour share and growth/cycles of the Japanese economy], in *Nihon no Shotoku to Tomi no Bunpai* [Distribution of Income and Wealth in Japan], T. Ishikawa (ed.) (Tokyo: University of Tokyo Press, 1994).

8. Minami, *The Turning Point*.

9. Moriguchi and Saez, "The Evolution of Income Concentration in Japan".

10. Y. Terasaki, "Senzenki Nihon no Shotoku Bunpu no Hendo: Tenbo" [Changes in the income distribution in prewar Japan: a survey], *Nagasaki Daigaku Kyoyo Gakubu Kiyo* 26(2) (1986) (volume for humanities).

11. R. Minami, *Nihon no Keizai Hatten to Shotoku Bunpai* [Japanese Economic Development and Income Distribution] (Tokyo: Iwanami Shoten, 1996), p. 6.

12. The interest on public and corporate bonds was separated from the Class III income tax records and formed part of the Class II income tax records.

13. Minami, *Nihon no Keizai Hatten to Shotoku Bunpai*, p. 5.

14. *Ibid.*, p. 18.

15. B. Nishizaki, B. Y. Yamada and E. Ando, *Nihon no Shotoku Kakusa* [Income Inequality in Japan] (Tokyo: Economic Planning Agency, 1988), p. 26. It should be noted that the Gini index is not an ideal measure of income inequality because it implicitly assumes a weighting of a unit of income for each person according to his/her position in the distribution, and it is sensitive to an income change in the lower income group (A. B. Atkinson, *Inequality: What Can Be Done?* (Cambridge, MA: Harvard University Press), p. 17).

16. H. Yazawa, Kindai *Nihon no Shotoku Bunpu to Kazoku Keizai: Kokakusa Shakai no Kojin Keiryo Keizaishigaku* [Income Distribution and Household Economies in Modern Japan: "Biogrametrical" Economic History on the Society with High Income Inequality] (Tokyo: Nihon Tosho Center, 2004).

17. In the case of the 1937 issue, the criterion of wealth was that a person paid more than 50 yen in Class III income tax or more than 70 yen in business profit tax.

18. Yazawa, *Kindai Nihon*.

19. H. Morikawa, *Zaibatsu: The Rise and Fall of Family Enterprise Groups in Japan* (Tokyo, 1992); T. Okazaki, "The Role of Holding Companies in pre-war Japanese Economic Development: Rethinking Zaibatsu in Perspectives of Corporate Governance", *Social Science Japan Journal* 4(2) (2001), pp. 243–68.

20. Yazawa, *Kindai Nihon*, pp. 96–7.

21. The average income of the adult population is obtained by dividing the national disposable income by the adult population. The disposable income is obtained from the Economic Planning Agency, *Kokumin Shotoku Hakusho* [White Paper on National Income], 1963 issue (Tokyo: Printing Bureau of Ministry of Finance, 1965), whereas the adult population is from the Statistics Bureau, Ministry of Internal Affairs and Telecommunication, *Shinban Nihon Choki Tokei Soran* [Historical Statistics of Japan, New Edition], Volume 1 (Tokyo: Japan Statistical Association, 2006).

22. The average assets of the adult population are obtained by dividing national private assets by the adult population. The data on national private assets in 1930 are from the Economic Planning Agency, *Fukkoku Nihon no Kokufu Chosa* [National Wealth Survey in Japan Reprinted] (Tokyo: Printing Bureau of Ministry of Finance, 1976).

23. Indeed, the bonuses of the corporate directors were very high. See T. Okazaki, "Corporate Governance", in *Japanese Economic System and Its Historical Origins*, Tetsuji Okazaki and Masahiro Okuno-Fujiwara (eds) (New York: Oxford University Press, 1999).

13

PIKETTY AND INDIA

Prasannan Parthasarathi

Thomas Piketty's *Capital in the Twenty-First Century* has been celebrated for bringing inequality to the forefront of political and policy discussions in the US and around the world. From the standpoint of the economic historian, the book, along with several earlier articles by Piketty and others, is also to be commended for compiling detailed data on the evolution of income and wealth across a number of nations, with a focus upon France, Britain and the US. France especially provides sources that are not found elsewhere, dating from the period of the French Revolution and allowing for a remarkable reconstruction of wealth and its distribution. For Britain and the US, abundant material allows for a detailed study of wealth and income over the long run.

In the case of India, Piketty has, along with Abhijit Bannerjee, assembled data on the evolution of top incomes from 1922 to 2000. Drawing upon income tax returns, which they note have several serious limitations, they identify some major shifts in the share of total income going to top earners. They find that this share followed a U-shape, with a decrease from the early 1940s until the early 1980s, when it began to increase. The fall in top incomes took place during the Second World War and the socialist planning period in India, while the rise begins about a decade before the implementation of neoliberal policies but accelerates with that economic policy shift.[1]

Data on income and wealth comparable to what Piketty provides for France, Britain or the US will never be assembled for India for the period before 1922. The sources that provide the empirical material for such an exercise in France and elsewhere do not exist for India, and there is no way to get around this limitation. As a result, we will never be able to construct for the Indian case the striking graphs which trace the evolution of income and wealth that Piketty provides for nineteenth- and twentieth-century France. Even more importantly, there are critical forms of Indian wealth that are not amenable to the quantification in which he engages. These are forms of wealth that pertain to things that were later not considered forms of property, as well as property that was contained in communities and embedded in and derived from political and social relations.

Piketty's use of the categories of capital and wealth has been criticized for its looseness and broadness. He uses the terms interchangeably, but they are not synonymous. As Keith Tribe, amongst others, has pointed out, capital refers to investments in the production process, which generate income for the owners of the assets as a consequence of the act of making something. Wealth refers to assets that generate income for their owner without reference to production. It includes land and residential real estate, and it therefore cannot be equated with capital.[2]

This chapter will not pursue this line of thinking, which points to the broadness of Piketty's definition of wealth; instead, it will focus on the definition's narrowness. It will depart from Piketty's approach, which is very much a modern one, and consider forms of wealth, as well as of property, that cannot be quantified, but which have historically been of extraordinary importance for livelihoods and well-being, and were critical in tempering the extent of inequality. These forms of property were firmly rooted in social and political relations, and depart radically from the definitions of property that dominate conventional economic history.

PROPERTY: COMMON AND COMMUNAL

The nineteenth century saw a narrowing of conceptions of property both in India and elsewhere in the world. Things that had long been taken to be forms of property were no longer recognized as such. The shape that property took also changed as complex, communal forms gave way to individual ones. One of these was a property in skill. Watchmakers in Coventry, England, described this form of property in a petition to Parliament in 1817:

> The apprenticed artisans have, collectively and individually, an unquestionable right to expect the most extended protection from the Legislature, in the quiet exclusive use and enjoyment of their several and respective arts and trades, *which the law has already conferred upon them as a property, as much as it has secured the property of the stock-holder in the public funds.*[3]

This property in skill had its origins in the apprenticeship that all artisans served to enter into their trades. The apprenticeship not only transmitted knowledge, i.e. skill, but also initiated a young man into the community of artisans. Therefore, the property in skill was a form of property that owed its existence to

238

a community. John Rule has argued that "even though it was in part an inheritable property which fathers could pass on to sons, *what was inherited was rather the use right to be exercised within the regulations and constraints imposed by the trade*".[4]

This form of property helped artisans to preserve their power and prerogatives in their relationship with merchants. However, it did so by excluding unskilled competitors from gaining access to trades. In particular, it excluded women from these lucrative activities, and maintained them as largely male preserves. John Rule writes: "It was an exclusive property and among those excluded were most women. Girls were more completely excluded from the skilled crafts in the period of manufacture than they had been in the guild era."[5]

We do not possess descriptions of property in skill for India. However, it is likely that such conceptions of property found resonances in India, where skill was contained in artisanal communities and transmitted to new generations through systems for training and education of youth. In Britain, these forms of property were not voiced until artisans were forced to defend themselves, beginning in the late eighteenth century, from attacks on their status and attempts to degrade their work. In India, while such a transformation also took place, it did not generate a written record of a property in skill that was being defended.[6]

In the Indian case, we know more about communal property systems in agriculture. While it is well known that there was no private property in land before the period of British rule, historians have paid less attention to other forms of agrarian property that were displaced in the nineteenth century. An important exception is Frank Perlin, who argues that there were two distinct forms of property, not in land but in what the land yielded in eighteenth-century western India. These property forms were rights to claim shares in the output. The first derived from rights granted by sovereigns, which typically took the form of the power to collect revenue and was known as *saranjam* (revenue rights). The second derived from rights granted by communities; these were known in Marathis as *vatan*. As Perlin explains, in the case of *vatan*:

> "Sovereignty", as it were, stopped at the frontiers of another's *vatan* property right, at the edge of the category over which another, in short, was already proprietor (*khavand*), or sovereign. In contrast to *saranjam*, property (*vatan*) could not be cancelled; it is *vatan* that lies at the centre of concepts and institutions comprising an ideology of corporate and egalitarian individualism.[7]

Similar dual property systems were found in South India. In Tamil, there were two words for property: *pattam*, or title, was a right to property that was granted to an individual from a higher authority, typically a political powerholder; and *pangu,* or share, was a form of property that was granted to individuals from community organizations, and these rights to shares were exercised within a communal context. As was the case with the *vatan* in western India, in the Tamil country we encounter property forms that combined community and individual elements.[8]

For our purposes, which have to do with inequality of income and wealth, the importance of property as *pangu* or share lies in its deep penetration of the social order in South India. Rights to shares of the harvest were held not only by the high castes that dominated the Tamil countryside, but also by the lowly labourers who did the work of cultivation. These labourers did not toil for a wage but for a return on their property, which is why it is incorrect to refer to them as agricultural labourers.[9] With the establishment of British rule and the transformation of shares of the harvest into private property in land, these labourers came to be dispossessed; they became property-less wage labourers. These agriculturalists challenged this change in British Indian courts, but the new legal order did not recognize *pangu* as a form of property right.[10]

With this shift in their status came heightened insecurity for rural labourers, and likely, over the next dozen decades, a decline in their remuneration. As Piketty has noted, there is a connection between inequality in wealth and inequality in income. The loss of wealth leads to loss of income, which is illustrated in the example of property as share in South India. This form of wealth had for centuries been critical to the well-being of those who occupied the lower rungs of the economic order, and their loss of this form resulted not only in the deterioration of their economic status but also in the disappearance, and subsequent forgetting, of an alternative regime of property and wealth.

ENTITLEMENTS

A second form of property and wealth that is critical to understanding economic life and well-being in India took the form of what Amartya Sen has labelled entitlements. Entitlements are economic or political resources that permit an individual to lay claim to commodities, the most critical of which for Sen was foodstuffs. Sen argues that the failure of entitlements is the primary cause of famines, and he presents this approach as an alternative to the conventional wisdom that famines are due to a decline in the availability of food.[11]

A number of things may be seen as entitlements, including the ability to do work in exchange for a wage, income-generating assets that one may own, and political prerogatives such as rationing coupons. While this brief list shows that only a subset of entitlements may be classified as property, and thus wealth, as a whole they are critical for the prevention of both famines and poverty. As Sen writes, "ownership of food is one of the most primitive property rights, and in each society there are rules governing this right".[12]

In the case of India, the common and communal property forms just described were, at the same time, entitlements and forms of wealth. To these we may add assets such as animals, which provided resources ranging from milk to meat, and garden plots, which could be used for supplies of vegetables, fruits and other foodstuffs and provide tradeable items, including flowers, betel leaves, coconuts and curry leaves. While both animals and garden plots provided commodities that could be exchanged for food, animals could also be sold in hard times, and the proceeds could be used to purchase food. However, the keeping of animals required access to grazing areas such as grasslands or forests, the supplies of which were reduced in the nineteenth and twentieth centuries, in part due to the loss of natural wealth, which is discussed in the next section.

Another very important type of entitlement took the form of political and social rights, which provided access to food during times of dearth as well as a secure income.[13] Under British rule in India, these rights were no longer respected, which was a major reason for both famine and poverty. Rajat Datta, for instance, has argued that the severe famine that struck Bengal in 1769–70, shortly after the establishment of British power in the region, may be seen as the first colonial famine, because the British, unlike their predecessors, did not take steps to alleviate the crisis. Datta writes:

> What the Company's state failed to do, and which surely increased the misery of the people, was to provide any form of institutional relief… Insignificant cash was spent in providing immediate assistance to the uprooted and hungry … the most important dimension of institutional relief is the material help given to support production and the producers… Here, the Company performed miserably.[14]

In the Indian context, these political and social rights were essential assets, which is clear from what happened when they were dismantled from the late eighteenth century onwards. The massive famines, which killed as many as twenty million in the final third of the nineteenth century and plunged tens of millions of Indians into poverty, stemmed from this dispossession.[15] Therefore, any historical discussion of wealth in India cannot ignore these institutions.

NATURAL WEALTH

In 2011, the per capita ecological footprint of India was 0.9 hectares. The ecological footprint is "a measure of how much area of biologically productive land and water an individual, population or activity requires to produce all the resources it consumes and to absorb the waste it generates, using prevailing technology and resource management practices".[16] From a global perspective, India's footprint is well below the world sustainability level of 1.6 hectares per person, which means that India's production and consumption is well under the capacity of the planet.

From a national perspective, however, India's situation looks less rosy. This is because in 2011 the per capita biocapacity of India was approximately 0.5 global hectares. The biocapacity is "the ecosystem's capacity to produce biological materials used by people and to absorb waste material generated by humans, under current management schemes and extraction technologies".[17]

Admittedly the ecological footprint is a rough measure. Nevertheless, it suggests that India is on the ecological edge, and most likely in ecological deficit, with production and consumption exceeding the biological capacity of the nation. This situation has existed since at least 1961, the year for which the first footprint estimates are available, but it is likely to be a longstanding problem that has its origins in the running down of the natural wealth of the nation. While this is no doubt a process with deep roots – very few still believe in a lost golden age in which man and nature lived in harmony – the loss of natural wealth accelerated in the nineteenth and twentieth centuries.

When it comes to the different forms of wealth that humans possess, natural wealth is the most important of them all, for its loss, which means the destruction of our planet, dims the possibilities for human life. At the moment, we are facing ecological collapse, with the widespread extinction of countless species with which we share our world; the loss or destruction of valuable resources and planetary systems; and the pollution of air, water and soil.[18] One of the critical tasks of economic history is to trace the exhaustion of our natural wealth; this is something that is not addressed in Piketty's work and rarely finds mention in the writings of economists, despite its centrality to the understanding of global inequality.

The research that is necessary to outline this process in India is in its infancy. While the environmental history of India has been an important field of study since the late 1980s, it is still only imperfectly connected with larger economic questions. Nevertheless, some sense of how the depletion of natural wealth happened may be gleaned from the transformation of forests and water systems in nineteenth- and twentieth-century South India. In the nineteenth century, vast tracts of forest were cut down in South India. Contrary to the conventional wisdom, which attributes deforestation to population growth driven by the need for more arable land, a far more important factor was the rise of what I call a new energy economy. Three new energy demands led to the felling of large extents of wooded area that lay within close distance of major population centres as well as zones of highly productive rice agriculture. The heart of this new energy economy was the growth of sugar and iron production for export, which demanded enormous quantities of wood for heat: the British building of Madras using exposed brick, which required fuel for firing; and, most importantly, the arrival of steam engine technology, which was not powered with coal, as was the case in the rest of the world, but with wood. Steam technology included powered spinning mills as well as railways, which together had a punishing impact on forested land in South India.[19]

The depletion of water took a different path, but this was also closely tied to fossil fuels. For nearly two millennia, South Indians had come up with ingenious methods by which to store and use surface supplies of water. While in a few areas the flood waters of rivers could be diverted into canals, and thus used directly to irrigate fields, in much of the region the water of rivers, streams and rains had to be channelled into storage tanks. The South Indian landscape was dotted with thousands of these structures, and they represented a significant accumulation of community wealth. The break-up of community property forms in the nineteenth century led to a breakdown in the communal systems that had maintained and invested in tanks. As a result, there was a slow decline in tank-based irrigation beginning in the nineteenth century, which accelerated after the Second World War.

In the aftermath of the horrific Madras Famine of 1876–8, British officials concluded that surface water irrigation systems were unreliable: if the rains failed, so too did they. So, they pushed for the expansion of wells for the watering of fields. Wells had long been a feature of irrigation in the region, but they were either drawn upon in emergencies, e.g. if water was badly needed to bring crops to maturity, or for the cultivation of high-value garden produce. Well use was limited because lifting water was expensive. This changed in the late nineteenth century, when oil pumps and then electric motors and diesel engines reduced the costs of bringing underground water to the surface. These lift technologies diffused rapidly after 1945, and wells supplanted tanks for irrigation.[20] This shift came at a high cost, however. Tanks relied upon a renewable resource: the annual rains of the monsoon. Wells drew upon a resource that had built up over many thousands, even millions, of years: water that slowly seeped from the surface to form underground aquifers. The result of this shift in irrigation source has been the exhaustion of aquifers in a number of places in South India, and thus the exhaustion of the natural wealth in water.

There are two more items that should be noted about the loss of water and forest resources. First, these losses do not register in standard economic analyses, which focus on the accumulation of capital in the form of machinery, i.e. spinning mills, railways, water pumping devices or permanent improvements such as wells. Such investment, according to the conventional wisdom, would have created the conditions for growth and future prosperity and are thus unequivocally good. From the perspective of natural wealth, however, such improvements came at the expense of the longer-term viability of the economic system and represented a net reduction in wealth. Second, the loss of natural wealth may be seen as a condition of modernity. It is a global phenomenon and has been documented for every nation in the world. In the Indian case, there was a dramatic depletion of natural wealth but with little to show for it. In Western Europe, North America and parts of East Asia, the wealth of the natural world was exchanged for economic growth and higher incomes, and perhaps even improved economic well-being. In the Indian case, there was little economic growth in per capita terms in the nineteenth century and none at all in the first half of the twentieth; poverty grew throughout this long period of 150 years. India presents a striking example of disaccumulation of natural wealth with growing immiseration.

CONCLUSION

While this chapter has been inspired by Thomas Piketty's *Capital in the Twenty-First Century*, it has argued that its author's concepts of wealth are too narrow to make sense of the economic history of India. A broader approach has been proposed here, and three forms of property and wealth for which no room is found in Piketty's account have been described: communal property, entitlements and natural wealth. All three are critical to understanding economic life in the Indian past and present.

Marx famously declared that capital is a "social relation of production". He then asked: "Are not the means of subsistence, the instruments of labour, the raw materials of which capital consists, produced and accumulated under given social conditions, in definite social relations?"[21] Just as capital emerges in specific social situations, property rights, too, are formed in political and social contexts. This was the case for the communal property systems and entitlements described in this chapter. These forms of property have a long history in India and were critical for the well-being of many. Historians should not allow them to be obscured because they declined in the nineteenth and twentieth centuries.

Marx also famously wrote: "Labour is *not the source* of all wealth. *Nature* is just as much the source of use values (and it is surely of such that material wealth consists!) as labour."[22] Marx did not develop this important insight. Nor does Thomas Piketty, and, alas, he is not alone in this among the ranks of economists and economic historians. Speaking of natural wealth – the loss of which is critical for understanding the modern economic history of India – remains the rare exception. However, as we enter a new geological era, the Anthropocene, and a new biological era, the sixth extinction, the neglect of the wealth of nature is no longer possible. By pointing to the failure of growth to reduce inequality, Piketty's *Capital in the Twenty-First Century* provides an important starting point, but there is much more to be done to identify the profound failures of economic growth.

Notes for Chapter 13

1. Abhijit Bannerjee and Thomas Piketty, "Top Indian Incomes, 1922–2000", *The World Bank Economic Review* 19(1) (2005), pp. 1–20. See also Amit Basole, "Dynamics of Income Inequality in India: Insights from World Top Incomes Database", *Economic and Political Weekly* 49(40) (2014), pp. 14–17. For an analysis of changes in wealth distribution in the 1990s, see Arjun Jayadev, Sripad Motiram and Vamsi Vakulabharanam, "Patterns of Wealth Disparities in India During the Liberalisation Era", *Economic and Political Weekly* 42(38) (2007), pp. 3853–63.

2. Keith Tribe, "Wealth and Inequality: Thomas Piketty's *Capital in the Twenty-First Century*", *Past & Present* 227 (2015), pp. 256–7.

3. Parliamentary Papers 1817, IV, "Report from Committee on the Petitions of the Watchmakers of Coventry", minutes, p. 47, cited in John Rule, "The Property of Skill in the Period of Manufacture", in *The Historical Meanings of Work*, Patrick Joyce (ed.) (Cambridge: Cambridge University Press, 1989), p. 105 (emphasis added).

4. Rule, "Property of Skill", p. 111 (emphasis added).

5. *Ibid.*, p. 107.

6. See Prasannan Parthasarathi, *The Transition to a Colonial Economy: Weavers, Merchants and Kings in South India, 1720–1800* (Cambridge: Cambridge University Press, 2001).

7. Frank Perlin, "Concepts of Order and Comparison, with a Diversion on Counter Ideologies and Corporate Institutions in Late Pre-Colonial India", *Journal of Peasant Studies* 12(2–3) (1985), p. 132.

8. For further elaboration see David Ludden, *Peasant History in South India* (Princeton, NJ: Princeton University Press, 1985), pp. 165–7.

9. For an elaboration on this point see Gyan Prakash's introduction to *The World of the Rural Labourer in Colonial India* (Delhi: Oxford University Press, 1992), which he also edited.

10. Ludden, *Peasant History in South India*, p. 175.

11. Amartya Sen, *Poverty and Famines: An Essay on Entitlement and Deprivation* (Oxford: Oxford University Press, 1981).

12. Sen, *Poverty and Famines*, p. 45.

13. These may be seen as counterparts to the social welfare and old-age provisions of today, which are described in this volume in the essays on Germany and Sweden.

14. Rajat Datta, *Society, Economy and the Market: Commercialization in Rural Bengal c. 1760–1800* (New Delhi: Manohar, 2000), p. 259.

15. Mike Davis, *Late Victorian Holocausts: El Niño Famines and the Making of the Third World* (London: Verso, 2002).

16. www.footprintnetwork.org/en/index.php/GFN/page/trends/india/ and www.footprint network.org/en/index.php/GFN/page/glossary/#biocapacity (accessed 24 February 2015).

17. *Ibid.*

18. For readable overviews, see J. R. McNeill, *Something New Under the Sun: An Environmental History of the Twentieth-Century World* (New York: Norton, 2000) and Elizabeth Kolbert, *The Sixth Extinction: An Unnatural History* (New York: Henry Holt, 2014).

19. For further details, see Prasannan Parthasarathi, "Forests and a New Energy Economy in Nineteenth-Century South India", in *Economic Development and Environmental History in the Anthropocene: Perspectives on Asia and Africa,* Gareth Austin (ed.) (London: Bloomsbury Academic, 2017).

20. For more details, see Prasannan Parthasarathi, "Water in Nineteenth-Century South India", *Modern Asian Studies*, forthcoming.

21. Karl Marx, "Wage Labour and Capital", in *The Marx–Engels Reader*, Robert C. Tucker (ed.), 2nd edn (New York: Norton, 1978), pp. 207–8.

22. Karl Marx, "Critique of the Gotha Program", in Tucker, *Marx–Engels Reader*, p. 524.

PART IV

PROSPECT

14

GOALS AND MEASURES OF DEVELOPMENT: THE PIKETTY OPPORTUNITY

Pat Hudson

> *The imperfect lessons that we can draw from history ... are of inesti-*
> *mable, irreplaceable value, and no controlled experiment will ever be*
> *able to equal them.*[1]

Thomas Piketty has put long-run shifts in inequality, and their importance, back at the centre of economics.[2] By addressing changes in income and wealth distribution over more than two centuries and across several parts of the globe, he has also given an important new impetus to the study of economic history. The first part of this chapter provides a commentary on Piketty's major achievement, seeking to draw out some of the implications of arguments made in the earlier chapters of this book. More importantly, a critical approach to Piketty's research and thesis is a necessary prelude to exploring the ways in which his work opens up new areas of debate for economists, economic historians and social scientists in general. In the second part of the chapter, we consider the "Piketty opportunity": a chance to question and to rethink some long-established and entrenched approaches, measures, assumptions and methods of economic history and economics. Comparative measures of the success or failure of economies, growth theory, definitions and measures of capital and wealth, technological innovation, ideas about convergence and divergence, and the central importance of politics and ideology in economic change can all be placed in the spotlight created by Piketty, with salutary implications.

PIKETTY'S ACHIEVEMENT: A COMMENTARY[3]

Inequality: elements and trajectory

Piketty forces us to put the meaning and measurement of inequality, as well as its trajectory, at centre stage when discussing the economic history of advanced economies over the past two centuries. In considering his achievement, one must be clear about the components of primary income and wealth inequalities.[4] They comprise a flow (income) and a stock (wealth), although the latter might largely be seen as the result of historical and intergenerational income flows, hence the importance given to the former.[5] But wealth differentials are generally higher than differentials in income, and this seems to have been increasingly the case in leading economies since the 1980s or so (as it was for sure in most economies of the nineteenth century and earlier). Whereas the average pre-tax pay of the top 10 per cent of earners in the UK is currently 27 times that of the lowest 10 per cent, and the same elite in the US enjoys around 48 per cent of total pre-tax income, the accumulated wealth of the top decile is over 70 per cent of total wealth in the US, and it is well over 60 per cent in Britain, France and Sweden. In the French case, which is better documented than any other, inherited wealth was 80–90 per cent of total wealth in the nineteenth century; this fell to less than 50 per cent by 1970, but it has now reached 70 per cent and looks set to keep rising. The top 10 per cent in modern societies can expect to receive inheritances equivalent to the lifetime incomes of the bottom 50 per cent, a factor that is crucial to Piketty's thesis about the progressive accumulation of wealth in certain families, the rise of a new patrimonial class, and the related threat to social democracy posed by the power of the wealthy elite.[6]

The forces that drive income inequality and wealth inequality are different. Circumstances and policies explaining rising inequality of earned income (wages and salaries) include the following: the supply and demand for skills; equality of access to education; technological change; institutions and rules that affect the operation of the labour market; salary levels and increases in top managerial pay (which are in turn influenced by changing company structures, incentives and norms, and by the level of top tax rates).[7] The distribution of incomes that arise from wealth ownership (interest payments, dividends and capital gains) is determined by savings and investment behaviour, laws relating to inheritance and real estate, and financial markets. Piketty mentions all of these factors, exploring some in detail but giving less attention than is deserved to others. Wealth inequality trends result from both earnings and investment-income flows in combination but, and this is a key point for Piketty, they are underpinned and endorsed by the degree to which wealth, with its accumulated gains, is passed from one generation to another.

It is largely in relation to his assumption of a continuously rising inequality of wealth in the future that Piketty's dystopian predictions and "fundamental laws" come into play. He fears the emergence of societies where patrimonial wealth becomes ever more concentrated in the hands of those who cannot be argued to have earned it. The wealthy elite will increasingly engineer the political and legal process to defend their economic interests, and the rewards to merit, skill and education in society will break down.[8] In the absence of radical policy changes to arrest it, the trajectory of growing economic inequality will continue until it creates a terminal crisis in the political and economic order, perhaps (depending upon the speed of change) by the middle of the twenty-first century. Although wars, capital destruction, revolutions, expropriations, nationalizations, welfare spending, deficit financing, financial crises and greater fiscal impositions on the rich may interrupt the "logic" in Piketty's schema, often for several decades (as they did, in his view, across many economies between 1914 and the 1970s or 1980s), the long-term and underlying driver of inequality, for Piketty, is the tendency for the returns to capital to exceed the rate of economic growth. The relatively high growth rates of the three decades following 1945 (ending with the oil price shocks of the 1970s, growth slowdown and the subsequent adoption of neoliberal deregulation and greater globalization) continued, in Piketty's view, to arrest the natural forces of capital accumulation and concentration. But in the US, the UK, Canada and Australia, income inequality by most measures had by 2007 regained the level obtaining under the old-style patrimonial systems of the late nineteenth and early twentieth centuries. France, Germany, Japan and Sweden also experienced declining inequality between 1914 and the 1950s, generally followed by increasing inequality, although the polarization of wealth and income in recent decades has been more modest than in the Anglophone economies. Despite variations between countries, the pattern is thus clear: there was a significant increase in the concentration of wealth accruing to the top 10 per cent, and even more so to the top 1 per cent or 0.1 per cent, in all of the major OECD economies between the 1970s and the end of the twentieth century. The common experience of the "Great Levelling" followed by renewed divergence in the distribution of incomes and wealth within so many countries demands that one asks whether there was a single common cause at work. This is the question that Piketty sets out to address.

An immediate difficulty arises from Piketty's insistence that the "Great Levelling" had a common set of causes that span victorious and defeated nations; combatants and non-combatants in wars and revolutions; countries with hyper-inflations, and those with stable prices; and states that increased their welfare expenditure, and those that did not. He suggests that the destructive impact of wars depressed wealth values and created uncertainty and pessimism that

spread from one country to another. But was the world asset market sufficiently connected to spread investor pessimism more or less equally across such
varied territories? The decline of population growth in industrialized countries,
and, hence, of their labour forces, exacerbated by an accelerated rise in labour
productivity, may have been more important common causal factors in this
period than Piketty accepts.

In searching for a common cause of growing inequality in recent decades,
Piketty pays little attention to changes in ideology, common trends in technology or the impact of the liberalization of global financial markets (all
discussed further in the next section of this chapter). Instead, he settles upon
a general thesis of the logic of capitalist accumulation. The difference between
r (the rate of return on capital) and g (the growth rate of the economy), and
the level of β (the capital–output ratio), are seen to be crucial. However, these
measures are only useful for discussing long-term trends in the accumulation of
wealth. They are only relevant in discussing the distribution of incomes (a major
driver of that wealth) to the extent that wealth holding, in itself, creates income.
Earned income (wages and salaries) accounts for between two-thirds and three-
quarters of total income in all of the leading economies that Piketty considers;
yet he focuses upon the growing importance of incomes from capital under the
assumption that this will become an ever larger share of the rewards of the top
10 per cent in the coming half century.[9] This introduces an element of *a priori*
circularity, since what might happen in the future is allowed to determine how
accumulation in the past and present is perceived. Capital's share of income
appears to have risen in major rich countries during the period 1975–2007,
while labour's share declined. But only if this continues (*ceteris paribus*) will
Piketty's thesis be vindicated.

It has been suggested that Piketty underestimates the extent to which modern
inheritance practices and conspicuous consumption tend towards the dissipa-
tion of wealth in rich families as well as the degree to which tax incentives
encourage charitable transfers and the attrition of family assets.[10] Furthermore,
although the collapse of share prices that occurred in the wake of the financial
crisis of 2007–9 might be seen as a short-term interruption in the rise of wealth,
interest rates have been very low for more than a decade, with a negative impact
upon the returns to some sorts of investments. But different assets are in play
through the wealth hierarchy. Low interest rates disproportionately disadvan-
tage risk-averse lowly savers and pensioners, while the wealthy elite tend to hold
equities that are advantaged by the low rates. Only time and the long-run will
tell if Piketty has identified the major mechanism, the ratio of r to g, that drives
long-term differences in inequality, and whether there is a long-term *intrinsic*
negative relationship between modern economic growth and economic equality.
At this point, it is justified to say that his equations are suggestive descriptions

of the data: statistical regularities that do not yet add up to a full explanation, let alone a law.[11]

Piketty might be another case of the owl of Minerva flying at night: setting out a thesis, like Kuznets, Malthus and others before him, at a time when the tide has turned, when the nature of the phenomena and the relationships concerned are changing. If, as Piketty argues, the Kuznets curve rested on shaky empirical foundations, was a product of the Cold War needed to maintain underdeveloped countries "within the orbit of the free world" and had more to do with the violent economic and political shocks of the period 1914–45 than with any longer-term or intrinsic character of mature capitalism or the "tranquil process of inter sectoral mobility",[12] is it not the case that Piketty's vision might be similarly conditioned by the ideology and the events of our time?

If we agree that the jury is still out regarding Piketty's fundamental laws but accept the trajectories of his valuable time series data (with caution, qualifications and close scrutiny), we must inquire, further than does Piketty, about the other causal factors at work, including technological change and its impact on the labour market; the balance of bargaining power in societies; the impact of globalization, particularly in financial markets; and the nature of politics and belief systems expressed in regulatory and fiscal regimes.

Primary income and private wealth

It is important to note that, throughout Piketty's analysis, only primary income (pre-tax and pre-social transfers) and private wealth are considered. This has the advantage of easier computation and is justified because Piketty sees the trajectories of primary income and private wealth accumulation as the main drivers of inequality. Real disposable incomes are seen as the product of contingent social and fiscal policies that can modify but not arrest the long-term trends in the generation of inequality.[13] Earlier chapters in this volume by Hesse, Hasselberg and Ohlsson, and Tomlinson have shown just how complex and relevant to the inequality debate are the impacts of fiscal and social welfare ideals, shifts and trends. One might justifiably advocate that the distribution of *disposable* incomes should be the major object of comparative analysis, and that the definition of wealth should also incorporate forms of entitlement and ownership of assets that are essentially communal or collective. These might include anything from communal grazing rights and access to clean water to legal claims on company or state pensions and claims upon state-provided health, security, educational or social services. These elements of entitlement are important in assessing the distribution of "wealth" as highlighted in the earlier chapters by Tribe, Hasselberg and Ohlsson, Hesse, and Parthasarathi, in particular. The determinants of public or collective capital include the nature of political regimes (whether extractive or

socialist), changing histories of public investment, nationalization and privatization policies and attitudes to state (including deficit) financing. In other words,
public wealth is wealth that is politically and socially determined, and to discuss
it is to discuss the determinants of social and political attitudes to redistribution.
These factors play an important role in Piketty's book (in his Chapters 3 and 5)
but, by *his* measures, the ratio of private to public wealth has stayed roughly at
6:1 in OECD countries over the past half century. It has changed little, despite
growing state intervention and market liberalization.[14] He is therefore able to
justify sidelining the determinants of social entitlements or collective capital in
his analysis, for recent decades at least. He suggests that it is roughly equivalent
to (and perhaps cancelled out by) sovereign debts and so can be ignored (for his
purposes). By the early 2000s, private housing was the largest single source of
capital in all nations under the Piketty microscope, except the US; although it
was highly significant there too. Piketty does not sufficiently focus on why this
became the case (see the discussion below), or on any implications, but it does
on the surface justify his concentrating on the generation of private assets and
their macroeconomic effects rather than public wealth in contemporary leading
economies. It will, however, be important to include public/collective wealth
in future studies, particularly those with a wide chronological or geographical
scope.

Inequality: measurement

Once decisions are made on the issue of how inequality might be defined, one
enters the difficult territory of how it might be mapped and measured, whether
temporally within one administrative unit or, for comparative purposes, across
societies and states with very different data sources and data constraints. Piketty's
approach is both temporal and comparative, focusing upon deciles but allowing
the importance of outliers to be observed, that is, the top and the bottom few
percentiles.[15] This is innovative in dealing with truncated tax data. Kuznets used
the same method in an earlier form, but for most of the intervening period the
standard measure of comparative income inequality has been the Gini coefficient, invented by the Italian organicist statistician Corrado Gini in 1912.[16] It
remains the central measure used by most economists, national governments
and the UN. The Gini coefficient is a measure for comparing how income distribution in one society compares with that in a hypothetical society with the same
vital characteristics but where everyone earns exactly the same amount. On
the Gini scale, inequality is measured between 0 (where everyone has the same
income) and 1 (where all income is earned by a single individual). In the UK,
for example, the coefficient is currently around 0.35, above the OECD average
but below that of the US at around 0.37.

The problem with the Gini coefficient is that it can be the same for societies exhibiting very different income distributions, and different for two societies experiencing a very similar polarization of wealth at the extremes. The Gini coefficient is a single measure of the concentration of income, not an index, and it is oversensitive to changes in the low end and middle of the distribution while being undersensitive to variations at the upper extremes. The coefficient does not capture well real changes in the top 10 per cent or changes in smaller percentile groups at the top or bottom of the distribution. For this reason, other measures have become more common in recent years, such as the Palma coefficient (which relies on the ratio between income going to the top 10 per cent and the bottom 40 per cent) and the Theil index (which aggregates the inequalities at each level of the hierarchy, improving upon the Gini by capturing the between-category scores).[17]

The practice of top-coding, or capping, the reported maximum value on tax returns, to protect earners' anonymity (and the existence of similar cut-offs at the bottom end representing those below the tax threshold), has hitherto truncated the tax data and distorted analysis of the distribution of incomes and wealth.[18] Piketty and his team "solve" the "top-coding problem".[19] Their approach maintains a degree of cross-national and chronological comparability but at the same time reveals the extremes hidden for so long by excessive use of the Gini. It enables the trajectory and impact of top incomes to be studied in a way that was not possible before. This does, however, open up the question of whether equivalent scrutiny of the experience of other percentiles in the distribution across time and space might modify Piketty's thesis, or even suggest another.

Where the lower deciles have been closely studied, it seems that their inequality trends (particularly manifested in a growing gap between salaries and wages) mirror those within the top decile and the history of the top decile's share of total income. This adds further to the evidence of fundamental shifts in inequality in recent decades but may indicate that causal factors, additional to those identified by Piketty, are at work. It has been suggested that the underlying causes of inequality across the board would be further revealed if all income gaps were converted into single rate-of-change accounting, along the lines of the Theil index.[20] This would enable changes in wage compared with salary rates to be studied, alongside top salaries and the impact of changing returns to marketable wealth, to reveal shifts in the income mix of different groups in the social hierarchy within (and between) nations. It is unclear from Piketty's thesis alone what might explain inequality lower down the social scale in ways entirely removed from the influence of β. Increased inequality since the 1970s may have much more to do with shifts in allocation between different sorts of earned income than with wealth. The reasons for low (as well as very high) wages in work, the expansion of casual and part-time work, zero-hours contracts and the significant growth of casual self-employment, as well as unemployment, would need to be brought into the analysis. Poverty might lack an agreed definition among social scientists, but the trajectory of experiences of the bottom 10, 1 or 0.1 per cent of the population may be as instructive about the "laws of capitalism", or other explanations, as that of the top 0.1 per cent.[21]

Patrimony: a twenty-first-century reversion or a new form?

Piketty argues that advanced economies are on course to revert to an older pattern of patrimonial capitalism that existed in Western European states in the eighteenth and nineteenth centuries; but is this really the case? Or are some of the manifestations of inequality the same, while the pattern is new? Is a "fundamental law" of capitalism reasserting itself, or are new forces at work? This question is important because Piketty's thesis demands a rent-seeking socio-political argument. He needs to explain why a high wealth-to-annual-income ratio determines a political economy that retards the erosion of profits beyond that expected by the neoclassical economists of the nineteenth century.[22]

Piketty himself admits that studying the polarization of wealth in aggregated deciles is no substitute for the careful analysis of various asset categories and their reflection in social and economic relations between countries and within nations over time.[23] The first big increases in inequality certainly took the form of capital accumulation. In nineteenth-century Western Europe, a small group of increasingly rich rentiers lived off their investment returns while the rest had to work for a living in a labour market that afforded them little regulation or protection. Agricultural land as a source of wealth was gradually replaced by business assets, urban real estate and foreign investment, but, by Piketty's measures, wealth inequality remained just as extreme, if not more so, at the end of the nineteenth century as it had been at the beginning. There was little taxation or inflation before 1914, so the gap $(1 - t)r - g$ (where t is the marginal rate of taxation) was particularly high in pre-First World War societies.

During 1914–45, physical destruction, high inflation, raised taxation and nationalizations resulted in the rate of return on capital (post-tax, post-capital losses and writeoffs) falling below the growth rate. This shift is reflected in the age–wealth profiles for France, for example.[24] Steeply rising age–wealth profiles at the top end of the scale in the nineteenth and very early twentieth centuries broke down during 1914–45. But they have been reasserted in recent decades. This unites the nature of society in the nineteenth century with that of the present day. It is important since within-age-group wealth distribution is substantially more unequal than within-age income distribution, a fact that is difficult to reconcile with conventional life cycle models of accumulation, and that hints at the importance of inherited wealth.

But the share of capital income today in France and Britain (and in Japan and elsewhere) remains significantly lower than it was in the late nineteenth century. Furthermore, the concentration of wealth within a small elite at the top in the US was much lower in the late nineteenth century than it was in Europe. There had been less time for dynastic wealth creation in the settler economy, and growth rates were higher than in Europe (in turn, partly due to a lower starting point and faster population growth). This would, in Piketty's schema at least, have retarded elite accumulation.[25] The fact that the time series of income and wealth inequality in the US exhibit a much clearer U-shape than in any other nation may not, therefore, hold up a pattern that will be followed elsewhere in the future. Rather, the US may be seen as an outlier among leading economies, as a result of its particular history and pattern of population, settlement, slavery and politics.[26]

In considering the nature of different forms of wealth-holding and patrimony, it is informative to recognize that hierarchies of wealth and income are often different rather than congruent. In some cases, the top shares of income and wealth correlate closely in the hands of the same individuals; in others, the social hierarchies of income and wealth are entirely different, as they were in what Piketty terms "traditional patrimonial societies". In 1930s Japan, as Okazaki demonstrates in this volume using individual-level data, there was a close correlation between wealth-holding and the income hierarchy among the top 100 income earners.[27] Today's rich are more likely to work than in the nineteenth or early twentieth centuries. In the UK, the top 1 per cent of income earners is almost congruent with the top 1 per cent of wealth holders. These are the working rich, who accounted for 13 per cent of national income in 2000, and who have largely (though not completely) replaced the "idle rich" rentiers of the past.[28]

This is an interesting observation, because although Piketty points to a reversion to patrimonial forms of capitalism of the past, the close coincidence of (earned) income and wealth hierarchies in leading economies is something new. It may reflect changes in aspects of society to which Piketty pays relatively little attention: for example, the impact of changing structures of ownership and management of firms, top pay, new technologies and the financialization of economies.[29]

Equally important, and a point that Piketty clearly recognizes and discusses, is that the extent to which these two dimensions of inequality differ in their nature and distribution may give rise to different social and moral ideas about the causes of inequality and the policies that might or might not be used to tackle them.[30] The divergence of wealth and income hierarchies may make inflated salaries and low wages or poverty seem more justified. Their coincidence may create a different, more interventionist, reaction. In the UK today, the lowering of wages has resulted in the rise of in-work poverty, which, to some degree, has been countered by the growth of in-work state bene- fits (principally "Income Support") that effectively represent a large subsidy to employers. This type of relief to the working poor last characterized the UK in the decades leading up to the New Poor Law of 1834, when it faced increasing criticism because of its supposed negative impact on incentives to work harder.[31] It is questionable, given the parallel, how long such a policy will last within a liberal political economy that favours the determination of wages by the market.

Of course, it is also important to emphasize that alongside some parallels in political economy, the nature of social democracy has changed since the nine- teenth century. It could be argued that change in the direction of social inclu- sivity *should* make it easier to combat inequality and challenge the political power of wealth than was the case in earlier centuries. In more autocratic soci- eties, as in the nineteenth century, such a potentially countervailing democratic force was in its infancy.

However, so far, middle-class voters have not reacted to their relative impoverishment as much as one might expect. Why have they been gener- ally opposed to compensating the losers of deindustrialization and the shift to the "knowledge economies", or even to protecting their own lack of rewards *vis-à-vis* the elite?[32] Electoral participation has been in near constant decline since the 1970s in all Western democracies. It has fallen by 12 percentage points since the 1950s, with decline especially strong among those whom one would expect to have the greatest interest in social benefits and redistri- bution from the top to the bottom of society.[33] Apathy and resignation, and declining respect for the integrity of politicians, are hallmarks of contempo- rary social democracies, to a greater or lesser degree. Can democracy counter growing inequality in such a context, where the dominant economic ideology justifies the reduction of wages and worker power in the interests of global competitiveness; where the power of trade unions has been so much reduced; and where each social class in the hierarchy is being made to feel that they need to hold out against those just below? Salaries are continuously creeping away from wages, and the long-term shift from manufacturing to services and finance is resulting in the rapid obsolescence of older skills, a "hollowing out" of middling incomes, and a polarization between a limited number of high-end and high-paid jobs on the one hand and very low paid, insecure and often part-time employment on the other. The recent referendum vote in the UK in favour of leaving the EU was fuelled by the contrasting fortunes of rich and poor during the half-century of membership. Thus, new patrimonial tendencies are intimately bound up not only with new causes of inequality but also with new trends in political economy and politics.

THE PIKETTY OPPORTUNITY: A PROSPECT

As Brad DeLong has pointed out, Piketty's book is "an attempt to reorient economists' discussions of issues rather than a contribution to the already-ongoing economic discussion".[34] This is where Piketty's real strength lies: in his insistence on the importance of understanding the dynamics and the implications of accumulation and inequality, he offers a new angle on development. In his preference for induction, the gathering of new data and descriptive rather than analytical statistics, and in his questioning of the utility of multiple regression analysis, especially in relation to complex cross-national data, he encourages a critique of approaches and methods that have dominated the fields of economics and economic history for decades.[35] He and his colleagues fundamentally unsettle the assumption that the night-watchman state and liberalized markets are good for growth. They show that for the three decades when the leading countries applied their historically highest tax rates on business, top incomes and inheritance, they had their best growth performance.[36] After 1980, US top tax rates came down along with capital gains tax, which palpably boosted the flow of wealth to the top 10 per cent, but the impact on growth was negligible.[37] Correlations cannot prove causality, but they challenge the idea that high taxes on wealth and top incomes will damage growth.[38]

Although Piketty says little about the negative impact of inequality on economic growth, aside from its potential to get out of control and dominate political systems in the future, his work opens up this issue to much more attention than it has hitherto received. The impact of inequality on the distribution of financial assets and investment patterns, on aggregate and differentiated patterns of demand (and, hence, of innovation and economies of scale), on human capital (through unequal access to education and training as well as nutrition and health) and on the nature of the state and political instability: Piketty's data and his thesis demand that all of these lines of research be given renewed attention.[39]

At the same time, *Capital in the Twenty-First Century* deflects attention from growth in favour of considering how levels of inequality might best shape our conceptions of the success or failure of economies. Although Piketty himself wishes to save capitalism from its major contradiction in order to create stronger (and more evenly distributed) growth, his work also gives rise to the possibility of focusing policy on inequality rather than growth, in and of itself, in leading world economies. It may be the case that if societies get distribution right, then (sufficient) growth will follow, rather than the other way around: that is, chasing ever faster and more growth in the hope of creating the trickle down that *might* sustain it (by ensuring a peaceable workforce and buoyant domestic demand).

In a world in which the environmental limits to growth are being reached, and where the scramble for fossil fuel energy is creating high levels of political violence and terrorism, it is vital not to miss the alternative perspectives that the Piketty opportunity creates.

Comparative measures of growth and development

Placing distribution back at the centre of things challenges our understanding of how best to measure economic development and progress. It also highlights the limits to capturing the essentials of growth or real wealth creation using standard tools. While it may be obvious to some that "an economy that is not creating benefits for most of its citizens is a failed economy",[40] most economists continue to use the yardstick of GDP per capita as *the* measure of success, or otherwise, of an economy, despite warnings by Kuznets (pioneer of the measure) that it should not be used for such purposes.[41] GDP per capita is commonly used as shorthand not only for judging the overall performance of an economy (often in comparative terms) but also for suggesting movements in living standards.[42] It has dominated the major debate in economic history in recent years about the "Great Divergence" between East and West and the "Little Divergence" between northern and western Europe and southern Europe from the early modern period onwards. In this manner, from shaky benchmark estimates and despite a lack of knowledge about how incomes and wealth were distributed, it has recently been used to suggest that Britain had left behind the Malthusian threat of population reverses by 1700 (or earlier).[43]

The attraction of using GDP per capita to calibrate changes in living standards has been increased by near-universal use of the Geary–Khamis dollar of 1990 ($GK1990). This has been applied as a standard comparator because of the ease with which it enables an average living standard above the poverty line to be identified. In 1990, the World Bank suggested that poverty be defined as an income of less than a dollar a day. Where populations elsewhere and in the past (from ancient times to the present) have been able to boast an annual per capita GDP of the same purchasing power as 365 $GK1990, or above, they have generally been seen to be thriving. Putting distribution back at the centre of economic history will hopefully temper such easy judgements.

Piketty uses estimates of national income as a benchmark against which his own calculations of different types of capital and wealth are set for comparative purposes, so he does not escape the problem of comparability of national accounts. Problems of comparability are integral to his measures of cross-temporal and cross-cultural change in inequality levels.[44] In order to generate comparative data on β and $r > g$, he essentially removes absolute growth in output and in population levels from his picture. It is valid to suggest that he is thereby "flattening" the historical record and "controlling for history" in ways that hide, as much as they reveal, differences in national and comparative trajectories of development.[45]

Divergence is the notion around which research and ideas have long been focused regarding global development, from the Middle Ages to the twentieth century. It has too often been seen to arise from market failure. The possibilities of convergence have, by contrast, tended to dominate analyses of the twentieth century; these are often seen as synonymous with greater globalization and market efficiencies. However, there are marked differences in intra-regional wealth and income inequalities, and their movements, in those parts of the globe that lie beyond Europe and the US, as several contributions to this volume have shown. Like the convergence of growth patterns, Piketty's general thesis about the mechanism of the relationship between capitalism and the polarization of wealth is not evidenced worldwide. Structurally high levels of inequality in Latin America, Africa, China and India, for example, appear to bear complex and varied relationships to any estimated values of β or the rate of economic growth. Many different patterns of growth have been accompanied by different levels of income and wealth inequality. Kuznets curves have been identified that rise and fall over time with little semblance of a linear or law-like trajectory.[46]

What is most obviously missing from Piketty's work and the debates currently surrounding it are transnational forces. His is a nation-state comparative study, not a globally connective one.[47] Just as variation in wealth and income disparities over time, within Piketty's core nations, have been, and are being, influenced by a variety of monopolistic and collusive practices, so too is the experience of income and wealth distribution transnationally. Colonial legacies, unbalanced growth, patterns of specialization, the location and use of R&D, technology gaps, economic and political volatility and the exercise of transnational power are likely to be the focus of global inequality research beyond Piketty.

Finally, the growth agenda must take more notice of the environmental limits to global growth equalization than do most of today's economists, including Piketty. Economics has given us few tools to calculate the full costs of global resource depletion or to challenge the advocates of growth at any cost.[48] As Bertola points out in his chapter, future developments in inequality will depend on how societies succeed in directing ICT, nanoscience, biotechnologies, and other technological shifts, in environmentally friendly ways, as well as on how new technologies will be distributed across the world.[49]

Defining and measuring capital and wealth

As Mary O'Sullivan makes clear earlier in this volume, the question of "what is capital?" is central to Piketty's investigation. So also is his definition and use of the term "wealth". Debate surrounding his conceptualizations has been vital in highlighting the difference between the investable capital available to society and the total of dispersed wealth in accounting terms. As with other aggregate and composite entities, especially in time series, sometimes an increase in *measured* wealth occurs because of the growth of previously unmeasured elements. Changes in the balance of power in the labour market can shift wealth from workers to owners (and top-salaried employees) of firms with market power.[50] The rise in the value of businesses is recorded, but the decreased wealth of workers is not. If banks use their size and political influence to retain more of their gains and receive bailouts in hard times, measured wealth in the financial sector increases, while the impact on taxpayers' wealth caused by bailouts escapes measurement. Similarly, if corporations such as major armaments or drug companies convince governments to overpay for their products and services, or are given access to public resources or services at below-market prices (as house-building, private health care, mining and fracking companies are), reported wealth increases while capital does not. If monopoly power grows such that businesses develop more sophisticated methods of exploiting customers, this will generate higher accounting profits, which are recorded as an increase in financial wealth. Social well-being and economic efficiency often fall even as wealth increases. The fact that capital in any productive sense is not increasing as fast as accounting wealth is important in explaining the failure of the return on capital to fall (as neoclassical modelling might suggest in the current circumstances) and even the failure of wages to rise.[51]

In considering inequality, total wealth holdings, including productive capital *and* idle investments, is the most relevant measure. Thus, Piketty defines "capital" as all assets held by private individuals, corporations and governments that can be traded on the market, whether the assets are being used productively or not. He includes land; real estate; housing; intellectual property rights; and consumer investments, such as art or jewellery. This seems reasonable because such idle assets are often appreciating (creating income and wealth) significantly without any further action being taken; they can be called into active investment or withheld from the market at will (in order to increase, through scarcity, the income of the capital that is in the production process).[52] The growth of productive capital or capital as a factor of production (K), the sort that combines with labour in a neoclassical-type production function to create output, is only one outcome of the ways in which the rich use or store wealth. These include investment in housing; forestalling and regrating; rents; intellectual property to create monopolies of knowledge; restrictions on competition to create quasirents; regulatory policies that favour a particular location or type of activity; and investment in the political system. Piketty's work has brought the rent-seeking and political-lobbying investments that create individual wealth to the forefront, even though they are not part of society's true "capital".[53]

It is, however, an inconsistency in Piketty's analysis that "capital" and the broader measures of wealth are used synonymously in much of his discussions, while in his equations relating to the production function, he maintains a more conventional definition of capital in order to calculate the commercial rate of return. To take the US as an example, capital is calculated for the period since the 1980s as stock market capitalization plus the declared corporate equity of households and other players. This is consistent with Piketty's reversion to neoclassical growth theory, from which he derives his "fundamental laws". The problem has been discussed a great deal by his critics, not least by Harcourt and Tribe and by O'Sullivan and Bertola earlier in this volume. As Charles Jones has suggested, if we subtract housing and real estate from Piketty's definition of wealth, his capital–output time series would look very different, and his *explanation* for increasing disparities of capital and income would become entirely questionable.[54]

As Harcourt and Tribe discussed in Chapter 2, definition and measurement were central to the Cambridge controversies over "capital" during the 1960s. Some way of valuing initial capital (K) independently of the market price of the output it creates was seen as vital in order to calculate a meaningful rate of return. The question of how capital can be valued independently of the value of the output it is used to produce, or how much it can be sold for in the market, perplexed many economists before Piketty. Not the least of the difficulties is the influence, upon the valuation of K, of market price fluctuations, which are difficult to separate from the amount of physical capital that actually enters production. It is fair to say that "the whole of neoclassical economic thought (which is the basis of Piketty's thinking) is founded on a tautology",[55] because the rate of return on capital, as generally measured (and also by Piketty), depends crucially on the rate of economic growth and market price variability. The value of K is heavily influenced by speculation and can be seriously warped by the characteristic booms and slumps of stock markets. The long-run trend in the rate of return on capital (around 5 per cent) that Piketty documents, but does not satisfactorily explain, is probably determined largely by the lack of an independent valuation of productive capital.

Finally, capital can be seen as a process as well as a thing: a process of circulation in which money is used, in production, to make a profit. If the rate of return on capital being used is high, it is often because part of the potentially available capital has been withdrawn from the market into other forms of wealth holding as well as less productive ways of making money. Capital is always a store of value as well as a source of income, and in some sorts of asset holding, such as land, real estate and housing, it is often viewed as both. Restricting the supply of capital for new investment in productive activities (as is currently happening in leading economies) ensures a high rate of return because of artificial scarcity. It can be argued that this "underpins the tendency of the rate of return on capital (no matter how it is defined and measured) to always exceed the rate of growth of income".[56] Piketty's work has opened up an old can of worms at the centre of neoclassical theorizing. Without reinventing the wheel, these old debates about capital now need revisiting.

Growth theory and fundamental laws: a challenge to neoclassical orthodoxy?

In standard theory, large increases in the wealth–output ratio would be associated with a subsequent fall in the return to capital and an increase in wages. But the return to capital has not diminished, and average wages have declined significantly in leading economies in recent decades. Thus, Piketty's data and thesis challenge the neoclassical orthodoxy of the Solow–Swan Cobb–Douglas-derived production function that has hitherto (with some important extensions) provided the simplified basis for expectations and predictions about economic growth. Above all, it has challenged the assumption that growth is balanced between factors in the long run. The law of diminishing returns is deep seated in the armoury of economists. If the amount of capital deepening that Piketty suggests is taking place, the rate of return on capital should fall.[57] If, on the contrary, it is rising, then it is necessary to rethink our basic models of the production function, well beyond what Piketty has to offer in his study.[58]

In neoclassical models, the equilibrium capital–output ratio increases with the savings rate and decreases with the long-run growth rate. However, in the US, the UK and many other countries the savings rate stagnated after the Second World War, and has decreased very markedly since the 1980s (while wealth has risen). It is now well below 5 per cent of disposable income in the UK and the US, for example, and household debt has risen. Even among the elite 10 per cent, savings are relatively low (they are currently around 35 per cent in the US, for example).[59] The growth rate has fluctuated over the same period of declining savings; it was more buoyant in the three decades following 1945 than it has been since. However, the wealth–output ratio does not reflect these changes well if we are relying on standard predictions. Stiglitz has suggested, for the US, that savings alone can only account for about half of the increase in the value of wealth that has occurred since the 1970s.[60]

These puzzles arise from the fact that much of the increase in wealth has had little to do with savings. This is another reason why it is important not to confuse productive capital with wealth. Wealth increases have in recent decades arisen largely from the increased value of land and real estate in general, particularly domestic housing, and a growth in the capitalized and accounting value of a range of other rents. The rising value of houses in the decade or so before the 2007–9 crisis, for example, inflated the value of the "stock of capital"; but capital inputs into the productive process (capital deepening) was probably unaffected. Plant and equipment for productive purposes may have increased little in relation to GDP, or even declined in leading economies. Similarly, the value of land has been rising on trend, but in real productive terms this does not make a society wealthier, as land is in fixed supply.

Piketty assumes that households save a constant proportion of their income. In other words, he assumes a constancy of the savings rate. He also adopts a saver-dominated view of capital accumulation in line with neoclassical growth theory. However, there is still much controversy about the determinants of business investment that his work provokes us to examine. The neoclassical assumption is that companies are relatively passive. They invest what savers choose to accumulate at equilibrium output, $I = S$. It is this, in combination with $r > g$, that generates Piketty's dire predictions. As David Soskice has pointed out, this leads to the strange result that companies responded to the trend fall in growth after the 1970s by increasing their investment relative to output, thus leading to increased inequality via the growing ratio of capital to output (β). He suggests that it would be more realistic to assume that businesses determine investment levels based on their expectations of output growth, but the implication of this model (as Robert Rowthorn has shown) is that β remains unchanged over the long run.[61]

As recent trends in both wealth and income have been driven almost entirely by rising values of real estate, and especially by rising house prices, it must be accepted that these have underlying causal mechanisms that are quite different from those emphasized by Piketty.[62] If β has not risen, at least in the relevant sense of business capital, we are left needing to explain how the rise in real estate and house prices is largely responsible for the increase in wealth and income inequality during the last four decades or so. But the relationship between the rising prices of property and growing inequality is not explained in Piketty's model.[63]

Soskice and Rowthorn both question the assumption that Piketty makes in his model that the elasticity of substitution between capital and labour is greater than 1. Until a decade ago, dominant use of the Cobb–Douglas production function in aggregate macro-models, especially in the US, assumed that the elasticity of substitution was 1 ($\sigma = 1$) and it was regarded, in reality, as often being below 1 ($\sigma < 1$).[64] But it is justifiable to argue that "the neoclassical assumption that $\sigma = 1$ was adopted to make sense of a world in which the labour and the wealth-holder shares of growth in income were roughly constant ... that is not the world in which we now live".[65] This is indeed Piketty's argument: "The Cobb–Douglas hypothesis is sometimes a good approximation for certain periods or sectors but it does not explain the diversity of patterns we observe."[66] Economists rarely apply it to data pre-1950, and they certainly do not apply it to the nineteenth century. It is difficult to predict how much greater than 1 the elasticity of substitution of capital for labour will be in the twenty-first century. But new growth theory and ideas about "directed technological change" (see below) indicate that Piketty might be right when he suggests, on the basis of the time series data, that an elasticity of between 1.3 and 1.6 is not out of the question.[67] If the world technological trajectory, especially via ICT, bio- and nano-technologies, is now impacting upon capital and labour in unprecedented ways, we will need "new theories for the new era".[68]

Wage reduction can lead to declining economic growth via another channel that lies outside the purview of the neoclassical aggregate production function. Luigi Pasinetti, as well as J. M. Keynes, long ago emphasized that wage repression can lead to secular stagnation by enriching the rentier, largely because lower economic activity reduces the bargaining power of labour (as well as consumer demand from the labour force). This argument has recently been applied by Lance Taylor as a riposte to Piketty's neoclassically derived thesis.[69]

There is an additional reason why the coincidence of wage stagnation and rising inequality, even as wealth increases, cannot be understood using standard neoclassical tools for analysing a market economy. This is because of the prevalence of rent-seeking and exploitation. As I write this chapter, a good example of this, the case of the UK retail giant British Home Stores (BHS), is hitting the headlines. It is to close after ninety years in operation with the loss of 11,000 jobs. It leaves a pension deficit of well over £500 million.[70] Sir Philip Green bought the chain for £200 million in 2000, at which point the pension *surplus* was £5 million. From 2002 to 2004, BHS shareholders received dividends of £442 million, the majority of which went to Green's family, including his wife, Tina, who resides in Monaco and pays no tax. In 2009, BHS merged with other companies owned by Tina, and the pension deficit soared to nearly £140 million. In 2015, BHS was sold for £1 to Retail Acquisitions, "a collection of little-known accountants and lawyers" headed by Dominic Chappell, who had been declared bankrupt three times. In the first few months of ownership, Retail Acquisitions extracted £25 million in "management and professional fees, salaries and interest", and by the end of 2015 the pension fund deficit was £226 million; by April 2016, it had risen to £571 million.[71] Arcadia, Philip Green's holding company, is a preferential creditor, set to be favoured by law over pension holders and redundant employees to the tune of £35 million. Governments in leading economies since the 1980s have created a legal and institutional framework in which it has been easier than in the past for corporations and the rich to exploit the bulk of society with impunity.[72] To understand this fully requires a cultural, political and sociological approach as well as economic analysis.

Piketty's work shines a torch on stories such as that of BHS, and on the marked growth of executive salaries and bonuses over the last thirty years or so. These are impossible to explain in terms of growing labour productivity. One of the biggest bonus schemes in the City of London's financial history is set to occur in December 2016, when it is forecast that 135 managers of Persimmon Homes will receive £600 million-plus in shares, with around £200 million going to just five of them.[73] The fact that much executive remuneration is, as here, now linked to stock market prices, and comprises share options whose value is determined by factors entirely separate from performance, has terminated any illusion that pay might be linked to contribution. It can only be explained by changes in corporate ownership and governance, plus a change in moral attitudes, which has also encouraged less transparent ways of increasing profits and executive pay.

The financialization of the economy and changes in technology, especially in ICT, have increased the power of network externalities and eased the processing of underhand financial transfers. Deregulation of financial institutions has encouraged more exploitation of clients and more hiding of wealth in tax havens. Weaknesses in corporate governance laws and the weakening of unions has made abuses harder to counter. The rising power of business, especially banks and their ability to make exploitative profits, can, without recourse to Piketty's fundamental laws, largely explain the stagnation of wages, the increase in the wealth–income ratio and the failure of the return to capital to fall (as would be predicted in a neoclassical framework of analysis).[74]

New growth theory, technology and directed technological change

Although the timing and pace of shifts might vary, most of the countries Piketty examines in detail have followed a similar technological path in recent decades. This suggests that his observations regarding inequality may be the result of similar technological choices driving economic specialization, the employment of labour and, therefore, the reward structure. This may produce a similar evolution of inequality in income, and perhaps in wealth, and also account for some of the cross-country variations.[75]

It has long been accepted that most productivity growth comes from technological change, but until recently (and within the classic Swan–Solow model) this was treated as a residual, indicated by total factor productivity growth (TFP), after the impact of greater capital intensity had been taken into account. Traditionally, technological change has also been viewed as factor neutral. New growth theory of the last two or three decades is concerned with the active modelling of innovation, including the impact of the ICT revolution, which has prompted much retheorizing of technological and organizational change.[76] Piketty largely neglects new growth theory, and this may be responsible for his underplaying the role of contemporary technological change in accounting for some common trends and differences in inequality between nations in recent decades. But new growth theory does support Piketty's suggestion that the elasticity of substitution between labour and capital may well increase well beyond unity with the rise and acceleration of skill- and capital-biased innovation (i.e. innovation that favours skilled over unskilled labour by raising its relative productivity and market power, and that, at the same time, involves capital investment to replace manpower). It is thus useful to consider Piketty in light of this literature.

Technological change during the late eighteenth century and in most of the nineteenth century, in western Europe and the US, saw capital being substituted for labour, and was capital- and unskill-biased, replacing manual skills and dexterity as well as muscle power in the workforce with powered machinery. Factories employing less skilled labour gradually took over much of the manufacturing of standard items previously produced by trained artisans, and many complex manufacturing processes were simplified, reducing the demand for skilled workers. At this point, however, industrialization also created many more jobs across the economy in areas of manufacture and services that absorbed both skilled and unskilled labour.[77] Industrialization occurred first in England, it is argued, because, compared with continental Europe (and, indeed, the rest of the globe), labour was expensive relative to capital and coal. Only when technology had advanced to become more factor neutral was it economical to innovate steam-powered technologies in manufacturing elsewhere in Europe and beyond.[78] This thesis of the origins of the British industrial revolution has gained much support in recent years. Although the high-wage argument is hotly contested,[79] there is no doubt that factor bias in innovation in the eighteenth and nineteenth centuries, and especially in recent years, along with its causes and its impact on the distribution of employment (including gender and class distribution) and wealth creation, requires much additional research.

Technological change since the advent of computer technology has radically unsettled the nature of factor substitution bias. Technological change in most of the second half of the twentieth century has been skill biased. This accelerated in the 1980s and early 1990s. Thus, the major changes in income distribution at that time were among different sorts of workers (i.e. salary–wage and skilled–unskilled differences, with skilled remuneration and salaries pulling away from the rest), rather than between labour and capital. For this reason, the academic literature for a time focused almost exclusively on skill bias, highlighting the rising premiums on education, skills and university degrees, and advocating the expansion of universities and skills training to keep up with the skills premium.[80]

It is no accident that from this time the use of the term "human capital" and the redefinition of labour as human capital became central in the literature.[81] But the college premium has stabilized or even fallen in the last decade, and, as Piketty points out, the possession of skill sets does not explain the polarization of income and wealth *within* the graduate or skilled population.[82] There is some evidence that a substantial part of innovation and technical change is now increasingly capital (as well as skill) biased, which would explain increasing unemployment in Europe and the decrease in the labour share of national income since the early 1990s.[83] This is particularly likely with the new wave of ICT and nanotechnology innovation. Krugman explains how the "rise of robots" has resulted in reshoring some branches of manufacturing back to the US, and how capital bias in technological change is a major element in shifting the distribution of income away from workers and towards the owners of capital.[84]

Acemoğlu suggests that there are two major determinants of the relative profitability of the different types of innovations (skill- and unskill-biased, and capital- or labour-biased): the price effect and the market size effect. Where relatively expensive goods are being produced, technologies often use the more expensive factor. If the market size is large it will encourage technologies that use the more abundant factor. The two effects compete because the price effect implies that there will be more rapid technological improvements favouring scarce factors, while the market size effect creates an incentive towards innovation that complements the abundant factor. Acemoğlu demonstrates that the elasticity of substitution between the two factors (labour and capital) determines the relative strengths of the two effects. When the elasticity of substitution is low, scarce factors command higher prices; this makes the price effect relatively more powerful, favouring those economies that produce high-price and high-value-added goods and services. He argues that if the elasticity of substitution is sufficiently large (greater than a certain threshold between 1 and 2), the induced bias in technology can overcome the usual substitution effect and increase the relative reward to the factor that has become more abundant. The induced bias in technical change can become so powerful that the relative abundance of a factor may in fact increase its relative reward.[85]

While theory dictated that all factors were supposed to be paid their marginal product, the concept of a "more expensive factor" did not make much sense and was never discussed. But now this sort of issue cannot be avoided. As technology has evolved, over the last century or so, capital has moved from being a substitute for human labour in the form of muscle power to being a complement to human labour in the form of electronic control of machines, data and information processing, etc. However, as the ICT revolution advances further, with biotechnologies and nanoscience, the factor bias is changing again. Technology is no longer amplifying the productivity of machines while creating more jobs, but rather eliminating employment, particularly on assembly lines and in routine clerical work.[86] The expansion of service sector jobs cannot replace such losses in number or in type. The jobs that remain are increasingly concentrated in the interstices of advanced economies, and in personal services, where no mechanical substitute is available. This lies behind Piketty's challenge to orthodoxy. His statement "that there is no reason why the technologies of the future should exhibit the same elasticity (*of substitution between capital and labour*) as in the past" demands attention and research.[87]

For these sorts of reasons, Lindert has argued that we should shift our attention from Piketty's main preoccupation, top income shares, to all income differentiation and its relationship to technological change.[88] Most countries that show a rise in top income shares since the 1970s also exhibit greater inequality across the spectrum of incomes.[89] In the US, the gap between the middle- and lower-income levels has widened beyond its level in 1929, and the pay gap between the 90th salary percentile and the median earner, which had fallen between the 1930s and 1950s, has increased thereafter. For the UK, ratios of middle incomes (of the 40th to 90th percentiles) to the bottom 40 per cent have risen on trend since the 1940s.[90] For Lindert, it seems more plausible to suggest that the causation runs from inequality in human earnings to wealth rather than the other way round. Studying the contemporary forces that make human earning power so unequal, including technological factors, should in that case be the priority.[91]

Piketty's data on wealth and incomes certainly demand greater understanding of the decline and technological transformation of the manufacturing sector in leading economies as well as the rise of the service sector, particularly ICT-based services. Similarly, in addressing inequalities on a global scale, technological diffusion and adaptation, and the control of both, must be central. Factors governing the siting of different sorts of high-technology manufacturing and R&D – together with technology gaps, the uneven distribution of social capabilities and path dependence in terms of the patterns of sectoral specialization – must continue to be the focus of work on global inequality beyond Piketty.

Financialization and financial liberalization

Because his neoclassically derived "laws" of the progressive widening of inequality in modern societies rest on shaky foundations, Piketty has forced us to consider more carefully not only the impact of new technologies and changing business structures on inequality but also the impact upon income and wealth distribution of the financialization of modern economies. This includes the results of the increasing liberalization of global credit and financial markets since the 1970s; the rise of debtor states as well as indebted individuals;

and the instability that has been created by global financial, investment and credit flows. The peculiar structure of the financial sector and its employment and remuneration practices also increase the opportunities for rent-seeking, exploitation and subterfuge that have an impact on income and wealth polarizations. These elements are only lightly touched on by Piketty, but his work and the debates surrounding it place renewed emphasis on the manifold impact of global financialization.

Piketty highlights the role of housing in capital accumulation in recent years, but he does not explore the causes and impact of the centrally important topics of housing credit and house price inflation. This is surprising, given the role of the housing bubble in precipitating the financial crisis of 2007–8, but perhaps it is consistent with Piketty's concentration on "laws" intrinsic to capitalism, rather than on the impact of globalization. The increasing pace of global liberalization of financial flows, starting with the breakdown of Bretton Woods (1971) and accelerated by policies particularly pursued by the Reagan, Thatcher, Clinton and Blair governments, is central here. In such a deregulated environment, lending effectively creates money to the extent that, and with the effect that, the globally available money supply is increasingly out of the control of the interest rate and monetary policies of the central banks. Speculative credit and investment funds find their highest secure returns by moving internationally into the extension of bank credit, particularly into the liberalized mortgage market and, hence, into the subprime sector, as evidenced in the crisis.[92]

The decline of savings ratios and the increase in household debt in developed economies in recent decades is partly linked to the exponential growth of house mortgages, but it has also been determined by the rise of other instruments of personal credit. Household debt in the UK was in 2015 around (the equivalent of) 150 per cent of GDP, having risen from around 50 per cent of GDP in 1970. This is similar to the experience of Canada and Sweden, but in Australia and Ireland it is more than 200 per cent, and in Denmark it is more than 300 per cent.[93] One implication of such household debt, plus the decline of reasonably well-paid, secure manufacturing jobs and the rise of low-paid employment, is the threat posed to the buoyancy of consumer demand across the leading economies. This has been shored up in recent decades with a rise in subsidies to low wages (and, hence, to business) via state benefits (such as Income Support in the UK).[94] But much more important in staving off under-consumption has been the continuing rise of personal debt to unprecedented heights. The introduction of credit cards from the 1960s revolutionized personal indebtedness as US and European businesses competed hungrily for the credit card market, persuading large numbers of people to take on what were in effect unsecured loans. By the 1990s, a sixth of the 30 million-plus credit card holders in the UK alone were in difficulties with their repayments. By 2007, at the unsustainable peak, debt advice charities were reporting large numbers of individuals presenting with debts on multiple credit cards of between £20,000 and £50,000.[95] Aggravated by easy self-validated mortgages and the rise of lending in other spheres, including student loans, the impact of personal debt on inequality has become a major factor, and it must be central to future analyses. The liberalization of credit and finance and the growth of deficit financing by governments that this has allowed (with its necessary redistributive fiscal implications), as well as growing personal debt, have underpinned the growth of inequality. According to Wolfgang Streek, these are the ways in which Western economies have been able to "buy time" to stave off the inevitable crises of capitalism and democracy.[96]

The financial sector in the UK, always important, has expanded in recent decades and now accounts for around 10 per cent of GDP; it is 8 per cent in the US and almost as high a percentage in Canada too. It is lower in other countries. It is interesting to note that the UK, the US and Canada are the countries that have experienced the most rapid polarization of wealth in recent decades. The financial sector accounts for a high percentage of corporate profits: around 40 per cent in the US just before the 2008 crisis, for example. There has, however, been relatively little to show for the activities of the financial services sector regarding overall growth rates during the period of its rapid expansion. Although this highlights Piketty's emphasis on $r > g$, it is difficult to reconcile the returns to the modern transnational financial sector with a neoclassical model.

Apart from the impact of growing state and personal debt and the global instability that has been created, today's financial sector is characterized by a variety of forms of what Stiglitz has termed "exploitation rents" that are likely to have contributed greatly to inequality at the top and bottom of society:

> Predatory lending and abusive credit card practices provide rents derived from exploiting the poor based upon imperfect information and knowledge; market manipulation, evidenced in the LIBOR and FOREX scandals, also generates rents based on imperfect and asymmetric information ... mainly exploiting people who are better off; the huge interchange fees associated with credit and debit cards create rents based on market power related to control of the payments mechanism. Insider trade and the sophisticated front running associated with high frequency trading ... generate other forms of rent, as does the trading in credit default swaps and derivatives.[97]

Global tax competition (reductions in business taxation) to attract international capital, tax havens and the instability inherent in global financial flows are likely together to hasten inequality trends. Greater international cooperation will be necessary to direct and control flows of capital and credit. Piketty's work thus highlights the necessity for greater understanding of not only internation-alization and financialization but also of the policies needed to direct them.

Politics, governance and institutions

Piketty's book opens up the possibility to place politics and governance back at the centre of economics and economic history. As he himself stresses, distribu-tion cannot be reduced to purely economic mechanisms: "The history of income and wealth is always deeply political, chaotic and unpredictable. How history plays out depends on how societies view inequalities and what kinds of politics and institutions they adopt to measure and transform them."[98] It is the inter-action, in his view, of the gap between r and g *and* the institutional and public policy responses, including progressive taxation of income, wealth and inheri-tance, that determines the dynamics and magnitude of wealth inequality.

Among the institutions that Piketty stresses are taxation policies with respect to income, wealth and inheritance; institutions of the welfare state; equality of access to high quality schools and universities; monetary regimes and central banking; labour market rules, including minimum wages; market regulation; legal property regimes and transmission rules; and fertility policies.[99] Piketty tries to develop a new historical and political economy approach to the study of institutions and their role in inequality dynamics. He emphasizes that beliefs and collective representations about social inequality and the role of government are formed and deeply influenced by their context. He cites in particular the First World War, the Great Depression, the rise of communism, the Second World War, the stagflation of the 1970s and the fall of the Soviet Union as having been fundamentally important in this respect.[100]

Despite these valuable pronouncements, Piketty spends much less time on politics and political economy, especially in recent decades, than on the evidence for and the logic of his "fundamental laws". If the growing size of β and the tendency of r to exceed g are the drivers of income and wealth inequality, it implies a certain fatalism. Better education will not do much to reduce inequality if the main rewards go straight to those with the most assets, and creating greater equality of opportunity in education and health care will not help much to reduce inequality if the most important asset you can have in life is your parents.[101] Stiglitz suggests that Piketty's inexorable laws divert attention from simple policy changes, "including higher capital-gains and inheritance taxes, greater spending to broaden access to education, rigorous enforcement of anti-trust laws, corporate-governance reforms that circumscribe executive pay, and financial regulations that rein in banks' ability to exploit the rest of society".[102] These, he argues, would markedly reduce inequality and increase equality of opportunity. Piketty's more radical fiscal solutions might also be viewed as a diversion from the changes in political economy and belief systems that are necessary before a wider raft of measures can be introduced. But he has at least started new debate about the close relationship between politics and economics, and he has pointed to the need for the latter to emerge from its disguise as a value-free and objective "science".

Acemoğlu and Robinson claim that Piketty neglects the role of institutions, but this is partly because they consider institutions in a different way.[103] Piketty is being generous in suggesting that their approach is consistent and complementary to his.[104] Instead, his work provides an opportunity to critique the way in which neo-institutionalism, especially in economic history, has developed since Douglass C. North and his followers first wrote on the subject.[105] This sort of neo-institutionalism is focused on the search for good and bad institutions: those that protect private property rights and then free up the market to do its work, and those that are seen harmfully to regulate or distort the market mechanism.[106] Piketty considers institutions in a different way, a way that enables one to see more clearly that institutions, in different contexts, can have contrary effects. Importantly, he insists that where there are strong beliefs in property-rights-centred institutions there tends to be a strong denial of inequality. Until 1914, the French elite often justified opposition to progressive income tax and indirect taxation by referring to the abolition of aristocratic privilege in the Revolution, the concept of liberty and the development of property rights for all.[107] The contemporary power of liberal ideologies in both politics and economics may currently be having a similar effect: denial of the negative social and political repercussions of grossly increasing inequality arises because institutions are seen as best confined to providing "equality of opportunity".

Conclusion

The cost of writing a brave book is the ease with which it can be both applauded and at the same time dismissed by economists and politicians on both the left and right, who have strong vested interests in their own views of long-term development and associated methodologies for defending them. The challenge is to find a way through this in order to emphasize the opportunity for debate and for methodological change that Piketty opens up, and which should not be missed. Because he tackles the most centrally important topic of economic history in our time, providing new data, a more inductive approach, a thought-provoking thesis and controversial policy proposals, the stage is set. The strutting and fretting over his book has passed. In order to move on from the opportunity that he has created, it will be necessary to question further the goals of growth and development: how to guarantee better social outcomes from economic growth, and how to reconcile growth with equity and sustainability.

The ways in which the success or failure of national economies (and of the international economy) might be measured will also need more sophisticated yardsticks than are currently being applied, yardsticks that place distributional issues back at centre stage. The role of new technologies in determining growth rates and income distribution, in less developed as well as in leading nations, will need more attention than Piketty allows. Above all, we must take Piketty's lead in finding better ways to link economics in the twenty-first century, nationally and internationally, to politics and to the exercise of economic and political power.

Notes for Chapter 14

1. Thomas Piketty, *Capital in the Twenty-First Century* (Cambridge, MA: Harvard University Press, 2014), p. 575.

2. Thanks to Keith Tribe, Gauthier Lanot and Jim Tomlinson for their comments on an earlier draft of this chapter.

3. I concentrate here upon Piketty's central arguments and some of his methods, avoiding the strengths and weaknesses of his data choices and sources, and his methods of data smoothing and manipulation, which are to some degree addressed elsewhere in this volume. On some key problems associated with Piketty's visual data manipulations, particularly the use of varied scales over the axes of individual graphs, see Noah Wright, "Data Visualization in *Capital in the Twenty-First Century*", University of Texas Inequality Project, Working Paper 70 (May 2015).

4. By primary income, I am here referring, as does Piketty, to variation in the distribution of income before taxation, welfare or other transfers.

5. Of course, this definition alludes only to what one might term economic inequality, which is easier to pin down than wider aspects that relate closely to, but cannot be subsumed within, the economist's standard tool kit. These include equality of access to education, health services, personal security, protection of human rights and the democratic process, for example.

6. The best summary of the inequality findings is Thomas Piketty and Emmanuel Saez, "Inequality in the Long Run", *Science* 344(6186) (2014), pp. 838–43. For a much more detailed and geographically wide-ranging summary of available data, see Jesper Roine and Daniel Waldenström, "Long Run Trends in the Distribution of Income and Wealth", Uppsala Center for Fiscal Studies, Working Paper 2014:5 (http://ftp.iza.org/dp8157.pdf; accessed 25 April 2016).

7. Thomas Piketty, "Putting Distribution Back at the Center of Economics: Reflections on *Capital in the Twenty-First Century*", *Journal of Economic Perspectives* 29(1) (2015), pp. 68, 72ff; Thomas Piketty, Emmanuel Saez and Stafanie Stantcheva, "Optimal Taxation of Top Labor Incomes: A Tale of Three Elasticities", *American Economic Journal: Economic Policy* 6(1) (2014), pp. 230–71. On changing company structures in the US, see O'Sullivan in this volume.

8. Jeffrey Frankel, "Piketty's Missing Rentiers", 18 September 2014 (www.project-syndicate.org/commentary/jeffrey-frankel-says-that-inequality-is-rising--but-not-for-the-reason-thomas-piketty-has-given; accessed 8 November 2015).

9. Piketty, "Putting Income Distribution Back", p. 76.

10. See p. 429 of Joseph E. Stiglitz, "The Origins of Inequality and Policies To Contain It", *National Tax Journal* 68(2) (2015), pp. 425–48.

11. David Harvey, "Afterthoughts on Piketty's *Capital in the Twenty-First Century*", *Challenge* 57(5) (2014), pp. 81–6, p. 82.

12. Cited by Piketty, *Capital*, p. 15.

13. For those who are not convinced by Piketty's inexorable long-term laws governing wealth concentration, the need to examine movements in disposable incomes becomes more urgent, since these are most influenced by fiscal and social policy determinants. For the same reason, such critics might argue that much more attention should be paid to inequality movements in the lower 90 per cent of the populations under study to see how twentieth-century shocks and political responses impact on their experience. See, for example, Peter H. Lindert, "Making the Most of *Capital in the Twenty-First Century*", National Bureau of Economic Research Working Paper 20232, June 2014 (www.nber.org/papers/w20232; accessed 15 January 2016). For the labour versus capital share in current income as a predictor of inequality, see the fullest summary of inequality statistics for various countries currently available: Roine and Waldenström, "Long Run Trends", especially Figure 5, p. 113. For discussion of the chronological and country variation in the usefulness as "predictors" of inequality of ratios of wealth or productive non-human capital to national product, see Lindert, "Making the Most of Capital". Lindert concludes that they are strong predictors before the First World War, especially in France and the US, but less so for twentieth-century trends in inequality. There is more correlation in Britain, France, Germany and the US than elsewhere. But, as Lindert points out, the same overall inequality movements show up in earnings figures that have little to do with wealth, such as wage rates in the middle- and lower-income ratios.

14. The term "neoliberalism" is not used by Piketty.

15. That Piketty concerns himself only with the top and not the bottom 10 per cent, or those in poverty, is an issue to which we return later.

16. Gini in turn built upon the work of Max Lorenz, who was the first to determine the visual representation of total equity in a straight-line graph.

17. The main advantage of the Theil over the Gini is that it can be decomposed between groups in a natural fashion. This arises because the Theil index behaves like an "average", whereas the Gini coefficient does not. The former is useful where one needs to see variation in the behaviour of regional and sub-group strata in the population.

18. At the extreme in the US, this could be seen as responsible for a betrayal of the middle classes: Jacob S. Hacker and Paul Pierson, *Winner-Take-All Politics: How Washington Made the Rich Richer – And Turned Its Back on the Middle Class* (New York: Simon & Schuster, 2010), p. 13.

19. They assume a Pareto distribution for the tails. Dividing by national income, they are then able to estimate the income of the top-income groups over the time series. Information on fiscal administration is used to estimate the various quintiles (for information on the procedures undertaken on the French data, see Annex B in Thomas Piketty, *Les Hauts Revenus en France au XXe Siècle. Inégalités et Redistributions* (Paris: Grasset, 2014).

20. Lindert, "Making the Most of Capital", pp. 14–15.

21. Poverty does not appear in the index of *Capital in the Twenty-First Century* and, as Soskice points out, it is only mentioned four times in relation to post-1914 developments in the "advanced" world: see p. 654 of David Soskice, "*Capital in the Twenty-First Century*: A Critique", *British Journal of Sociology* 65(4) (2014), pp. 650–66.

22. J. Bradford DeLong, "Mr Piketty and the 'NeoClassics': a suggested interpretation", *National Tax Journal* 68(2) (2015), pp. 393–408, p. 402.

23. Piketty, "Putting Distribution Back", p. 72.

24. Thomas Piketty, Gilles Postel-Vinay and Jean Laurent Rosenthal, "Wealth Concentration in a Developing Economy: Paris and France, 1807–1994", *American Economic Review* 96(1) (2006), pp. 236–56. See also Thomas Piketty, Gilles Postel-Vinay and Jean Laurent Rosenthal, "Inherited vs Self-Made Wealth: Theory and Evidence from a Rentier Society (1872–1927)", *Explorations and Economic History* 51(1) (2014), pp. 21–40.

25. Piketty discusses this in Chapters 10 and 11.

26. See the O'Sullivan chapter in this volume for a discussion of the peculiarities of the US, and the impact of chattel slavery on conceptions and measurement of income and wealth inequalities.

27. Okazaki, Chapter 12, p. 230–33.

28. The proportion relates here to the UK. How much work they actually do is, of course, in question; drawing a salary from a firm, whether as a member of a family firm or as a top shareholder, is not always or often indicative of real roles.

29. Some of these forces are likely to lie behind the explosion of top salaries, as Piketty has acknowledged.

30. Piketty, *Capital*, p. 20; Piketty, "Putting Distribution Back", p. 73.

31. See Tomlinson, Chapter 10, pp. 183–84.

32. Soskice, "*Capital in the Twenty-First Century*", pp. 653–4.

33. Wolfgang Streek, *Buying Time: The Delayed Crisis of Democratic Capitalism* (London: Verso, 2014), p. 54.

34. See DeLong, "Mr Piketty and the 'Neoclassics'", p. 394.

35. Piketty's equations may best be viewed as empirical generalizations derived inductively from the mass of data assembled. Savage has pointed out that this may be an intentional challenge to the deductive approach of mainstream economics in order to assert the significance of history: see p. 593 of Michael Savage, "Piketty's Challenge for Sociology", *British Journal of Sociology* 65 (2014), pp. 591–606.

36. Piketty, *Capital*, pp. 505–8; Piketty, Saez and Stantcheva, "Optimal Taxation of Top Labour Incomes".

37. Piketty's work suggests that many fiscal changes tend to have a bigger impact on redistribution than on growth, even if they are largely designed to improve growth. This is another potentially important research area highlighted by Piketty's work and data.

38. For a recent (IMF-sponsored) analysis of the negative relationship between inequality and growth, including the impact of taxation, see Era Dabla-Norris, Kalpana Kochhar, Nujin Suphaphiphat, Frantisek Ricka and Evridiki Tsounta, "Causes and Consequences

of Income Inequality: A Global Perspective", 15 June 2015 (www.imf.org/external/pubs/cat/longres.aspx?sk=42986.0; accessed 18 March 2016).

39. Addressed variously in Anthony B. Atkinson, *Inequality: What Can Be Done?* (Cambridge, MA: Harvard University Press, 2015); Robert Reich, *Saving Capitalism for the Many Not the Few* (New York: Knopf, 2015); Joseph E. Stiglitz, *The Price of Inequality: How Today's Divided Society Endangers Our Future* (London: Penguin, 2012); Richard Wilkinson and Kate Pickett, *The Spirit Level: Why More Equal Societies Almost Always Do Better* (London: Allen Lane, 2009).

40. Stiglitz, "The Origins of Inequality", p. 426; Wilkinson and Pickett, *The Spirit Level*.

41. Simon Kuznets, "International Differences in Income Levels: Reflections on Their Causes", *Economic Development and Cultural Change* 2(1) (1953), pp. 3–26; Pat Hudson, "GDP per Capita: From Measurement Tool to Ideological Construct" (http://blogs.lse.ac.uk/businessreview/2016/05/10/; accessed 19 August 2016).

42. Of course, this relies upon the assumption of a strong trickle-down effect.

43. Stephen Broadberry, Bruce M. S. Campbell, Alexander Klein, Mark Overton and Bas van Leeuwen, *British Economic Growth 1270–1870* (Cambridge: Cambridge University Press, 2015), p. xxxix.

44. As Manning and Drwenski highlight (Chapter 11), Net National Product (NNP) is likely to be a much more accurate and comparable measure than GDP because it takes account of international financial transfers such as profit repatriation and wage remittances that are significant for many economies, especially African economies, and which can impact substantially upon measures of both growth and inequality.

45. Savage, "Piketty's Challenge for Sociology", p. 594.

46. Branko Milanovic, "Introducing Kuznets Waves: How Income Inequality Waxes and Wanes over the Very Long Run" (http://voxeu.org/article/introducing-kuznets-waves-income-inequality; accessed 11 July 2016) . See also François Bourguignon, *The Globalization of Inequality* (Princeton, NJ: Princeton University Press, 2015); Peter H. Lindert and Jeffrey G. Williamson, *Unequal Gains: American Growth and Inequality Since 1700* (Princeton, NJ: Princeton University Press, 2016); Branko Milanovic, *Global Inequality: A New Approach for the Age of Globalization* (Cambridge, MA: Harvard University Press, 2016); François Bourguignon and Christian Morrison, "Inequality Among World Citizens: 1820–1992", *American Economic Review* 92(4) (2002), pp. 727–44.

47. Galbraith insists that in order to understand real differences that have real effects, inequality must be examined through both smaller and larger administrative units than the nation state; at subnational levels within and between states and provinces, in multinational continental economies as well as at a global level. See *Inequality and Instability: A Study of the World Economy Just Before the Great Crisis* (New York: Oxford University Press, 2012), pp. 20–46.

48. See Parthasarathi, Chapter 13. Also W. D. Nordhaus and C. Kokkelenberg (eds), *Nature's Numbers: Expanding the National Economic Accounts to Include the Environment* (Washington, DC: National Academy Press, 1999); W. D. Nordhaus and J. Tobin, "Is Growth Obsolete?", in *Economic Research: Retrospect and Prospect*, Nordhaus and Tobin (eds), Volume 5 ("Economic Growth") (London: NBER, 1972)

(www.nber.org/chapters/c7620.pdf; accessed 8 March 2014); Tim Jackson, *Prosperity Without Growth: Economics for a Finite Planet* (London: Routledge, 2009).

49. Bertola, Chapter 10.

50. There is an important if only partially resolved debate about the relationship between monopoly power, exploitation rents and neoliberalism, both in theory and in practice, from the 1950s onwards: see Rob Van Horn, "Reinventing Monopoly and the Role of Corporations: The Roots of Chicago Law and Economics", in *The Road from Mont Pèlerin,* Philip Mirowski and Dieter Plehwe (eds) (Cambridge, MA: Harvard University Press, 2009), pp. 204–37. Compare Joseph Stiglitz, "The Origins of Inequality".

51. Stiglitz makes most of these points: *Ibid.*, pp. 432–4.

52. Social or public capital per capita and natural wealth resources might also be added in more sophisticated accounting, as already discussed; but this is not Piketty's focus.

53. Stiglitz, "The Origins of Inequality".

54. Charles Jones, "Pareto and Piketty: The Macroeconomics of Top Income and Wealth Inequality", *Journal of Economic Perspectives* 29 (2015), p. 41; Harvey, "Afterthoughts", p. 85.

55. Harvey, "Afterthoughts", p. 85.

56. *Ibid.*, p. 85.

57. According to Rognlie, for example, given the realistic assumption of diminishing returns to capital accumulation, increased capital will only erode the economy-wide return on capital: Matthew Rognlie, "A Note on Piketty and Diminishing Returns to Capital", Working Paper, 15 June 2014, pp. 16–18 (www.conta-conta.ro/economisti/Thomas_Piketty_file%2030_.pdf).

58. Stiglitz, "The Origins of Inequality", p. 430.

59. *Ibid.*, p. 429.

60. *Ibid.*, p. 430.

61. Soskice, *"Capital in the Twenty-First Century"*; Robert Rowthorn, "A Note on Piketty's *Capital in the Twenty-First Century*", *Cambridge Journal of Economics* 38 (2014), pp. 1275–84.

62. Rognlie, "A Note on Piketty and Diminishing Returns"; Rowthorn, "A Note on Piketty's *Capital in the Twenty-First Century*".

63. See Offer and Tomlinson, Chapters 4 and 9.

64. See also DeLong, "Mr Piketty and the 'Neoclassics'".

65. *Ibid.*, p. 403.

66. Piketty, *Capital*, pp. 218–21.

67. *Ibid.*, p. 221.

68. See Kanbur and Stiglitz, Chapter 15.

69. Lance Taylor, "The Triumph of the Rentier? Thomas Piketty versus Luigi Pasinetti and John Maynard Keynes", *International Journal of Political Economy* 41(3) (2014), pp. 4–17.

70. Only part of this will be covered by the Pension Protection Fund (PPF), which was set up in 2005 to address the growing problem of the impact of insolvencies on pensions and to cover minimum pension rights. Funding for the PPF comes from a levy on all other pension schemes.

71. *The Guardian*, 3 June 2016, pp. 1, 15.

72. In a recent example, a French tribunal ordered Société Générale to pay 450,000 euros in damages to Jérôme Kerviel for unfair dismissal even though he had almost bankrupted the bank by recklessly accumulating trading losses of 4.9 billion euros: www .theguardian.com/business/2016/jun/07/former-trader-jerome-kerviel-wins-unfair -dismissal-case; accessed 10 June 2016). For his analysis of why so little government action has been taken to regulate abuses and to combat financial opacity see Thomas Piketty, "Why Have Governments Done So Little since 2008 to Address Financial Transparency?", *The Observer*, 10 April 2016, p. 7; see also "BHS and the Moral Vacuum in Big Business", *The Observer*, 5 June 2016, p. 44.

73. *The Guardian*, 13 June 2016. This follows a long sequence of high bonus payments in recent years, despite the fact that standards of construction and safety at Persimmon have been frequently criticized.

74. See Reich, *Saving Capitalism*, and Paul Krugman's review in *New York Times*, 17 December 2015 (www.nybooks.com/articles/2015/12/17/robert-reich-challenging -oligarchy/).

75. See Robert Reich, *The Work of Nations: Preparing Ourselves for 21st Century Capitalism* (New York: Vintage, 1992).

76. See Daron Acemoğlu, "Directed Technical Change", *Review of Economic Studies* 69 (2002), pp. 781–809; Daron Acemoğlu, "When Does Labor Scarcity Encourage Innovation?", *Journal of Political Economy* 118(6) (2010), pp. 1037–78; Philippe Aghion and Peter Howitt, *The Economics of Growth* (Cambridge, MA: MIT Press, 2009).

77. See, for example, Raphael Samuel, "The Workshop of the World: Steam Power and Hand Technology in mid-Victorian Britain", *History Workshop Journal* 3(1) (1977), pp. 6–72.

78. R. C. Allen, *The British Industrial Revolution in Global Perspective* (Cambridge: Cambridge University Press, 2009).

79. See, for example, Jane Humphries, "The High Wage Economy and the Industrial Revolution: A Restatement", *Economic History Review* 68(1) (2015), pp. 1–22; Peer Vries, *Escaping Poverty: The Origins of Modern Economic Growth* (Vienna: V&R Unipress, 2013), pp. 199–214.

80. Claudia Goldin and Lawrence Katz, *The Race Between Education and Technology* (Cambridge, MA: Harvard University Press, 2008).

81. See Geoffrey Hodgson, "What is Capital? Economists and Sociologists Have Changed Its Meaning: Should It Be Changed Back?", *Cambridge Journal of Economics* 38 (2014), pp. 1063–86. Piketty deliberately rejects both the term "human capital" and its inclusion in conceptions of capital.

82. Piketty, *Capital*, pp. 314–15.

83. R. J. Caballero and M. Hammour, "Jobless Growth: Appropriability, Factor Substitution and Unemployment", *Carnegie-Rochester Conference Proceedings* 48 (1998), pp. 51–94.

Only time will tell if this is a phase rather than a longer-term trend: O. Blanchard, "The Medium Run", *Brookings Papers on Economic Activity* 1997(2) (1997), pp. 89–158 (www.brookings.edu/~/media/projects/bpea/1997-2/1997b_bpea_blanchard_nordhaus_phelps.pdf).

84. Paul Krugman, "Rise of Robots", *New York Times,* 8 December 2012; Paul Krugman, "Capital Biased Technological Change: An Example", *New York Times,* 26 December 2012.

85. Acemoğlu, "Directed Technical Change"; Blanchard finds that in the 1990s the computer industries had the highest elasticity of substitution between factors in the US: Blanchard, "The Medium Run". But see arguments by commentators on his paper: William Nordhaus and Edmund S. Phelps, *Brookings Papers on Economic Activity* 1997(2) (1997), pp. 142–56 (www.brookings.edu/about/projects/bpea/papers/1997/the-medium-run-blanchard) (Piketty himself appears to be making this argument: *Capital*, p. 221). As regards these various models, there is rarely any discussion of how to gauge the price of labour relative to capital; and if capital and labour both become less homogeneous in future, old-style modelling will become more complex and difficult. Many patterns of allocation within a period may be consistent with a particular path for the aggregate return on capital. The analysis would require one to deal with composition changes. I am grateful to Gauthier Lanot for this comment.

86. Bradford DeLong, "Mr Piketty and the 'Neoclassics'", p. 404; Caballero and Hammour, "Jobless Growth".

87. Piketty, *Capital*, p. 221.

88. See Anthony B. Atkinson, *The Changing Distribution of Earnings in OECD Countries* (Oxford: Oxford University Press, 2008), which covers earnings disparities in twenty OECD countries since the mid-twentieth century; Chartbook of Economic Inequality (www.chartbookofeconomicinequality.com). See also Roine and Waldenström, "Long Run Trends".

89. UK (1978–2013), US (1948–2012), Portugal (1982–2000), Canada (since the 1950s), Australia (1975–2012), New Zealand (1986–2012), Portugal (1982–2000) and Sweden (1983–2011). The two notable exceptions are Germany (1978–2010) and Switzerland (1994–2010), but they were also unusual in that their top 1 per cent share also remained stable. Lindert, "Making the Most of *Capital in the Twenty-First Century*", p. 13ff.

90. *Ibid.*, Figures 1 and 2, pp. 22–4.

91. *Ibid.*, p. 14; Reich, *The Work of Nations*.

92. Joseph E. Stiglitz, *Freefall: Free Markets and the Sinking of the Global Economy* (New York: Norton, 2009); Joseph E. Stiglitz, *The Roaring Nineties: A New History of the World's Most Prosperous Decade* (New York: Norton, 2003); Wolfgang Streek, *Buying Time: The Delayed Crisis of Democractic Capitalism* (London: Verso, 2013). See also Offer, Chapter 4, and his 2016 Tawney Lecture at www.ehs.org.uk/multimedia/tawney-lecture-2016-the-market-turn-from-social-democracy-to-market-liberalism.

93. https://data.oecd.org/hha/household-debt.htm.

94. Jim Tomlinson discusses the rise of a "new Speenhamland system" in the UK in Chapter 9.

95. BBC Radio 4, "Plastic Revolution: 50 Years of the Credit Card", broadcast 19 June 2016.

96. Streek, *Buying Time*. Galbraith provides additional insights on the same developments in *Inequality and Instability*.

97. Stiglitz, "The Origins of Inequality", p. 432–3. On high frequency trading, see Michael Lewis, *Flash Boys: A Wall St. Revolt* (New York: W. W. Norton, 2014).

98. Piketty, *Capital*, pp. 20, 35; Piketty and Saez, "Inequality in the Long Run", pp. 842–3.

99. Piketty, "Putting Distribution Back", p. 69. See also Piketty, "Why Governments Have Done So Little since 2008".

100. Piketty, "Putting Distribution Back", p. 85.

101. Krugman, "Rise of Robots"; Krugman, "Capital Biased Technological Change".

102. Stiglitz, "Democracy in the Twenty-First Century", Project Syndicate, 1 September 2014 (www.project-syndicate.org/commentary/joseph-e--stiglitz-blames-rising-inequ ality-on-an-ersatz-form-of-capitalism-that-benefits-only-the-rich; accessed 8 November 2015).

103. Daron Acemoğlu and James Robinson, "The Rise and Decline of General Laws of Capitalism", *Journal of Economic Perspectives* 29(1) (2015), pp. 3–28. Daron Acemoğlu and James Robinson, *Economic Origins of Dictatorship and Democracy* (Cambridge: Cambridge University Press, 2006).

104. Piketty, "Putting Distribution Back", pp. 84–5.

105. See Douglass C. North, *Understanding the Process of Economic Change* (Princeton, NJ: Princeton University Press, 2005).

106. For a critique of the neo-institutionalism of Acemoğlu and Robinson, see Vries, *Escape from Poverty*, pp. 120–40.

107. Piketty, "Putting Distribution Back", p. 85.

15

WEALTH AND INCOME DISTRIBUTION:
NEW THEORIES NEEDED FOR A NEW ERA

Ravi Kanbur and Joseph E. Stiglitz

Six decades ago, Nicholas Kaldor put forward a set of stylized facts on growth and distribution for mature industrial economies.[1] The first and most prominent of these was the constancy of the share of capital relative to that of wealth in national income.[2] At about the same time, Simon Kuznets put forward a second set of stylized facts: he stated that while the interpersonal inequality of income distribution might increase in the early stages of development, it declines as industrialized economies mature.[3]

These empirical formulations brought forth a generation of growth and development theories, whose object was to explain the stylized facts. Kaldor himself presented a growth model that claimed to produce outcomes consistent with constancy of factor shares, as did Robert Solow. Kuznets also developed a model of rural–urban transition consistent with his prediction, as did many others.[4]

KALDOR–KUZNETS FACTS NO LONGER HOLD

However, the Kaldor–Kuznets stylized facts no longer hold for advanced economies. The share of capital as conventionally measured has been on the rise, as has interpersonal inequality of income and wealth. Of course, there are variations and subtleties of data and interpretation, and the pattern is not uniform. But these are the stylized facts of our time. Bringing these facts to centre stage has been the achievement of research leading up to Piketty's *Capital in the Twenty-First Century*.

It stands to reason that theories developed to explain constancy of factor shares cannot explain a rising share of capital. The theories developed to explain the earlier stylized facts cannot very easily explain the new trends, or the turnaround. At the same time, rising inequality has opened once again a set of questions on the normative significance of inequality of outcomes versus inequality of opportunity. New theoretical developments are needed for positive and normative analysis in this new era.

What sort of new theories? In the realm of positive analysis, Piketty has himself put forward a theory based on the empirical observation that the rate of return to capital, r, systematically exceeds the rate of growth, g; the famous $r > g$ relation. Much of the commentary on Piketty's facts and theorizing has tried to make the stylized fact of rising share of capital consistent with a standard production function $F(K,L)$ with capital K and labour L. However, in this framework a rising share of capital can be consistent with the other stylized fact of rising capital–output ratio only if the elasticity of substitution between capital and labour is greater than unity; this is not consistent with the broad empirical findings.[5] Further, what Piketty and others measure as wealth W is a measure of control over resources, and not a measure of capital K in the sense that that is used in the context of a production function.

DIFFERENCES BETWEEN K AND W

There is a fundamental distinction between capital K, thought of as physical inputs to production, and wealth W, thought of as including land and the capitalized value of other rents that give command over purchasing power. This distinction will be crucial in any theorizing to explain the new stylized facts. K can be going down even as W increases, and some increases in W may actually lower economic productivity. In particular, new theories explaining the evolution of inequality will have to address directly changes in rents and their capitalized value.[6] Two examples will illustrate what we have in mind.

Consider first the case of all sea-front property on the French Riviera. As demand for these properties rises, perhaps from rich foreigners seeking a refuge for their funds, the value of sea frontage will be bid up. The current owners will get rents from their ownership of this fixed factor. Their wealth will go up and their ability to command purchasing power in the economy will rise correspondingly. But the actual physical input to production has not increased. All else constant, national output will not rise; there will only be a pure distributional effect.

Consider next the case where the government gives an implicit guarantee to bail out banks. This contingent support to income flows from ownership of bank shares will be capitalized into the value of these shares. Of course, there is an equal and opposite contingent liability on all others in the economy, particularly on workers: the owners of human capital. Again, without any necessary impact on total output, the political economy has created rents for share owners, and the increase in their wealth will be reflected in rising inequality. One can see this without going through a conventional production function analysis. Of course, the rents once created will provide further resources for rentiers to lobby the political system to maintain and further increase rents. This will set in motion a spiral of increasing inequality, which again does not go through the production system at all, except to the extent that the associated distortions represent a downward shift in the productivity of the economy (at any level of inputs of K and labour).

Analysing the role of land rents in increases in inequality can be done in a variant of standard neoclassical models – by expanding inputs to include land; but explaining the increase in inequality as a result of an increase in other forms of rent will need a theory of rents that takes us beyond the competitive determination of factor rewards.

DIFFERENCES IN INEQUALITY: CAPITAL INCOME VERSUS LABOUR INCOME

The translation from factor shares to interpersonal inequality has usually been made through the assumption that capital income is more unequally distributed than labour income. Inequality of capital ownership then translates into inequality of capital income, while inequality of income from labour is assumed to be much smaller. The assumption is made in its starkest form in models in which there are owners of capital who save and workers who do not.

These stylized assumptions no longer provide a fully satisfactory explanation of income inequality because (i) there is more widespread ownership of wealth through life cycle savings in various forms, including pensions, and (ii) increasingly unequal returns to increasingly unequally distributed human capital has led to sharply rising inequality of labour income.

This sharply rising inequality of labour income focuses attention on inequality of human capital in its most general sense: (1) unequal prenatal development of the foetus; (2) unequal early childhood development and investments by parents; (3) unequal educational investments by parents and society; and (4) unequal returns to human capital because of discrimination at one end and use of parental connections in the job market at the other end. Discrimination continues to play a role not only in the determination of factor returns, given the ownership of assets, including human capital, but also in the distribution of asset ownership.

At each step, inequality of parental resources is translated into inequality of children's outcomes.

An exploration of this type of inequality requires a different type of empirical and theoretical analysis from the conventional macro-level analysis of production functions and factor shares.[7]

In particular, intergenerational transmission of inequality is more than simple inheritance of physical and financial wealth. Layered upon genetic inequalities are the inequalities of parental resources. Income inequality across parents, due to inequality of income from physical and financial capital on the one hand and inequality due to inequality of human capital on the other, is translated into inequality of financial and human capital of the next generation. Human capital inequality perpetuates itself through intergenerational transmission just as wealth inequality caused by politically created rents perpetuates itself.

Given such transmission across generations, it can be shown that the long-run, "dynastic" inequality will also be higher.[8] Although there have been advances in recent years, we still need fully developed theories on how the different mechanisms interact with each other in order to explain the dramatic rises in interpersonal inequality in advanced economies in the last three decades.[9]

HIGH INEQUALITY: NEW REALITIES AND OLD DEBATES

The new realities of high inequality have revived old debates on policy interventions and their ethical and economic rationale.[10] Standard analysis, which balances the trade-off between efficiency and equity, would suggest that taxation should now become more progressive to balance the greater inherent inequality against the incentive effects of progressive taxation.[11]

One counter-argument is that what matters is not inequality of "outcome" but inequality of "opportunity". According to this argument, so long as the prospects are the same for all children, the inequality of income across parents should not matter ethically. What we should aim for is equality of opportunity, not income equality. However, when income inequality across parents translates into inequality of prospects for children, even starting in the womb, then the distinction between opportunity and outcome begins to fade, and the case for progressive taxation is not undermined by the "equality of opportunity" objective.[12]

CONCLUDING REMARKS

The new stylized facts of our era demand new theories of income distribution. First, we need to break away from competitive marginal productivity theories of factor returns and model mechanisms that generate rents with consequences for wealth inequality. This will entail a greater focus on the "rules of the game".[13] Second, we need to focus on the interaction between income from physical and financial capital and income from human capital, not only in determining snapshot inequality, but also in determining the intergenerational transmission of inequality. Third, we need to further develop normative theories of equity that can address mechanisms of inequality transmission from generation to generation.[14]

Notes for Chapter 15

1. This chapter was originally published online in 2015 on VoxEU (www.voxeu.org/article/wealth-and-income-distribution-new-theories-needed-new-era); we are grateful to Richard Baldwin, editor in chief of VoxEU.org, the Policy Portal of the Centre for Economic Policy Research (CEPR), and to the authors for permission to reprint the essay in this collection.

2. Nicholas Kaldor, "A Model of Economic Growth", *Economic Journal* 67 (1957), pp. 591–624.

3. Simon Kuznets, "Economic Growth and Income Inequality", *American Economic Review* 45 (1955), pp. 1–28.

4. Ravi Kanbur, "Does Kuznets Still Matter?", in *Policy-Making for Indian Planning: Essays on Contemporary Issues in Honor of Montek S. Ahluwalia,* S. Kochhar (ed.) (New Delhi: Academic Foundation, 2012), pp. 115–28.

5. Joseph E. Stiglitz, "New Theoretical Perspectives on the Distribution of Income and Wealth Among Individuals", in *Inequality and Growth: Patterns and Policy. Volume 1: Concepts and Analysis,* Kaushik Basu and Joseph E. Stiglitz (eds) (London: Palgrave Macmillan, 2016).

6. Stiglitz, "New Theoretical Perspectives".

7. J. Heckman and S. Mosso, "The Economics of Human Development and Social Mobility", *Annual Reviews of Economics* 6 (2014), pp. 689–733.

8. Ravi Kanbur and Joseph E. Stiglitz, "Dynastic Inequality, Mobility and Equality of Opportunity", CEPR Discussion Paper 10,542 (2015).

9. For early discussions of such transmission processes, see Joseph E. Stiglitz, "Distribution of Income and Wealth Among Individuals", *Econometrica* 37 (1969), pp. 382–97 (presented at the December 1966 meeting of the Econometric Society in San Francisco), and D. Bevan and Joseph E. Stiglitz, "Intergenerational Transfers and Inequality", *Greek Economic Review* 1 (1979), pp. 8–26.

10. Joseph E. Stiglitz, *The Price of Inequality: How Today's Divided Society Endangers Our Future* (New York: Penguin, 2012).

11. Ravi Kanbur and M. Tuomala, "Inherent Inequality and the Optimal Graduation of Marginal Tax Rates", *Scandinavian Journal of Economics* 96 (1994), pp. 275–82.

12. Ravi Kanbur and Adam Wagstaff, "Inequality of Opportunity: Useful Policy Construct or Will o' the Wisp?", VoxEU (10 June 2015), www.voxeu.org/.

13. Joseph E. Stiglitz *et al.*, "Rewriting the Rules of the American Economy", Report, Roosevelt Institute (2015).

14. Developments in this area are exemplified by J.E. Roemer and A. Trannoy, "Equality of Opportunity", in *Handbook of Income Distribution*, A.B. Atkinson and F. Bourguignon (eds), Volumes 2A–2B (Amsterdam: Elsevier, 2014).

INDEX

Italic page numbers indicate tables; bold page numbers indicate figures.

Abel-Smith, B. 183
Abramovitz, M. 144, 145, 152, 162
Acemoğlu, D. 269, 274
Africa 217
  capital and inequality 213–16
  capital invested from abroad 214–16, *214*
  changing inequality 210
  comparison of tax record and survey data
    measuring top 10 per cent share of
    incomein South Africa **213**
  context and overview 207–9
  data deficiencies 208, 213–14
  domestic capital formation 217
  funded debt 215, **215**
  future research 219–20
  Gini coefficient **210**, **211**
  gold mining 214–16
  income inequality 207, 208, 209–13
  income per capita 210–11
  levels of inequality 207–8
  modelling inequality with transfers 216–18
  national income 208, 222
  Piketty's view 219
  poverty 212
  remittance rates 218
  top 10 per cent income shares in select
    economies **212**
  top decile income share 209, **209**
  top incomes for South Africa **213**
  transfers and inequality 218–19
  transfers out 218–19
aggregate production function model 16–17,
    20, 27, 266
agriculture 15, 68, 93, 146, 227, 243
  India 239
  United States 146–7

Albertini, J. 77, 84
allemansfonder 126
American Revolution 146
"An Essay in Dynamic Theory" (Harrod) 17–18
animal spirits 23
Arrighi, G. 156
Arrow–Debreu general equilibrium 21, 56
Åsbrink, P. 121
assets
  capital 90, 95, 97, 103, 177
  financial 57, 74, 115 f., 142, 230, 259
  income 57, 230–33
  private 38, 53, 68, 70, 223, 230 ff., 236, 238,
    252 f., 262, 273, 285
  turnover 150
  types of 19, 262
  and wealth 57, 177, 253
Atkinson, A. 7–8, 30–31, 42, 47, 49, 50, 82,
    104, 129, 176–7, 185 ff., 220 f., 234–5,
    278, 281, 288
Attlee government 169–71, 173
automation 76–7, 269

Balogh, T. 23, 27
bank bail-outs 262, 284
Bannerjee, A. 237
bargaining 34, 56, 113, 141, 155, 177, 199,
    253, 263, 266
Barr, N. 179
Beatty, C. 181
Bengtsson, E. 113
Bhaduri, A. 21, 22, 27
biocapacity, India 242, 246
birth, advantages and disadvantages of 39, 41
Blundell, R. 79, 85, 189
Bohlin, J. 198, 204

Booth, C. 34, 36, 48–49
Bourguignon, F. 6, 7, 129, 201, 204, 275–8
Bowley, A. L. 37, 49
Branting, H. 122
Braudel, F. 156
Britain
  Capital Gains Tax 174, 259
  economic growth as priority 174
  housing 167 *ff.*
  Industrial Revolution 4–5, 8, 47, 196, 202,
    268, 280
  Labour party policy 40, 169–78
  mortgage interest tax relief 174
  New Labour 168, 179, 184–5, 189
  payments in kind 172
  public spending 175
  responses to 1970s crises 176–80
  self-employment 178, 185, 189
  service sector 181–2
  shareholding 177
  Social Contract 175
  taxation 169–70, 176–7, 179
  unemployment 169, 178, 180 *ff.*
  wages 33, 34, 36, 45, 50, 170, 176 *f.*, 178, 181,
    183, 189
  wealth distribution 178
  wealth inequality 170
British Home Stores (BHS) 266–7
business investment 265
business, power of 267

Cambridge capital debate 20–21, 26, 161, 198,
  263
Cannan, E. 134
capital
  accumulation 98, 131, 160, 251, 256, 265,
    271, 279
  aggregation of 22, 139
  collective and public 127, 253–4, 279
  concept of 139–43
  concept of profit 199
  defining 133–5, 141–2, 261–4
  as distinct from wealth 238, 284–5
  domestic capital formation, Africa 217
  dual role 140, 156
  financial organization of 156–9
  financial vs. productive 157–8
  and income 67 *f.*, 96, 111, 113 *f.*, 128, 141 *f.*,
    177, 224, 252, 257, 263, 285, 287
  and inequality in African economies 213–16
  marginal productivity 139, 141, 143, 161
  market value 198, 199, 207, 217
  measurement of 19, 20–22, 24, 135–8, 160,
    198

Piketty's concept of 24, 55
  productive organization 146–52
  residential 135
  return on 68, 71, 96, 105–6, 199, 207, 224,
    256, 264, 284
  rewards to 140–6
  role of 139–40, 146, 153
  as social relation 199, 244
  US history of 132–3
  utilization of 143, 146, 150, 156
  and wealth 3, 19, 21, 23, 25, 55, 57, 68, 71, 89,
    93, 103, 112 *ff.*, 177, 238, 262 *f.*, 264
capital deepening 22, 264 *f.*
Capital in the Twenty-First Century
  achievement 53, 250–8
  approach taken 6, 69–70, 110, 131 *ff.*, 167 *f.*,
    195–7, 252, 259, 275
  contextualization 197–8
  criticism of 3, 24, 100, 250–8
  model 53–58, 264–7
  summary of Piketty's view 198–9, 250–8
capital–income ratio 90, 101, 109, 132 *f.*, 137,
  161, 216, 219, 222
capital income vs. labour income 285–6
capital intensity 140, 146, 149, 150 *f.*, 267
Capital (Marx) 14, 15, 21, 23 *f.*, 113, 195, 244
capital–output ratio 18, 133, 136, 150, 201,
  252, 264, 284
capital-saving 149–50, 163
capital stock 17, 18, 68, 90, 112, 132, 136, 141,
  144, 160, 162, 207–8, 216 *f.*, 219, 222, 224,
  235
Capital Theory and the Rate of Return (Solow)
  21
capitalism
  and inequality 2, 16, 131
  laws of 22, 90, 99, 102, 197, 256, 271
  organization of 22–23, 132, 153, 159
  patrimonial 19, 31, 256, 257
Caradog Jones, D. 34
Carnegie, A. 149
Carnegie Company 152
Cartwright, N. 55
censuses of wealth 136
Central Statistical Office (CSO), Britain
  172, 174
Chandler, A. D. 148–9, 151
Child Trust Fund 179
China 200
civil servants
  Germany 98–99
  Sweden 119
Clark, T. 178
Coatsworth, J. H. 201

Cobb–Douglas model 18, 54–56, 141, 265–6
collective agreements, France 78
collective pension wealth 117–18
collective wealth
  and accumulation of wealth 119 ff.
  collective pension wealth 117–18
  contribution of 126
  defining 112–13
  determinants of 253–4
  distribution 114
  as equality insurance 127–8
  formation 109–10, 111
  general supplementary pension (*Allmän Tilläggs Pension* (ATP)) 119–22
  institutionalization 126
  international comparisons 117–19
  and power 114
  private sector 115–16
  wage-earner funds 122–6
  see also Sweden; wealth
collusive distribution 202
comparability, problems of 9, 255, 260
comparative measures, of growth and development 260–1
computer technology 268–9
Connolly, S. 182
consumer demand 61, 271
consumption 15, 21, 27, 33, 57, 61, 74, 91, 173, 176, 198, 242, 252, 271
contribution sociale generalisee (CSG) 74
convergence 101, 196, 202 f., 220, 249, 261
convergence/divergence debate 196, 201–4
corn model 24
corporate governance 267
corporate valuations 137–8, 142
cost accounting 24–25
cotton-spinning industry, pre-war Japan 226, **226**
credit 59 ff., 96, 182, 230, 270, 271 f.
credit cards 84, 271–2
credit flows 272
creditors, movement of wealth 54–55
Cripps, S. 170
Crosland, A. 40, 171, 172
cross-country wealth data 117
Currency Reforms, Germany 90–91, 94, 96, 97

Dalton, H. 42, 170
data deficiencies, Africa 208
data, Piketty's use of 55, 57, 67, 69 f., 82, 88, 89, 103, 135, 138, 139, 228, 234, 237, 253, 259, 264, 266, 270, 274, 275, 276, 277
Datta, R. 241
Daunton, M. 176

De Tocqueville, A. 38
debt
  Africa 215, **215**
  household 184, 271
  personal 271–2
  sovereign 19, 88, 90, 141, 254
debt servicing 54, 60–61
deciles, use of 30–31, 41, 69, 77, 254 ff.
deficit financing 251, 254, 272
deforestation, India 242–4
deindustrialization 183, 258
Dell, F. 87, 89, 95, 96
DeLong, B. 8, 84, 259, 277, 279, 281
democratic capitalism 89
demography 69, 72
deregulation, financial institutions 2, 106, 158, 251, 267, 271
Deutscher Gewerkschaftsbund (DGB) 124
development
  capitalist 6, 14 f., 203
  economic 4, 16, 36, 38, 68, 140, 200, 224, 226 f., 260
  of income inequality 69, 75, 92, 223
  laws of 13 f.
  new growth theory 162, 266–8
  path of 4, 6, 13, 69, 260 ff.
  of wealth 114, 256 ff.
difference, and diversity 31–32
differentials, wealth and income 250
differentiation, Phelps Brown's perspective 44–45
discrimination, effects of 285
distribution and growth in the world economy **198**
distributional analysis, data sources 69
divergence 13, 181, 196, 201, 202 f., 220, 249, 251, 257
diversity, and difference 31–32
division of labour, and wealth 33
Donaldson Brown, F. 149–50
DuPont 149–50
DuPont formula 150

earnings distribution, Britain 178
ecological footprints 241–2
economic authority 38
economic democracy 122–3, 124, 127
economic historians, research opportunities 101–3
economic modelling 26, 196, 216, 262, 267, 281
  definitions used in 18
  simplification 5–6
economic science, Piketty's understanding of 196

economic trajectories, diversity 4–7
Economics of Welfare (Pigou) 42, 44
economies, success/failure 259
economists, future-orientation 15, 274–5, 285 *ff.*
economy, visions of 21
education 268–9
elasticity of substitution, capital and labour
    141–2, 265–6, 269–70
electoral participation 258
elite accumulation 257
employment 4, 18, 26, 34, 36, 37, 41, 49, 61,
    72, 77, 80, 95, 99, 267, 292
  full 2, 18, 22 *f.*, 59, 123, 127, 169, 258
  self-employment 72, 181, 185, 189
  unemployment 7, 22, 31, 48, 79 *f.*, 92, 126,
    178, 180 *ff.*, 190, 269
endogenous money theory 59–60
energy demands, India 242–4
Engerman, S. 147
entitlements 240–1, 253, 254
entrepreneurial function 153
entrepreneurial wealth 58
environment 241–4
  and growth 259, 261
equality 4, 114, 117, 119, 129, 167 *f.*, 175, 179,
    250, 252, 273, 275, 286
equality of opportunity 274, 286
"Equality" (Tawney) 37
Erlander, T. 121–2
Erzberger, M. 93
Essay on Population (Malthus) 14
Essays on the Welfare State (Titmuss) 171
Estate Duty 170
EU referendum 258
Eulenberg, F. 95–96
Eurocentrism 199–200
euthanasia of the rentier 20, 180
executive remuneration 267
executive salaries and bonuses 267
exploitation 75, 147, 266 *f.*, 271 *f.*, 279
exploitation rents 272

factor shares, Britain 177
Family Credit, Britain 184
Family Expenditure Survey (FES), Britain
    172, 174
famine, India 241, 243
Feldt, K.-O. 125
Felipe, J. 22
fictive goods 113
Field, A. 149
financial flows 272
financial institutions, deregulation 267, 271
financial organizations, of capital 156–9

financial sector, United Kingdom 272
financial speculation, United States 157
financialization 3, 46, 54, 156–8, 188, 257, 267,
    270 *ff.*
  Britain 184
  and financial liberalization 270–3
  United States 156–9
First World War
  effects in Germany 90, 94, 95
  political and economic effects 5
fiscal reform, in Piketty's analysis 81
Fisher, F. M. 22, 25
Fisher, I. 21, 143
food subsidies 169
4 October Movement (Sweden 1983) 125–6
France
  collective agreements 78
  conflicts in evidence 68–69
  demography 72–73, 75
  economic development 68–69
  employment 72, 77, 79–80
  employment contracts 78–79
  income inequality 81
  jobs 76–77
  labour costs 79
  labour laws 78–79
  labour market reforms 79–81
  measurement of inequality 67–68, 69–71
  pensions 73, 75
  Piketty's approach 69–70
  population ageing 72–73, 75
  population distribution 72
  production 72
  public spending 73
  savings 99
  taxation 73–74
  technological progress 75–78
  trajectory of inequality 67, 70–71
  wealth inequality 71
Frankel, S. H. 214–16
Fujino, S. 226
funded debt, Africa 215, **215**

G20 180
Galbraith, J. K. 24
Gates, B. 154
GDP per capita, as measure of success 260
Geary–Khamis dollar of 1990 ($GK1990) 260
general equilibrium project 21, 56
Germany
  civil servants 98–99
  Currency Reforms 90–91, 94, 96, 97
  economic historians 101–3
  economic miracle 91

home ownership 100–101
house prices 100–101
housing 93, 98, 100 f., 106, 107
hyperinflation 90, 95–97
income inequality 88, 89, 90, 91, 92, 99
inequality research 88–92
jobs 77
pensions 98–99
redistribution 94–95
research opportunities 102–3
savings 96–97, 99
tax legislation 92–95
taxation 89
wealth inequality 90, 91, 95, 96, 99
wealth taxation 93–95
welfare capitalism 97–99
Ghosh, J. 19
Gini, C. 254
Gini coefficient 254–5, 276
    Africa 208, **210**, 211, 212, 213
    Britain 59, 178 f., 190
    Germany 91–92, 104
    Japan **228**, 229, 235
    methodological problems 91–92, 208, 254 ff.
globalization 2, 3, 251, 253, 261, 271
    connections, and inequality 7
    connectivity 261
    financial crisis, 2007–9 2–3, 7, 26, 29, 252, 271, 272
    inequality 7, 270
    perspective 261
    policy debate 180
    tax competition 272
    tax on wealth 61
    trade 75–76
    view, of inequality 201–4
gold mining 214–16
gold standard 59
Golden Age 202
Goldsmith, R. 136, 138, 139
governance, politics and institutions 273–4
Great Depression 90, 133, 157, 273
Great Divergence 260
Great Levelling 251–2
Great Moderation 59
Gregory, M. 182
growth
    accounting 136, 144–5
    actual 17–18
    comparative measures 260–1
    and environment 259, 261
    international relative 202–4
    and taxation 259
    and technological progress 202–4, 266–7

theory 56, 134, 145, 162, 249, 263, 264 ff.
    warranted 17
    see also development
Growth of British Industrial Relations (Phelps Brown) 44

Harrod, R. 17–18
Hausman, D. 55
Hautcoeur, P.-C. 73
hierarchies, of wealth and income 257
high inequality 286
Hilferding, R. 156
Hills, J. 178
Hirschman, A. O. 97
historical regularity 53–54
historical research, strength of 102
history, linking with theory 6
Hoenack, S. 136
home ownership 100 f., 174, 179, 184
Hont, I. 33, 47, 50
house prices
    Germany 100–101
    increase in 60–61
    international comparisons 100
household debt 264, 271
Household Tax Act, Japan 229
housing 19, 34, 48, 53, 57–58, 59 ff., 63, 68, 77, 133, 142, 160, 217, 254, 262 f., 265, 271
    Britain 174–5, 179, 182, 184, 187 f., 190
    and capital accumulation 271
    Germany 88, 93, 98, 100 ff.
    taxation of 61
    value of 264–5
    and wealth 77
human capital 177, 198, 217, 259, 269, 276, 280, 284 ff.
human rights 4, 275
humbug production function 22
Hutton, W. 179
hyperinflation, Germany 90, 95–97

ideology
    effects of 253, 258
    liberal 274
in-work benefits 179, 182–5, 258
income
    and assets 230–3
    capital vs. labour 285–6
    disposable 236, 253, 264, 276
    diverse sources 177
    forms of 74, 257
    minimum 44
    sources of 73–74, 252

income distribution 2, 29 f., 30 ff., 41, 69, 91 f.,
    111, 118, 143, 169, 172 f., 177 f., 184, 199,
    209, 221, 223, 226, 228 f., 234, 255, 268,
    275, 286
  within-age-group 256
  Germany 92
  individual, pre-war Japan 228–30
  international comparisons 224
  Kuznets's view 16
  need for new theories 283–7
  pre-war Japan 223–7
Income Distribution and Social Change
  (Titmuss) 171–2
Income Distribution (Pen) 30
income inequality 1, 7, 30 ff., 42, 46, 67, 81,
    88 ff., 99, 181, 201, 207, 208–9, 212, 216,
    220, 223, 228, 234 f., 250, 251, 254, 285 f.
  Africa 207, 208, 209–13
  France 81
  Germany 88, 89, 90, 91–92, 99
  Japan 223
  Latin America 201, 209
  measurement of 42
  pre-war Japan 234
  South Africa 216
income redistribution 171, 184
India
  agrarian property 239
  agriculture 239
  biocapacity 242
  British rule 240, 241
  conceptions of property 238–40
  data availability 237
  deforestation 242–4
  ecological footprint 241–2
  energy demands 242–4
  entitlements 240–1
  famine 241, 243
  forms of wealth 237–8
  irrigation 243
  natural wealth 241–4
  political and social rights 241
  water demands 243
industrial development, United States 147–9
industrial growth, United States 151–2
inequality vii, ix–xi, 1, 2 ff., 16, 25, 29 ff., 38 ff.,
    42, 44 ff., 53, 55, 58, 59, 61, 67 ff., 77 ff., 92,
    94 ff., 102, 127, 131, 155, 161, 167 ff., 177 ff.,
    197 f., 201 f., 207 ff., 220 ff., 228, 234–5,
    237, 240, 242, 249–50, 251 ff., 283 ff.
  causation 31, 255–6
  changes over time 210
  costs of 31
  as difference 45

dimensions of 180
distribution and democratic order 37–41
dynamic perspective 34–36, 37
economic and social ix, 2, 31, 33, 34, 38, 40 f.,
    87 ff., 97, 101 f., 109 ff., 123, 210, 220
economists' perspectives 30
elements and trajectory 250–3
explaining decline in 55–56
explanations for 70–71
and growth 199–201
historical perspective 32–46
impact of 259
international comparisons 37–38
and labour market 78–79
and labour market reforms 79–81
measurement of 67–68, 69–71, 201, 254–6
measures to reduce 168
outcome vs. opportunity 284
and potential of society 38
property ownership 37–38
and reform 79–81
resurgence 58–61
and social differentiation 32–36
as synonymous with divergence 201–2
and technological progress 75–78
and welfare 41–46
Inequality of Pay (Phelps Brown) 44
information transparency 71
infrastructure outputs, difficulties of estimating
  19
inheritance 70–71, 111, 122, 207, 250, 252
institutional frameworks, for exploitation
  266–7
institutions, politics and governance 273–4
interest rates 54, 57, 59, 252
intergenerational transmission 285–6, 287
international comparisons 70
International Monetary Fund (IMF) 175, 180,
  277
international networks 75–76
international relative growth 202–4
international transfers 208, 216–19
intra-regional variations 261
investment
  business investment 148, 151, 158, 265
  government vs. private 19
  public 19, 26, 112, 126, 254
irrigation, India 243

Japan, income inequality 223
  see also pre-war Japan
Jerven, M. 213–14
job polarization 76–77
jobs, changing types 77

Jones, C. 135, 263
Jostock, P. 96

K/Y ratio 151, 224, 225
Kaldor, N. 16, 23, 135, 173, 283
Kalecki, M. 23
Kapuria-Foreman, V. 16
Karabarbounis, L. 113
Keynes, J. M. 17, 19–20, 22–23, 26–27, 120,
    126, 164, 180, 190, 199, 266, 279
Knoll, K. 100
Korpi, W. 123
Krugman, P. 8, 162, 269, 280 *ff.*
Krupp, B. 87
Kuznets's curve 29, 88, 91, 100, 195, 200, 253,
    261
Kuznets, S. 2, 16, 46, 253, 254, 260, 283

labour laws, France 78–79
labour market 30, 34, 68 *f.*, 76–81, 92, 99, 123,
    181 *ff.*, 201, 250, 253, 256, 262, 273
  France 78–79
  position of women 182
labour market reforms
  France 79–81
  in Piketty's analysis 80–81
Labour Party (Britain) 40, 49, 172, 175 *f.*, 185
land ownership, Sweden 112–13
land rents 285
land values 198–9, 264–5
Lastenausgleichsgesetz 94
Latin America 200–1, 209
law of diminishing returns 264
Le Capital au XXIe siecle see *Capital in the
    Twenty-First Century*
Le Grand, J. 173
Le Quéré, F. 73
legal frameworks, for exploitation 266–7
legitimacy, of managerial control 158
Leicester, A. 178
lending 60
Les hauts revenus en France au XXe siecle
    (Piketty) 69
Lewis, A. 226, 227, 234
liberal socialism 175
life expectancy 31, 98, 177
Lindert, P. H. 269–70
Little Divergence 260
Lucas, R. 2, 8, 47

Machin, S. 182
Madsen, J. 136
Malthus, T. R. 13–15, 33, 176, 253, 260
managerial control, legitimacy of 158

managerial organization, United States 148–9
managerialist ideology, United States 157–8
marginal productivity of capital 139, 141, 143
marginal productivity theory of distribution
    20, 22
mark to market concept 57
market liberalization, rationale for 2
market mechanisms, and wealth 77
market prices, effects of fluctuations 263
market, resurgence 151
market values 43, 137, 198–9
markets, unequal effects 30
Marris, R. 25
Marshall, A. 152
Martin, R. 87
Marx, K. 13, 14, 15, 23, 195, 244
Marxist economics 15–16
Massachusetts Institute of Technology (MIT)
    20–1
McCombie, J. 22
McGowan, J. J. 25
Meade, J. 175, 176, 188, 191
means testing 172
measurement
  of capital 19 *ff.*, 67, 113, 131, 135 *ff.*, 144,
    187, 263
  of inequality 30 *ff.*, 42, 69 *ff.*, 250, 254 *ff.*, 277
Meidner, R. 123
meritocracy 39–40
methodological inconsistency 56–57
middle class 173–4, 185, 258
Milanovic, B. 201, 209
Mill, J. S. 43, 55
Minami, R. 223–4, 225, 229
Minsky, H. 156
Mitsui, T. 231
modern business enterprise 147–9
modern management, United States 148
monetarism 23, 59
money 58–60
moral perspectives 257–8
Moriguchi, C. 223, 228
Morrison, C. 201
mortgage interest tax relief, Britain 174
mortgages 60, 100, 142, 173–4, 189, 271–2

nanotechnology 140, 203, 269
national dividend 43–44
national income, Africa 208, 222
National Insurance, Britain 169, 170, 172, 173,
    189
national minimum wage, Britain 179, 182, 273
National Superannuation 171
natural rate of growth 17–18

natural resources 200–1, 261
natural wealth 241–4
Neiman, B. 113
Nell, E. 23
neo-institutionalism 196, 274, 282
neoclassical analysis 54
neoclassical approach 139–45, 264–7
neoliberalism 8, 183–4, 276, 279
new egalitarianism 184, 185
new growth theory 162, 268
New Labour 168, 173, 178, 179–80, 184, 189
New Right, reassertion 59
normative theories of equity 287
North, D. C. 274

OECD
  collective pension wealth as share of GDP
    in 2014 **118**
  collective wealth 117–19
Ohkawa, K. 224
Ohlin, B. 121, 122, 127
Ohlsson, H. 114
oil crisis, Sweden 123
Okazaki, T. 257
Ono, A. 223–4, 225, 229
opportunity 274, 286
origins, effects of 41
ownership 61*f.*, 100–101, 112*f.*, 120, 124*f.*, 128,
    157, 164, 170*f.*, 174, 178*ff.*, 184, 187, 241,
    250, 253, 257, 266, 267, 284*ff.*

Palma coefficient 255
Panama Papers 46
pangu 240
parental resources, and children's outcomes
    285–6
parents, income inequality 286
Pareto optimum 56
participation income 185
Pasinetti, L. 21, 22, 266
patrimonial capitalism *see* capitalism
patrimonial wealth 58
patrimony 256–8
pattam 239–40
Pay As You Earn (PAYE) taxation 169
payments in kind 172
Pen, J. 30
Penrose, E. 25
pension funds, as intervening institutions 109,
    116–17, 120–21, 129
pensions 73, 75, 83, 88, 98–9, 113–14, 115,
    118*ff.*, 126, 129*f.*, 177, 185, 280, 285
  contributory 171
  occupational 115, 171

private 6, 129
  state 88, 253
Perlin, F. 239
Perlman, N. 16
perpetual inventory method (PIM) 136–8
Persimmon Homes 267
Phelps Brown, H. 30, 44–45
Pickett, K. 31
Pigou, A. C. 42–44, 50
Piketty, Thomas *passim.*
Polanyi, K. 113
policy development, focus 259
"Political Aspects of Full Employment"
    (Kalecki) 23
political change 4
politics, governance and institutions 273–4
Poor Law Amendment Act 1834 183, 281
population ageing 72–73, 75, 177
positive analysis 284
poverty 31, 34–35, 36, 48, 49, 50, 169, 171,
    179*ff.*, 190, 196, 212, 240*f.*, 244–5,
    257*f.*, 260, 276, 277, 288, 282
  defining 260
  in-work 183, 257–8
  mapping 34
  over life cycle **35**
  Piketty's inattention to 212
  rediscovery of 171
power 4, 7, 38, 46, 110*ff.*, 118*f.*, 121*ff.*, 157–8,
    168, 170, 175, 188, 195, 197, 201, 239,
    243, 267
  bargaining 34, 57, 141, 253, 266
  economic 157, 168, 170
  market 71, 76, 153, 199, 268, 272
  monopoly 279
  political 58, 196, 199, 239, 241, 258, 275
  purchashing 53, 92, 119, 260, 284
  social 23, 45, 127, 196, 199
pre-war Japan
  assets as determinant of income **233**
  capital share 224–6, **225, 226**
  change over time in capital share in
    non-agricultural sector **224**
  correlation between assets and income **233**
  cotton-spinning industry 226
  functional distribution of income 223–7
  Gini coefficient **228**, 229
  household tax 229
  income inequality 234
  indices of income inequality **228**
  individual income and assets 230–3
  individual income distribution 228–30
  international comparisons 224
  Lewis turning point **227**, *227*

taxation 228–9, 230–1
top 1 per cent income share **228**
top 100 income earners *231*
top 104 asset holders *232*
wealth distribution 230
see also Japan
precariat 41
prediction 55
present-centrism 6
price stability 58–59
primary income, and private wealth 253–4
Principles of Political Economy, and Taxation
    (Ricardo) 14–15
private wealth, and primary income 253–4
privatization 46, 99, 201
  Britain 178–9
  rationale for 19
production, France 72
production function 16, 17, 19, 20, 26, 27, 54,
    55, 56, 61, 82, 141, 152, 262–4, 266, 284,
    285, 289, 294
productivity 76
profit, as social relation 199
profits 2, 5, 17, 19 *f.*, 24, 25, 73, 141, 147, 149,
    153 *f.*, 170, 197, 201 *ff.*, 215 *ff.*, 219 *ff.*,
    267, 273
  excess 94, 123
  long-run rate 14–15
  monopoly 25
  untaxed 124
  war profits 94
progressive taxation 110–11, 113, 126
property
  agrarian 239
  communal 238–9
  conceptions of 238–40
  entitlements 240–1
  material goods 241
  political and social rights 241
  skill as 238–9
property ownership 37–38
property values 57, 284
property windfalls 61
public housing 174–5
public pension reserve funds, Sweden 114,
    116–17, 126
  and wage-earner funds 124–5
public–private partnerships, rationale for
    19
public spending
  Britain 169, 175
  France 73
  redistributive effects 173
public wealth, determinants of 253–4

quantity theory of money 59

railroads 148, 156–7
rate of return on capital 68, 71, 96, 105–6, 199,
    207, 224, 251, 256, 264
rates of growth, warranted, actual and natural
    17–18
Rawls, J. 30, 175, 188
real estate 264–5
recording, and reporting 262
redistribution, Germany 94–95
redistributive transfer payments 46
Rehn–Meidner proposals 171
Reich emergency levy 94
rent-seeking 256, 262–3, 266, 271
rents, creation of 284–5
reported taxation, use of 24
research needs 259
researcher training 102
reserve army of labour 15, 23
reshoring 269
residential capital 135
retirement provision 98–99
return on capital 68, 71, 96, 99, 105–6, 199,
    207, 264
  changes over time 256
  and economic growth 251, 284
  pre-war Japan 224
  United States 140–6
Ricardo, D. 14–15, 33
right to buy, United Kingdom 60
Robinson, J. 20, 21, 274
robots 269
Rognlie, M. 142
Roine, J. 114
Rowntree, S. 34–36
Rowthorn, R. 137–8, 265
Royal Commission into the Taxation of Profits
    and Wealth (Britain) 173
Royal Commission on the Distribution of
    Income and Wealth (Britain) 176
Rule, J. 239

Saez, E. 223, 228
salaries
  executive salaries and bonuses 267
  and wages 258
Samuelson, P. 20–21, 27, 161
saranjam 239
Savage, M. 40–1
savings 18, 37–38, 61, 68, 90, 94 *ff.*, 119, 123,
    128, 197, 250, 264 *f.*, 271, 285
Say's law 22
schools 19, 40, 41, 173, 273

Schularick, M. 100, 102
Schumpeter, J. 134, 153
Second World War 5, 67 *ff.*, 72 *f.*, 90, 94, 98,
    100–101, 237, 243
secondary education 40
Seers, D. 172
Sen, A. 30, 240
service sector, Britain 181–2
Shaikh, A. 21–22
shareholder value 158
shareholding, Britain 177
Sidgwick, H. 42–43
skill, as property 238–9
skill bias 268
Sköld, P.-E. 120
slavery 132, 147, 197, 201, 257, 277
Smith, A. 32–33, 45, 100, 134
Smyth, R. 136
social attitudes, to income and wealth 257–8
social change 4
    and taxation 176–7
Social Class in the 21st Century (Savage) 40–41
social classes 34, 36
Social Contract, Britain 175
social democracy 55 *f.*, 122, 168, 174–5, 188,
    190, 258
    and inequality 55–56
social differentiation, and inequality 32–36
social inclusion 258
social invisibility 53
social mobility 31, 38, 40, 41, 49
social progress 33
social security
    Britain 169, 171, 172, 182–3
    France 73, 74
    Sweden 122
social services, Britain 169
Social Survey of Merseyside (Caradog Jones)
    34
social wealth 46
socialization 122, 171
societal capital direction 122
Sokoloff, K. 147–8
Solow, R. 16–17, 18, 21, 22, 134, 139, 143
Solow–Swan Cobb–Douglas derived
    production function 264
Solow–Swan model of economic growth 143,
    267
Sonnenschein–Mantel–Debreu conditions 56
Soskice, D. 212, 265
South Africa 211–13
    comparison of tax record and survey data
        measuring top 10 per cent share of
        income **213**

income inequality 216
    top incomes **213**
Speenhamland system 183, 281
spillovers 203
Sraffa, P. 24, 199
stagflation, Sweden 123
stakeholder capitalism 179
Stamp, J. 37
standard analysis 286
static theory of distribution, in dynamic
    setting 143
steel industry, United States 149, 152
Steger, T. 100
Stiglitz, J. 264, 272–3, 279
stock market capitalizations 142
store of wealth concept 55
strategy of equality 168
Streek, W. 272
student fees, Britain 179–80
stylized facts 16, 283–4, 286–7
super managers 155
surplus approach 199
Swan–Solow model 143, 267
Swan, T. 16–17, 18
Sweden
    collective financial assets as share of net
        wealth **116**
    collective financial assets as share of total
        financial assets **115**
    collective wealth and accumulation of
        wealth 119
    collective wealth as equality insurance 127–8
    economic democracy 122–3, 124
    general supplementary pension (*Allmän
        Tilläggs Pension* (ATP)) 119–22
    individual and collective wealth 114–17
    labour movement policy 123
    land ownership 112–13
    motives for reform 126–7
    oil crisis 123
    pension fund management 121
    pensionsberedning 120–1
    Rehn–Meidner proposals 171
    social democracy 122
    stagflation 123
    wage-earner funds 122–6
    wealth inequality 110
    see also collective wealth; public pension
        reserve funds; wage-earner funds
Swedish Employers' Confederation, attitude to
    wage-earner funds 125
Swedish Trade Union Confederation,
    committee, 1973 123–4
Szirmai, A. 196

Tawney, R. H. 37–38, 40, 45, 168–9, 185
taxation 44, 110–12
  avoidance and evasion 46
  Britain 169–70, 173, 174, 175, 178, 179
  distributed and undistributed profits 170
  elite 274
  France 73–74
  Germany 89, 92–95
  global competition 272
  global tax 30, 57, 61, 185
  and growth 259
  of housing 61
  of inheritance 170
  in Piketty's model 56, 81
  pre-war Japan 228–9, 230–1
  progressive taxation 110–11, 113, 126
  and property values 57
  reported 24
  and social change 176–7
  of wealth 71
Taylor, L. 19, 22, 266
technological change 2, 14, 25, 77, 162, 200 ff.,
    250, 253, 266, 267, 268, 270
technological progress 75–78, 202–4, 267
technology, elimination of employment 269–70
Thatcher government 177–9
Thatcher, M. 59, 175
Theil index 255
Theory of Justice (Rawls) 30
Titmuss, R. 171–2, 173
top-coding/capping 255
total factor productivity (TFP) 143–5, 267–8
Towards a Dynamic Economics (Harrod) 17–18
Townsend, P. 183
trade, global 75–76
trade unions 30, 120, 127, 175, 258
  Britain 178, 179
  formation 34
  France 78
transnational forces 261
transparency, of information 71
trends, aggregation of 5–6

unemployment see employment
United Nations University–World Income
    Inequality Database (UNU–WIID) 212
United States
  aftermath of Revolution 146–7
  agriculture 146–7
  autonomy of corporate sector 157
  bargaining 155
  capital–output ratio 135–7
  Civil War 132
  composition of capital 133

confronting history of capital 145
cross-national comparison of capital–output
    ratio excluding land and housing 135
definition of capital 133–5
emergence of modern enterprises 148
fallacy of productive factors and their rewards
    152–6
financial organizations of capital 156–9
financial speculation 157
financialization 156–9
"hard-driving" capital in retail industry
    150–1, 150
history of capital 132–3
industrial development 147–9
industrial growth 151–2
industrial organization 148
labour productivity growth 144, 144
land values 132–3
legitimacy of managerial control 158
levels of capital 132–3
managerial organization 148–9
managerialist ideology 157–8
measurement of capital 135–8
modern management 148
organizational revolution 148
ownership and control of business 156–7
political and economic development 5
productive organization of capital 146–52
productivity growth 147–8
profits 153–4
railroads 148
ratio of total market value to the book value of
    equipment, structures and land 138
residential capital 135
rewards to capital 140–6
role of capital 139–40, 146
sharing corporate success 155
steel industry 149
technological progress and employment 77
utilization of capital 146
wealth inequality 257
see also capital
universalism 172–3
universities, differentiation 41
unlimited labour supply model 226
utility, as measure of value 43

vatan 239–40
Veblen, T. 134
Verspagen model 202–3
visions, of economy 21

wage-earner funds 114, 122–7
wage-fund doctrine 33

wage rates
  governing factors 33–34, 76–77
  repression 266
wages
  Britain 181–2
  Malthus's view of 14
  and salaries 258
Waldenström, D. 114
Walmart 150–1
warranted rate of growth 17–18
water demands, India 243
wealth
  accumulation of 88, 95, 98, 99, 114, 116,
    120, 126, 253
  and capital 177
  collective and public 253–4
  collusive distribution 202
  cross-country wealth data 117
  defining 112, 261–4
  as distinct from capital 238, 284–5
  and division of labour 33
  entitlements 240–1
  factors affecting 113
  forms of 257
  global tax on 61
  and housing 77
  wealth–income ratio 101, 111, 129, 197, 267
  lack of attention 30
  and market mechanisms 77
  meaning of 31
  measurement of 19
  natural 241–4
  nature of 68
  as occupation 58
  ownership 113
  ownership of 285
  Piketty's concept of 24
  Piketty's view of 19
  polarization 272
  progressive taxation 110–11, 113, 126
  ratio private to public 254
  realization of 57
  recording and reporting 262
  and security 57–58
  social 46
  sources of 244–5, 264–5
  Sweden 114–17
  value of 57
  see also collective wealth

wealth accumulation and income distribution
    68
Wealth and Welfare (Pigou) 43–44
wealth censuses 136
wealth distribution 31
  within-age-group 256
  Britain 178
  need for new theories 283–7
  polarization 29
  pre-war Japan 230
wealth inequality 250, 256, 261, 273, 286, 287
  Britain 170
  components of 250
  factors in 250
  France 71
  Germany 90, 91, 92, 95, 96, 99
  Labour party policy development 170
  levels of 251
  Sweden 110
  United States 257
Wealth of Nations (Smith) 134
wealth of nations, Smith's view of 32–33
wealth–output ratio 264
wealth redistribution, Germany 94–95
wealth taxation 71, 93–95
welfare 41–46
welfare capitalism, Germany 97–99
welfare economics 42–44, 56
welfare states
  Britain 171
  payments in kind 172
  price stability 59
Whiting, R. 175
Wigforss, E. 122
Wilkinson, R. 31
Wilson government 174
women, in labour market 182
working poor 183, 257–8
working rich 180
World Bank Migration Remittance Project
    218
World Income and Wealth Database 211
World Panel Income Distribution database
    209

Yazawa, H. 230
Yearbook of German Millionaires (Martin) 87
Young, M. 38–40
youth unemployment, France 79–80